Select Registry – Travel's Safest Bet

Two of the hottest buzz words in Epicurean circles are "local" and "organic," and for good reason. Discerning people want the best quality food possible, and they know that locally grown and cultivated food is better in so many ways than the mass-produced. And discerning travelers want the same in their lodging. SELECT REGISTRY represents the "local" and "organic" version of accommodations and hospitality.

And just how organic food must be inspected and certified, so too must SELECT REGISTRY properties pass a rigid, 200-point inspection. As a traveler, you want the best value for your money and rely upon all kinds of information to make your final decision. It's one thing to sift through a ton of online reviews to discover the truth about the quality of a place, and it's another to know that before you hit the "Book Now" button, this place has been checked out by a real pro.

Our SELECT REGISTRY travelers know a good thing when they see it - the SELECT REGISTRY logo. Just like there is comfort and confidence when you see that "Certified Organic" logo in your favorite grocery store, so too should you have the confidence that staying at a SELECT REGISTRY B&B, inn or boutique hotel will be a memorable and wonderful experience....the best of breed in lodging and hospitality.

Go ahead. Book your next stay at a SELECT REGISTRY property. In a world where one traveler gives a place one star, and the next person gives the same place five stars, you can relax knowing that staying at one of our member properties is one of the safest bets you can make in travel.

Enjoy.

Jay Karen, CAE
Chief Executive Officer

For four decades, a brand and a directory you can count on...

SELECT REGISTRY, Distinguished Inns of North America—the premier guide to exceptional travel and lodging for more than 40 years—invites you to find that special place that will make your next trip unforgettable.

Whether you're traveling for business or pleasure, by yourself or with your family, this guidebook will help you to locate extraordinary places to stay throughout the U.S. and Canada. And, no matter what the season or the type of property that you find most appealing, SELECT REGISTRY likely has something for you.

Most importantly, you can rest assured that our member properties have been selected as among the most comfortable and welcoming—unique and quality assured lodging alternatives in an increasingly cluttered and impersonal travel marketplace.

In years past, the registry book in the lobby of hotels and inns welcomed guests and provided a connection between innkeepers and travelers. The historical registry "quill"—the original instrument of guest registration—has been incorporated into our Association's graphic identity, and the predicates of hospitality, comfort, and authenticity establish our members as "the best of the best"—select properties that will exceed your highest expectations when it comes to lodging.

Look for the plaque with the quill on it when you visit our members' inns, and you'll know that you are "traveling the SELECT REGISTRY way..."

SELECT REGISTRY

DISTINGUISHED INNS OF NORTH AMERICA

se·lect (sĭ-lĕkt') *v.* **-lect·ed**, **-lecting**, **-lects**. —*tr.* To choose from among several; pick out, —*intr.* To make a choice or selection. —*adj.* Also **se·lect·ed** (-lĕk'tĭd). **1.** Singled out in preference; chosen. **2.** Of special value or quality; preferred. —*n.* One that is select. [Lat. *seligere*, select-: se-, apart+legere, to choose.] —**se·lect'ness** *n.*

In the late 1960s, one man had an interesting idea. A travel writer named **Norman Simpson** drove throughout North America in a paneled station wagon. He identified unique places offering exceptional hospitality and what he called good honest lodgings, good honest food, and good honest feeling. He was hailed as the father of country inn travel. Through his pioneering book, *Country Inns and Back Roads*, Simpson introduced an entirely new type of lodging experience to the traveling public.

What we consider routine in the travel industry in 2014 is certainly different than in 1972 when Norman Simpson first organized our association. Airline travel is commonplace. Gasoline is no longer 40 cents per gallon. Computers, smart phones and tablets accompany business travelers as well as tourists.

The association begun by Norman Simpson with just a handful of New England properties now includes more than 300 of the finest country inns, B&Bs and small hotels from California to Nova Scotia.

Simpson was an innovator, and his vision and tireless promotion fundamentally changed the public perception of inns in North America. Today, Select Registry, the association that was his brainchild, is alive and well, and we continue to represent the very best the travel industry has to offer.

How to use this book

This guidebook is organized in alphabetical order, by state and province (our Canadian members have a separate section that begins on page 383). A map of the state or province at the beginning of each section shows the location of each property relative to major cities and highways. For the most recent list of members and larger map images, please go to the SELECT REGISTRY website, **www.selectregistry.com**.

Generally speaking, properties are grouped within each state or province by travel area, north to south, east to west. When searching by state, inns are listed alphabetically for your convenience.

For the convenience of our guests, an index of properties by state and province is provided at the front of the book. At the back of the book, you'll find an alpha-listing of all member properties.

Each SELECT REGISTRY member property is represented with its own page of information in this guidebook. The page includes two pictures, a brief description of the experience a guest can expect at that property, contact information, and a QR code to that inn's page on the SELECT REGISTRY website. The owners/innkeepers are listed so you know who your hosts will be. ❶

The Rooms/Rates section gives the number of rooms and pricing structure for the property. ❷ Cuisine describes the food and beverage specialties for which our members are famous, including whether the property serves only breakfast or is full service. ❸ The nearest Airport(s) tells you where you might fly in. ❹

Because food and wine are important compliments to many of our properties, some members are proud to have received prestigious DiRoNa (Distinguished Restaurants of North America) or *Wine Spectator* Awards. These awards are noted on participating Inns' guidebook page(s), as is any AAA Award the inn has received (confirmed by Official Appointment by AAA.) ❺

Each of our inns has a slightly different mix of food and beverage services. Although these are often described in more detail in the Cuisine section for each inn, we want to give our guests a quick snapshot of what each inn offers in-house. The icons near the top of each page tell you whether the inn serves breakfast, lunch, and/or dinner, and whether or not wine or cocktails are available. Also in this area, the inn will indicate if they have handicap accessible facilities; please check with the inn directly to determine availability and the extent of those facilities, if applicable. ❻

| Breakfast | Lunch | Dinner | Wine/Cocktails | Handicap Accessible |

SelectRegistry.com

For quickly moving from this guidebook to the member inn's page on the SELECT REGISTRY website, a QR code is provided for each member inn. Using a QR code reader application on a smartphone, you can take a picture of the code and link directly to that inn's page on the SELECT REGISTRY website. You may also see links to the member inn's social media pages here. ❼

We hope these instructions help you utilize your guidebook as you plan your travels. The SELECT REGISTRY guidebook is also available in digital format at **http://digitalguidebook.selectregistry.com** or by using the QR code on page 6.

For many additional pages of information on each member property, visit us online at: **www.selectregistry.com**.

Rabbit Hill Inn
www.rabbithillinn.com
48 Lower Waterford Rd, Lower Waterford, VT USA 05848
802-748-5168 • 800-76-BUNNY • Fax: 802-748-8342
info@rabbithillinn.com   *Member Since 1990*

Vermont
Lower Waterford

Innkeepers/Owners
Brian & Leslie Mulcahy

AAA
Four Diamond
Award

Even in these fast-paced, continuously connected times, there are still a few places in the world where one can escape to unwind and spend some "adult-only" time with that special someone. Named One of the World's Top 100 Hotels by Travel+Leisure Magazine, Rabbit Hill Inn offers all the luxuries that one would come to expect - fireplaces, double spa tubs, fine bath amenities, and more; yet what sets Rabbit Hill apart from just any nice place to stay is the warmth, comfort, and personal caring provided by its long-time hands-on innkeepers and wonderful staff. Dining at the inn is truly outstanding. Sophisticated, locally sourced food at an intimate, candlelit table adds to a most romantic evening - comfortable and always unpretentious. A myriad of seasonal activities -- everything from adrenaline pumping adventurous pursuits to relaxing in-room massage is available year-round. Zagat Guide said it best: "...this just might be the most romantic place on the planet...!" Free wifi available; non-smoking.

Rates
Including breakfast, afternoon sweets, turndown service, and gratuity for staff - Classic: $170-$250; Superior w/fireplace: $255-$305; Luxury w/whirlpool & fireplace: $330-$405. Rates vary by season. Check for specials! Number of Rooms: 19

Cuisine
Full country breakfast and afternoon tea and pastries included. Dinner features a frequently changing, modern and innovative menu. Beer, wine, and spirits available in our Snooty Fox Pub.

Nearest Airport
Manchester, NH (MHT)-2 hrs; Burlington, VT (BTV)-2 hrs; Logan Int'l (BOS)-3 hrs

320   SelectRegistry.com

Quality Assurance

Watch a behind-the-scenes video of an undercover inspection online at www.youtube.com/stayselect.

Perhaps the most important distinction between a SELECT REGISTRY member inn and others is our system of quality assurance. SELECT REGISTRY periodically conducts a quality assurance inspection of each of its nearly 350 inns. This program involves an independent firm, Quality Consultants, LLC—not employees of SELECT REGISTRY—with years of experience in the hospitality industry.

The inspectors arrive anonymously, spend the night, and evaluate the inn based on a detailed point system, which translates into a pass/fail grade for the inn. Inns applying for membership are inspected as are existing member inns on a regular basis.

No other organization of innkeepers has a comparable inspection program.

Not all inns have what it takes to pass inspection. Thus, this practice provides a guarantee to the traveling public that a SELECT REGISTRY inn is in a class of its own. A recent Internet directory identified over 20,000 country inns and B&Bs in the United States and Canada, and only a select few are members of SELECT REGISTRY. No other online directory or organization of innkeepers has a comparable inspection program. In fact, a recent *New York Times* article noted that the proliferation of "inns" has resulted in an industry that is misrepresented, lacks quality control, and charges widely varying room rates. With its rigorous inspection program, SELECT REGISTRY has established quality as a hallmark of its member properties.

SELECT REGISTRY doesn't rank its members with diamonds or stars, although many of our members carry the high ratings you'd expect from various groups who evaluate inns and B&Bs. If you're a member of SELECT REGISTRY, you're the cream of the crop. All of our inns are "the best"—and our inspections prove it!

Gift certificates

The gift of an overnight stay or a weekend at an exceptional inn or B&B can be one of the most thoughtful and appreciated gifts you can give your parents, children, or dear friends. Employers are discovering that a gift certificate for a "getaway" is an excellent way of rewarding their employees, while at the same time giving them some much-needed rest. A few ideas:

- **Weddings** • **Anniversaries** • **Holiday & Birthday gifts** •
- **Employee rewards/incentives** • **Retirement** •
- **Thank you or Appreciation** •

Our gift certificates are valid at any of our nearly 350 member properties. We process orders daily, packaging certificates with our complimentary Association guidebook and your personal message. If you need a gift certificate immediately, you can order our online electronic version. The next time you think about gift giving, think about our collection of celebrated properties and our gift certificate program—the perfect gift for that special person, **1-800-344-5244** or online at **www.SelectRegistry.com/gift-shop.**

You're selective. So are we.

SELECT REGISTRY
DISTINGUISHED INNS OF NORTH AMERICA

The Select Rewards Program

allows you to accumulate points toward a Reward Certificate
by staying at any Select Registry Inn or B&B.

Visit **www.selectregistry.com/rewards**
for complete details and to register, confirm
and track your Reward Points online.

Rewards

Guest Loyalty:

We believe that loyalty should be rewarded. That's why we developed the SELECT REGISTRY **Select Rewards Program**. This rewards program allows you to accumulate points toward a reward certificate by staying at any SELECT REGISTRY inn or B&B.

For each night of lodging at a SELECT REGISTRY property, you earn one Reward Quill Point. Once a total of twelve (12) Quill Points are earned, you will receive a $100 reward certificate for use at ANY SELECT REGISTRY inn or B&B in North America.

Visit **www.selectregistry.com/rewards** for complete details and to register, confirm and track your Quills Points online.

Are you on Facebook? As a special incentive for Facebook users, you can earn an extra Quill Point FREE, just for "Liking" us. Visit **www. facebook.com/selectregistry** and click on "SELECT REGISTRY Select Rewards" to register and receive your free Quill Point.

SELECT REWARDS

U.S Map

Alaska

Nunavut

British Columbia (pg. 370)

Alberta

Saskatchewan

Manitoba

Washington (pg. 348)

Montana

North Dakota

Minn.

Oregon (pg. 252)

Idaho

South Dakota

Iowa

Wyoming (pg. 364)

Nevada

Utah

Nebraska

California (pg. 28,29)

Colorado (pg. 55)

Kansas

Arizona (pg. 19)

New Mexico (pg. 198)

Oklahoma (pg. 249)

Pacific Ocean

Texas (pg. 303)

Kauai

Niihau

Oahu

Molokai

Lanai

Maui

Kahoolawe

Hawaii

Hawaii

Mexico

Gulf of Mexico

© 2013 Christmas Mapping Services Inc. Licensed for use in the 2013 Select Registry.

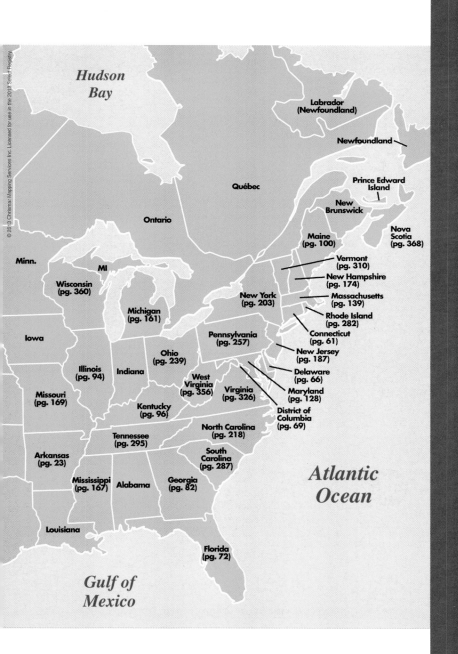

Hudson Bay

Labrador (Newfoundland)

Newfoundland

Québec

Prince Edward Island

New Brunswick

Ontario

Maine (pg. 100)

Nova Scotia (pg. 368)

Minn.

MI

Vermont (pg. 310)

Wisconsin (pg. 360)

New York (pg. 203)

New Hampshire (pg. 174)

Massachusetts (pg. 139)

Michigan (pg. 161)

Rhode Island (pg. 282)

Iowa

Pennsylvania (pg. 257)

Connecticut (pg. 61)

Ohio (pg. 239)

New Jersey (pg. 187)

Illinois (pg. 94)

Indiana

West Virginia (pg. 356)

Delaware (pg. 66)

Virginia (pg. 326)

Maryland (pg. 128)

Missouri (pg. 169)

Kentucky (pg. 96)

District of Columbia (pg. 69)

Tennessee (pg. 295)

North Carolina (pg. 218)

Arkansas (pg. 23)

South Carolina (pg. 287)

Atlantic Ocean

Mississippi (pg. 167)

Alabama

Georgia (pg. 82)

Louisiana

Florida (pg. 72)

Gulf of Mexico

Get Social with Select Registry

Today's travelers rely on the power of social media to get the inside scoop on what our inns and B&Bs have to offer. Here's your chance to moonlight as a travel writer and share your SELECT REGISTRY experience with friends on your favorite social network.

We look forward to connecting with you on...

/selectregistry

Share updates about your stay: the room, the meals or just relaxing with an afternoon cocktail. Tag the inn and "check-in" on Facebook when you arrive.

@selectregistry

Tweet about your stay, nearby attractions, even your friendly innkeepers. Tag your tweets with **#stayselect** and we'll re-tweet them to our followers.

/selectregistry

Pin pictures of the inns' gardens, interesting decór, accoutrements and, of course, the food. Tag us in a pin and we'll repin it to our pinboards.

/stayselect

Watch videos of the undercover inspections to see why our Distinguished Inns are a cut above. Posting a video from your stay? Share it with us.

@selectregistry

Document the little things that make your experience unique (retro filters, optional). Share with fellow inn-goers by tagging your photos with **#stayselect**.

SelectRegistry.com

Index by State or Province

SelectRegistry.com

Index by State or Province

Index by State or Province

SelectRegistry.com

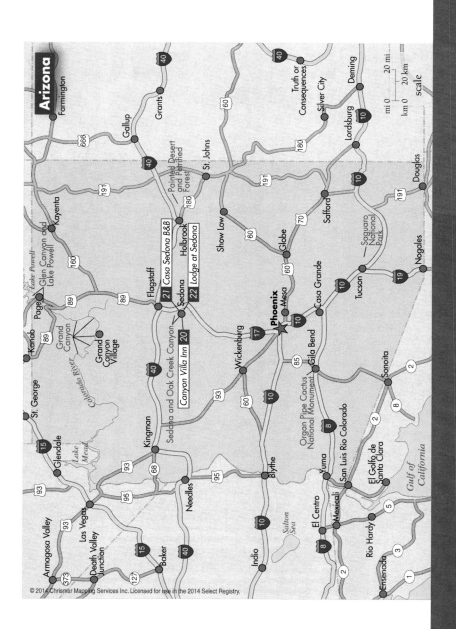

Arizona

Farmington

Gallup

Grants

666

40

Truth or Consequences

Deming

Silver City

60

20 mi

20 km

mi 0
km 0

scale

191

Kayenta

St. Johns

40

Painted Desert and Petrified Forest

180

191

Lordsburg

10

Douglas

191

10

Glen Canyon and Lake Powell

160

21 *Casa Sedona B&B*

Holbrook

22 *Lodge at Sedona*

Show Low

70

Safford

Saguaro National Park

Page

Lake Powell

89

Flagstaff

Sedona

60

Globe

60

Nogales

19

Casa Sedona B&B

Kanab

89

89

Grand Canyon

Grand Canyon Village

Colorado River

Sedona and Oak Creek Canyon 20

Canyon Villa Inn 20

Wickenburg

17

Phoenix

Mesa

10

Casa Grande

10

Tucson

St. George

40

Kingman

93

60

10

Gila Bend

85

Sonoita

2

Organ Pipe Cactus National Monument

8

Glendale

15

Lake Mead

93

68

95

Blythe

95

Needles

Yuma

San Luis Rio Colorado

2

El Golfo de Santa Clara

8

Gulf of California

Armagosa Valley

93

Las Vegas

95

Indio

10

Salton Sea

El Centro

Mexicali

8

Rio Hardy

5

Death Valley Junction

373

127

Baker

15

40

2

Ensenada

3

1

© 2014 Chrismar Mapping Services Inc. Licensed for use in the 2014 Select Registry.

Canyon Villa Bed & Breakfast Inn

www.canyonvilla.com
40 Canyon Circle Drive, Sedona, AZ USA 86351
800-453-1166 • 928-284-1226
canvilla@sedona.net

Member Since 1995

Approved

Owners/Innkeepers
Les & Peg Belch

Canyon Villa Inn is uniquely located and custom designed to capture the visual experience of Sedona's world famous Bell Rock & Courthouse Butte. Large common areas and themed intimate guestrooms open from glass doors onto private balconies or lush garden patios. Guestrooms include cable TV, DVD players, free Wi-Fi, phone, clock radios, irons, hair dryers, and 4 have fireplaces. Private ceramic bathrooms include jetted tubs, personal amenities, irons, hair dryers, makeup mirrors, and bath & pool robes. Three course breakfast and appetizer hour each day. 1000 volume library with over 100 DVDs, guest computer, and printer. Guests relax daily under the warm Arizona sun by a glass tiled swimming pool, hike desert trails from the premises, & stargaze cool evenings outdoors by fireside. Ranked in the Top 10 "Best U.S. Inns and B&Bs" 3 of the last 7 years by TripAdvisor Traveler's Choice Awards. Past recipient of "Best U.S. Bed and Breakfast" award from Harper's "Hideaway Report." Recommended by Frommers and admitted to Diamond Collection status by BedandBreakfast.com.

Rates
10 Red Rock View Rooms $199-$349. 1 Limited View Room $189-$199. Discounts for AAA, AARP, Military. Other savings may include Multi-Night discounts as high as 20%. Fares vary by season and are subject to change as per inn's website. Number of Rooms: 11

Cuisine
Three course hot served breakfasts include our award winning Cinnamon Rolls. Afternoon refreshments and appetizers. Guests welcome to bring their own spirits. Harney & Son teas served with original light desert throughout each evening.

Nearest Airport
Phoenix Sky Harbor (PHX) is most popular. Also available is Phoenix-Mesa Gateway (AZA) & Flagstaff (FLG),

SelectRegistry.com

Casa Sedona Inn

www.casasedona.com
55 Hozoni Drive, Sedona, AZ USA 86336
928-282-2938 • 800-525-3756
casa@sedona.net

Member Since 2004

Approved
♦ ♦ ♦

Owner/Innkeeper
Kimberly Komara

Casa Sedona is a world-renowned inn located at the base of Thunder Mountain in a quaint and quiet area of West Sedona. We are just minutes from the bustling "uptown" area, and a short walk or drive to some of the best dining and hiking that Sedona has to offer. Relax in our serene and landscaped gardens or on your private patio or balcony. Our Chef-prepared Southwest gourmet breakfast is served seasonally on our shaded Juniper Garden Patio, offering spectacular red rock views or in our newly renovated dining room. Guest rooms are well appointed with luxurious 600 thread-count pima cotton sheets and down comforters.

Rates
Low season $149-$299 and high season $189-$349. Number of Rooms: 16

Cuisine
Chef-prepared gourmet breakfast leisurely served in our newly renovated dining room or seasonally on the patio.

Nearest Airport
Phoenix Sky Harbor

The Lodge at Sedona

www.LODGEatSEDONA.com
125 Kallof Place, Sedona, AZ USA 86336
800-619-4467 • 928-204-1942 • Fax: 928-204-2128
Info@LODGEatSEDONA.com

Member Since 2003

"Romance and Intrigue, Comfort and Luxury, Escape and Adventure – the Lodge at Sedona has it all." – AZ News. Elegant and Secluded Mission/Arts and Craft Estate set on two acres of grand seclusion in the very heart of Sedona, Arizona. Awarded Top 10 Inns in US by Forbes.com, Best B&Bs by Phoenix Magazine. Recommended by Small Elegant Hotels, Historic Lodging Directory, Bon Appetit, Mobil Three Star, Fodors.com, and Frommer's. Close to hiking trails, biking, golf, tennis, art galleries, and shopping. Spectacular Red Rock views, sculpture gardens, fountains and a magical labyrinth. King suites with fireplaces, jet tubs, spa robes, large decks, stereo TV. Massage Services, complete concierge service and full gourmet breakfast and snacks included daily. Check our Seasonal Specials and Hot Deals." The Lodge at Sedona is one of the most romantic Inns in Arizona." – AZ Foothills Magazine. Imagine staying in the very heart of Sedona protected by acres of serenity, nature and comfort. Come and experience the Lodge at Sedona.

Rates
14 Rooms & King Suites: $199/$349 B&B. King Suites w/ fireplaces, tubs, private decks, private entrances, stereo TV. Our rooms are all romantic, well appointed, and intimately casual. Number of Rooms: 14

Cuisine
Professionally prepared and served gourmet breakfast including Sedona Gold coffee, Lodge granola & our vanilla honey yogurt. Sunset appetizers, drinks & snacks included daily. Enjoy the culinary delights outdoors & indoors. Guest beverages welcome!

Nearest Airport
Phoenix (PHX), Flagstaff (FLG), Sedona (KSEZ)

SelectRegistry.com

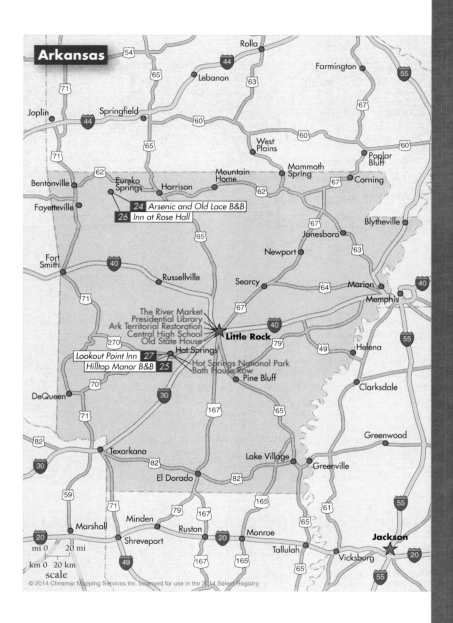

Arkansas

54
65
Rolla
44
Lebanon
63
Farmington
55
71
Joplin
Springfield
44
60
West
Plains
60
60
65
Mammoth
Spring
Poplar
Bluff
62
Bentonville
Eureka
Springs
Harrison
Mountain
Home
62
67
Corning
Fayetteville
24 Arsenic and Old Lace B&B
26 Inn at Rose Hall
67
Blytheville
65
Jonesboro
Newport
63
Fort
Smith
40
Russellville
Searcy
64
Marion
40
71
The River Market
Presidential Library
Ark Territorial Restoration
Central High School
Old State House
67
40
Little Rock
79
Memphis
270
Hot Springs
49
Helena
55
Lookout Point Inn 27
Hilltop Manor B&B 25
Hot Springs National Park
Bath House Row
Pine Bluff
70
30
167
65
Clarksdale
DeQueen
71
Greenwood
82
Texarkana
82
Lake Village
Greenville
30
El Dorado
82
55
59
165
61
65
71
79
167
Marshall
Minden
Ruston
Monroe
20
Jackson
20
mi 0   20 mi
Shreveport
20
Tallulah
Vicksburg
20
km 0   20 km
49
167
165
65
55
scale
© 2014 Chrismar Mapping Services Inc. Licensed for use in the 2014 Select Registry.

Arsenic and Old Lace B&B

www.eurekaspringsromancebb.com
60 Hillside Avenue, Eureka Springs, AR USA 72632
866-350-5454 • 479-253-5454
ArsenicOldLaceBB@gmail.com

Member Since 2006

Arkansas

Eureka Springs

Innkeepers/Owners
Beverly and Doug Breitling

Arsenic and Old Lace is located on a heavily wooded hillside in the Historic District of Eureka Springs. The beautiful Ozark Mountains surround the inn that is a step back to a quieter, more relaxed time. From our Morning Room, or the Chantilly Rose room balcony, guests enjoy the mixed white squirrels, birds, chipmunks and sometimes even deer. A short walk through a wooded area will bring guests to the shops, historic homes and buildings of the Historic Loop. The mood of the inn is relaxed luxury, as your hosts strive to make each guest feel as if they are at home. The relaxed feel continues into your room, where you will find comfortable furnishings, jetted tubs, Comphy micro-fiber sheets, individual thermostats, luxury showers, televisions, VCR/DVD players, CD players and Wireless Internet access. Enjoy the video library to watch a movie, curl-up with a good book or your loved one. Rest, Relax and Recreate! You've stepped back in time without leaving modern necessities. Excite all of your senses with an unforgettable experience!

Rates
$115/$299. Rates vary seasonally and midweek. Number of Rooms: 5

Cuisine
Enjoy custom blended coffee, tea or hot chocolate; our full gourmet breakfast starts with a delicious fruit course, breakfast breads or scones, and a unique main course. Enjoy complimentary homemade snacks all day and a well stocked refrigerator.

Nearest Airport
NW Arkansas Regional (XNA)

$\mathscr{F}$ **SelectRegistry.com**

Hilltop Manor Bed & Breakfast

www.HilltopManorHotSprings.com
2009 Park Avenue, Hot Springs, AR USA 71901
501-625-7829
info@HilltopManorHotSprings.com

Member Since 2010

Arkansas Hot Springs

Innkeepers/Owners
Jennifer DeMott & Joanna Brooks

Legends such as Jesse James and Al Capone have spent time on the Hilltop Manor estate. Is it your turn now? Come visit this award winning 1910 craftsman manor which has been restored to classic elegance. Take refuge from life's stress on this five acre estate which borders the National Park forest and was awarded a "Beauty Spot". Gaze at the waterfall from the expansive front porch. Wander the grounds and explore rock walls and buildings from the past. Meander through the grove of Magnolia trees and stop to smell a rosebud. Whatever you choose to do, we are here so that you can relax. We offer five unique, well-appointed suites most with king-sized bed, whirlpool tub, fireplace, refrigerator and microwave. All with decadent linens, robes and a fully plated breakfast each morning. Relish the morning meal which is served in your private suite, the front porch or the dining room with antique lighting overhead. Named "Top 10 Inns in US" by BedandBreakfast.com. Located just 5 minutes from Historic Downtown Hot Springs.

Rates
Standard Suites $170-$250, Perfect for an anytime escape! Deluxe Suites $250-$350, 2 Person Jacuzzi Tub, Fireplace, King Bed, 40" Flat Screen TV, Spa Therapy Sound Machine and More. Perfect for a Special Romantic Getaway! Number of Rooms: 5

Cuisine
Hilltop Manor is known for its delicious breakfast that is unique each day. There is always a bread item, fruit dish, egg dish and sweet. We promise you won't go away hungry. Happy to accommodate dietary needs; let us know when making your reservation.

Nearest Airport
Hot Springs Memorial Field Airport - 6 Miles, Bill & Hillary Clinton National Airport in Little Rock - 55 Miles

Inn at Rose Hall

www.InnAtRoseHall.com
56 Hillside Ave., P.O. Box 110, Eureka Springs, AR USA 72632
479-253-8035 • 800-544-7734
innkeeper@innatrosehall.com
Member Since 2013

Owners/Innkeepers
Zoie Kaye & Faryl Kaye

The Inn at Rose Hall sits in the heart of the Ozarks in a tiny Victorian Village in Eureka Springs. The narrow, steep hills are reminiscent of early San Francisco. It is an easy ten-minute walk to downtown on history-filled streets lined with Victorian painted ladies.

The Inn provides you a respite from life and the ultimate in a luxurious and relaxing getaway. Select the room that appeals to your personality and sense of comfort. Start your holiday with a treat from the guest pantry, soak in your jetted tub for two, curl up in front of the fireplace and unwind with a movie. The beds have plush toppers, luxurious linens and pillow options to give you a perfect nights sleep. The smell of fresh baked goods and specialty house coffee announces a sumptuous gourmet breakfast.

A guest review says it all: "We're hooked on The Inn at Rose Hall...smelled the cookies baking, welcomed as if we were old friends. The extra pillows, homemade chocolate truffles, and sumptuous breakfast - We love it!"

Rates
Midweek $129-$155, Weekend $149-$185 plus tax. Fireplaces, double jetted tubs, flat screen televisions with DVD players, mini-refrigerators and free Wifi in all rooms. Number of Rooms: 5

Cuisine
Gourmet breakfasts. Individual tables in the Morning Room or in-room service in king rooms. Arrival refreshments and sweet treats in the evening. Guest Pantry available 24 hours with coffee, selection of teas, hot chocolate, and snacks.

Nearest Airport
Northwest Arkansas (XNA) Fayetteville, AR (1 hour); (BKG) Branson, Missouri (1 hour); (TUL) Tulsa, OK (3 hour).

Lookout Point Lakeside Inn

www.LookoutPointInn.com
104 Lookout Circle, Hot Springs, AR USA 71913
866-525-6155 • 501-525-6155 • Fax: 501-525-5850
info@LookoutPointInn.com

Member Since 2005

Arkansas Hot Springs

Innkeepers/Owners
Ray & Kristie Rosset

Enjoy peace and tranquility, comprehensive pampering, and luxury. Relax with the views of Lake Hamilton and the low-lying Ouachita Mountains from your guest room. Experience an exceptional inn, with fine attention to detail as its hallmark. Delicious breakfasts from one of the Eight Broads in the Kitchen (www.EightBroads.com) starts your day splendidly. The gardens with waterfalls and meditation labyrinth provide a perfect backdrop for small, intimate weddings. Canoe the bay, watch the birds, nap in the hammock, or soak in the nearby historic Hot Springs bathhouses. In addition to the inn's guest rooms, a one or two bedroom lakeside condominium, called Lakeview Terrace, invites guests to enjoy the 36 ft. deck right at water's edge. The condo is perfect for a family to enjoy all of Hot Springs' fun. Chosen Top Ten B&B/Inn in the U.S. by TripAdvisor Travelers Choice Awards.

Rates
$159/$399 for rooms and suites. $299/$509 for 1 or 2 bedroom condo. Rates based upon type of room and season. Corporate weekday rates available. Wedding, romance and family fun packages available. Number of Rooms: 13

Cuisine
Fresh and hearty breakfast plus Innkeeper's Reception features dessert, appetizers, wine and tea. Complimentary snack bar. Soups, salads and hot/cold sandwiches available. Gourmet dinner for two by private chef, with dining by the waterfalls.

Nearest Airport
Little Rock, 60 miles. Air service to Hot Springs airport available from Memphis & Dallas.

California

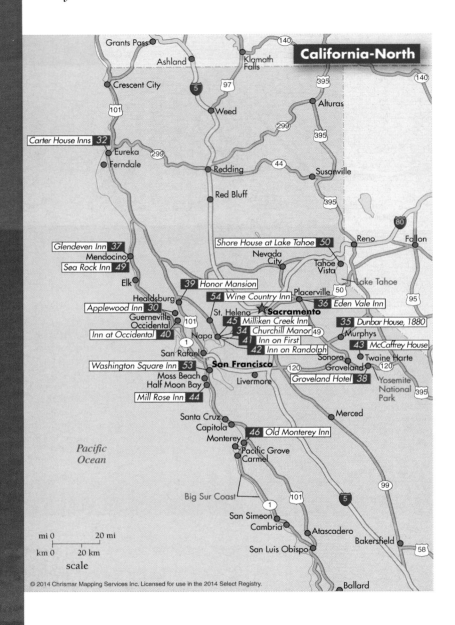

SelectRegistry.com

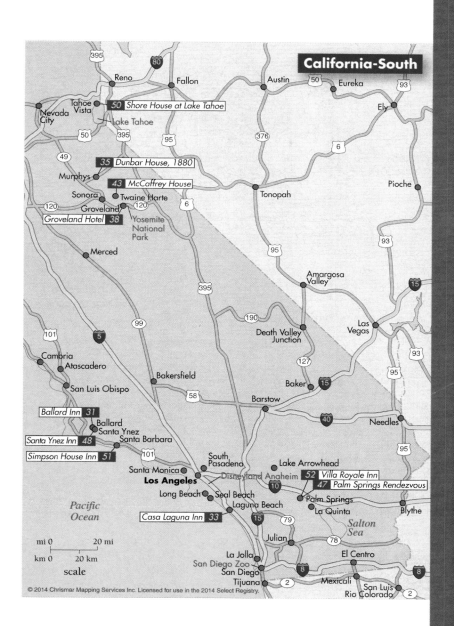

California-South

395
80
Reno
Fallon
Austin
50
Eureka
93
Tahoe
Vista
50 Shore House at Lake Tahoe
Ely
Nevada
City
Lake Tahoe
50
395
95
376
6
49
35 Dunbar House, 1880
Murphys
Pioche
43 McCaffrey House
Sonora
Twaine Harte
120
Tonopah
120
Groveland
6
Groveland Hotel 38
Yosemite
National
Park
95
93
Merced
Amargosa
Valley
15
395
99
190
101
5
Death Valley
Junction
Las
Vegas
Cambria
127
93
Atascadero
Baker
95
San Luis Obispo
Bakersfield
15
58
Barstow
Ballard Inn 31
Ballard
40
Needles
Santa Ynez
Santa Ynez Inn 48
Santa Barbara
95
Simpson House Inn 51
101
South
Pasadena
Lake Arrowhead
Santa Monica
Los Angeles
Disneyland Anaheim 52 Villa Royale Inn
10
47 Palm Springs Rendezvous
Long Beach
Seal Beach
Palm Springs
Laguna Beach
La Quinta
Blythe
Pacific
Ocean
Casa Laguna Inn 33
15
79
Salton
Sea
mi 0   20 mi
Julian
78
km 0   20 km
La Jolla
El Centro
scale
San Diego Zoo
San Diego
8
8
Tijuana
2
Mexicali
San Luis
Rio Colorado
2

© 2014 Chrismar Mapping Services Inc. Licensed for use in the 2014 Select Registry.

iOi iOi ℞ Applewood Inn

www.applewoodinn.com
13555 Hwy 116, Guerneville, CA USA 95446
800-555-8509 • Fax: 707-869-9170
relax@applewoodinn.com

Member Since 2004

Approved
♦ ♦ ♦

Owners
Carlos Pippa and Sylvia Ranyak

A lovely and verdant meadow guarded by towering Redwoods in the heart of Sonoma's
Russian River Valley (one of the world's premier growing regions for Pinot Noir &
Chardonnay grapes) is home to Applewood Inn and its acclaimed restaurant which is
recommended by Zagat and has earned a Michelin star for 2011. Splashing fountains
and whimsical statues add texture and interest to the terraced courtyard and gardens
that separate the tile roofed and stuccoed villas of this gracious Mediterranean complex.
The old-world atmosphere of a "Gentleman's Farm" is evoked in lovingly maintained
orchards and kitchen gardens that supply the restaurant through the Summer and early Fall.
Gourmet picnic baskets provided by Applewood's kitchen help make a day of exploring the
wine country and dramatic Sonoma Coast all the more enjoyable while Day Spa services
add a touch of indulgent pampering. Located within a short drive of wineries in both the
Napa and Sonoma Valleys, the Sonoma coast and Armstrong State Redwood Reserve.

Rates
$165/$375. Number of Rooms: 19

Cuisine
The Michelin starred restaurant at Applewood offers Mediterranean inspired wine
country fare paired with a Sonoma wine list. The inn's romantic dining room features
lovely views over a garden courtyard & towering redwoods. Adv reservations
suggested.

Nearest Airport
San Francisco/Oakland/Sonoma County

SelectRegistry.com

The Ballard Inn

www.ballardinn.com
2436 Baseline Ave., Ballard, CA USA 93463
800-638-2466 • 805-688-7770 • Fax: 805-688-9560
innkeeper@ballardinn.com

Member Since 1993

California Ballard

AAA Four Diamond Award

General Manager
Christine Forsyth

Voted one of America's Top Ten Most Romantic Inns, our comfortably elegant 4 diamond country inn is nestled among vineyards and orchards in the charming, historic township of Ballard. Each of the fifteen rooms possesses its own special charm and character reflecting local history. Many of our rooms have fireplaces, creating an especially romantic retreat. Borrow a bicycle and take a picnic lunch for an adventurous tour of the Santa Ynez Valley wine country. A tasting of local wine & hors d'oeuvres, bed turn down service with home-made cookies, and a full breakfast are included in your stay. The acclaimed Ballard Inn Restaurant features French-Asian cuisine in an intimate 12 table dining room complete with a magnificent marble fireplace. Our Restaurant is open to the public Wednesday-Sunday. AAA Four Diamond.

Rates
$265-$345 not including taxes or service charge. Closed Christmas Eve & Christmas Day. Number of Rooms: 15

Cuisine
Breakfast: A delicious full breakfast, included with your stay, is served in our dining room each morning.
The Restaurant: The Chef's award winning French Asian fare melds the flavors of eastern & western cuisines to create mouthwatering dishes.

Nearest Airport
Santa Barbara
Santa Maria

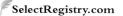

Carter House Inns

www.carterhouse.com
301 L Street, Eureka, CA USA 95501
800-404-1390 • 707-444-8062 • Fax: 707-444-8067
reserve@carterhouse.com

Member Since 2003

California

Eureka

GRAND AWARD 2013

Innkeepers/Owners
Mark Carter and Christi Carter

Northern California's premier inn is perched alongside Humboldt Bay in Eureka, California. The luxurious accommodations at Carter House Inns and the sumptuous dining at its Restaurant 301, featuring 3500 wines and the Grand Award from Wine Spectator since 1998, is considered among Northern California's best restaurants and offers a full bar with our own Kentucky Bourbon. Drive through the giant redwood forests, walk rugged Pacific beaches and experience the other wonders of Redwood Coast. Our accommodations and service are unparalleled; our award-winning cuisine is prepared with local organic products and fresh herbs, greens, and vegetables harvested daily from the inn's extensive gardens. The inn also produces its own wines at our winery in Calistoga—Envy Wines (www.envywines.com) and Carter Cellars (www.cartercellars.com) which specializes in limited production of cabs & merlots from the finest vineyards in Napa Valley with a perfect wine scoring 100 points from Robert Parker. Check out all our specials and packages and accommodations in the heart of the Redwood Empire!

Rates
9 Rooms, $179/$385 B&B, 2 Suites, $312/$595 B&B. Open year-round. Number of Rooms: 11

Cuisine
Full service award-winning restaurant open nightly, full breakfast, full bar, Wine Shop with 3,500 wine selections. With a recent perfect wine scoring of 100 points from Robert Parker, Carter Cellars wine is quickly becoming a cult classic.

Nearest Airport
Eureka-Arcata Airport is 16 miles north of Eureka.

SelectRegistry.com

Casa Laguna Inn & Spa

www.casalaguna.com
2510 South Coast Highway , Laguna Beach, CA USA 92651
800-233-0449 • 949-494-2996 • Fax: 949-494-5009
innkeeper@casalaguna.com

Member Since 2004

California Laguna Beach

General Manager
Kathryn Mace

Created as a tranquil alternative to bustling family-style resorts, Casa Laguna Inn & Spa is the perfect place for a romantic getaway or a relaxing escape from work and worry. Built on a terraced hillside, our inn is often compared to the Mission-style villas of Spain. In order to assure a romantic, calming ambiance, room occupancy is limited to a maximum of two persons regardless of age. Massage can be reserved in our candlelit indoor spa or in our ocean-view garden, accompanied by a therapeutic soak. Beautiful Victoria Beach is just a 10-minute walk away. Casa Laguna is also within walking distance of two superb restaurants. As you snuggle down in one of our acclaimed luxurious beds, dream of our famous gourmet breakfast, chosen from a full menu of delicious seasonal entrees. Our inn is just 1.5 miles from downtown Laguna Beach shops, restaurants, art galleries, and renowned summer art festivals. Casa Laguna has been recognized as one of the Top 25 Small Hotels and Top 10 Hotels for Romance in the United States, as well one of the Top Ten Luxury Inns in the world.

Rates
Rooms, suites & a cottage: $159 to $679 subject to weekend/seasonal adjustments. All rooms have luxurious bedding, AC, flat-panel HDTV, DVD player, & free WiFi. Some rooms have jetted tubs. Most have ambiance or gas fireplaces. Number of Rooms: 22

Cuisine
Our inn has become a well-known "foodie" destination. Guests choose from a menu of 7 to 9 gourmet breakfast entrees & sides. A selection of wine & gourmet hors d'oeuvres is served at our evening reception. A hot/cold beverage bar is open all day.

Nearest Airport
Orange Co, John Wayne(SNA); Los Angeles(LAX); San Diego(SAN); Ontario(ONT)

♿ 🍴 ♀

Churchill Manor

www.churchillmanor.com
485 Brown Street, Napa, CA USA 94559
800-799-7733 • 707-253-7733 • Fax: 707-253-8836
be@churchillmanor.com

Member Since 2013

California
Napa

Innkeeper/Owner
Joanna Guidotti

Built in 1889, Churchill Manor is the first private residence in Napa County to be placed on the National Register of Historic Places. Churchill Manor is an exquisite mansion offering the exclusivity of only ten guest rooms and an abundance of shared spaces for guest use inside our 10.000 square foot mansion. Enjoy the expansive front parlor with original unpainted woodwork, historic dining room, entertainment parlor, and solarium. A massive wrap-around veranda allows many vantage points from which to contemplate our beautiful grounds with numerous varieties of roses, manicured lawns, and mature trees.

Our experienced staff is delighted to assist you in planning winery excursions and making dinner reservations both in advance of or during your stay.

Guest rooms are individually decorated and offer fireplaces and private bathrooms, most with claw foot bathtubs and all with showers. The beds are very comfortable with luxurious bedding. Plush microfiber robes and slippers are provided for the use of our guests.

Rates
Rates are $179 to $389 depending on time of year, room chosen, and days of the week. Number of Rooms: 10

Cuisine
Churchill Manor offers a two hour wine and appetizer reception each evening, a gourmet three course breakfast each morning, and fresh baked cookies in the afternoon.

Nearest Airport
The San Francisco, Oakland, and Sacramento airports are all within a 75 minute drive, except peak traffic times.

f 🐦 📌 👀 g+

🖋 **SelectRegistry.com**

Dunbar House, 1880

www.dunbarhouse.com
271 Jones Street, Murphys, CA USA 95247
209-728-2897
dunbarhouse@dunbarhouse.com

Member Since 2001

Innkeepers/Owners
Richard & Arline Taborek

Step into Dunbar House, 1880 and step back into a piece of history, where homes were beautifully decorated with a casual elegance. This AAA Four Diamond Italianate home is filled with Old World Charm, and offers guests a private haven of relaxation, comfort and ease. Located two hours east of San Francisco, nestled between Lake Tahoe and Yosemite in the Sierra foothills, Murphys has not changed much since the Great Gold Rush. Just steps across the bridge over Murphys Creek are restaurants, galleries, wineries, seasonal events, and live theatre. Our lovingly tended historic rose garden and surrounding floral gardens are the jewels of our property. Water fountains and lush greenery abound, surrounded by a white picket fence with many private sitting areas. Read a good book, or take a long nap in our hammock for that ultimate, lazy afternoon. An appetizer plate and local bottle of wine await guests in their rooms each day. Grab a fresh baked cookie, a cup of hot chocolate, or a glass of Rosemary Lemonade or Iced Tea, and just sit on our veranda and watch the world go by.

Rates
$199-$290. Special rates for 3 & 4 nights, also Corporate rates. In room refrigerator stocked with appetizer plate, wine, beer & water. TV/DVD, AC, gas stove, Free WiFi, and private porches. 2-person Jacuzzi in Cedar and Sequoia. Number of Rooms: 5

Cuisine
Enjoy your beautifully presented gourmet breakfast & our own special freshly brewed roasted coffee blend, served in our cozy dining room by the fire or in our beautiful century-old garden. Our breakfasts are cooked with love and served with pride.

Nearest Airport
SFO-San Francisco, SAC-Sacramento, SJC-San Jose

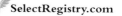

Eden Vale Inn

www.EdenValeInn.com
1780 Springvale Rd, Placerville, CA USA 95667
530-621-0901
innkeeper@EdenValeInn.com

Member Since 2013

California
Placerville

Innkeepers/Owners
Mark Hamlin and Gayle Erbe-Hamlin

Featured in Sunset Magazine, and chosen as one of "America's Top 10 Most Romantic Inns" by iLoveInns.com, this contemporary inn offers all the modern amenities in a unique resort environment on a rustic 10 acre setting. All of the guest rooms are newly reconstructed with fireplaces, in-room controlled air and heat, and free WiFi, satellite HDTV/DVD, parking and telephone. You'll stay in a uniquely styled room with a private luxury bath. Breakfast can be enjoyed in the sun room or on the decks overlooking the gardens. The inn includes extensive gardens, wedding pavilion, swimming pond and an onsite Spa for therapeutic massages. This superb rural Sierra Foothills setting is located east of Sacramento near Placerville and Coloma, the site of the California Gold Discovery State Park. Area activities include Gold Rush History, Apple Hill Family Farms, all season Hiking, Rafting and Wine Tasting. Lake Tahoe is only an hour and a half away. Within an hour of the inn are over 100 Sierra Foothill wineries which continue to take Gold Medals at the State Fair year after year.

Rates
Rates start at $169 per night, depending on the room selected and length of stay. Visit our website or call us for seasonal specials. Accommodations for 4 people and pet friendly options available for an additional fee. Number of Rooms: 7

Cuisine
Full breakfast featuring fresh fruit, homemade baked goods, juices and hot entree using locally sourced ingredients. Early morning coffee/tea. Local wine available for purchase on premise. Full use of guest kitchen and BBQ. Quality restaurants nearby.

Nearest Airport
Sacramento Int'l SMF, 1 hr; San Fran Int'l SFO, 2.5 hrs; Reno-Tahoe Int'l RNO, 2 hrs.

SelectRegistry.com

Glendeven Inn

🍽️ 🍽️ 🍽️ 🍷

www.glendeven.com
8205 North Highway One, P.O. Box 914, Mendocino, CA USA 95460
800-822-4536 • 707-937-0083
innkeeper@glendeven.com

Member Since 2002

California Mendocino

Proprietor
John Dixon

Offering exceptional experiences daily, this ocean view, luxury farm-stay property focuses on service and amenities that are comfortable, detailed, and personal. Seen in many national publications, this well appointed, 8-acre farmstead offers wood-burning fireplaces, gourmet in-room breakfasts with farm-fresh eggs, featherbeds, outstanding gardens, over 50 local wines in its Wine Bar[n] and a complimentary wine & hors d'oeuvres hour. Glendeven is a multi-building 1867 farmstead situated on a headland meadow with grazing llamas, roaming chickens, manicured gardens & an organic edible garden. Located 2 minutes south of the historic Mendocino village, Glendeven offers trails to the Pacific headland cliffs, to the beach & to its own Forest Trail connecting to Fern Canyon trail along Little River. Its Wine Bar[n] features flight tastings of local Mendocino County wines. There is a 2,000 sq ft vacation rental onsite, perfect for couples traveling together. A four-course, Farm-to-Table, wine paired, ocean-view dinner is available three times weekly at Glendeven's farm table.

Rates
Six rooms & 4 suites among four separate historic buildings plus two vacation rental houses. $150 to $380. King & Queen beds. 2-6 people per unit. Open year-round.
Number of Rooms: 12

Cuisine
Breakfast is 3-courses served in-room with their farm eggs. A Farm-to-Table dinner is 3 times weekly with wine pairing at a shared table. Wine & appetizers in the Wine Bar[n] nightly. Coffee, teas & baked goods always available in the farmhouse lounge.

Nearest Airport
San Francisco, Oakland, and Sacramento

SelectRegistry.com

37

& |O| |O| |O| ♀
# Groveland Hotel

www.groveland.com
18767 Main Street, P.O. Box 289, Groveland, CA USA 95321
800-273-3314 • 209-962-4000 • Fax: 209-962-6674
guestservices@groveland.com   *Member Since 2005*

Wine Spectator
BEST OF
AWARD OF
EXCELLENCE
2013

Innkeeper/Owner
Peggy Mosley

Savor a lazy morning in the most luxurious feather bed you'll never want to get out of, snuggle into one of our cozy bathrobes, and enjoy a cup of freshly-brewed coffee on our veranda. The Groveland Hotel is just 23 scenic miles from the gate of Yosemite National Park, and is a peaceful, playful, pet-friendly place to rest during your Sierra adventures. World-class whitewater river rafting is just five minutes away. Explore California's gold rush history, wildflowers, and diverse wildlife of the region, which includes bears, mountain lions and bald eagles. One of Country Inn's US Top 10 Inns, Sunset Magazine called us "A West's Best Inn." Enjoy fine yet casual dining in the Cellar Door Restaurant, featuring California fresh cuisine with local fresh ingredients. Explore our Wine Spectator Best of Award of Excellence wine list with over 640 labels, kept cool in our natural stone wine cellar, hand-laid in 1849 when the hotel was built (we're on the National Register of Historic Places). FREE parking, WiFi, and a full hot breakfast are all included with your stay.

Rates
Suites: $235-$349. Rooms: $145-$249, seasonal pricing. Rates are for 2 guests. Additional guests: $25 per person. Pets Welcome - $20/pet/night includes treats and use of bowls. $4.50 Energy Surcharge. Number of Rooms: 17

Cuisine
Gourmet breakfast, lunch for groups and full service fine yet casual dining, open to the public. Summer Courtyard dining and music. Special holiday menus. Full service saloon and Wine Spectator Best of Award of Excellence wine list.

Nearest Airport
Approx. 2.5 hours from Sacramento (SAC), Oakland (OAK), or San Francisco (SFO), 5 mins from E45 in PML.

f 𝕏 𝔭 ⊚⊚

The Honor Mansion, A Wine Country Resort

www.honormansion.com
891 Grove Street, Healdsburg, CA USA 95448
800-554-4667 • 707-433-4277 • Fax: 707-431-7173
innkeeper@honormansion.com

Member Since 1998

Owners
Steve & Cathi Fowler

The only AAA 4 Diamond property in Healdsburg since 1998. A TripAdvisor Traveler's Choice winner 2014 #1 top 25 Romantic Hotels US, #11 top 25 Romantic Hotels World, #2 top 25 Small Hotels US, #3 Top 25 Luxury Hotels US & the recipient of 2 perfect quality inspections in a row from Select Registry, this luxuriously intimate resort awaits your arrival. Imagine world-class amenities & service with hometown hospitality. Pool, tennis, PGA putting green, bocce, croquet, basketball, massages & gardens, all situated on 4 acres of landscaped grounds. A pleasant walk to the downtown square which is replete with shops & restaurants. The perfect romantic special occasion get-away. Healdsburg, voted one of the top 10 small towns in America by Fodor's, is at the confluence of the world-renowned wine growing regions of Dry Creek, Alexander & Russian River Valleys, with over 150 wineries. Come enjoy our passion for this incredible area & discover some of our boutique wineries. Our fully trained concierge staff is at your service. Come, let us pamper you!

Rates
13 Rooms: $240/$600, 2 guests per room. K & Q beds, fireplaces, soaking tubs, private decks, spa tubs, wifi and more. Number of Rooms: 13

Cuisine
Full gourmet breakfast buffet, as well a limited list of enhancements available with 24 hour notice, complimentary evening wine and appetizers, sherry, and bottomless cookie jar. Complimentary soda, water, coffee & tea always available.

Nearest Airport
Oakland and San Francisco

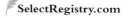

♿ 🍽

Inn at Occidental

www.innatoccidental.com
3657 Church Street, P.O. Box 857, Occidental, CA USA 95465-0857
800-522-6324 • 707-874-1047 • Fax: 707-874-1078
innkeeper@innatoccidental.com   *Member Since 1995*

California

Occidental

Innkeepers/Owners
Jerry & Tina Wolsborn

Inn at Occidental of Sonoma Wine Country--according to The Wine Spectator, "One of
the Top Five Wine Country Destinations." The antiques, original art and decor provide
charm, warmth and elegance exceeded only by the hospitality you experience." Tops our
List as the Most Romantic Place to Stay" is what Bride and Groom said of the featherbeds,
down comforters, spa tubs for two, fireplaces and private decks. The gourmet breakfast and
evening wine and cheese reception add to a memorable experience. Excellent boutique
wineries, Armstrong Redwoods State Reserve, Russian River, the dramatic coast and
scenic drives along country backroads make for a great destination and the perfect hub for
exploring the pristine area. Hiking, biking, horseback riding and golfing nearby. Concierge
service. All reasons why AAA VIA says of The Inn "The Best Bed and Breakfast in the
West." An Andrew Harper Recommendation.

Rates
3 Suites, 13 Rooms: Fireplaces, Spa Tubs, Decks $199/$379, 2 BR Vacation House
$689. Number of Rooms: 18

Cuisine
Full gourmet breakfast. Local wines and cheeses and freshly-baked cookies provided
nightly. Wonderful dining nearby. Special Functions: Wedding, Corporate Retreat,
Celebrations.

Nearest Airport
San Francisco (SFO), Oakland (OAK), Santa Rosa (limited service)

𝝏 **SelectRegistry.com**

The Inn on First

www.theinnonfirst.com
1938 1st Street, Napa, CA USA 94559
707-253-1331
innkeeper@theinnonfirst.com

Member Since 2008

California Napa

Approved

Innkeepers/Owners
Jim Gunther and Jamie Cherry

We have set the new standard for the Napa Bed and Breakfast Inn. We cater to a new generation of B&B guests who want something more than doilies, egg bakes, and cheap sherry. With no televisions in the rooms, we choose to be counter-cultural and encourage our guests to disconnect from the world in order to reconnect with each other.

We are attracting guests who want great food for breakfast. The Inn on First is where you are able to experience a chef's creative innovation each morning, in one of his 118 recipes for breakfast such as Corndog Omelets, Tomato and Egg Soup with Grilled Cheese Croutons, or S'mores French Toast with house made Marshmallows.

The Inn boasts 10 comfortable, elegant rooms, each uniquely appointed. A long list of amenities includes free internet access, fireplaces, whirlpool tubs and private baths in every room accompanied by complimentary sparkling wine, specialty refreshments, house-made confections and snacks.

Rates
10 rooms, 5 Mansion and 5 Garden Suites. Rates vary by season. Winter (November-February): $150-$250; Spring (March-May): $200-$300; Summer (May-July): $275-$325; Peak (August-October): $295-$400. Number of Rooms: 10

Cuisine
Exciting, California Contemporary Comfort food. Guests are served in two courses. The first consists of house-made granola and pastry, fresh fruit salad, and yogurt. The second is a unique and whimsical creation that keeps guests returning.

Nearest Airport
1-Sacramento. 2-Oakland. 3-San Francisco. Although OAK and SFO are closer than SAC, there is less traffic to SAC.

♿ 🍽️   🍷

Inn on Randolph

www.innonrandolph.com
411 Randolph Street, Napa, CA USA 94559
707-257-2886
innkeeper@innonrandolph.com

Member Since 2013

Owner/Innkeeper
Karen Lynch

The Inn on Randolph brings fresh vitality to the world of boutique inns. Chosen by the Wall Street Journal as part of a new crop of trophy B&Bs, this stunningly restored historic property is run by innovative and savvy owners with a keen eye for design and comfort. With their finger on the pulse of Napa, they provide guests with the most current wine country experience. Whether it's booking restaurant reservations, suggesting the perfect winery or a beautiful trail to hike, your hosts will exceed expectations.

The Inn on Randolph strikes the perfect balance between peaceful refuge and the comfort and convenience derived from the most modern of amenities. Seemingly secluded, it sits in the heart of all that downtown Napa has to offer. A gourmet breakfast prepared by one of Napa's rising culinary stars completes the unique experience.

"A thoroughly modern inn with 10 next-generation guest rooms boasting luxuries like heated bathroom floors. Need further proof that this isn't your grandma's B-and-B? The gourmet kitchen just so happens to be gluten-free." – Forbes

Rates
$225-$450 Rates vary by season. Heated bathroom floors, spa tubs, fireplaces, flat screen TV's, private garden areas and conference rooms. Complimentary half bottle of wine, free wi-fi and parking. Number of Rooms: 10

Cuisine
Full gourmet breakfast created in our gluten-free kitchen with fresh ingredients sourced from our gardens. Start the day with homemade granola, fresh organic fruit, and creamy yogurt before moving onto a creative main dish prepared daily by our chef.

Nearest Airport
OAK - Oakland, CA; SAC - Sacramento, CA; SFO - San Francisco, CA

f 𝓟 ◎◎ 8+

McCaffrey House

www.mccaffreyhouse.com
23251 Highway 108, P.O. Box 67, Twain Harte, CA USA 95383
888-586-0757 • 209-586-0757
innkeeper@mccaffreyhouse.com

Member Since 2004

California · Twain Harte

Innkeepers/Proprietors
Michael & Stephanie McCaffrey

Pure elegance...in a wilderness setting. This AAA Four Diamond inn is a delightfully warm and enchanting mountain lodge nestled in a quiet forest hollow of the High Sierra - near Yosemite National Park. Guestrooms are artfully decorated with gas fire place, private bath with tub & shower, flat screen TV, DVD player, free WiFi, iPod Dock and parking, plus exquisite views of the forest that envelops the inn. McCaffrey House was designed and built by your hosts, Michael and Stephanie. They had one essential theme in mind: refined luxury blended with comfort and modern convenience. General gathering areas are spacious and beautifully decorated with a fascinating collection of furniture and art. All appointments have such a welcoming touch that they extend an invitation to come often and stay awhile. In summer, breakfast is served on the decks which surround the inn. Enjoy the romance of this mountain lodge, the pleasure of a family vacation, or take over the inn for a reunion, a business meeting or a small wedding. Well behaved children and pets are welcomed at McCaffrey House.

Rates
$169/$225. Number of Rooms: 8

Cuisine
Awaken to the aroma of fresh coffee. Relax in the dining room for a full country/gourmet breakfast prepared by Stephanie. Enjoy fresh fruits & juice, hot entrees, potatoes, muffins, scones, Decadent French Toast, delicious egg casseroles & quiches.

Nearest Airport
Approximately 2.5 hours from SAC, SFO, SJC, OAK
Check website under location for directions to the inn.

Mill Rose Inn

www.millroseinn.com
615 Mill Street, Half Moon Bay, CA USA 94019
800-900-7673 • 650-726-8750
info@millroseinn.com

Member Since 2008

California Half Moon Bay

AAA
Four Diamond
Award

Innkeepers/Owners
Terry & Eve Baldwin

For guests who expect extraordinary personal service, warm hospitality and meticulous attention to detail, the Mill Rose Inn of Half Moon Bay is a destination not to be missed. This award-winning boutique Inn is renowned for an exuberant garden of year round color, sinfully comfortable rooms and suites, decadent culinary treats and an easy five-minute walk to beaches, numerous shops, galleries and restaurants of vibrant Half Moon Bay. The Mill Rose Inn invites you to relax and be pampered in the comfortable luxury of an English country garden by the sea. The innkeepers and their staff welcome you into a world of tranquility and romance. Ideally located 30 minutes south of San Francisco and 45 minutes north of the heart of Silicon Valley on the breathtakingly beautiful California coast, the Inn is the perfect venue for a special celebration, a reunion, or a business meeting, as well as an elegant garden wedding and reception. A Mill Rose Inn massage treatment coupled with our spa enhances your total escape. Owned and operated since 1982. Four-diamond AAA rating since 1992.

Rates
Baroque Rose Room $175-$230,
Burgundy and Briar Rose Rooms $235-$280,
Botticelli Rose Room $265-$310,
Renaissance and Bordeaux Rose Suites $295-$360 Number of Rooms: 6

Cuisine
Our Lavish gourmet champagne breakfast served to you in your room or dining room gets rave reviews from all our guests. Fresh and homemade emphasized!

Nearest Airport
We are 30 mins. from San Francisco Intl. & 45 mins. from Oakland Intl. & San Jose Intl.

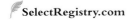

Milliken Creek Inn & Spa, A Four Sisters Luxury Inn

www.millikencreekinn.com
1815 Silverado Trail, Napa, CA USA 94558
888-622-5775 • 707-255-1197 • Fax: 707-255-3112
millikencreekinn@foursisters.com

Member Since 2014

California
Napa

Innkeeper
David Jessup

Milliken Creek Inn & Spa is an elegant Napa hotel in California's esteemed wine country. Hidden away on three verdant acres overlooking the idyllic Napa River, discover a place unlike any other Napa hotel. Here you will encounter five-star luxury that emphasizes thoroughly sophisticated service and style in a tranquil, intimate ambiance.

In this peaceful setting, simply sumptuous accommodations are bathed in serene colors and accented with an exotic flair. Thoughtful touches invite pampering and romance, such as flickering fireplaces, canopy beds with the finest linens, rain showers and oversized hydrotherapy tubs. Combining the best signature service of larger Napa hotels with a very exclusive and intimate ambiance.

The spa at Milliken Creek Inn is the perfect place to restore mind, body and soul. Massage, body treatments and aesthetic services available.

Rates
$449-$799. Number of Rooms: 12

Cuisine
A gourmet breakfast served in the privacy of your room or al fresco anywhere on the property. At day's end, unwind at our complimentary wine and cheese reception, and of course, enjoy our delicious, homemade cookies served throughout the day.

Nearest Airport
San Francisco International Airport
Sacramento International Airport
Oakland International Airport

Old Monterey Inn

www.oldmontereyinn.com
500 Martin St. , Monterey, CA USA 93940
800-350-2344 • 831-375-8284 • Fax: 831-375-6730
omi@oldmontereyinn.com

Member Since 1993

Innkeepers/Owners
Lawrence and Katy Havlick

"The level of service and accommodations here would rival most any inn or hotel we've visited," says The San Francisco Chronicle. Set amidst an acre of spectacular gardens on a quiet, oak-studded Monterey hillside, the Old Monterey Inn exudes romance and warmth. The 1929 half-timbered English Tudor Inn's rooms all overlook the uniquely beautiful gardens. Inside, guests find the attention to detail, which is the hallmark of the Inn-- memorably fluffy featherbeds and 24-hour access to mineral waters, juices, tea and coffee. A full gourmet breakfast is served bedside or in our Heritage dining room, or, weather permitting, in our gardens. The owner imbues every element with the extra touches that help the Inn achieve near perfection. Recommended by prestigious Harper's Hideaway Report, Conde Nast Gold List, and Travel & Leisure (as seen on a recent Today Show Dream Getaway Segment).

Rates
Cottage, 3 Suites and 6 Rooms with sitting areas - fireplaces, spa tubs, private baths, air conditioning $199-$499. Number of Rooms: 10

Cuisine
Gourmet breakfast. Evening wine and hors d'oeuvres. Extraordinary restaurants nearby. Port and fresh fruit.

Nearest Airport
Monterey Airport - 10 min. San Jose Airport - 1 hr. 15 mins. SFO - 2 hrs. 30 mins.

SelectRegistry.com

Palm Springs Rendezvous

www.palmspringsrendezvous.com
1420 North Indian Canyon Drive, Palm Springs, CA USA 92262
800-485-2808 • 760-320-1178 • Fax: 760-320-5308
info@palmspringsrendezvous.com

Member Since 2009

California Palm Springs

General Manager
John-Michael Cooper

TripAdvisor Travelers' Choice Award for Top 10 Romance & Bargain properties! Top 25 Relaxation & Spa by TripAdvisor Users! Enter Rendezvous through custom frosted glass doors and hear nostalgic '50s music wafting through the air. Pass into the sunny courtyard with pristine pool, hot tub, and blue carpeted deck. Settle into a lounge chair, wrap yourself in a plush towel, bake in the beautiful desert sun while looking at high mountain peaks. Choose the '50s theme of the 10 rooms – Elvis, Marilyn, The Rat Pack, Lucy, or Route 66. Each room opens to the pool and courtyard and has a King Bed, 32" Flat Panel TV, DVD & MP3 Player, sitting area, refrigerator, microwave, coffee maker, plush robes, organic bathroom amenities, tiled showers, and luxury linens. 8 rooms have 2 person whirlpool tubs. Single or couples massage in our creekside massage studio. Rendezvous is known for its amazingly attentive staff, who make you feel at home, set you up with reservations at all the best local restaurants and activities, and pamper and entertain you from the moment you step through the door!

Rates
$139-$269 depending on room and season. Includes use of complimentary cruiser bikes to ride around the glamorous movie-star neighborhoods of the '50s, and into town. Fresh baked treats delivered to your room daily. Number of Rooms: 10

Cuisine
Guests marvel at our award-winning 3 course breakfasts - fresh fruit smoothies, a daily fruit creation, and a creative main course. Enjoy a RendezBlu martini and appetizer each evening poolside. We cater to individual dietary needs. Cookbook available

Nearest Airport
Palm Springs International airport is 5 miles away. Ontario, Los Angeles & San Diego airports 50-110 miles away.

Santa Ynez Inn

www.santaynezinn.com
3627 Sagunto St., Santa Ynez, CA USA 93460
800-643-5774 • 805.688.5588 • Fax: 805.686.4294
info@santaynezinn.com

Member Since 2004

California

Santa Ynez

Innkeeper/Owner/General Manager
Douglas Ziegler/Rick Segovia

Our Wine Country Getaway awaits in 14 individually decorated luxury guest rooms. Accommodations feature unique antique furnishings, queen or king-sized beds with Frette linens, remote-controlled gas fireplaces, steam showers and whirlpool tubs in deluxe marble baths. Most rooms offer a semi-private balcony or patio to savor the beauty and serenity of the Santa Ynez Valley. Take advantage of all that Santa Barbara County has to offer, from wine tasting and antique shopping, to Glider rides and Jeep tours. There's something for everyone in Santa Ynez. After a day of Southern California sightseeing adventures, you may wish to unwind in the heated outdoor whirlpool, lounge on the sundeck, or take a leisurely stroll through the gardens of the Inn. Whatever your needs--whether you wish to arrange for wine tasting tours, shopping, dining, glider rides, bicycle rentals or spa treatment--our concierge service is eager to assist you.

Rates
$245/$445. Number of Rooms: 14

Cuisine
Full Gourmet breakfast, Evening Wine & Hors d'oeuvres and Nightly Desserts.

Nearest Airport
Santa Barbara Airport

Sea Rock Inn

www.searock.com
11101 Lansing Street, Mendocino, CA USA 95460
800-906-0926 • 707-937-0926 • Fax: 707-676-9008
innkeeper@searock.com

Member Since 2005

California Mendocino

Innkeepers/Owners
Andy & Susie Plocher

One of the few inns in Mendocino with ocean views from every hillside accommodation, The Sea Rock Inn beckons with crashing surf and inviting firelight rooms. From your suite or cottage you will experience the true beauty of the Mendocino Coast with spectacular panoramic views of the ocean and dramatic rocky cliffs of the Mendocino Headlands State Park. The setting is perfect for a memorable getaway. Hand-hewn wood treatments accent luxuriously comfortable coastal contemporary design and appointments of virtually every amenity imaginable. Stroll through colorful gardens, curl up by the fire, or relax on your deck and watch the sunset from your private ocean view cottage or suite. Hiking trails abound nearby, as does ocean and river kayaking, canoeing and many other outdoor activities. Gourmet dining is a short walk or minute's drive away, and the charming village of Mendocino is a National Historic Register community laden with special shops and attractions. Great rooms, stunning views and nice people...The Sea Rock Inn.

Rates
6 Cottages, 4 Jr. Suites, 4 Suites: $179/$395. Number of Rooms: 14

Cuisine
Guests enjoy an attractive breakfast buffet with daily changing quiche, hard boiled eggs, yogurt, fresh pastries, juices, fruit and more. Upon check in to the room, guests may relax with a complimentary split of fine local wine.

Nearest Airport
SFO or Oakland, 3 1/2 hrs

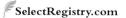

♿ 🍽 🍷

Shore House at Lake Tahoe

www.shorehouselaketahoe.com
7170 North Lake Blvd., P.O. Box 499, Tahoe Vista, CA USA 96148
800-207-5160 • 530-546-7270 • Fax: 530-546-7130
innkeeper@shorehouselaketahoe.com   *Member Since 2000*

California

Tahoe Vista

Innkeepers/Owners
Marty Cohen and Margie Rugger

The Shore House is the ultimate romantic getaway at the water's edge of spectacular Lake Tahoe. Balconies surrounding each room offer fabulous views of our pristine lake and mountains. Relax in our large outdoor lakefront hot tub. Enjoy fine lakefront restaurants, art galleries, and casinos close by. This winter wonderland offers world class downhill and x-c skiing at 20 resorts, ice skating, snow shoeing, snowmobiling, and sleigh rides. Summer activities include spectacular hiking, biking, golf, tennis, rafting, para-sailing. Kayak or Paddle Board right from the Shore House. Enjoy a romantic couples' massage in our on site massage studio overlooking the Lake and Mountains. The Shore House specializes in intimate lakefront Weddings with Marriage License and Minister on site. Wedding, Honeymoon, Anniversary and Birthday Packages are also offered.

Rates
All King or Queen Rooms, $154-$397 depending upon season. Each room has a gas log fireplace, custom-built log furnishings, 32" Flat Screen TV, Coffee Maker, Refrigerator, Hair Dryer and Robes. Beach Towels available at water front. Number of Rooms: 9

Cuisine
Award-winning Gourmet Breakfasts and Wine & Appetizers served daily in our lakefront dining room or lakefront lawns and gardens. Fresh Baked Treats delivered to your room each day. Enjoy many extraordinary Lake Tahoe restaurants.

Nearest Airport
Reno Tahoe International

SelectRegistry.com

Simpson House Inn

www.simpsonhouseinn.com
121 East Arrellaga Street, Santa Barbara, CA USA 93101
800-676-1280 • 805-963-7067 • Fax: 805-564-4811
reservations@simpsonhouseinn.com

Member Since 1993

California Santa Barbara

Owners
Glyn & Linda Davies

Located in the heart of downtown Santa Barbara, Simpson House Inn is a boutique hotel that blends historic charm with modern day luxuries. This elegantly restored 1874 Historic Landmark Victorian Estate is nestled amongst an acre of award-winning, beautifully landscaped English gardens and offers 15 diverse guestrooms, suites and cottages. All rooms feature fireplaces, whirlpool tubs, Kiehl's bath and body products and complimentary Netflix. Spa treatments, ranging from Swedish massages to European facials, can be arranged in the comfort of your guestroom. Each morning guests enjoy a delicious gourmet breakfast followed by a sampling of local wines and hors d'oeuvres each evening, all of which are complimentary. Additional complimentary amenities include bicycles and beach equipment. Just a five-minute walk away from the countless restaurant, shopping and theater offerings in the downtown area and a short trolley ride to the beach, Simpson House Inn is perfectly placed to allow guests to enjoy the best that Santa Barbara has to offer.

Rates
Victorian Estate Home & the Garden Room from $230-$475. Carriage House Rooms from $425-$675. Garden Cottages from $535-$675. Sun-Thurs and seasonal rates available. Number of Rooms: 15

Cuisine
Full vegetarian gourmet breakfast delivered to your room or served at individual tables on the veranda or in the dining room. Afternoon refreshments on arrival. Mediterranean hors d'oeuvres buffet with local wine tasting & evening dessert.

Nearest Airport
Santa Barbara Municipal Airport. Flights from Denver, Los Angeles, Phoenix & San Francisco. www.flysba.com.

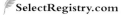

Villa Royale Inn

www.villaroyale.com
1620 S. Indian Trail, Palm Springs, California 92264
800-245-2314 • 760-327-2314 • Fax: 760-322-3794
info@villaroyale.com

Member Since 2006

California Palm Springs

Innkeeper/Owner
David Shahriari

Framed by breathtaking mountain views, the Villa Royale's intimate three acres echo an ancient Tuscan estate. Wander through tranquil courtyards overflowing with fragrant citrus, jasmine and lavender, gently cascading fountains, two heated pools and a large jacuzzi. AAA's Westways magazine calls the Villa Royale's AAA Four Diamond Europa Restaurant "a charming hideaway where you'll feel as if you have been transported to an intimate castle in Europe." Europa's bar, with its pool and mountain views, prides itself on its extensive offerings awarded by Wine Spectator Magazine. Luxurious full-service amenities, including full complimentary breakfast and fine dining, a daily newspaper, in-room spa services, and an attentive and caring staff make the Villa Royale Inn your ultimate Palm Springs romantic getaway.

Rates
Four room styles from $99 to $450 (Seasonal). Pool Side, Private Patios, & Fire Places are available. Number of Rooms: 30

Cuisine
Cook to Order Complimentary Breakfast. Dinner with Four Diamond cuisine served fireside or by trickling fountains. Small private dinning room for up to 12 ideal for a special occasion or intimate wedding celebration.

Nearest Airport
Five minutes from downtown Palm Springs and the Palm Springs International Airport.

Washington Square Inn, A Four Sisters Inn

www.wsisf.com
1660 Stockton Street, San Francisco, CA USA 94133
800-388-0220 • 415-981-4220 • Fax: 415-397-7242
washingtonsquareinn@foursisters.com

Member Since 2006

California San Francisco

Innkeeper
Brian Montanez

Situated in the very heart of San Francisco's legendary North Beach, the Washington Square Inn welcomes guests with the charm and comfort of a small European hotel. Whether traveling for business or recreation, enjoy a European-style breakfast, evening wine and hors d'oeuvres and complimentary WiFi.

No two rooms are alike in the beautifully renovated 1910 Washington Square Inn. Choose from king, queen, double or twin beds to suit your needs and preference. All rooms come with a private bath, appointed with luxurious bath amenities and flat panel televisions. Rooms have high quality linens and are individually decorated in warm, subdued tones. Some rooms offer bay windows with window seats, fireplaces, or views of North Beach landmarks such as Coit Tower, Washington Square, or Saints Peter and Paul Church.

Rates
There are 15 guest accommodations (15 with private baths). Double occupancy rate is between $199 and $409. Number of Rooms: 15

Cuisine
Breakfast served in your room or our lobby, includes fresh juices, tea assortment, muffins, croissants, pastries, fresh fruit, yogurt or toast. Fresh coffee every morning and afternoon wine and hors d'oeuvres.

Nearest Airport
San Francisco International Airport
Oakland International Airport
San Jose International Airport

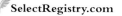

The Wine Country Inn

www.winecountryinn.com
1152 Lodi Lane, St. Helena, CA USA 94574
888-465-4608 • 707-963-7077 • Fax: 707-963-9018
romance@winecountryinn.com

Member Since 1978

Innkeeper
Jim Smith

For more than 30 years, 3 generations of the Smith family have been welcoming guests to this slice of Heaven. The stone and wood Wine Country Inn is a tranquil, hidden oasis in the heart of Napa Valley, America's center for fine wine and eclectic dining. The tree-lined drive, welcoming common room and friendly greeting set the mood for a memorable experience. Smells of freshly baked granola or evening cookies raise expectations of meals to come. With antique-filled guest rooms, panoramic vineyard views, lush gardens, a sun-drenched pool with warming hot tub, and a massage tent almost in the vineyards, guests find it difficult to leave. But for those who do, the staff are eager to help map out truly memorable days of sampling the finest the area has to offer. At the end of the day, guests gather with the innkeepers to compare experiences over more great wine and tables laden with homemade appetizers. To increase enjoyment, the inn offers a free evening restaurant shuttle servicing the area's fine restaurants as well as guided day-tours they call Inn-Cursions.

Rates
20 rooms, 4 suites, 5 luxury cottages. Rates are $220/$610 Off-season and $285/$680 Harvest Season. Rates include a full buffet breakfast, afternoon wine social and evening restaurant shuttle. Call for seasonal special packages. Number of Rooms: 29

Cuisine
Innovative egg dishes, fresh fruit, juices, home-made granola and nut-breads as well as a fun bagel/waffle bar. Family-recipe appetizers with great local wines in afternoon.

Nearest Airport
Sacramento, San Francisco, or Oakland

🖋 **SelectRegistry.com**

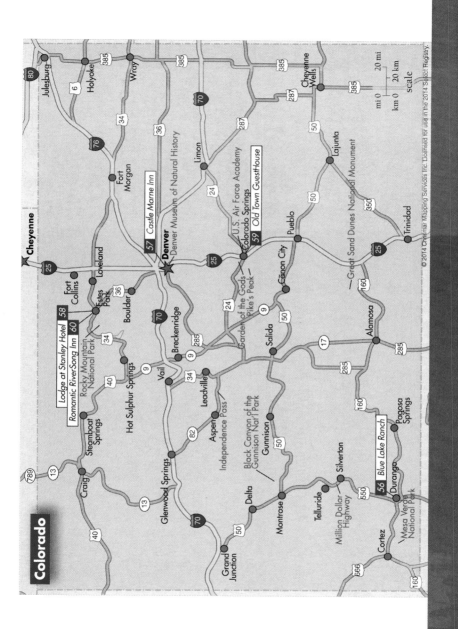

Colorado

Cheyenne

Colorado

57 Castle Marne Inn
Denver Denver Museum of Natural History

U.S. Air Force Academy
59 Old Town GuestHouse

Lodge at Stanley Hotel **58**
Romantic RiverSong Inn **60**

56 Blue Lake Ranch

Garden of the Gods — Pike's Peak
Great Sand Dunes National Monument
Black Canyon of the Gunnison Nat'l Park
Million Dollar Highway
Mesa Verde National Park
Rocky Mountain National Park

Julesburg, Holyoke, Wray, Cheyenne Wells, Fort Morgan, Limon, Colorado Springs, Pueblo, Lajunta, Trinidad, Cañon City, Salida, Alamosa, Pagosa Springs, Durango, Cortez, Silverton, Telluride, Montrose, Delta, Gunnison, Aspen, Leadville, Vail, Breckenridge, Hot Sulphur Springs, Steamboat Springs, Craig, Glenwood Springs, Grand Junction, Boulder, Estes Park, Fort Collins, Loveland, Independence Pass

© 2014 Chelmar Mapping Services Inc. Licensed for use in the 2014 Select Registry.

scale
20 mi
20 km
mi 0
km 0

♿ 🍴
Blue Lake Ranch

www.bluelakeranch.com
16919 Hwy 140, Durango, CO 81326
970-385-4537 • Fax: 970-403-1156
bluelakeranch@gmail.com

Member Since 2013

Owners
Shirley and David Alford

Blue Lake Ranch, a Durango Bed & Breakfast, is located on a private 200 acre estate, just 15 minutes from the bustling frontier town of Durango, Colorado. Centrally located just 30 minutes from Mesa Verde National Park and 10 minutes to spectacular mountain activities and off-road adventure, our guests enjoy year round outdoor activities from skiing to hiking, fishing, and hunting. Counted among the top bed and breakfast inns in the United States by Country Inns, Conde Nast Traveler, and Travel + Leisure, Blue Lake Ranch remains a quiet and affordable getaway for the sophisticated and casual traveler alike. Ideally situated upon 200 secluded acres with its own trout-filled lake, Blue Lake Ranch is tucked in a spring-fed valley, well off the county road. Famous for its sumptuous breakfasts made from homemade recipes, spectacular garden, and mountain views, the Ranch offers unparalleled year-round sensory delights, from the quiet of a winter's snowfall to the fragrance of 10,000 irises in summer bloom.

Rates
$139-$259. Rooms and Suites with romantic fireplaces, hand crafted furniture and decor, original Native American and Southwest inspired art. Number of Rooms: 16

Cuisine
Full breakfast.Start the day with our famous Southwest inspired breakfast buffet. Freshly brewed coffee, seasonal fresh fruit, gourmet house made granola, fresh pastries, with rotating hot items including quiche and pinion pancakes.

Nearest Airport
Durango-La Plata County Airport only 30 minutes away.

The Historic Castle Marne Inn

www.castlemarne.com
1572 Race Street, Denver, CO USA 80206
303-331-0621 • 303-331-0622 • Fax: 303-331-0623
info@castlemarne.com

Member Since 1991

Colorado

Denver

Innkeepers/Owners
The Peiker Family: Diane, Jim, Melissa, Louie, Louie J, Charlie & Liz

Denver's grandest historic mansion is located on Capitol Hill and listed on the National & Local Registers. Castle Marne, built in 1889, features hand-hewn lava stone, called Rhyolite. The interior includes hand-rubbed imported woods, four balconies, a four story octagonal tower and among several other stained glass windows, the famous seven foot diameter "Peacock Window". Beautiful antiques and family heirlooms are used at the Castle, creating a charming Victorian atmosphere. The Castle features Denver's finest examples of Victorian Ceiling Art. The Dining Room is paneled in the original Cherry wood. Your plated gourmet breakfast is served at two seatings. In season, enjoy Jim's gardens and roses and relax beside the bubbling fountain. Special afternoon teas and Candlelight Dinners are enjoyed by reservation. Small weddings and honeymoon packages available, and elopements are our specialty. Available for small meetings and other special events. The AIA says " Castle Marne is one of Denver's great architectural legacies."
Come – Experience the "Castle Way To Stay!"

Rates
9 Rooms, $125/$320. 2 Suites with Jacuzzi tubs. 3 Rooms with private outdoor hot tubs. Reservations required for luncheons, and dinners. Call for pricing and availability. Number of Rooms: 9

Cuisine
Full gourmet breakfast featuring homemade muffins and breads & artistically presented fresh fruit. Elegant Private 4 course Dinners served in the original formal dining room. Afternoon Tea and Luncheons. Evening Sleepy Time Tea and fresh baked cookies.

Nearest Airport
Denver International

¶◎¶ ¶◎¶ ¶◎¶ ♀
The Lodge at the Stanley Hotel

www.stanleyhotel.com
333 East Wonderview Ave, Estes Park, CO USA 80517
800-976-1377 • 970-577-4000
mknerr@stanleyhotel.com

Member Since 2012

Innkeeper
Midge Knerr

Located 7,500 feet "above the ordinary" The Lodge at the Stanley is a recently renovated 40-room boutique hotel located in picturesque Estes Park surrounded by the majestic Rocky Mountains. Formerly The Manor House, The Lodge is adjacent to The Stanley Hotel and was where single men resided in the 1900s. The Lodge at the Stanley has spacious common areas and guest rooms with a nod to Colorado's early beginnings through furnishings, photography and curios. Relaxing on the front porch and taking in the views of the breathtaking nearby views is a favorite with guests as is sitting by the fireplace in Manor Hall or Ranch Room. The Lodge is also dog-friendly with homemade biscuits as a welcome treat. As The Lodge is part of The Stanley Hotel, guest have access to fine dining in Cascades Restaurant & Lounge - an upscale American Steakhouse also featuring The Whiskey Bar lounge-with over 500 selections. The fitness center, spa, gift shop, fire engine tours, hotel tours and hunts round out the unique activities available to The Lodge guests.

Rates
The Lodge at The Stanley is a comfortable, elegant getaway for those looking to enjoy the beautiful scenery of the Rocky Mountains. Rates start at $199 per night and range up to $399 per night for spacious Lodge Suites. Number of Rooms: 40

Cuisine
Guests are privileged to vistas of Longs Peak as Innkeeper Midge Knerr prepares a "Continental Divide-style American breakfast" - a bounty of handmade pastries, house granola and fresh jars of curd and jams from the kitchen adorn the rustic tables.

Nearest Airport
Denver International Airport (DIA) is conveniently located just 90 minutes from Estes Park, Colorado.

SelectRegistry.com

Old Town GuestHouse

www.oldtown-guesthouse.com
115 South 26th Street, Colorado Springs, CO USA 80904
888-375-4210 • 719-632-9194 • Fax: 719-632-9026
Luxury@OldTown-GuestHouse.com   *Member Since 2001*

Approved
▼ ▼ ▼

Innkeepers/Owners
Don & Shirley Wick

The three-story brick guesthouse is in perfect harmony with the 1859 period of the surrounding historic Old Colorado City. The contemporary Inn offers upscale amenities for discerning adult leisure and business travelers. Our elevator allows the entire inn to be accessible and the African Orchid room exceeds ADA specifications. The soundproof, uniquely decorated guestrooms have private baths and 7 rooms have fireplaces and/ or porches overlooking Pikes Peak. Relax in the library or out on the umbrella-covered patio for afternoon wine, beer and snacks, then walk to some of Old Town's many fine restaurants, boutiques and galleries. End your evening with a soak in your own private two-person hot tub or your relaxing ensuite steam shower. Your morning starts with a gourmet 3 course breakfast served in our dining area. And then it's off to one of the many attractions and activities that the area has to offer (Pikes Peak, Garden of the Gods, Cave of the Winds). Member Pikes Peak Lodging Association, Bed & Breakfast Innkeepers of Colorado and other local community organizations.

Rates
$99/$199. Corporate and military rates available. Private baths, hot tubs, steam showers, fireplaces. Lower winter rates November and April, with few seasonal blackout dates. Check our website for periodic discounts and packages. Number of Rooms: 8

Cuisine
Full 3 course sit-down breakfast. Hot entree, fruit in season, muffin or sweet bread and a cereal buffet. Evening with wine, beer and light snacks. Dine on our veranda (weather permitting) or in front of the fireplace with semi-private seating.

Nearest Airport
Colorado Springs Airport (20 min.); Denver International Airport (1hr 30 min.)

Romantic RiverSong Inn

www.romanticriversong.com
P.O. Box 1910, 1766 Lower Broadview Road, Estes Park, CO USA 80517
970-586-4666 • 970-586-3223
romanticriversong@gmail.com

Member Since 1987

Colorado

Estes Park

Innkeepers/Owners
Sue & Gary Mansfield

Romantic RiverSong represents the classic country inn rarely found in the West. Located on a quiet backroad, we were personally chosen by Select Registry's founder Norman Simpson... his choice for a unique place that offered "exceptional hospitality" and "good honest lodging." Secluded on 27 wooded acres with towering Blue Spruce and Ponderosa Pines, the inn offers quiet ponds, hiking trails and tree swings. Romantic RiverSong is a refuge for guests, as well as for wildlife. With only ten guest rooms, the inn has achieved a marvelous balance with its luxurious rooms (radiant-heated floors, jetted tubs for two, crackling fireplaces) and surrounding nature with the melodies of songbirds and a rushing mountain stream. After exploring nearby Rocky Mountain National Park and the variety of quaint shops in town, come home to a relaxing "streamside massage." Then, later that evening enjoy our own chef-prepared candlelight gourmet dinner. Our warm hospitality will make your memories of Romantic RiverSong linger long after you've gone from this little bit of heaven in Colorado.

Rates
5 Rooms from $175-$195 junior suites ; 5 Suites, $245-$350 with Jetted tubs for 2; real wood burning fireplaces, private decks or flowered patios. Free Wifi on property. Hiking sticks and packs available without charge. Guided hikes. Number of Rooms: 10

Cuisine
Mountain morning chill is lifted by a crackling fire and fresh brewed coffee followed by John Wayne Casserole and Happy Trail muffins. Dinner is served on fine china enhanced by soft jazz & a glass of wine the perfect end to a day of adventure and fun.

Nearest Airport
Denver International (DIA) only 1 hour 45 minutes away , no mtn passes to cross !! Open year round to Estes Park.

SelectRegistry.com

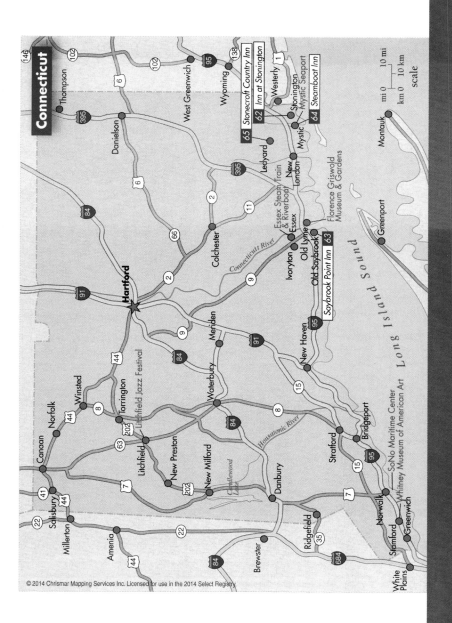

Inn at Stonington

www.innatstonington.com
60 Water Street, Stonington, CT USA 06378
860-535-2000 • Fax: 860-535-8193
innkeeper@innatstonington.com

Member Since 2005

Connecticut

Stonington

Innkeeper/Owner
William Griffin

Named by Travel + Leisure as Inn of the Month, this 18 room waterfront inn is located in the heart of Stonington Borough, one of the last untouched and 'historic' villages in New England. The inn offers individually decorated guest rooms with gas fireplaces, baths with oversized soaking Jacuzzi tubs and separate walk in showers. Seaside rooms have private balconies with views of Stonington Harbor and beyond. Common areas include a top floor sitting room with breathtaking views, an intimate bar with adjoining breakfast room, the cozy living room, and a well equipped gym. During your stay, stop by one of the local wineries, visit downtown Mystic or simply take a stroll down Water Street and enjoy the specialty shops and some of the finest antique shops in the area. Enjoy our complimentary wine and cheese before walking to dinner at one of five fabulous restaurants in the village. Area attractions: small beach within walking distance, Stonington area vineyards, Mystic Seaport, Mystic Aquarium, Mohegan Sun and Foxwood Casinos, Watch Hill beaches.

Rates
18 Guest rooms. Seasonal rates $160/$445. Open Year Round. Number of Rooms: 18

Cuisine
Continental breakfast of fresh baked treats, fruit & locally roasted coffee.
Complimentary wine and cheese hour nightly.

Nearest Airport
T.F. Green- Providence, RI or Bradley Internation Airport- Windsor Locks, CT.

Saybrook Point Inn

www.saybrook.com
2 Bridge Street, Old Saybrook, CT USA 06475
800-395-2000 • 860-395-2000 • Fax: 860-388-1504
info@saybrook.com

Member Since 2010

Connecticut Old Saybrook

Innkeeper/Managing Owner
Stephen Tagliatela

Authentic hospitality proudly delivered is the hallmark of this family owned, AAA Four Diamond Inn, Spa & Marina. Located where the Connecticut River meets the Long Island Sound, breathtaking views, elegant spacious accommodations, unique amenities and our New England Main Street town provide the ideal backdrop for the perfect getaway. Newly renovated Spa 'Sanno,' delivers customized well-being experiences 'your way.' In and outdoor salt water pools overlook the water. Our Health Club has up-to-date equipment and fitness classes. Fresh Salt, a fresh food experience, features modern American seafood, farm to table cuisine, a wonderful oyster bar, outdoor dining, and seasonal entertainment. Our Marina, like the Inn, is recognized for sustainable environmental leadership and is designated an Atlantic Cruising Guide perennial 5 Bell Marina. The Saybrook Point Inn has awards for not only being the first hotel in Connecticut to be certified a Green Hotel by the state, but for continued leadership as a Green Lodging property. Available by Amtrack with courtesy shuttle.

Rates
$229 to $629, vary seasonally and on weekday and weekends. Number of Rooms:
80 Rooms

Cuisine
Modern American seafood. A proud founding member of the Connecticut Farm to Chef Program.

Nearest Airport
Bradley, Hartford and T.F. Green, Providence. Both about one hour away.

Steamboat Inn

www.steamboatinnmystic.com
73 Steamboat Wharf, Mystic, CT USA 06355
860-536-8300 • Fax: 860-536-9528
info@steamboatinnmystic.com

Member Since 2009

Owners/Innkeeper
Paul Connor/John McGee/Sandra Chapman

The Steamboat Inn offers eleven elegant rooms overlooking the beautiful Mystic River. Located in the heart of Historic Downtown Mystic, Steamboat Inn is just steps from fabulous shopping and fine dining; just minutes away are Mystic Seaport, Mystic Aquarium, Foxwoods Resort & Mohegan Sun Casinos, plus four local wineries. Each of our rooms are uniquely decorated with antiques and individually climate controlled. The rooms have private baths with single or double whirlpool tubs or luxury rain shower. Six of our rooms have wood burning fireplaces. Enjoy breathtaking river views from ten of our rooms. Complimentary wireless internet is offered throughout the inn. Enjoy a full breakfast each morning in our common room or stop by in the evening for our delicious cookies and sherry. Awarded "most unique setting" two years in a row by Lanier Bed and Breakfast – chosen by the guests of over 8,500 B&Bs worldwide. Be among the guests who visit Steamboat Inn year after year. Come explore Steamboat Inn today.

Rates
Seasonal Rates $150-$330. Open Year Round. Number of Rooms: 11

Cuisine
Buffet Breakfast includes fresh baked pastry, scrambled eggs, bacon, turkey sausage, fruit filled pancakes or savory quiche, fresh fruit, yogurt, cereal, granola, cheeses, bagels, oatmeal, coffee, tea, and juices. Sherry and cookies served nightly.

Nearest Airport
T.F. Green Airport, Providence, RI Bradley Int. Airport, Windsor Locks, CT.

Stonecroft Country Inn

www.stonecroft.com
515 Pumpkin Hill Road, Ledyard, CT USA 06339
800-772-0774 • 860-572-0771 • Fax: 860-572-9161
innkeeper@stonecroft.com

Member Since 2002

Connecticut

Ledyard

Innkeeper
Jim and Marcie Townsend

Relax in quiet country elegance on an 1807 sea captain's six-acre estate, less than 10 minutes from Mystic Seaport, Foxwoods and Mohegan Sun casinos.

Historic stone walls and lush green lawns surround the inn, consisting of The 1807 House, a sunny Georgian colonial, and our converted 19th century post & beam barn. Romantic guestrooms feature French, English and American country decor, with fireplaces, whirlpool tubs and heated towel bars, wide-screen TV/DVDs (barn only) and free Internet access. Savor an exquisite country breakfast in our elegant granite-walled dining room or the outside garden terrace.

One Inn . . Two Styles . . Endless Charm.

Rates
$149 - $329. Please check our website for current rates, specials and packages at www.stonecroft.com. Number of Rooms: 10

Cuisine
Full country breakfast in our dining room or on the stone terrace. Enjoy a selection of fresh baked goods, seasonal fruits, and specialty entrees created by our Innkeepers!

Nearest Airport
TF Green (Providence) - 45 minutes, Bradley (Hartford) - 60 minutes

Delaware

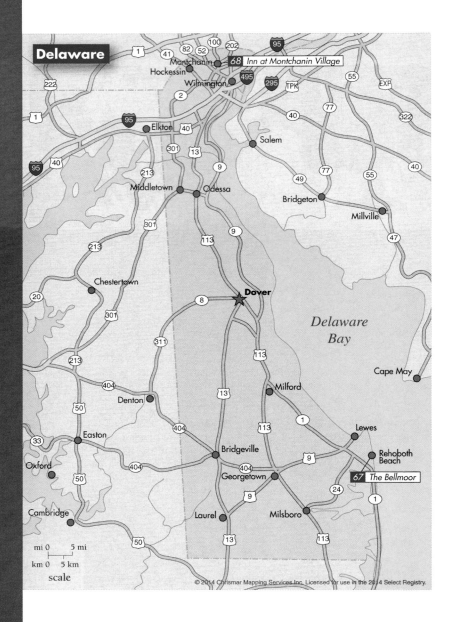

Delaware

Montchanin
Hockessin
Wilmington
68 Inn at Montchanin Village
Elkton
Salem
Middletown
Odessa
Bridgeton
Millville
Chestertown
Dover
Delaware Bay
Milford
Cape May
Denton
Lewes
Easton
Bridgeville
Rehoboth Beach
Oxford
Georgetown
67 The Bellmoor
Cambridge
Laurel
Milsboro

mi 0   5 mi
km 0   5 km
scale

© 2014 Chrismar Mapping Services Inc. Licensed for use in the 2014 Select Registry.

The Bellmoor

www.thebellmoor.com
6 Christian Street, Rehoboth Beach, DE USA 19971
800-425-2355 • 302-227-5800 • Fax: 302-227-0323
info@thebellmoor.com

Member Since 2004

Proprietors
The Moore Family

Quiet moments in the garden...sunrise on the beach...the crackle of the fire in the Jefferson Library...a leisurely walk to unique boutique shopping and fine dining restaurants...a favorite book in the Sunroom. Our Day Spa offers over 30 services to restore and rejuvenate body and spirit. Whether you choose a seaweed wrap, hot stone pedicure or a soothing springtime facial, you can leave the world behind and experience refined relaxation and well-being. Additional complimentary services: concierge, bellman, high speed Internet access, wireless access, guest computer room, two pools, hot tub, and a fitness room. Enjoy complete relaxation in our beautifully appointed accommodations of unsurpassed comfort combining the warm, residential feel of a B&B with the efficient, professional service of a small European hotel. Enjoy the privacy and comfort of our newly renovated 4th floor Club Suites.

Rates
55 rooms, $125/$465 B&B. 23 suites, $150/$695 B&B; suites include marble bath, fireplace, whirlpool, wet bar. Number of Rooms: 78

Cuisine
Full American breakfast served in the Garden Room or in the garden. Afternoon refreshments. 24 hour coffee service. Rehoboth Beach offers many fine dining options within walking distance of the Inn. Entire property non-smoking.

Nearest Airport
Philadelphia and Baltimore are both within a 2 hour drive.

🍴 🍴 🍴 ♍

The Inn at Montchanin Village & Spa

www.montchanin.com
Rte 100 & Kirk Rd, GPS 528 Montchanin Rd., Wilmington, DE,
Montchanin, DE 19710
800-269-2473 • 302-888-2133 • Fax: 302-888-0389
inn@montchanin.com   *Member Since 2002*

Delaware

Montchanin

General Manager
Vera C. Palmatary

Listed on the National Historic Register, The Inn at Montchanin Village was once a part
of the Winterthur Estate and was named for Alexandria de Montchanin, grandmother
of the founder of the DuPont Company. One of the few remaining villages of its kind,
the settlement was home to laborers who worked at the nearby DuPont powder mills.
In eleven carefully restored buildings dating from 1799 to 1910, there are 28 richly
furnished guest rooms/suites appointed with period and reproduction furniture, marble
baths with all the amenities for the demanding and sophisticated traveler. Most rooms
have beautifully manicured private courtyards and several have cozy fireplaces. The Spa at
Montchanin is an innovative facility that offers facials, body treatments, and massages in a
luxurious and peaceful environment. Nestled in the Brandywine Valley, 10 minutes NW of
Wilmington and 25 minutes South of Philadelphia. Centrally located to all major museums
– Winterthur, Longwood Gardens, Hagley Museum, Nemours Mansion, Brandywine River
Museum, and Delaware Museum of Natural History.

Rates
Rooms: $192-$244; Suites: $290-$399. Free parking on site, European turndown, coffee
maker, microwave, beverage area with icemaker, daily paper, free wireless Internet, and
fitness room. Please see website for package information. Number of Rooms: 28

Cuisine
Once the village blacksmith's shop, Krazy Kat's Restaurant is famous for it's fresh
nouvelle cuisine and whimsical decor. They serve breakfast, lunch, Sunday brunch, and
dinner. Our private dining room, The Crow's Nest, may accommodate up to 40 guests.

Nearest Airport
Philadelphia International (PHL) Airport: 20 miles
New Castle Airport: 10 miles
Baltimore (BWI) Airport: 82.8 miles

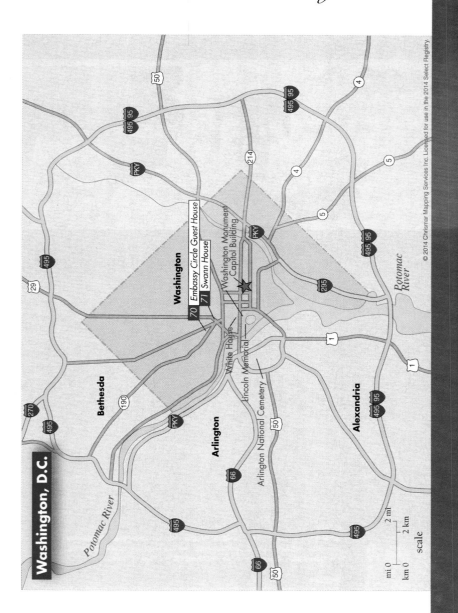

Washington, D.C.

Washington

Bethesda

Arlington

Alexandria

70 Embassy Circle Guest House
71 Swann House

Washington Monument
Capitol Building
White House
Lincoln Memorial
Arlington National Cemetery

Potomac River

Potomac River

scale

mi 0 · 2 mi
km 0 · 2 km

© 2014 Chrismar Mapping Services Inc. Licensed for use in the 2014 Select Registry.

Embassy Circle Guest House

www.dcinns.com/embassy.html
2224 R ST NW, Washington, DC USA 20008
202-232-7744 • 877-232-7744
embassy@dcinns.com

Member Since 2011

Innkeepers
Laura & Raymond Saba

Embassy Circle Guest House is a spectacular historic mansion renowned for elegance and warm, personal hospitality. Explore the house and discover its wealth of architectural detail, original artwork and collection of Murano glass chandeliers. Settle into one of our spacious guest rooms, individually furnished for your comfort and enjoyment with superb beds, fine linens, vibrant original art and stunning Persian carpets. Start the day with our sumptuous breakfast buffet and enjoy Laura's French toast or Raymond's omelets. Begin your evening with our very popular "wine buffet." Join owners and fellow guests as you sample Laura's wine selections and Raymond's favorite IPAs, while trading travel tales, sightseeing tips and restaurant recommendations. Enjoy the extraordinary amenities offered by our Dupont Circle neighborhood – embassies, art galleries and grand private homes: easy access to DC's Metro (subway) system; outstanding local restaurants and sidewalk cafes; and great bookstores and coffee shops. Fodor's Choice. Diamond Collection. Top 10 Urban B&Bs.

Rates
$240-$310 in season. $180-$240 off season. Rate includes double occupancy, buffet breakfast, afternoon snacks, evening wine, and free high-speed Internet access. Limited parking is available for an additional fee. Number of Rooms: 11

Cuisine
Sumptuous breakfast buffet featuring a daily hot entree, fresh-cut fruit salad and organic honey yogurt, smoked salmon with creamed cheese and capers, organic breads, and great coffee. World's best brownies every afternoon! Evening wine and snacks.

Nearest Airport
Ronald Reagan National Airport (DCA) - 5 miles
Dulles International Airport (IAD) - 26 miles

SelectRegistry.com

Swann House

www.swannhouse.com
1808 New Hampshire Ave. N.W., Washington, DC USA 20009
202-265-4414
stay@swannhouse.com

Member Since 2002

Innkeeper
Isabelle Hauswald

Located on a tree-lined avenue in the heart of the Dupont Circle Historic District, Swann House welcomes you to the Nation's Capital and our 1883 Richardson Romanesque gem. Crystal chandeliers, elaborately carved fireplaces and original plaster moldings reflect just a portion of the nineteenth century craftsmanship that can be seen throughout our inn. Each individually decorated guestroom comes well appointed with sumptuous bathrobes, sateen sheets, down featherbeds and luxurious bath amenities. Select rooms include whirlpool baths, fireplaces and private decks for added luxury. Dozens of restaurants and cafes are just steps away allowing our guests to experience one of Washington's most vibrant and beautiful neighborhoods. Just 12 blocks from the White House and close proximity to several universities, galleries and conference venues, Swann House makes for a wonderful respite whether here for a romantic escape, business meeting or well-deserved getaway. "The Inn that launched 1,000 marriages" - Frommer's. "Fodor's Choice Gold Award" - Fodor's Guide.

Rates
9 Rooms $169/$369; 3 Suites $249/$369. 6 w/fireplaces, 4 w/whirlpool tubs, 2 w/ private deck. Seasonal Rates. Free WiFi, Cable TV, guest computer, robes, hairdryers, secret garden pool. Limited parking by reservation for add'l fee. Number of Rooms: 12

Cuisine
Sumptuous breakfast buffet includes hot entree plus home-made pastries & granola, seasonal fruit, Greek yogurt, cereals, meats & cheeses. Afternoon refreshments, evening sherry & all-day coffee & tea. Dozens of fine restaurants within walking distance

Nearest Airport
Reagan National (DCA) 6 miles, Dulles International (IAD) 26 miles

Florida

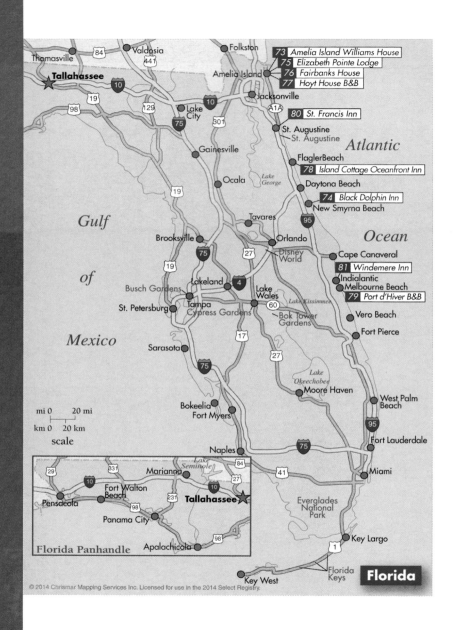

Thomasville
Valdosta
84
441
Folkston

Tallahassee
10
19

98
129
75
301
Lake City
10

73 *Amelia Island Williams House*
75 *Elizabeth Pointe Lodge*
76 *Fairbanks House*
77 *Hoyt House B&B*

Amelia Island
Jacksonville
A1A

80 *St. Francis Inn*

St. Augustine
St. Augustine

Atlantic

Gainesville

19

FlaglerBeach

78 *Island Cottage Oceanfront Inn*

Ocala
Lake George
Daytona Beach

74 *Black Dolphin Inn*

New Smyrna Beach

Gulf

Tavares
95

Brooksville
75
Orlando
Disney World
27

Ocean

of

19
Lakeland
4
Cape Canaveral

81 *Windemere Inn*

Busch Gardens
Tampa
Lake Wales
60
Bok Tower Gardens
Lake Kissimmee
Indialantic
Melbourne Beach

79 *Port d'Hiver B&B*

St. Petersburg
Cypress Gardens

Vero Beach

Mexico

Sarasota
17
27

Fort Pierce

75

Lake Okeechobee
Moore Haven

West Palm Beach

mi 0   20 mi
km 0   20 km
scale

Bokeelia
Fort Myers

95

Fort Lauderdale

Naples

75

Miami

Lake Seminole
29
331
Marianna
84
27
41

Everglades National Park

10
Fort Walton Beach
231
Tallahassee
10
4

Pensacola
98
Panama City
98

Key Largo

Florida Panhandle
Apalachicola
4
1
Florida Keys

Florida

Key West

SelectRegistry.com

Amelia Island Williams House

www.williamshouse.com
103 South Ninth Street, Amelia Island, FL USA 32034
800-414-9258 • 904-277-2328
info@williamshouse.com

Member Since 2007

Innkeepers/Owners
Byron & Deborah McCutchen

Amelia Island Williams House is a beautiful antebellum mansion, circa 1856, where romance, relaxation, and history combine to whisk you away to another place and time. Choose from our elegantly decorated guest rooms with private baths and antique furnishings, some featuring original working fireplaces with hand carved mantels, whirlpool tubs, and a private hot tub. Sweeping verandas invite you to come and relax. Enjoy a delicious gourmet breakfast served each day in our dining room. Sip wine beneath our 500 year-old live oak tree in our flower lined courtyard. We are located in the historic seaside village of Fernandina Beach on Amelia Island, FL, just one block from downtown boutiques, bistros, antiques, art galleries,and world class restaurants. We offer complimentary bikes for exploring the island, beach equipment, WiFi, and all the comforts of home. We offer packages for romance, birthdays, girls getaways, Christmas and other holidays. We are the perfect venue for weddings and family gatherings.

Rates
$175-$275, weekend rates. Romantic getaway and spa packages available. Midweek discounts. Christmas and other holiday packages. We are open year round. Number of Rooms: 10

Cuisine
Breakfast is served each morning in our dining room and consists of a fruit course followed by a savory or sweet dish with fresh ground coffee and juice. Each evening during our social hour we offer complimentary choice of wine and cheese.

Nearest Airport
Jacksonville, Florida - 20 min drive to the inn. Take I-95 N to exit 373. East on AIA, right on Beech, left on 9th.

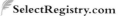

Black Dolphin Inn

www.blackdolphininn.com
916 South Riverside Drive, New Smyrna Beach, FL USA 32168
386-410-4868 • 855-410-4868 • Fax: 386-410-4899
info@blackdolphininn.com

Member Since 2013

Owners/Innkeepers
Brett P. and Taylor C. Smith

Florida

New Smyrna Beach

A quaint Old Florida Beach town is the setting for this elegant Spanish Isle boutique inn overlooking the Indian River on Florida's east-central Atlantic Coast. Opened in 2013, the Black Dolphin Inn is the recipient of the TripAdvisor Travelers Choice Award as one of the Top 10 Inns in the US, AAA Four Diamond Award, BedandBreakfast.com Top 10 Beach B&Bs worldwide and ILoveInns.com Top 10 Romantic Inns in the United States. The Black Dolphin features 14 luxurious rooms, each individually designed with vintage furniture, fine art, eclectic accents and spa baths. Just as every gemstone is unique, so too are the rooms of the Black Dolphin Inn. Our interior designers have mixed Mid-century style with classic Old Florida woods and materials. Eclectic ceiling fans, vintage art, and tropical spa-inspired baths come together to create a unique oasis for your escape. Located less than an hour from Orlando, Cocoa Beach and St. Augustine, the town is blessed with bays, lagoons, and waterways for boating, fishing, and water sports. Wildlife and water are your constant companions.

Rates
Room rates range from $109 to $319 per room per night - based on single/double occupancy. Add'l guest: $25 per person. Pets Welcome - limited to ground level units. Rates subject to change - holiday rates and minimum stay may apply. Number of Rooms: 14

Cuisine
The Black Dolphin Inn takes the term "bed and breakfast" to a new level. Breakfast is served from 8:00 – 10:00 each morning and is prepared from scratch in our professional "open air" exhibition kitchen, seamlessly integrated into our Lobby.

Nearest Airport
Orlando Intl (MCO), Sanford Intl (SFB), Daytona Beach Intl (DAB), Jacksonville Intl (JAX).

SelectRegistry.com

Elizabeth Pointe Lodge

www.elizabethpointelodge.com
98 South Fletcher Avenue, Amelia Island, FL USA 32034
888-757-1910 • 904-277-4851 • Fax: 904-277-6500
info@elizabethpointelodge.com

Member Since 1998

Florida

Amelia Island

Approved
💎 💎 💎

Innkeepers/Owners
Jim, Gay and Brandon Dunlop

Rated "One of the 12 Best Waterfront Inns" in America and Voted the #3 Top Resort in Florida in the Conde Nast Traveler Reader's Choice Awards, the Pointe sits directly on the beach overlooking the Atlantic Ocean. The inn is a Nantucket "shingle style" architecture with broad porches around. Each room is individually outfitted with all contemporary accommodations and a choice of soaking tub or large Rainforest glass shower. The Lodge provides a full seaside breakfast and a 24/7 staff able to exceed your expectations. A selection of soups, salads, sandwiches, desserts and room service are available 24 hours a day. Complimentary WiFi DSL Internet service encompasses the property, USA Today or Wall Street Journal is delivered to your room daily. Beach umbrellas, loungers and towels are set each day for your enjoyment. Parking is complimentary. Elevator to all floors. Focusing on individualized attention, Concierge assistance is available for day trips, bicycle touring and other Island experiences.

Rates
20 Rooms, $230/$380; 4 Oceanhouse deluxe rooms $295/$495; 1 Cottage, $445/$540. Open year-round. Number of Rooms: 25

Cuisine
Complete tended buffet breakfast in the Sunrise Room or on the deck overlooking the ocean. Lunch and casual dinner menu available plus room service. Complimentary social hour evenings at 6 p.m. Our culinary staff accommodates special dietary requests.

Nearest Airport
Jacksonville International approximately 35 minutes away.

The Fairbanks House

www.fairbankshouse.com
227 South 7th Street, Amelia Island, FL USA 32034
888-891-9880 • 904-277-0500
email@fairbankshouse.com

Member Since 1998

Florida

Amelia Island

Innkeepers/Owners
Bill & Theresa Hamilton

Named as the #1 property in Florida on the Conde Nast Gold List, Fairbanks House is an 8000 sq. ft. Italianate villa rising above a quiet Victorian village on Amelia Island. Surrounded by soaring magnolias and live oaks with dripping Spanish moss, the mansion, its cottages, organic gardens, gazebo and pool rest on a strikingly landscaped acre where guests enjoy a serene, smoke-free stay. Rooms are casually elegant with period antiques, romantic reproductions and comfortable seating. Numerous upscale amenities are designed for a carefree getaway, honeymoon or vacation. King beds, Jacuzzis, robes, bikes, beach gear and full concierge service are but a few examples of our attention to detail. Most rooms are quite spacious and give honeymooners and vacationers room to spread out. Walk to shops, restaurants, carriage and boat tours; bike to secluded beaches and a state park. Ask for details on seasonal specials, Romance Packages, Elopements, major holiday packages and Girls Just Wanna Have Fun Getaways. If you don't see it on the website, just ask. We're happy to accommodate.

Rates
5 large rooms from $185 to $230, 3 cottages from $230 for two to $395 for four, 4 very large suites from $275 for two to $450 for a private floor for four B&B. Open year-round except for two weeks after Labor day in September. Number of Rooms: 12

Cuisine
Breakfast from our organic gardens in our formal dining room, or on piazzas and patios amid our hidden gardens by the pool. Lively daily social hour with beverages, hot/cold hors d'oeuvres. 3 minute walk to cafes, taverns and fine-dining restaurants.

Nearest Airport
Jacksonville, FL - 30 minutes from the inn. Pre-arranged cab service available for approximately $50 each way.

SelectRegistry.com

Hoyt House Bed & Breakfast

 ♿ 🍽 🍽   🍷

www.hoythouse.com
804 Atlantic Avenue, Amelia Island, Florida United States 32034
904-277-4300 • 800-432-2085 • Fax: 904-277-4305
innkeeper@hoythouse.com

Member Since 2012

Approved
◈ ◈ ◈

Innkeeper
Myrta Defendini

A luxurious Bed & Breakfast that has it all under one roof in beautiful Amelia Island. The Hoyt House offers 10 spacious guest rooms, luxuriously appointed king & queen guest chambers all with private baths and some with jetted tubs, flat screen DVD TV & WiFi throughout. A heated swimming pool and hot tub, 3 public salons with original hand-tiled fireplaces and The Amelia Lounge complete with English Pub and full liquor license to service all of your libations poolside or in-room. Tucked under 500 year old oak trees and located in the Historic District where you can find shopping, antiquing, food and drink galore of our 47 restaurants all within a few blocks of the Inn. Enjoy our complimentary cocktail hour, new bikes, DVD library and secure off street parking. Gilchrist & Soames complete your bathroom amenities. If your breakfast is just as important as your bed having 600 count Egyptian cotton linen, then you are in for a treat. Our breakfast serves up our signature warm sticky buns with warm pecans and raisins in a caramel butter bath. We will exceed your expectations.

Rates
Our rates for the mansion are $229 to $310 per night weekday and $249 to $350 per night on the weekend. Additional packages and add-ons can be arranged on-line or speak to Myrta at 904-277-4300 about your personal needs. Number of Rooms: 10

Cuisine
The Hoyt House offers a true culinary experience that will stimulate your pallet as well as your eyes. Our three course breakfast gives you a choice of 6 appetizers & 7 entrees to choose from. French Press Coffee table side. Daily afternoon English Tea

Nearest Airport
Jacksonville International Airport 35 minutes. Fernandina Beach Airport 3 miles for private planes & small jets.

Island Cottage Oceanfront Inn & Spa

www.islandcottagevillas.com
2316 S. Oceanshore Blvd., Flagler Beach, FL USA 32136
386-439-0092 • 877-662-6232
icv@cfl.rr.com

Member Since 2007

Florida

Flagler Beach

Owner/Innkeeper
Toni Treworgy

Tucked away in a tiny beach community along the Atlantic shoreline, this quaint "Key West" styled jewel is appreciated for its warmth, romantic ambiance & pampering. From the moment you enter this enchanting oasis of tranquility, you'll want to kick off your shoes & relax in barefoot comfort as gentle music mentally transports you to a secluded tropical paradise.

Plan to indulge in a couples massage or facial at the Inn's exclusive Spa, or just sit back & enjoy the sparkling pool, the sounds of the surf & the scent of fresh sea air. Rooms feature ocean vistas, private decks, king beds, fireplaces, Jacuzzis & kitchenettes. The on-site "Wine & Gift" shop showcases original watercolors of the innkeeper, art prints, exquisite hand made jewelry, soaps & candles plus an eclectic collection of fine estate wines from around the world.

Guests are treated to "Afternoon Tea" & home baked cookies 4 to 8 pm each day. Breakfast is an optional upgrade that adds $40 per couple per night (with advanced reservation only) allowing you to choose the getaway that suits you best!

Rates
Without Breakfast ---- $189 to $450 / night based on season
With Breakfast -------- $229 to $490 / night based on season
Sorry, we do not accept "drive-ups." ------ Advanced reservations required.
2 Night Minimum in most cases --- Number of Rooms: 6

Cuisine
Guests who wish breakfast to be added to their stay receive a delicious, individually prepared hot entree accompanied by fresh fruit, mountain grown coffee, imported teas, juice & mimosas elegantly served by candlelight in the Inn's private dining room.

Nearest Airport
Daytona - Just 22 miles /// Jacksonville & Sanford - 90 miles /// Orlando - 100 miles

SelectRegistry.com

Port d'Hiver Bed & Breakfast

www.portdhiver.com
201 Ocean Avenue, Melbourne Beach, FL USA 32951
866-621-7678 • 321-722-2727 • Fax: 321-723-3221
info@portdhiver.com

Member Since 2008

Florida

Melbourne Beach

Innkeepers/Owners
Mike and Linda Rydson, Erika Fadden

Port d'Hiver Bed and Breakfast is old Florida luxury at its finest. A comfortable yet elegant retreat just 200 feet from the Atlantic Ocean. Port d'Hiver has ocean views, private porches, a bubbling spa pool and winding brick paths through a private compound of Island style buildings surrounded by lush tropical landscaping. Soak away the world in a large spa tub in one of our spacious new cabana rooms or watch the sunrise over the ocean from the deck of your beautifully restored historic room. Enjoy breakfast either on your porch or in our cheerfully inviting dining room. We also offer wine and refreshments at 5 o'clock in the main house, complimentary concierge services, wireless high speed Internet inside and out, flat screen TVs, evening turn down service & the finest amenities. Fish, surf, dine, or watch the sea turtles... Melbourne Beach is a barrier island only .7 miles across from the ocean to the Indian River Lagoon. Port d'Hiver is a 2013 AAA Diamond property and in 2012 was named TOP 10 B&Bs in the United States by BedandBreakfast.com.

Rates
$200/$525. Number of Rooms: 11

Cuisine
Casually elegant 3 course breakfast w/choice of entrees served individually in our dining room or on your private deck. Special vegetarian, lactose and gluten free diets are no problem. Wine & appetizers at 5 PM, cookies, coffee & snack room 24 hours.

Nearest Airport
Melbourne International - 7 miles, Orlando International - 69 miles

St. Francis Inn

www.stfrancisinn.com
279 St. George Street, St. Augustine, FL USA 32084
800-824-6062 • 904-824-6068 • Fax: 904-810-5525
info@stfrancisinn.com

Member Since 2002

Innkeepers/Owners
Joe & Margaret Finnegan

Guestrooms and suites with antiques, balconies with rocking chairs and swings, fireplaces and whirlpools add to the tranquil ambiance. Walk to everything from the Inn's Old City location. This historic inn overflows with hospitality, set in a lush tropical courtyard on brick paved streets with horse-drawn buggies passing by. A historic treasure, but modern comforts abound! Great value, with many guest amenities: swimming pool, gourmet Southern breakfasts, brunch on weekends and holidays, bicycles, social hour, evening sweets, DVD, WiFi, health club privileges, private parking, free and discounted attraction tickets, coffee and inn-baked cookies, sherry and flowers in your room. Add in-room massages, gift baskets, in-room breakfasts, picnic baskets, flowers, champagne and other ala carte extras. Tropical setting provides endless outdoor activities, plus sightseeing, historic landmarks, cultural events and celebrations steps away. Many packages available to enhance your stay with added value and savings, themed for romance, history, and more.

Rates
12 Rooms $159/$319; 4 Suites $209/$309; 2-BR Cottage for 4 $279/$359. Each with queen or king bed, private bath, central heat/air, WiFi, cable TV, mp3/iPod connection. Several with fireplaces, whirlpool, fridge. Great amenities! Number of Rooms: 17

Cuisine
Homemade breakfast entrees, in our dining room, your room, on a private balcony or in the courtyard. Mimosas, Bloody Mary's at weekend/holiday breakfast. Social hour appetizers; evening sweets; cookies all day. Specialty lattes, cappuccinos, espressos.

Nearest Airport
St. Johns County (SGJ); Jacksonville International (JAX)

SelectRegistry.com

Windemere Inn By The Sea

www.windemereinn.com
815 S. Miramar Avenue (A1A), Indialantic, FL USA 32903
800-224-6853 • 321-728-9334
stay@windemereinn.com

Member Since 2005

Florida

Indialantic

Owners/Innkeeper
Chuck & Jackie Leopold/Bonnie De Lelys

Imagine... a luxury, oceanfront bed and breakfast, only an hour east of Orlando. Guest rooms and suites are furnished with antiques and fine linens, most with ocean views, some with balconies, porches, whirlpool tubs and TVs. Start each morning with a full breakfast. Social Hour upon request is from 5-6 pm. Windemere is the ideal spot for your small wedding, honeymoon or special getaway, corporate retreat, for watching a rocket launch from Kennedy Space Center, or witnessing sea turtles nest and hatch. The grounds have several gardens, including herbs for cooking. The central point is a koi pond alive with marine plants and animals. Sit on our beach-side pergola and watch dolphins and surfers play in the waves, or the sun/moon rise.

Windemere is 45 minutes south of Kennedy Space Center, an hour east of Orlando and 10 minutes from Historic Downtown Melbourne with shopping, arts entertainment, and casual and fine dining. Visit www.windemereinn.com.

Rates
King and queen size beds all with private baths, luxury amenities, flat screened TVs, hair dryers Please view all rooms at www.windemereinn.com. We answer the phones from 9 am-6 pm EST, or you may book online. Number of Rooms: 11

Cuisine
Start each day with sunrise over the Atlantic and a full breakfast. A fruit course is followed by alternating daily sweet and savory dishes and freshly baked breads and muffins. Social Hour upon request is from 5-6 p.m.

Nearest Airport
Melbourne International Airport 15 minutes with free shuttle service, Orlando International Airport 1 hour west.

Georgia

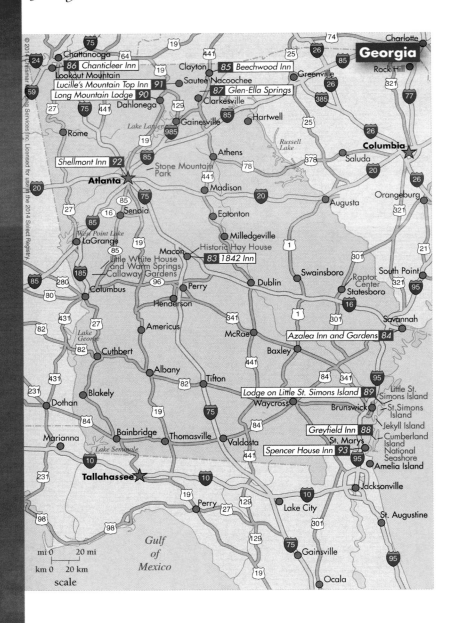

Georgia

Charlotte
Chattanooga
86 Chanticleer Inn
Lookout Mountain
Lucille's Mountain Top Inn 91
Long Mountain Lodge 90
Dahlonega
Clayton
85 Beechwood Inn
Greenville
Rock Hill
Sautee Nacoochee
87 Glen-Ella Springs
Clarkesville
Gainesville
Hartwell
Columbia
Rome
Lake Lanier
Athens
Russell Lake
Saluda
Shellmont Inn 92
Stone Mountain Park
Atlanta
Madison
Augusta
Orangeburg
Senoia
Eatonton
LaGrange
West Point Lake
Milledgeville
Historic Hay House
83 1842 Inn
Macon
Little White House and Warm Springs
Callaway Gardens
Perry
Dublin
Swainsboro
South Point
Raptor Center
Statesboro
Columbus
Henderson
Americus
McRae
Savannah
Lake George
Cuthbert
Baxley
Azalea Inn and Gardens 84
Albany
Tifton
Dothan
Blakely
Lodge on Little St. Simons Island 89
Little St. Simons Island
Waycross
Brunswick
St. Simons Island
Marianna
Bainbridge
Thomasville
Valdosta
Greyfield Inn 88
Jekyll Island
Cumberland Island National Seashore
St. Marys
Spencer House Inn 93
Amelia Island
Tallahassee
Jacksonville
Perry
Lake City
St. Augustine
Gulf of Mexico
Gainsville
Ocala
mi 0   20 mi
km 0   20 km
scale

SelectRegistry.com

1842 Inn

www.the1842inn.com
353 College Street, Macon, GA USA 31201
800-336-1842 • 478-741-1842 • Fax: 478-741-1842
management@1842inn.com

Member Since 1994

Georgia Macon

Owner
Edmund E. Olson

The 1842 Inn welcomes you to step back in time and enjoy the beauty of the mansion built as a private home in the year of 1842 in the beautiful historic district of Macon, Georgia. Experience true southern hospitality grand antebellum style. Come and enjoy a mint julep on the beautiful columned veranda. Meet guests in the parlors daily during our hospitality hour. The 1842 Inn boasts 19 luxurious rooms among the mansion and the 1900 guest house. Public areas are tastefully designed with fine English antiques, tapestries and paintings. A quaint garden courtyard greets guests for cocktails or breakfast. Nightly turndowns and fresh flowers enhance many other gracious grand hotel amenities. Rooms available with whirlpool tubs and fireplaces. High level of service. Considered 'One of America's Top 100 Inns in the 20th Century' by the International Restaurant and Hospitality Rating Bureau.

Rates
19 Guest Rooms, $189/$240 B&B. Rates subject to change without notice. Open year-round. Number of Rooms: 19

Cuisine
Full breakfast and hors d'oeuvres included. Full service attended cash bar.

Nearest Airport
Macon, Atlanta

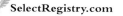

Azalea Inn and Gardens

www.azaleainn.com
217 East Huntingdon Street, Savannah, GA USA 31401
912-236-6080 • 800-582-3823 • Fax: 912-236-0127
Info@AzaleaInn.com

Member Since 2012

Georgia

Savannah

Innkeepers/Owners
Teresa and Micheal Jacobson

Experience the gracious Southern hospitality of Savannah at the Azalea Inn and Gardens. Savannah visitors are fascinated with the easy-going appeal found at our romantic inn located in the Landmark Savannah Historic District -- within two walking blocks of Forsyth Park, the city's infamously captivating "Central Park". Proving you can 'travel well on little' in historic Savannah, or indulge to your heart's content, Innkeepers Teresa and Micheal Jacobson and staff spoil their guests with casual dining, nightly wine socials, and tips on where to go to personally experience historic Savannah character.

Whether you are looking for a romantic escape, a reunion with longtime friends, business retreat or honeymoon getaway, the inn has a package to exceed your desires.

Rates
$199-$429. Many rooms have working fireplaces and private balconies while others may have jet-air tubs and private decks. Our 2-unit Cottage Garden house is ideal for longer stays. Number of Rooms: 10

Cuisine
Bountiful hot Southern breakfast - Sweet Georgia Shrimp served over Georgia Grits, Spiced Apple and Pear French Toast with local fruits. Evening wine and house-made appetizers. At the end of the day, evening sherry and a fresh-made dessert await you.

Nearest Airport
Savannah-Hilton Head International Airport;
Jacksonville International Airport, Jacksonville, FL is 2 hours by car.

 SelectRegistry.com

Beechwood Inn

www.beechwoodinn.ws
220 Beechwood Dr, P.O. Box 429, Clayton, GA USA 30525
706-782-5485
info@beechwoodinn.ws

Member Since 2005

Georgia Clayton

Innkeepers/Owners
David & Gayle Darugh

Beechwood Inn – Georgia's Premier Wine Country Inn: Selected "Best Inn in Georgia 2013" by Georgia Magazine. It's about the food - we use fresh local products, much from our own gardens. Both Chefs selected as "Best Chefs America 2014." It's also about the wine - Beechwood Inn offers daily wine-thirty featuring our own wines made from Georgia grapes. The Inn's restaurant features a Wine Spectator Award of Excellence selection of vintages. Wine Enthusiast Magazine places Beechwood Inn in the Top 5 Destinations "for your next wine and food-focused escape." Don't forget the comfort. Travel writer Becky Lamb says: "Beechwood Inn is the closest thing to a Napa Valley Bed and Breakfast we have in Georgia." Luxury suites all with private baths, most have fireplaces, private porches and mountain views. The Inn's beautifully landscaped 5 acre property is perfect for weddings, receptions, and group functions. Eco-Friendly: low carbon footprint, re-cycling center, NWF Certified Habitat, Electric Vehicle Charging Station, Awarded a Trip Advisor "Gold Level GreenLeader" designation.

Rates
7 guest suites, 2 cabins $179/$259. Private baths, fireplaces, porches, mountain views, free WIFI, MP3/Bluetooth, 600 thread count sheets, hair-dryers, complimentary soft drinks, itinerary planning and daily "Wine-Thirty." Number of Rooms: 9

Cuisine
Multi-course breakfast of local foods. Farm to table "Chefs Tasting Dinners" feature specialties fresh from our gardens. Wine Spectator Award of Excellence. Cooking classes, wine tastings & live music events. Two "Best Chefs America 2014" on staff.

Nearest Airport
Atlanta, GA, Asheville, NC and Greenville, SC each 90 minutes away

‡©‡ Chanticleer Inn Bed & Breakfast

www.stayatchanticleer.com
1300 Mockingbird Lane, Lookout Mountain, GA USA 30750
866-999-1015 • 706-820-2002 • Fax: 706-820-7976
info@stayatchanticleer.com

Member Since 2003

Lookout Mountain

Innkeepers/Owners
Robert & Audrey Hart

Located high atop historic Lookout Mountain and only 10 minutes from downtown Chattanooga, TN. The inn is directly across the street from Rock City Gardens and two banquet facilities all with spectacular views of the Chattanooga Valley. Nearby are hiking trails, waterfalls, views, golf courses, restaurants, shopping, and many other attractions. Built in 1927, the Chanticleer Inn B&B offers 17 French cottage style guest rooms nestled around the inn's courtyard, swimming pool, bocce court and fire pit. While the mountain stone exterior retains its original charm, the interior spaces have been completely renovated. Antique furnishings create a unique and inviting atmosphere in each guest room. Amenities include private bath, individual central heat and air, DVD player, flat screen TV and WiFi. Some rooms feature private patio, fireplace and/or whirlpool and/or steam shower. Family owned and operated, the inn serves a full home-made breakfast each morning and afternoon desserts.

Trip Advisor Travelers Choice 2013 Winner.

Voted "Top 25 Bed & Breakfast/Inn in USA."

Rates
$150-$265/night. Rates include: full breakfast, evening cookies/desserts, bottled water, coffee/tea. Some rooms/suites offer whirlpool, steam shower, fireplaces and mini frig. All rooms have private baths, TV, Keurig and WIFI. Number of Rooms: 17

Cuisine
A complimentary breakfast is freshly prepared by our chef each morning along with homemade cookies/desserts and each evening. Made to order European Cheese Platters, Chocolate Covered Strawberries and more are available for an extra charge.

Nearest Airport
Chattanooga, 25 Minutes; Atlanta, 2 hours; Nashville, 2 hours; Birmingham, 2 hours

ℱ **SelectRegistry.com**

Glen-Ella Springs Inn & Meeting Place

& 🍴 🍴 🍴 ⚲

www.glenella.com
1789 Bear Gap Rd, Clarkesville, GA USA 30523
888-455-8786 • 706-754-7295 • Fax: 706-754-1560
info@glenella.com

Member Since 1990

Innkeepers/Owners
Ed and Luci Kivett

RELAX...RESTORE...REJUVENATE! This historic inn is located in the foothills of the Blue Ridge Mountains just 90 miles north of Atlanta. Over a century old, Glen-Ella Springs Inn & Meeting Place features 16 rustic yet elegant rooms all with private baths and complete with amenities expected by today's discriminating traveler. The inn's fine dining restaurant is open most evenings by reservation and has been named as one of Georgia's Top Dining Destinations since 2004. Located on 17 acres, the property has a 12 acre meadow with extensive perennial herb and flower gardens, as well as an open air swimming pool. If outdoor adventure peaks your interest, you will find numerous hiking trails and waterfalls close by. Tallulah Falls State Park and Black Rock Mountain State Park are within 30 minutes of the inn offering some of the area's most beautiful vistas. Shopping enthusiasts will find original art, hand thrown pottery and antique galleries all around the region and guests can also plan to visit one of the many north Georgia wineries all within a short drive of the inn.

Rates
16 Rooms, $160/275 plus applicable sales tax. Availability may be checked by calling the inn directly or by visiting our website. Number of Rooms: 16

Cuisine
A freshly prepared breakfast is included with your room. The inn's fine dining restaurant features American Continental cuisine prepared with a southern flare and is open most evenings. Please call the inn to check restaurant availability.

Nearest Airport
Greenville, SC or Atlanta, GA

¡O¡ ¡O¡ ¡O¡ ♀
Greyfield Inn

www.greyfieldinn.com
P.O. Box 900, Fernandina Beach, FL 32035, Cumberland Island, GA USA
32035
888-243-9238 • 904-261-6408 • Fax: 904-321-0666
seashore@greyfieldinn.com   *Member Since 1982*

Georgia Cumberland Island

Innkeepers/Owners
The Ferguson Family

This turn-of-the-century Carnegie mansion is on Georgia's largest and southernmost
coastal island. Miles of trails traverse the island's unique ecosystems along with a beautiful,
undeveloped white sand beach for shelling, swimming, sunning and birding. Exceptional
food, lovely, original furnishings, and a peaceful, relaxing environment provide guests with
a step back into another era. Overnight rate includes an island outing with our naturalist,
bicycles and kayaks for exploring the island, round-trip boat passage on our private ferry, all
meals and pantry snacks throughout the day and all non-alcoholic beverages.

Rates
$425/635 AP. Open year-round. Number of Rooms: 16

Cuisine
Hearty southern breakfast, delightful picnic lunch, gourmet dinner. All meals focus
on local southern foods and traditions, including island grown produce and locally
caught seafood. Full bar, wine, beer, liquor, and cocktail hour with hors d'oeuvres.

Nearest Airport
Jacksonville, Florida

Lodge on Little St. Simons Island

🍴 🍴 🍴 ❦

www.LittleSSI.com
PO Box 21078, 1000 Hampton Point Dr, Little St. Simons Island,
GA USA 31522
888-733-5774 • 912-638-7472 • Fax: 912-634-1811
Lodge@LittleSSI.com

Member Since 1993

General Manager
Scott Greene

Nature prevails on this pristine Georgia island where 10,000 acres are shared with no more than 32 overnight guests at a time. Accessible only by boat, Little St. Simons Island unfolds its secrets to those eager to discover a bounty of natural wonders. Seven miles of shell-strewn, private beaches meet acres of legendary moss-draped live oaks, glistening tidal creeks, and shimmering salt marshes to provide an unparalleled setting for a host of activities and total relaxation. Guests enjoy guided interpretive tours, birding, canoeing, kayaking, fishing, beachcombing, hiking, and bicycling. Creature comforts include gracious accommodations, delicious regional cuisine, and warm Southern hospitality. The Lodge on Little St. Simons Island was recently voted one of the "Top 20 Resorts in the South" in Conde Nast Traveler's 2012 Readers' Choice Awards as well as selected for the 2013 Conde Nast Traveler's "Gold List".

Rates
All-inclusive rates range from $450-$775 per night, double occupancy. Rates include boat transfers to/from the island, all meals & beverages, evening cocktail reception, naturalist-led island tours, & use of recreational gear. Number of Rooms: 16

Cuisine
Delicious regional cuisine including island grown USDA certified organic produce and local seafood served family-style. Rates include breakfast, lunch and dinner daily, all beverages including beer and wine, snacks, and a complimentary cocktail hour.

Nearest Airport
Brunswick, GA (BQK), Savannah, GA (SAV), and Jacksonville, FL (JAX).

Long Mountain Lodge

www.longmountainlodge.com
144 Bull Creek Rd, Dahlonega, GA USA 30533
706-864-2337
longmountainlodge@gmail.com

Member Since 2013

Georgia

Dahlonega

Owners/Innkeepers
Dianne & Tim Quigley

Sunset mountain views from every guest room! Get away to beautiful wine country in
the North Georgia Mountains. On the slope of Long Mountain in the Chattahoochee
National Forest, Long Mountain Lodge offers peace, serenity and classic amenities. Ten
minutes from the historic city of Dahlonega and close to waterfall hikes, the Appalachian
Trail, cycling, unique shopping and owner-run restaurants. Dahlonega is one of the
top destinations in Georgia. Dianne is a former chef, and restaurant and bakery owner.
She takes great pride in her well regarded breakfasts and has published two cookbooks.
Two trout ponds invite you to try catch and release fishing or just enjoy the trails, small
waterfalls, and gardens on the property. The main lodge has a two-story rock fireplace in
the great room, plus in-room wood burning fireplaces, jetted garden tubs, free trade coffee,
WiFi, and Direct TV. Four of the rooms have private entrances with balconies or patios.
Afternoon wine, teas, light snacks, and homemade cookies. There is also a rare book store
in the lodge for guests to enjoy.

Rates
$139 to $209 with king or queen beds. One room ADA compliant. Two night weekend
stays for some holidays, festivals and during the high season September to mid-
November. Active duty and retired military discounts. Number of Rooms: 6

Cuisine
Three course candlelit breakfast varies daily with signature dishes such as: baked
pears in vanilla cream sauce, "lighter than air waffles", homemade sausage, cranberry
scones, rhubarb coffee cake, homemade granola & fruit parfaits, and egg souffles.

Nearest Airport
Atlanta, GA 82 miles; Chattanooga, TN 107 miles. Wimpy Airport - Dahlonega, GA for
private aircraft 3 miles.

Lucille's Mountain Top Inn & Spa

www.LucillesMountainTopInn.com
964 Rabun Road, Sautee Nacoochee, GA. USA 30571
706-878-5055
stay@LucillesMountainTopInn.com

Member Since 2012

Innkeepers/Owners
Jim Matthews & Jerry Morris

Sitting atop a mountain overlooking the Blue Ridge Mountains and the beautiful Sautee Valley of North Georgia, Lucille's is a luxury inn and day spa designed for your comfort and relaxation. Located just 90 minutes north of Atlanta in the heart of Georgia's wine country, you can spend the afternoon tasting award-winning wines at the many nearby wineries. Explore the quaint shops of the Village of Sautee, visit an historic grist mill or wander through one of the many art galleries and pottery studios in the area. Or spend the day outdoors hiking to mountain waterfalls, horseback riding across a scenic valley, fly fishing on a pristine mountain river or playing a round of golf. After your adventures return to Lucille's for an afternoon at the spa, relaxing with a soothing Swedish Massage, Hydrating Facial or relaxing Feet-in-the-Clouds treatment. Then sit back on the deck to watch the sunset over the mountains with a glass of wine or a craft beer, followed by dinner at a nearby restaurant. Lucille's Mountain Top Inn & Spa is "where relaxation meets the mountains".

Rates
Valley View Rooms $169-$229; Mountain View Rooms with Jacuzzi tubs and fireplaces $189-$279; ADA Compliant Main Level Rooms $159-$249; Mountain Suite with bubble massage tub, fireplace and outdoor shower $269-$349. Number of Rooms: 11

Cuisine
A full two-course gourmet breakfast of fresh fruits, home-baked breakfast treats and savoury egg dishes served tableside, overlooking the Blue Ridge Mountains and Sautee Valley. And save room in the evening for one of Lucille's home-made desserts!

Nearest Airport
Hartsfield-Jackson Atlanta Airport and Greenville-Spartanburg Airport

Shellmont Inn

www.shellmont.com
821 Piedmont Ave. N.E., Atlanta, GA USA 30308
404-872-9290 • Fax: 404-872-5379
innkeeper@shellmont.com

Member Since 1994

Georgia

Atlanta

Innkeepers/Owners
Ed and Debbie McCord

The Shellmont Inn is an award-winning premier Urban Inn offering all the luxurious amenities found in an upscale boutique hotel. Located in Atlanta's theater, restaurant and cultural district, this crowning jewel is an urban oasis just steps from Atlanta's Midtown Mile and bustling Peachtree Street. Business travelers find us technologically savvy, while leisure travelers find our inn romantic and tranquil. Whether here on business or pleasure, Shellmont Inn offers outstanding personal service in a sophisticated, elegant atmosphere. Indulge in a sumptuous breakfast. Relax in a spa tub. Unwind on a wicker-laden veranda. When your travels bring you to Atlanta, Shellmont Inn will always exceed your expectations. THE EXPERIENCE IS UNFORGETTABLE!

Rates
Rooms $175/$225; Deluxe Whirlpool Suites $225/$295; Carriage House Cottage $275/$375. Elegant Atlanta Elopement Package $1750/$1950. Open year-round. Number of Rooms: 5

Cuisine
A Southern Regional inspired full gourmet breakfast features fresh local ingredients and herbs grown in our garden. Complimentary beverages and delicious afternoon refreshments served daily. Evening turn-down service with treats and fresh fruit basket.

Nearest Airport
Hartsfield-Jackson Int'l - 8 miles south of inn

SelectRegistry.com

Spencer House Inn

www.spencerhouseinn.com
200 Osborne Street, St. Marys, GA USA 31558
912-882-1872 • 888-840-1872 • Fax: 912-882-9427
info@spencerhouseinn.com

Member Since 2003

Georgia St. Marys

Innkeepers/Owners
Mike & Mary Neff

Spencer House Inn is located nine miles east of I-95 on the Georgia/Florida border by
the St. Marys River. For your convenience, the Inn has an elevator and an outside ramp.
Spencer House Inn, built in 1872, is in the heart of the St. Marys Historic District within
walking distance to restaurants, shops, museums and the ferry to Cumberland Island
National Seashore. We can assist you in making ferry reservations and also pack a picnic
lunch for you as you head off for your day of adventure on a beautiful, undeveloped and
pristine barrier island – the beach was voted "one of the best wild beaches" by National
Geographic Traveler magazine – and we are on the Colonial Coast Birding Trail, too.
You will enjoy relaxing in the cypress rockers on the Inn's verandas. Take a leisurely stroll
around the historic village to the waterfront park, fishing piers, boat ramp and marsh walk.
There are golf courses nearby and outfitters available for a kayak trip. Okefenokee Wildlife
Refuge is 45 minutes away. The beaches of Jekyll, St. Simons and Amelia Islands are a
short drive.

Rates
$135/$245. Rates subject to change. All private baths. Elevator & outside ramp.
Complimentary wireless access. Daily paper. Flat screen TV with cable, HBO, ESPN
& DVD player. Open year-round. Pick up from marina or St. Marys airport. Number
of Rooms: 14

Cuisine
Full buffet breakfast with hot entree. Picnic lunches available. Walk to restaurants for
lunch and dinner. Guest refrigerator. Afternoon iced tea, coffee, hot tea and homemade
treats.

Nearest Airport
Jacksonville, FL (JAX).

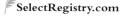

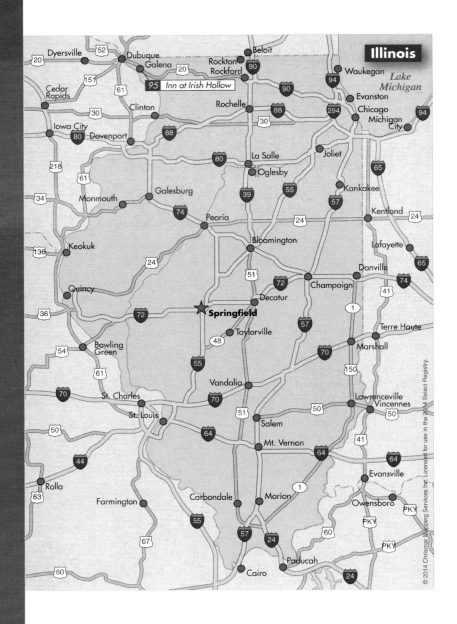

Illinois

Dyersville · Dubuque · Galena · 20 · Beloit · Rockton · Rockford · 90 · Waukegan · Lake Michigan

20 · 52 · 151 · 95 Inn at Irish Hollow · Evanston · 94

Cedar Rapids · 61 · Clinton · Rochelle · 88 · 294 · Chicago · Michigan City · 94

30 · 30 · 90

Iowa City · 80 · Davenport · 88 · 80 · La Salle · Joliet · 294

218 · Oglesby · 65

61 · Galesburg · Kankakee

34 · Monmouth · 39 · 55 · 57 · Kentland · 24

74 · Peoria · 24

Keokuk · 136 · 24 · Bloomington · Lafayette · 65

Quincy · 51 · 72 · Champaign · Danville · 74

36 · 72 · ★ **Springfield** · Decatur · 41 · 1

48 · Taylorville · 57 · Terre Haute

54 · Bowling Green · 55 · 70 · Marshall · 150

61 · Vandalia · Lawrenceville · Vincennes · 50

70 · St. Charles · 70 · 51 · 50 · 41

St. Louis · 50 · 64 · Salem · Mt. Vernon · 64 · 64

44 · Evansville

Rolla · 63 · Farmington · Carbondale · 55 · Marion · 1 · Owensboro · PKY

67 · 57 · 24 · 60 · PKY

60 · Cairo · Paducah · 24 · PKY

© 2014 Chrismar Mapping Services Inc. Licensed for use in the 2014 Select Registry.

Inn at Irish Hollow

www.irishhollow.com
2800 S. Irish Hollow Road, Galena, IL USA 61036
815-777-6000
innkeeper@irishhollow.com

Member Since 2010

Owners/Innkeepers
Bill Barrick, Tony Kemp, Matthew Carroll

Irish Hollow is the ultimate romantic, pampering and inspiring inn, set in the magnificent rolling hills of the Galena countryside. Secluded on an amazing 500-acre farm estate, I.H. features spectacular cottages, superb amenities, magical meals, and the perfect background for your personal journey. Located near historic Galena, a stone's throw from the Mississippi River, down the valley from Downhill Skiing and surrounded by thousands of acres of Trail-carved Conservation Land, I.H. offers the ideal setting for everyone. Spend an awesome day on snowshoes, bikes, woods, wandering or just sitting by the Creek. WiFi and IPod stations keep you connected...while the roaring wood-burning fireplaces, private candlelit dinners in the woods, double spa tubs, rain showers for two, horse-drawn buggy rides and couples massage reconnect the two of you! I.H. specializes in all-natural and homegrown cuisine, outdoor fitness, special diet accommodation, great wine and personalized service...all in a scrumptious setting. Our "CREATE YOUR OWN STAY" menu lets you design your ultimate visit!

Rates
5 Private Cottages and 3 Luxury Suites nightly $195-$450. Seasonal Packages (visit IrishHollow.com for details and rates), Full Country Breakfast, Farmhouse Dinners, Organic Beds, Spa Tubs, Wood Fires, BodyWorks Treatments. Number of Rooms: 8

Cuisine
Internationally acclaimed All-Natural Cuisine. Country Gourmet Breakfast (with delivery option) 7-course Farmhouse Dinner, Luscious Picnic, Private Campfire in the Woods, Special Diets including Vegan, Gluten-Free, Hand-Crafted Bakery, Great Wine List.

Nearest Airport
Dubuque Regional Airport, 30 minutes. O'Hare International Airport, 2.5 hours.

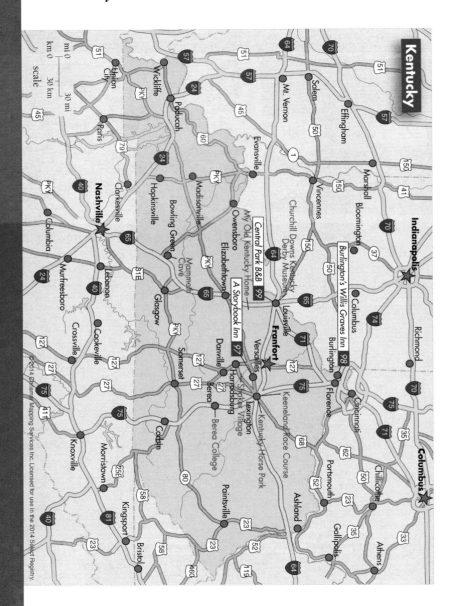

Kentucky

Central Park B&B

My Old Kentucky Home 99

A Storybook Inn 97

Burlington's Willis Graves Inn 98

SelectRegistry.com

© 2014 DeLorme Mapping Services Inc. Licensed for use in the 2014 Select Registry.

A Storybook Inn

www.storybook-inn.com
277 Rose Hill Avenue, Versailles, KY USA 40383
859-879-9993 • Fax: 859-873-0332
stay@storybook-inn.com

Member Since 2007

Owner/Innkeeper
C. Elise Buckley

A Storybook Inn has been likened to a small European luxury inn. It is so refreshing to find an award-winning historic place that is meticulously restored, yet so very welcoming! A Storybook Inn is on acreage in the historic district of quaint Versailles, within walking distance to shops and restaurants. Our suites are tastefully designed and furnished to reflect the classic movie each is aptly named for. Our health-conscious "skip-lunch" full breakfasts and afternoon snacks are served in our lovely, bright 50-ft long Conservatory overlooking the garden and water feature in our ancient stone pond. We use as many local, organic ingredients as possible. If you kindly call ahead, we would be glad to assist you with horse farm tours, dinner reservations, and en-suite massages by a professional Massage Therapist. Our stand-alone 3.5 BR/BA Huntsman Chase guesthouse with great room and full kitchen is fantastically appointed. We look forward to welcoming you to A Storybook Inn in World Class Horse Country! Close to Everything; Worlds Apart!

Rates
Regular Season: $269-$345 (double occupancy) April & October $295-$379. Derby: $324.-$417 (double occupancy) .Midweek discount excludes April, October Discount active military/clergy; must let us know at time of booking. Number of Rooms: 7

Cuisine
Gorgeous full breakfast w/fresh fruit, homemade scones or muffins, freshly prepared sweet or savory entree each morning. Fresh ground coffee, juice, filtered water. Guests are served in our lovely 50 ft. glass Conservatory overlooking the courtyard.

Nearest Airport
Lexington Bluegrass Field is a very convenient 10 mins from the inn. Louisville Airport is an hour.

Burlington's Willis Graves Bed & Breakfast Inn

www.burligrave.com
5825 North Jefferson Street, Burlington, KY 41005
888-226-5096 • 859-689-5096 • Fax: 859-689-0528
inn@burligrave.com

Member Since 2007

Innkeepers/Owners
Bob & Nancy Swartzel

Experience sophisticated charm and relaxed country living at this award-winning inn on the edge of a small town, just twenty minutes from Cincinnati. Choose between two masterfully restored early and mid-1800s buildings, the Willis Graves Federal brick homestead and William Rouse log cabin, furnished with appropriate antiques and reproductions. Attention to detail and luxurious touches are obvious everywhere. For your comfort and relaxation, we offer whirlpool baths, steam showers, plush robes and towels, fireplaces, triple sheeting with fine linens, down comforters, top quality mattresses, and fresh baked cookies. Guests may also enjoy in-room massage, wireless Internet, cable television, DVD and CD players, a comprehensive movie collection, and our inviting porches. Each morning, a full gourmet breakfast is served at individual tables set with white tablecloths, cloth napkins, and fine china. Suites offer in-room dining as an option. Gracious hospitality and beautiful surroundings create the perfect setting for your next romantic getaway, reunion, or business retreat.

Rates
$110-$235, special rates available. Number of Rooms: 5

Cuisine
A full gourmet breakfast is offered daily with a fresh fruit course to start. French roast coffee, assorted teas, juices, breads, and made from scratch entrees are served from our menu. Complimentary water and homemade cookies are in each room.

Nearest Airport
Cincinnati/Northern Kentucky International Airport

SelectRegistry.com

Central Park Bed & Breakfast

www.centralparkbandb.com
1353 South 4th St., Old Louisville Historic District, Louisville, KY 40208
877-922-1505 • 502-638-1505 • Fax: 502-638-1525
centralpark@win.net

Member Since 2006

Kentucky Louisville

Approved

Proprietors
Robert and Eva Wessels

Come and bask in the ambiance of a Gilded Age mansion facing Central Park. We are located in one of the largest Victorian neighborhoods in America. Relax and have a glass of wine on the veranda or sip a cup of tea by the 19th century grand piano in the parlor. We have created a Victorian dream for a romantic get away for any special couple wanting to soak in a tub for two or lounge in a king size bed dressed in luxury linens by the fireplace. It can be a romantic interlude or a corporate retreat. Whether you are a traveler searching for a luxurious respite or the business traveler looking for more than a hotel, we have the place for you. We prepare a delicious three course breakfast daily. Our coffees are specially blended for the inn, and we always have specialty teas, treats and wine available each evening. We are centrally located close to downtown (1.5mi), the Expo Center, Churchill Downs (1mi), or the airport (10min). All rooms have a private bathroom, a fireplace, television, comfortable sitting area, and Internet access. The Inn's antiques are of the Victorian period.

Rates
Queens $135/$145, Kings/suites $185/$195, Carriage House (Child and pet friendly) $185. Corporate rates for single business travelers (Please call for rates). Number of Rooms: 7

Cuisine
Creative 3-course breakfast served in dining room or on the veranda overlooking the courtyard. Fresh roasted coffee, teas, juices, and fresh baked goods. Afternoon beverages and desserts. Fine and casual dining less than 2 blocks from Inn.

Nearest Airport
Louisville International (SDF), 10-min.

Maine

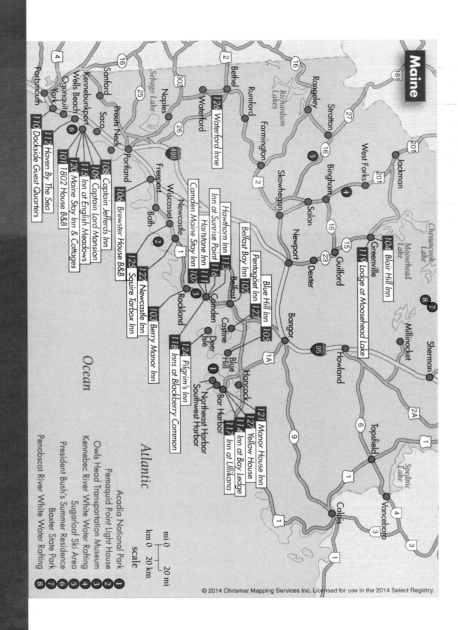

Maine

Portsmouth
York
Ogunquit
Wells Beach
Kennebunkport
Sanford
Saco
Prouts Neck
Portland
Naples
Sebago Lake
Waterford
Rumford
Bethel
Farmington
Rangeley
Stratton
Bingham
Salon
Skowhegan
Newport
Dexter
Guilford
Greenville
West Forks
Jackman
Moosehead Lake
Chesuncook Lake
Millinocket
Sherman
Howland
Bangor
Belfast
Camden
Rockland
Bath
Wiscasset
Freeport
Newcastle
Castine
Deer Isle
Blue Hill
Hancock
Bar Harbor
Northeast Harbor
Southwest Harbor
Topsfield
Vanceboro
Calais
Spednic Lake
Richardson Lakes

112 Haven By The Sea
110 Dockside Guest Quarters
101 1802 House B&B
120 Maine Stay Inn & Cottages
115 Inn at English Meadows
109 Captain Lord Mansion
108 Captain Jefferds Inn
106 Brewster House B&B
126 Waterford Inne
116 Inn at Sunrise Point
113 Hawthorn Inn
111 Harstone Inn
107 Camden Maine Stay Inn
102 Pentagoet Inn
122 Newcastle Inn
125 Squire Tarbox Inn
103 Berry Manor Inn
118 Inns at Blackberry Common
124 Pilgrim's Inn
123 Belfast Bay Inn
105 Blue Hill Inn
104 Blair Hill Inn
119 Lodge at Moosehead Lake
121 Manor House Inn
127 Yellow House
114 Inn at Bay Ledge
117 Inn at Ullikana

Atlantic Ocean

Acadia National Park
Pemaquid Point Light House
Owls Head Transportation Museum
Kennebec River White Water Rafting
Sugarloaf Ski Area
President Bush's Summer Residence
Baxter State Park
Penobscot River White Water Rafting

scale
mi 0 — 20 mi
km 0 — 20 km

© 2014 Chrismar Mapping Services Inc. Licensed for use in the 2014 Select Registry.

100

f SelectRegistry.com

1802 House B&B Inn

www.1802house.com
15 Locke Street, Kennebunkport, ME USA 04046
800-932-5632 • 207-967-5632
info@1802inn.com

Member Since 2013

Teri and Roger Walker
Innkeepers/Owners

Approved

The 1802 House Bed and Breakfast is one of Kennebunkport's finest historic Inns. Located in a serene, quiet neighborhood, Dock Square's shops, restaurants and galleries are only a short stroll away. The friendly informal innkeepers and staff, and the beautiful house and property, create a relaxing home away from home. Set amidst towering pines and landscaped gardens, this Inn offers six beautiful guest rooms whose gracious appointments are inspired by a sense of traditional charm mixed with modern hospitality. To ensure your comfort, guest rooms are furnished with private tiled baths, Jacuzzi tubs, flat screen TVs, radios with iPod/iPhone docking, air conditioning, romantic gas fires, premium bedding, complimentary Wi-Fi and deluxe toiletries. Guests are treated to a three course gourmet breakfast and inn-baked snacks every afternoon. Sit in front of the fire with a cup of hot chocolate or spend a lazy afternoon on the porch in rocking chairs enjoying the sunset over the golf course. This inn is perfect for all seasons.

Rates
Six rooms: $149/$369, including full three-course gourmet breakfast. Open year around. Fireplaces and air conditioning. Complimentary Wi-Fi and parking. Number of Rooms: 6

Cuisine
Three-course gourmet breakfast prepared fresh daily using local Maine ingredients. Your meal begins with assorted fruit juices, and tea or coffee followed by a delicious homemade bread, seasonal fruit and a hot main entree.

Nearest Airport
Portland Jetport, ME; Logan Airport, Boston, MA

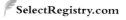

Belfast Bay Inn

www.belfastbayinn.com
72 Main Street, Belfast, ME USA
207-338-5600 • Fax: 207-338-9100
info@belfastbayinn.com

Member Since 2009

Maine
Belfast

Innkeepers/Owners
Ed and Judy Hemmingsen

You are invited to Belfast's only AAA Four Diamond Award winning Boutique Hotel with upscale accommodations featuring luxuriously appointed 2-person guest suites. We are located in the heart of downtown Belfast, a quaint seaside city declared "Coolest Small Town" by Budget Traveler and ranked one of the top ten art communities in America. We are surrounded by shops, galleries, restaurants, and we are steps to the waterfront at the town pier. We fully restored these mid-1800 Greek Revival row houses to offer refined and sophisticated guest suites for discerning tastes. Each gracefully decorated suite has distinctive features including hardwood and stone floors, crown moldings, granite counter tops, classic original oil paintings, carefully chosen furniture and fine upholstery. Some suites have gas fireplaces, balconies and water views. Treat yourself to our many guest amenities by scheduling an in-suite massage. Enjoy breakfast delivered to your suite each morning. Select a movie from our gallery or browse our wine collection at our Molly Amber gift shop.

Rates
6 Suites and 2 Rooms $198-$378. Number of Rooms: 8

Cuisine
Hearty breakfast of homemade breads and sweets, fresh juices and fruits, granola and a changing menu of hot entrees. Evenings enjoy fresh baked cookies, coffee and tea.

Nearest Airport
Bangor International Airport

102

SelectRegistry.com

Berry Manor Inn

www.berrymanorinn.com
81 Talbot Avenue, P.O. Box 1117, Rockland, ME USA 04841
800-774-5692 • 207-596-7696 • Fax: 207-596-9958
info@berrymanorinn.com

Member Since 2007

Innkeepers/Owners
Cheryl Michaelsen & Michael LaPosta, Jr.

Named as one of the Best US B&Bs by Trip Advisor (2013 & 2008), the Berry Manor Inn offers guests the elegance and grandeur of the Victorian era, the luxury and modern conveniences today's travelers expect, and exceptional warm and gracious hospitality without the pretense. Our spacious guest rooms are uniquely decorated in the colors of the Victorian era with a pleasing balance of elegance, comfort and privacy. Guest rooms have in room heat & AC, flat screen TVs, WiFi, fireplaces and private luxury baths (many whirlpool tubs or body jet showers). The inn is located in a quiet, residential neighborhood away from busy Rt.1, but within walking distance to the harbor, historic downtown shops, museums, art galleries and an array of great restaurants. Located just south of Camden, Rockland is the ideal home base for your travels along the coast of Maine. Enjoy the area's lighthouses, succulent Maine lobsters, renowned museums and year round activities as you savor the flavors, arts and adventures of Midcoast Maine. Experience the real Maine—Experience the Berry Manor Inn.

Rates
$145-$325 June–Late Oct; $120-$235 Late Oct-May. Private baths, in-room heat/AC, fireplaces, flat screen TVs and free WiFi. Rates include breakfast, concierge services and homemade pie. Exciting packages available. Open Year Round. Number of Rooms: 12

Cuisine
Breakfast served at private tables & features homemade multi-course entrees that vary daily. Dietary restrictions accommodated w/notice. Complimentary Guest Pantry area stocked w/soda, teas, ice & Mom's homemade pies as featured on the Food Network.

Nearest Airport
Rockland (RKD) 5 min CapeAir/JetBlue @ Boston; Portland (PWM) 1.5hrs; Bangor (BGR) 2 hrs. Train & Bus service also.

Blair Hill Inn

www.blairhill.com
351 Lily Bay Road, Greenville, ME USA 04441
207-695-0224 • Fax: 207-695-4324
info@blairhill.com

Member Since 2005

Maine

Greenville

Innkeepers/Owners
Dan & Ruth McLaughlin

"Arguably the finest inn in all of inland Maine (and quite possibly the entire state), Blair Hill Inn is pure North Woods fantasy." Travel + Leisure Magazine

Few places possess such dramatic landscape and magnitude of lake, sky & mountain views. Set atop 20-ft high, 900-ft long fieldstone walls, the panoramic views of Moosehead Lake will captivate your imagination. Reminiscent of the grand country hotels that once graced this fabled lake & mountain region, Blair Hill Inn was originally built in 1891 as the centerpiece of a 2,000-acre gentleman's farm. The inn's equally captivating interior, is restored to pristine perfection. The beautifully proportioned and light-filled rooms are tailor-made for a stylish life. Paired with renowned dining, a relaxed atmosphere & an abundance of thoughtful services, Blair Hill Inn has become a destination for discerning travelers from around the world. Open May through October.

AAA four-diamond, Forbes Travel Recommended, Rated # 1 by TripAdvisor.

Rates
5 king guest rooms, 2 queen guest rooms & 1 two-bedroom suite @ $325-$495: each with gorgeous designer baths, fresh flowers, thoughtful amenities and breathtaking views from huge windows that open to stunning vistas & cool breezes. Number of Rooms: 8

Cuisine
The inn's award winning, 4 & 1/2 star restaurant is reason alone to stay here, and the farm-to-table cuisine is inspired. Serving Thursday, Friday and Saturday evenings. Along with delicious and creative breakfasts, this is a haven for "Foodies."

Nearest Airport
Bangor International and Portland International

SelectRegistry.com

The Blue Hill Inn

www.bluehillinn.com
40 Union Street, P.O. Box 403, Blue Hill, ME USA 04614
207-374-2844 • 800-826-7415
sarah@bluehillinn.com

Member Since 1994

Innkeeper/Owner
Sarah Pebworth

The coastal village of Blue Hill wraps around Blue Hill Bay and is centrally located for exploring Acadia National Park, Deer Isle, Castine, and the peninsula. This area offers rocky coastlines, blueberry fields, lighthouses, fine galleries, and small town charm, perfect for strolling under evening skies filled with stars. Blue Hill offers the very best of Maine; it's a seaside village with a lot to offer. The 1830 Federal inn is a short walk to the bay, Kneisel Chamber Music Hall, a steel drum band street dance, and Blue Hill Mountain. The Blue Hill Inn, on the National Historic Register, retains many original features and was recognized as Editors' Choice Best Traditional Inn in Yankee Magazine in 2013. After a day of hiking, sailing, kayaking, bird-watching, gallery hopping, or reading in the garden, you'll be pampered with afternoon treats, evening hors d'oeuvres, luxurious linens, air conditioned rooms, free wifi, and staff attentive to every detail of your memorable stay. The inn is proud to be designated a Maine Environmental Leader and a TripAdvisor GreenLeader.

Rates
Vary with season. 11 rooms, 2 pet-friendly suites with kitchens, all with private baths. May-October, rates include our three-course breakfast, with lots of guest-friendly choices; afternoon treats; and evening hors d'oeuvres. Number of Rooms: 13

Cuisine
Enjoy a complimentary three-course breakfast, served in our sunny dining room on a schedule that fits your day's plan. Choices range from vacation decadent to watching one's waistline. A full bar and fine wines are available with hors d'oeuvres.

Nearest Airport
Hancock Co.-Bar Harbor (BHB) in Trenton - 40 min., Bangor (BGR) - one hour, Portland (PWM) - three hours.

Brewster House Bed & Breakfast

www.BrewsterHouse.com
180 Main Street, Freeport, ME USA 04032
207-865-4121 • 800-865-0822 • Fax: 207-865-4188
info@brewsterhouse.com

Member Since 2010

Innkeepers
Scott & Mary Gile

Brewster House Bed & Breakfast is a comfortable and inviting 1888 Queen Anne Victorian home located among other historic homes, yet just steps from L.L. Bean, Freeport outlet shops & fabulous restaurant choices! Built by a Mayflower descendant, Brewster House offers comfortable elegance, gas fireplaces, bay windows and large private baths. Relax in your room or in our cozy parlor and enjoy our afternoon refreshments after your visit to the Freeport shops and outlets, or your day trips to nearby lighthouses, coastal beaches and state parks, golf or boating adventures on Casco Bay. We'll provide maps, directions, and suggested itineraries to help you explore the Maine coast and find your way to lighthouses and lobster shacks. In addition to our 5 king or queen rooms, we have two 2-room suites for up to 3 or 4 guests. Three of our rooms have gas fireplaces, and all have fine linens, luxurious robes and slippers, Keurig coffee/tea service, satellite HDTVs, clock radios with iPod docks, air conditioning, and individual heat. There is complimentary WiFi throughout the house.

Rates
$189-$219 king/queen rooms, $259-$299 suites, seasonal rates, packages and specials. Open all year. Number of Rooms: 7

Cuisine
We serve a full, hot, gourmet breakfast daily. We begin with either a hot or cold fruit course, and alternate between sweet and savory main courses daily, as well as light alternatives. We bake fresh cookies and offer refreshments every afternoon.

Nearest Airport
Portland, Maine (PWM) 20 minutes, Manchester, NH (MHT) 1:45 hours, Boston (BOS) 2 hours

SelectRegistry.com

Camden Maine Stay Inn

www.camdenmainestay.com
22 High Street (US 1 North), Camden, ME USA 04843
207-236-9636 • Fax: 207-236-0621
innkeeper@camdenmainestay.com

Member Since 1995

Owners/Innkeepers
Roberta & Claudio Latanza

Relaxed, cozy, romantic and very friendly, the Maine Stay Inn is a grand old home located in the historic district of one of America's most beautiful seaside villages, known as the place "where the mountains meet the sea." It projects the true essence of New England, its history, its tradition. To visit the Maine Stay Inn is to literally step into a venerable piece of history. Built in 1802 by a direct descendant of John Alden, the striking main house, attached carriage house and four-story barn are an outstanding example of the progressive farm buildings common to 19th century Maine. Our three parlors are tastefully decorated with antique Italian furnishings, paintings and ceramics. Winner of Karen Brown Reader's Choice Award for "Warmest Welcome in New England." Chosen by Frontgate as one of America's Finest Homes. In the words of Vacations Magazine, "Down east hospitality at its very best." Frommer's comments, "Camden's premier Bed and Breakfast," and Fodor's agrees: "Camden's best B&B." Welcome to the History and the Tradition of Maine...with an Italian accent!

Rates
From $130 to $290 per night. Each room has individual style and character. Many of them have original wide plank pine flooring and Vermont Castings stoves. All rooms are very romantic with private baths. Open year-round. Number of Rooms: 8

Cuisine
Gourmet breakfast, which may be enjoyed at our antique harvest table in the dining room or at a table for two on our sun porch overlooking our large beautiful garden. Tea, coffee and cookies in the afternoon. Nearby casual and fine dining restaurants.

Nearest Airport
Rockland (RKD); Bangor (BGR); Portland (PWM); Boston (BOS)

Captain Jefferds Inn

www.captainjefferdsinn.com
P.O. Box 691, 5 Pearl Street, Kennebunkport, ME USA 04046
207-967-2311 • 800-839-6844
captjeff@captainjefferdsinn.com

Member Since 2008

Maine

Kennebunkport

Innkeepers/Owners
Erik & Sarah Lindblom

For travelers seeking a unique escape, the Captain Jefferds Inn holds particular appeal. Perhaps it's the historic lines of this 1804 sea captain's home tucked away within the heart of the historic residential district of Kennebunkport. Maybe it's the inn's beautifully manicured gardens, the siren song of ocean waves, or the ease of access to recreational activities. Then again it might be the absolute comfort and attention to detail found in each thoughtfully decorated room. Find yourself selecting from a wonderful assortment of home baked goodies, light hors d'oeuvres and seasonal hot and cold beverages. Find yourself experiencing personalized service and little touches to enhance your stay like wireless Internet access throughout the property and beach cruiser bicycles. Find yourself lounging on the Kennebunk Beaches or taking a five minute stroll to explore Dock Square's specialty boutiques, art galleries, antique shops and restaurants ranging from casual to five-diamond rated. Regardless of what leads you to Kennebunkport, find yourself at the Captain Jefferds Inn.

Rates
$149/$399 Seasonally adjusted. Open year-round. Number of Rooms: 16

Cuisine
Full served 3-course gourmet breakfast with fresh flowers, candlelight and fireplace in the cooler months. Afternoon tea with home baked goods and light hors d'oeuvres. Fine wines and champagne are available for purchase.

Nearest Airport
PWM - Portland Jetport, MHT - Manchester Boston Regional Airport, BOS - Boston Logan International Airport

SelectRegistry.com

Captain Lord Mansion

www.captainlord.com
6 Pleasant Street, P.O. Box 800, Kennebunkport, ME USA 04046-0800
800-522-3141 • 207-967-3141 • Fax: 207-967-3172
innkeeper@captainlord.com

Member Since 1975

Innkeepers/Owners
Bev Davis and Rick Litchfield

Make enduring memories at our intimate B&B! Your comfort, serenity and total satisfaction are vitally important to us. We strive to provide warm hospitality together with lots of personal service. Our central location, extensively landscaped grounds and large, beautifully-appointed guest rooms are dedicated to maximize your satisfaction. Each guest-room offers such amenities as an oversize bed, gas fireplace, flat screen TV, A/C and a heated bathroom floor. Several baths have multiple body-jet showers; 9 have double jetted tubs. The inn also offers freshly-prepared, family-style breakfasts, afternoon refreshments, and complimentary evening dessert wine. We offer a nice selection of bottled wine or by the glass. Delight in our on-premises, romantic, couple's spa. The inn's scenic location is situated at the head of a beautiful sloping green, overlooking the Kennebunk River. Our picturesque, quiet, yet convenient neighborhood affords you a terrific place from which to walk to explore the shops, restaurants and galleries in the historic village of Kennebunkport.

Rates
15 Rooms, $189/$449 B&B; 1 Suite $349/$549 B&B. Open year-round. Number of Rooms: 16

Cuisine
Full 3-course breakfast. Also, casual afternoon tea, with available fresh fruit, cheese and crackers as well as freshly-baked sweets. The Inn also offers a selection of fine wines, chocolate-covered strawberries and fruit platters for purchase.

Nearest Airport
Portland, ME; 35 Miles north of inn.

🍽️ 🍽️ 🍽️ 🍷

Dockside Guest Quarters

www.docksidegq.com
22 Harris Island Rd., York, ME USA 03909
800-270-1977 • 207-363-2868 • Fax: 207-363-1977
info@docksidegq.com

Member Since 1975

Maine

York

Innkeepers/Owners
Eric & Carol Lusty

The Dockside is a special place that captures the essence of the Maine seacoast, with its natural beauty, gracious hospitality, abundant sights, recreation and activities. Uniquely situated on a private peninsula overlooking York Harbor and the Atlantic Ocean, each room has a panoramic water view. Accommodations are in the Maine House, a classic New England Cottage, furnished with antiques and marine art. The large wrap around porch, complete with wicker rocking chairs and iced tea, offers great views of the harbor activities. The multi-unit buildings at the water's edge offer several different room types, all with private decks and water views. Each room is tastefully and individually decorated. There is plenty to do on site and close by: pristine beaches, nature walk, golf, boat rentals, art galleries and antique shops. The Dockside Restaurant boasts a water view from every table. Our creatively diverse menu and extensive wine list will ensure a truly memorable dining experience. You can also dine or enjoy your favorite beverage from the screened porch.

Rates
19 water-view rooms $148-$288, 6 suites $269-$335. One 3-bedroom unit $2,050 to $3,500 weekly. Off season rates, weekly discounts. Maine Escape package - dining and lodging. Number of Rooms: 25

Cuisine
Our restaurant is a favorite with locals and visitors alike. Lunch or dinner on the porch, overlooking York Harbor is a special experience you are sure to enjoy. Our cozy bar or harbor view deck is great for a light meal or beverages.

Nearest Airport
Portland, ME 50 mins; Manchester, NH 1 hr; Boston, MA 1.5 hrs.

Hartstone Inn

www.hartstoneinn.com
41 Elm Street, Camden, ME USA 04843
800-788-4823 • 207-236-4259 • Fax: 207-236-9575
info@hartstoneinn.com

Member Since 2002

Owners
Mary Jo Brink and Michael Salmon

Steps from Camden Harbor! AAA 4 Diamond hideaway in the heart of Camden village that Fodor's considers "An elegant and sophisticated retreat and culinary destination," this Mansard style Victorian built in 1835 offers a unique experience in pampered luxury. "From luscious linens in the guest rooms to the world-class cuisine in the dining room and the collection of 400 orchids, Mary Jo and Michael Salmon get absolutely everything right," says the Maine Explorers Guide. Each air conditioned guestroom combines carefully chosen furnishings to create a mood of lavish comfort and romance. Luxurious amenities include: on site massage room, iPads, WiFi, fireplaces, Jacuzzi Tubs, soft robes, Flat Screen w/dvd. The Cuisine at the Hartstone has been recognized by The American Culinary Federation with their Achievement of Excellence Award. For your vacation in Camden choose the Hartstone Inn and reward yourself with a sumptuous multi-course breakfast, Join the fun at happy hour with specialty cocktails & complimentary hors d'oeuvres. Critics and repeat guests say, "Don't miss dinner!"

Rates
6 rooms, 8 suites, $105/$280 B&B. Gourmet Getaway, Chef for a Day, Cooking Class and Spa packages available. Preview all of our packages www.hartstoneinn.com
Number of Rooms: 14

Cuisine
Sumptuous multi-course breakfast, afternoon cookies and tea, happy hour w/specialty cocktails and complimentary hors d'oeuvres. Memorable five-course dinner is available nightly by reservation. Full bar and Wine Spectator award winning wine list.

Nearest Airport
Bangor or Portland

Haven By The Sea

www.havenbythesea.com
59 Church Street, Wells Beach, ME USA 04090
207-646-4194 • Fax: 207-646-4194
jarvis@havenbythesea.com

Member Since 2006

Maine

Wells Beach

Owners/Operators
John & Susan Jarvis

Known as a Wells Beach oceanside premier property and just steps back from one of
Maine's most beautiful beaches, Haven By The Sea is a place so charming, so welcoming,
so relaxing, you will return time and time again. This seaside property is located in
a quiet residential neighborhood and has been uniquely restored as one of Southern
Maine's destination spots. Experience breakfast in the multi-level dining room or terrace
with its breeze from the ocean and surrounding marshlands. Enjoy a refreshment at
"Temptations," the inn's bar. Some guestrooms and suites have private decks and balcony
water views. Original hardwood floors give the building a sense of history, warmth
and old-world charm. Large common areas, all with fireplaces, offer a comfortable
setting to relax and unwind. Historical colors and tasteful decor treat the eye. The inn
is conveniently located between the historic towns of Ogunquit and Kennebunkport
with specialty shops and dining experiences nearby. A Foder's Choice & TripAdvisor's
Certificate of Excellence award.

Rates
Guest Rooms: $239/$279, Suites: $319/$329. King and Queen Beds, Private Baths,
Cable TV, Wireless Internet and Central Air Conditioning. Number of Rooms: 6

Cuisine
Full breakfast served in the Dining Room or Terrace. Complete bar service available
select hours (Monday - Saturday). Guest Services area offers a refrigerator, cold
Maine Poland Spring water; gourmet coffee and tea available 24 hours.

Nearest Airport
Portland, ME 45 Min. Manchester, NH 1 Hr./15 Min. Logan, MA 1 Hr./30 Min.

SelectRegistry.com

Hawthorn Inn

www.camdenhawthorn.com
9 High Street, Camden, ME USA 04843
866-381-3647 • 207-236-8842 • Fax: N/A
info@camdenhawthorn.com

Member Since 2008

Maine

Camden

Owner/Innkeeper
Maryanne Shanahan

The Hawthorn Inn is an elegant, 1894 Queen Anne-style Victorian mansion situated on 1.2 acres of lawn and beautiful gardens just north of Camden Village and steps from Camden Harbor. One of 66 homes listed in the National Register of Historical Places in the High Street Historic District, the inn offers spacious accommodations with beautiful decor, Jacuzzis, soaking tubs, gas fireplaces, private decks, seasonal views of the Harbor from most rooms. Guests experience the romance of this elegant retreat in pampered luxury. They love to savor the Inn's renowned gourmet breakfast on the terrace and decks in summer and in the sunny dining room or cozy library in winter. The Hawthorn has a reputation for its warm and welcoming atmosphere, offering the perfect balance in comfort and sophistication. Attention to detail in decor and guests needs is in abundance at the inn. With just a short walk to town and the Harbor steps away from the back gate, the Hawthorn offers a peaceful oasis close to the Village and a beautiful, year-round venue for weddings, reunions and retreats.

Rates
Suites and rooms, $130/295. Weddings, commitment ceremonies, elopements, family and corporate retreats. Open year-round. Packages and Specials. Number of Rooms: 10

Cuisine
Full, gourmet breakfast. Local and organic foods. Afternoon refreshments.

Nearest Airport
Knox Municipal (RKD), Bangor (BGR), Portland Jetport (PWM)

Inn at Bay Ledge

www.innatbayledge.com
150 Sand Point Road, Bar Harbor, ME USA 04609
207-288-4204 • Fax: 207-288-5573
info@bayledge.com

Member Since 2002

Innkeepers/Owners
Jack & Jeani Ochtera

Amidst the towering pines, The Inn at Bay Ledge literally clings to the cliffs of Mt. Desert Island, which is locally and aptly referred to as "The Eden of New England." The veranda, appointed with comfy wicker, overlooks the spectacular coastline and is extremely inviting. Guests may enjoy a swim in our pool, relax in a hammock or take a stroll along our private beach. The elegant bedrooms compliment the style of the inn which was built in the 1900s and possesses an upscale country ambiance. Beautifully decorated with antiques, all rooms are unique with views of Frenchmen Bay. King and queen beds are covered with designer linens, down quilts and feather beds. The Summer Cottage sits just 25 feet from the cliff's edge, and every room has a bay view! Fireplace flanked by French doors with panoramic views of Frenchmen Bay. Air conditioned for your comfort! For your special holiday, the Summer Cottage will make it perfect.

Rates
8 rooms, $125/$375 low season; high season $165/$475. 4 cottages $125/$375 low season; high season $175/$475. Number of Rooms: 12

Cuisine
Full gourmet breakfast served in the sunroom overlooking the bay. Afternoon tea & refreshments on the porch.

Nearest Airport
Bar Harbor 15 minutes, Bangor 1 hour, Portland 3 hours, Boston 5 hours

Inn at English Meadows

www.englishmeadowsinn.com
141 Port Road, Kennebunk, ME 04043
207-967-5766 • 800-272-0698
innkeeper@englishmeadowsinn.com

Member Since 2012

Maine

Kennebunk

Innkeepers
Liz and Eric Brodar

Set in a newly renovated mid-1800s Greek revival home in Kennebunk's Lower Village, just an 8-minute walk to Kennebunkport's Dock Square, The Inn at English Meadows is the perfect Hideaway. This contemporary, luxury bed and breakfast is a unique combination of modern furniture, fixtures and impeccably maintained original moldings and floors.

The Inn at English Meadows offers two dramatically decorated common rooms filled with art, art deco, and Chineses from the owner's personal collection that will delight your senses and appeal to your inner self. The five rooms, five suites and pet-friendly bungalow show off the modern style of the Inn. Elegant amenities, including Frette fine linens, bath robes, slippers, towels, and toiletries by Malin & Goetz and beds by Vera Wang, await our guests. A variety of special touches are offered, such as guest iPads, WiFi Internet access, docking stations, flat-screen TVs, and fireplaces. The highlight of your stay will be the three-course gourmet breakfast and homemade refreshments that are served each morning and afternoon.

Rates
$179-$425. Number of Rooms: 11

Cuisine
Guests of The Inn have expressed that the freshly prepared three course gourmet breakfast is nothing short of divine. Menu items prepared by Liz, the culinary creative, are strongly influenced by her time spent traveling abroad.

Nearest Airport
PWM Portland Jetport, MHT Manchester, BOS Boston Logan

Inn at Sunrise Point

www.sunrisepoint.com
P.O. Box 1344, 55 Sunrise Point Road, Lincolnville, ME 04849, Camden, ME USA 04843
207-236-7716 • Fax: 207-236-0820
info@sunrisepoint.com

Member Since 2005

Maine

Camden

Innkeeper/Owner
Daina H. Hill

Four Diamond Award

A pampering seaside haven, this Andrew Harper's Best Hideaways-recommended bed and breakfast inn offers spectacular ocean views and all the luxuries you can expect from a AAA Four-Diamond property. Set on five secluded acres, this oceanfront hideaway is five minutes from picturesque Camden. Sleep soundly in the wonderful sea air, comforted by the gentle murmur of waves outside your window. Awaken to extraordinary sunrises across Penobscot Bay before enjoying a sumptuous breakfast in the Inn's sunlit conservatory or ocean room. Later, relax in the cherry-paneled library with a glass of fine wine and watch the moonrise over the Bay. Stay in a beautifully furnished room in the main house -- a wonderfully restored cedar shingled Maine summer "cottage," or in one of the romantic, luxury cottages at the water's edge, or choose one of the spacious suites set high among the trees. A luxurious, romantic and elegant retreat for discerning travelers. Ocean views, private decks, fireplaces, free wireless and more in all accommodations.

Rates
3 rooms $320-$420 cottages $380-$670. Loft and Suites $360-$510. Open Mid-April to Mid-November. Rates vary within range depending on dates. Number of Rooms: 12

Cuisine
Sumptuous three course breakfast in oceanfront conservatory, featuring Maine specialties and local produce; complimentary afternoon refreshments; full bar; fine dining and casual local seafood nearby for dinner.

Nearest Airport
Portland (PWM), Bangor (BGR), Rockland Municipal (RKD)

Inn at Ullikana

www.ullikana.com
16 The Field, Bar Harbor, ME USA 04609
207-288-9552 • Fax: 207-288-3682
relax@ullikana.com

Member Since 2000

Innkeepers/Owners
Helene Harton and Roy Kasindorf

Ullikana, a secluded, romantic haven, overlooking the harbor, is one of the few remaining cottages from the 1800s in Bar Harbor. Only a minute walk from the center of town, our quiet location offers a haven of hospitality. Watch the lobster boats in the harbor from the garden or the patio, where sumptuous breakfasts are served. Relax in the casual elegance of this historic inn, where art is an important part of our decor. "Everything blends perfectly here. Few innkeepers have mastered the art of hospitality as well as Roy and Helene," says Moon Handbooks. Maine, An Explorer's Guide, writes: "This is our top pick in downtown Bar Harbor, steps from both Main Street and the Shore Path, yet with an away-from-it-all feel." We invite you to share the history and hospitality of Ullikana with us.

Rates
10 Rooms, high season: $185/$355; low season: $160/$285. All our rooms have king or queen beds. All have private baths. Some have porches overlooking the harbor. Some rooms have fireplaces. All have air conditioning. Number of Rooms: 10

Cuisine
We serve a full breakfast on our patio, looking out on the water where our guests also enjoy afternoon refreshments. "The elaborate breakfast is a real treat" says Fodor's.

Nearest Airport
Bangor and Bar Harbor

Inns at Blackberry Common

www.innsatblackberrycommon.com
82 Elm Street, Camden, ME USA 04843
800-388-6000 • 207-236-6060 • Fax: 207-236-9032
innkeepers@blackberryinn.com

Member Since 2006

Maine

Camden

Innkeepers/Owners
Jim & Cyndi Ostrowski

Just three blocks to the picturesque schooner filled harbor, our Inns are a quiet romantic oasis surrounded by over an acre of Maine gardens. Maine Explorer's Guide says "the prettiest interior in Camden." Three gracious parlors of the 1849 Victorian boast original tin ceilings and ornate moldings. Our extensive gardens, complete with a blackberry patch, are a quiet retreat after a day of sailing, hiking or kayaking. Choose an elegant guestroom in Maine's only recognized "Painted Lady" Victorian. Select a suite room in our restored Carriage House tucked amid the gardens. Or stay in a stately guestroom in our Federal Colonial or in the delightful Tinker's Cottage. Amenities include lavish featherbeds, fine linens, gas fireplaces, cable TV and soaking clawfoot or whirlpool tub for extra pampering. WiFi and A/C throughout. Create a special memory! Seasonal Dinner and Culinary packages. Fine selection of wines and spirits. Featured in "Gourmet Getaways: 50 Top Spots to Cook and Learn" 2009. Lighthouses and bicycling are our specialty.

Rates
$99/$289. Open all year. Fireplaces, whirlpools, WiFi & A/C. Seasonal lighthouse, dining and culinary packages. Number of Rooms: 18

Cuisine
Multi-course breakfast of local Maine specialties and our fresh garden herbs and berries served in our dining room or on the garden patio. Complimentary afternoon refreshments. Gourmet dinner service for guests. Excellent selction of wines daily!

Nearest Airport
Portland Jetport; Bangor International

SelectRegistry.com

Lodge at Moosehead Lake

www.lodgeatmooseheadlake.com
368 Lily Bay Road, P.O. Box 1167, Greenville, ME USA 04441
800-825-6977 • 207-695-4400 • Fax: 207-695-2281
innkeeper@lodgeatmooseheadlake.com

Member Since 1995

Maine

Greenville

Proprietors
Dennis & Linda Bortis

Only The Lodge at Moosehead Lake captures the essence of the Maine North woods while pampering guests with luxurious amenities. Unspoiled vistas of Moosehead Lake against a mountain background provide the setting for this one of a kind country inn. Guests marvel at incredible sunsets from the dining room, pub, common areas, private decks and eight of the nine lodging rooms. Each room is individually decorated to reflect the natural surroundings of Moosehead Lake while providing the ultimate in luxury in every detail. You will enjoy a stone fireplace, one-of-a-kind hand carved beds, relics from the turn of the century logging era and twig furniture that defines the unique Moosehead Lake Region. A visit to the Lodge need never be the same twice! The travel and leisure industry has recognized the Lodge for its hospitality and uniqueness. This amazing spot is perfect for enjoying nature and incredible wildlife viewing. The goal is to make your visit as pleasant and stress free as possible. There are few places quite like this. Come see for yourself.

Rates
5 Lodge Rooms, 4 Suites; $250 to $695. King or Queen luxurious beds. Open all year except for April and November. Number of Rooms: 9

Cuisine
Hearty delicious breakfast included. Dinner features Up North Cuisine Friday-Sunday from Mid-June through Mid-October. Safari Camp Dinners on Sunday evenings in July and August only. Winter suppers Friday and Saturday from January-March. Full bar.

Nearest Airport
Bangor, Maine; Portland, Maine; Manchester, New Hampshire

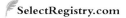

Maine Stay Inn & Cottages

www.mainestayinn.com
34 Maine Street, PO Box 1800, Kennebunkport, ME USA 04046
800-950-2117 • 207-967-2117
innkeeper@mainestayinn.com

Member Since 1996

Maine

Kennebunkport

Approved

Innkeepers/Owners
Judi and Walter Hauer

Experience relaxed sophistication at the Maine Stay Inn, where exceptional warmth and hospitality greet you at our door. Listed on the National Register of Historic Places, the Maine Stay is located steps from the quaint seaside village of Kennebunkport, known for its fine restaurants, shops, and galleries. And don't miss the area's incredible beaches, coves, and nature reserves! Enjoy afternoon tea and freshly baked cookies on our wrap-around porch or before the living room fire – a perfect opportunity to meet fellow guests and innkeepers. Or relax in your luxurious guest room with cable television, complimentary WiFi, fine linens, and many with whirlpool tubs and/or gas fireplaces. Choose a Victorian Inn Room/Suite, an intimate Romantic Cottage Suite, or a stylish Contemporary Cottage Suite. Our Classic Cottage Suites offer spacious accommodations, perfect for families or friends traveling together. Cottage Suite guests often choose to have the gourmet breakfast delivered to their door – the ultimate in luxury! Enjoy classic elegance with modern comforts.

Rates
4 Inn Rooms, $129/$329; 2 Inn Suites, $189/$399; 11 Cottage Rooms/Suites, $149/$489. Open year-round. Number of Rooms: 17

Cuisine
We strive to serve the freshest & most interesting breakfasts possible & offer guests different gourmet entrees daily. Enjoy summer fruit bruschetta w/candied nuts one day and savory French toast with baby greens the next. Afternoon refreshments daily.

Nearest Airport
Portland, ME

SelectRegistry.com

Manor House Inn

www.barharbormanorhouse.com
106 West Street, Bar Harbor, Maine USA 04609
800-437-0088 • 207-288-3759 • Fax: 207-288-2974
info@barharbormanorhouse.com

Member Since 1998

Approved

Maine Bar Harbor

Innkeepers/Owners
Ken & Stacey Smith

Manor House Inn was built in 1887 as the 22 room Cottage "Boscobel." The house has been authentically restored to its original splendor and devotedly cared for through the years. Proudly listed on the National Historic Register, Manor House now includes the Victorian era Chauffeur's Cottage, 2 airy Garden Cottages and the Acadia Cottage. The moment you step into our front entry a romantic Victorian past becomes your present. Enjoy casual comfort, quiet convenience, and privacy while staying within easy walking distance of Bar Harbor's fine shops, restaurants, and ocean activities. Each morning begins with the aroma of coffee and the smells of a delicious home baked breakfast. After a day spent enjoying the natural beauty of Acadia National Park and exploring all that Mount Desert Island has to offer, return to the Inn and take tea with us in the gardens and enjoy some sweets from the kitchen. Or simply relax on one of our many wicker filled porches surrounded by cool green ferns and the fresh ocean air. We look forward to welcoming you to our special place in the world.

Rates
18 Rooms with Cottages and suites. $165/255. Low season rates $90/$210
Manor House Inn opens in mid April and closes in late October. Number of Rooms: 18

Cuisine
Each morning a full country breakfast is served buffet style from our Butler's Pantry, complete with fresh fruit, hand made breads, hot and cold cereals and hot entrees that vary daily. Afternoon tea with sweets is a daily restorative tradition.

Nearest Airport
Bar Harbor (BHB)~20 min; Bangor International (BGR)~1 Hour; Portland Jetport (PWM)~3 Hours; Logan (BOS)~5 Hours

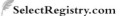

Newcastle Inn

www.newcastleinn.com
60 River Road, Newcastle, ME USA 04553
207-563-5685
info@newcastleinn.com

Member Since 1990

Maine

Newcastle

Innkeeper/Owner
Julie Bolthuis

Located in Maine's MidCoast, at the top of the Pemaquid Peninsula, Newcastle Inn has been welcoming guests since 1911. All guestrooms have a private bathroom, air conditioners for those rare occasions when it is needed and complimentary WiFi is available throughout the property. Two rooms are dog friendly. The variety of common areas provide opportunity to mix and mingle with other guests, or if you prefer, there are spaces for you to find your own "private corner." Complimentary coffee, tea, cold beverages, snacks, and the "bottomless cookie jar" are available in the Guest Pantry. A delicious, made-from-scratch breakfast is served in the dining room, or weather permitting, outside on the deck which overlooks the gardens and the river. After a day exploring the area with its beaches, lighthouses, art galleries and antique shops, our pub is the perfect place to relax and enjoy a glass of wine or a Maine micro-brewed beer. Newcastle Inn is centrally located for all you want to see and do on your trip to MidCoast Maine.

Rates
$185/$275 high season; $145/$230 quiet season. Corporate rates are available. The dog fee is $35/night, limit one dog in the room. Number of Rooms: 14

Cuisine
A full breakfast is served each morning. The breakfast entree changes daily. There is always yogurt, granola and a variety of cereals to choose from as well. You won't leave the table hungry!

Nearest Airport
Portland Jetport, Portland, ME - 1 hour south of inn.

SelectRegistry.com

Pentagoet Inn

www.pentagoet.com
26 Main Street, Castine, ME USA 04421
800-845-1701 • 207-326-8616 • Fax: 207-326-9382
stay@pentagoet.com

Member Since 2005

Maine
Castine

Innkeepers/Owners
Jack Burke & Julie Van de Graaf

The Pentagoet Inn has been welcoming guests since it was built as a steamboat era hotel in 1894 and continues a tradition of gracious hospitality. This authentic Queen Anne Victorian has a wraparound porch, three story turret, extensive perennial gardens and renowned window boxes. You will feel at home with the charming mix of antiques and collectibles, fine linens and amenities. Overlooking Penobscot Bay the vintage seaside village of Castine is on the National Historic Register. Our concierge can plan itineraries for kayaking, sailing, hiking, antiques and art galleries, there are guest bikes for a sunset pedal to the lighthouse. We are centrally located for day trips to Camden, Blue Hill, Deer Isle, Stonington, Acadia and Bar Harbor. We invite you to dinner in our nationally recognized restaurant. Enjoy our exceptional home cooking that honors the classics in its soulful simplicity, bowing to the seasons and our local farms. Have a nightcap in our cozy old world bar, the inn's "utterly fascinating Passports Pub," according to Andrew Harper's Hideaway Report.

Rates
16 Rooms, all private baths, $125-$295. Open May-October. Seasonal packages and specials. Number of Rooms: 16

Cuisine
Full country breakfast, afternoon tea, evening hors d'oeuvres, guest coffee/tea bar. Dinner features local, organic produce, lobster, native fish and meat, New England specialties, fine desserts. Full bar, specialty cocktails, well stocked wine cellar.

Nearest Airport
Bangor (BGR) 1 hr, Bar Harbor (BHB) 50 min, Portland (PWM) 2.5 hrs

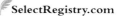

Pilgrim's Inn

🍴 🍴 ♀

www.pilgrimsinn.com
P.O. Box 69, 20 Main Street, Deer Isle, ME USA 04627
888-778-7505 • 207-348-6615
innkeeper@pilgrimsinn.com

Member Since 1980

Innkeeper/Owner
Tony Lawless & Tina Oddleifson

Overlooking Northwest Harbor and a tranquil pond, this 1793 colonial is surrounded by the unspoiled beauty of remote Deer Isle in Penobscot Bay. Glowing hearths, colonial colors, pumpkin pine floors and antique furnishings, combined with warm hospitality and flavorful meals in the cozy Whale's Rib Tavern have pleased many contented guests. Day trips to picturesque seaside villages and Acadia National Park make it an ideal location for an extended stay. The area is a kayaking, sailing and hiking paradise and is home to many artists, writers and the world renowned Haystack Mountain School of Crafts. The Inn is listed on the National Register of Historic Places and is a member of the Bed&Breakfast. com Diamond Collection. It has been chosen as an Editors' Choice in Yankee Magazine's Travel Guide to New England; one of the Country's Best B&Bs by Forbes.com, and recently featured in the US edition of "1000 Places to See Before you Die." In addition to 12 rooms in the inn, three cottages on the property are perfect for families with children and pets.

Rates
12 Rooms and 3 cottages; $119/$259, B&B. Most rooms have views of the pond or Northwest Harbor. All rooms have private baths. Open Mid-May through Mid-October. Number of Rooms: 15

Cuisine
Full country breakfast; refreshments available all day; and dinner at the Whale's Rib Tavern featuring American heritage cuisine and creative daily specials.

Nearest Airport
Bangor International Airport

🪶 **SelectRegistry.com**

The Squire Tarbox Inn

www.squiretarboxinn.com
1181 Main Road, Westport Island/Wiscasset, ME USA 04578
207-882-7693 • Fax: 207-882-7107
innkeepers@squiretarboxinn.com

Member Since 1974

Innkeepers/Owners
Roni, Mario & Lara De Pietro

The inn offers you peace and tranquility, away from tourist crowds, but convenient to coastal adventures. 15 Minutes from Wiscasset named "The Prettiest Village in Maine."

Relax with a drink on our screened in deck watching the beautiful sunsets, or sit in the old barn sitting room along with other guests and maybe play some games or do a puzzle. Dine leisurely and enjoy the ambiance in our 1763 dining room or on the deck with meals created by our Swiss/owner chef Mario along with daughter Lara, using local organic produce and vegetables from both our own farm as well as our son's nearby organic farm. Enjoy an amazing breakfast which includes fresh eggs cooked to order, from our own chickens. Wander through our 12 acres of fields and woods and check the wildlife out down at the salt water marsh. Sleep with the luxury of new mattresses in all our rooms. On the National Register of Historic Places.

Enhance your stay with a cooking class.

Rates
$115/$199 double occupancy. Open mid April - Dec. 31. $35 for an extra person in a room. Number of Rooms: 11

Cuisine
A mouthwatering hot breakfast served between 8 & 9:15. Cookies all day; full liquor license. Farm to table gourmet kitchen with an a la carte dinner "world cuisine" menu prepared by Swiss owner/chef Mario & daughter Lara. Served daily except Tuesdays.

Nearest Airport
Portland Jetport

The Waterford Inne

www.waterfordinne.com
Box 149, 258 Chadbourne Road, Waterford, ME USA 04088
207-583-4037 • 207-542-3630 • Fax: 207-583-4037
inne@gwi.net   *Member Since 1979*

Maine

Waterford

Innkeeper/Owner
Barbara Vanderzanden

This 19th century farmhouse midst 25 acres of fields and woods remained in the same family for generations until Barbara arrived in 1978 and created a true country inn. Elegance pervades the common rooms where art comes in a variety of forms from books and carvings to prints and paintings. Wandering throughout one is drawn in by beautiful and exotic artifacts constantly discovering something previously overlooked. An intimate library beckons with an eclectic collection. Step outside for an invigorating morning walk or bicycle ride--just remember the terrain is rolling--yes, that means hilly! Or relax on a porch swing and gaze out at the gardens; listen to the quiet, the birds, the frogs on the farm pond. Return inne-side to pamper your palate with country chic cuisine. This is a small inn, one where innkeepers Barbara and Jan are ready to answer questions or requests, make reservations, or simply to chat. Even breakfast is a festive occasion where conversation and laughter easily flow and tempt you to return and re-create your spirit with a trip back to the country.

Rates
8 uniquely decorated guestrooms. 6 rooms with bath en suite $160-$200. 2 rooms with semi-private bath (excellent for families) $125 each. Open year round (with a few breaks between January and April.) Number of Rooms: 8

Cuisine
Full breakfast included. Fine dinners available with advance reservation. We do not offer a menu, but prepare a fine meal (with attention to guests' preferences and dietary restrictions.) $45 fixed price. Guests are invited to bring their own spirits.

Nearest Airport
Portland, ME The inn is approximately 60 miles NW of Portland.
Boston Logan Airport is a three hour drive.

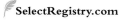
SelectRegistry.com

Yellow House

www.yellowhousemaine.com
15 The Field, Bar Harbor, ME USA 04609
207-288-5100
innkeeper@yellowhousemaine.com

Member Since 2000

Innkeeper/Owners
Pat & Chris Coston

Maine cottage chic in the heart of Bar Harbor. Yellow House Bed & Breakfast is located on a quiet road and offers comfort and style for sophisticated travelers. Our flavorful breakfasts will prepare you for whatever the day may offer, and late afternoon socials on the porch provide time for a sip and a chat about the day! Staying at Yellow House is like being a guest among friends in a Maine country cottage. Our six spacious guest rooms are named after the sprawling guest cottages and reflect the graciousness of Bar Harbors Golden Era. The Yellow House offers private, off-street parking, 24-hour coffee & tea in the butler's pantry, concierge service, and unlimited Wi-Fi. We are steps away from the historic shore path, boutique shops, art galleries, and top-notch restaurants. Concierge service at its best so plan on calling us ahead so you avoid missing that boat trip or romantic dinner at that special restaurant. Bar Harbor is located on Mount Desert Island, home to Acadia National Park, a destination that welcomes more than 2 million travelers a year.

Rates
Spacious guest rooms all with private ensuite baths. Open mid-May to late October. High season $250-$295; Low season $165-$240. Number of Rooms: 6

Cuisine
Served on the spacious wrap-around porch or in the colorful parlor we offer a delicious full breakfast with a creative flair. Gourmet coffee & teas available 24/7 in the butler's pantry. Late afternoon social hour, time for a sip of wine and a chat!

Nearest Airport
Bar Harbor airport is located 20 minutes away, Bangor International 1 hour, Portland International 3 hours

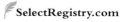

Maryland

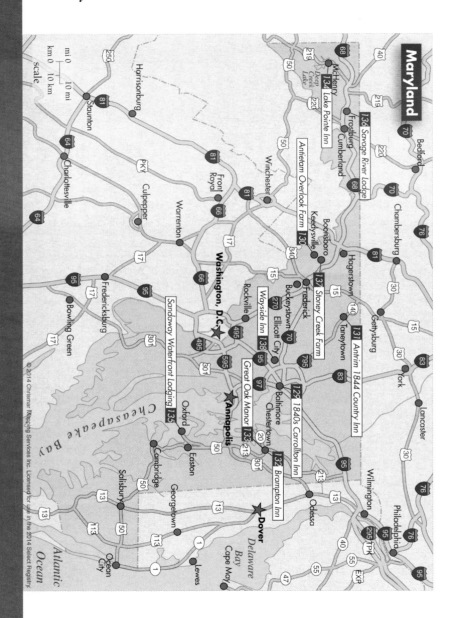

Maryland

136 Savage River Lodge
134 Lake Pointe Inn
McHenry
Frostburg
Cumberland
Antietam Overlook Farm 130
Keedysville
Boonsboro
137 Stoney Creek Farm
Buckeystown
Frederick
Ellicott City
Wayside Inn 138
Rockville
Washington, D.C.
131 Antrim 1844 Country Inn
Taneytown
Hagerstown
Gettysburg
129 1840s Carrollton Inn
Baltimore
Chestertown
Great Oak Manor 133
97
132 Brampton Inn
Sandaway Waterfront Lodging 135
Oxford
Annapolis
Easton
Cambridge
Georgetown
Salisbury
Ocean City
Dover
Lewes
Cape May
Odessa
Chesapeake Bay
Atlantic Ocean
Delaware Bay

scale
mi 0   10 mi
km 0   10 km

Staunton
Harrisonburg
Charlottesville
Front Royal
Winchester
Warrenton
Culpeper
Fredericksburg
Bowling Green
Bedford
Chambersburg
York
Lancaster
Wilmington
Philadelphia

1840s Carrollton Inn

www.1840scarrolltoninn.com
50 Albemarle Street, Baltimore, MD USA 21202
410-385-1840 • Fax: 410-385-9080
info@1840scarrolltoninn.com

Member Since 2008

General Manager
Timothy Kline

This boutique bed and breakfast comprised of a series of interconnected rowhomes, some dating back to the early 19th century, surrounds a central courtyard adjacent to the 1840s Plaza. The inn boasts historic quality antiques and decorator furnishings. Located at the center of historic Jonestown, the 1840s Carrollton Inn is within a short walk of Inner Harbor attractions, Little Italy's fine dining and the nightlife at Power Plant Live. The 1840s Carrollton Inn, next door to the historic Carroll Mansion, celebrates the life of Charles Carroll of Carrollton, the longest lived and only Catholic signer of the Declaration of Independence. Guests retreat to the comfort of overnight rooms with beds featuring handcrafted Kingsdown mattresses, large baths with whirlpool tubs and fireplaces topped with mantles of marble and oak. Business and leisure travelers alike enjoy the convenience of complimentary WIFI access, flat-screen cable television, in-room telephone, refrigerator and microwave. Romance, spa, all-inclusive and elopement packages available as well as monthly specials!

Rates
Room rates range from $150-$350 per night. Corporate, government and military rates available. Monthly and seasonal special rates, add-on and all-inclusive packages also available. Visit our website for details. Number of Rooms: 13

Cuisine
A full breakfast is served from a menu each morning, prepared to order, and included with overnight accommodations. Guests may enjoy dining in the charming garden courtyard, the historic first floor parlor or in the privacy of their room or suite.

Nearest Airport
Baltimore/Washington International Airport (BWI) is located just 10 miles from the Inn (a 20-minute drive).

Antietam Overlook Farm

www.antietamoverlook.com
4812 Porterstown Rd., Keedysville, MD USA 21756
800-878-4241 • 301-432-4200 • Fax: 301-432-5230
Reservations@antietamoverlook.com

Member Since 1992

Maryland

Keedysville

Owner/Innkeeper
Mark Svrcek

Experience Antietam Overlook & 95-acres of mountaintop beauty. Elevation: 1000' at the edge of the Battlefield & 40 mile views of four states. The inn is built of hand crafted timber frame, rough-cut pine & hardwood. Warm fireplaces & comfortable furnishings create an atmosphere that even the men appreciate. In the winter months, guests are invited to relax by the main fireplace where interesting conversation adds to the Antietam experience. The views are spectacular year round, but in the spring, summer & fall, the "Overlook" porch with its Western view for sunsets, is breathtaking. Spacious suites include fireplaces, comfy queen & king beds, soaking tubs, private baths and private screened porches. Enjoy the Hot Tub under the stars. While our seclusion & tranquility are unparalleled, guests also enjoy visiting The Antietam National Battlefield, Harpers Ferry, Shepherdstown WV & Gettysburg. Antiquing? We have the route planned for you. Outdoor adventures and activities are abundant and nearby. Oh, bring your horses and ride the 4200 acres of Battlefield. It is allowed.

Rates
6 Suites, $185/$350 B&B. Generals Quarters $395. Open year-round. Attractions: Antietam National Battlefield, Harpers Ferry, antiquing, Charlestown horse races, Hollywood Casino, hiking, biking, horseback riding and relaxing. Number of Rooms: 6

Cuisine
3 course gourmet breakfast is always included. Many dining experiences are nearby. Our House Chef is usually available to create your dream dining experience. Enjoy a Five Course Dinner with 5 wines for an added fee of $150 per person.

Nearest Airport
Reagan National, BWI & Dulles are 1 Hour. Hagerstown airport is 25 minutes away.

Antrim 1844 Country Inn

www.antrim1844.com
30 Trevanion Road, Taneytown, MD USA 21787
800-858-1844 • 410-756-6812 • Fax: 410-756-2744
mail@antrim1844.com

Member Since 1993

Proprietors
Dorothy and Richard Mollett

You are cordially invited to relive the elegance and hospitality of this National Historic Trust Antebellum Plantation. Antrim 1844 is located amidst 24 manicured acres of countryside accentuated by softly lit romantic walkways, rose gardens and bronze fountains. Embrace the comfort of one of the masterfully restored guestrooms adorned with lavish antique decor, fireplaces and Jacuzzis. Savor a six-course fine dining experience in Antrim's renowned Smokehouse Restaurant or dine privately in the Wine Cellar which boasts over 19,000 bottles of fine wine. Wine Spectators "Best of Award of Excellence" for over a decade as well as a proud member of DiRōNA, Distinguished Restaurants of North America.

Rates
40 Guest Rooms and Suites. $165/$400. Open year-round. Number of Rooms: 40

Cuisine
Afternoon tea. Evening hors d'oeuvres. Elegant six-course prix-fixe dinner $72 per person. Morning wake-up tray delivered to your door & full served breakfast. Enjoy a drink in the Pickwick Pub or privately dine in the Wine Cellar.

Nearest Airport
Baltimore Washington International (BWI), Reagan National and Dulles

Brampton Bed and Breakfast Inn

www.bramptoninn.com
25227 Chestertown Road, Chestertown, MD USA 21620
410-778-1860 • 410-778-1860
innkeeper@bramptoninn.com

Member Since 2001

Innkeepers/Owners
Michael & Danielle Hanscom

Brampton is the quintessential romantic oasis offering gracious hospitality on Maryland's upper Eastern Shore. Set on 20 acres, the inn beautifully blends the grand elegance of a historical estate with the comfort and amenities today's discerning travelers deserve. The spacious, very private and well-appointed guest rooms, suites, and cottages have wood-burning or gas fireplaces and modern bathrooms. A full a-la-carte breakfast is served daily at individual tables or can be delivered to the cottages upon request. Attention to detail, personal service, and friendly innkeepers will make your visit a memorable one. Brampton is located less than a mile outside of historic Chestertown, a colonial village on the banks of the Chester River. Chestertown is the home of Washington College ca. 1782, unique shops, art galleries and fantastic restaurants. It serves as a perfect base for exploring all that the Eastern Shore of Maryland and the Chesapeake Bay area has to offer.

Rates
13 rooms, suites and secluded cottages with en-suite bathrooms featuring whirlpool tubs and/or showers. All our rooms have working wood or gas fireplaces. Rates vary by season and day of the week $229-$429. Number of Rooms: 13

Cuisine
Our complimentary full breakfast includes fresh seasonal fruit, fresh muffins or scones & choice of entree using local organic eggs, meat & vegetables. Daily afternoon refreshments. Beverages & home baked cookies 24/7. Proud member of eightbroads.com.

Nearest Airport
Baltimore (BWI) or Philadelphia (PHL) 90 min, Washington DC (IAD) or (DCA) 2 hrs, NYC (JFK) 3 1/2 hrs

SelectRegistry.com

Great Oak Manor

www.greatoakmd.com
10568 Cliff Road, Chestertown, MD USA 21620
800-504-3098 • 410-778-5943
info@greatoakmd.com

Member Since 2003

Innkeeper
Jennifer Donisi

F. Scott Fitzgerald wrote of blue lawns and country houses, such is Great Oak Manor. From the estate's walled garden bordered by 65-year old boxwoods and its circular drive on the estate side, to its magnificent view of the Chesapeake Bay and private beach on the water side, this country estate provides the appropriate setting for a relaxing getaway or a romantic weekend. Our guest and public rooms are spacious and beautifully furnished. Built at a time when grandeur was more important than cost, guests are swept away by the majesty of the house. This is a true Manor House with fine details, beautiful furnishings, Orientals, and an 850 volume library. The Manor has a glass conservatory and a private beach. The Manor will meet your every need, with 1,200 ft. of waterfront lawn and towering trees on the Chesapeake Bay, and the most beautiful sunsets on the Eastern Shore of Maryland. A perfect place to rejuvenate your soul. Our Conservatory which overlooks the Bay, is popular for small business retreats, weddings or family reunions.

Rates
9 rooms,$159/$315,3 suites,$249/$315.Elegant spacious rooms, fireplaces, massage therapy available. Number of Rooms: 12

Cuisine
Sumptuous Country Breakfast at private tables in the dining room or on the patio overlooking the bay. Fresh baked goods cooked daily, fresh. Afternoon refreshments, coffee,tea,water,and soda. Complimentary evening Port and Sherry.

Nearest Airport
BWI Baltimore MD.(90 min.), PHL (90 min.)

Lake Pointe Inn

www.deepcreekinns.com
174 Lake Pointe Drive, Deep Creek Lake, MD USA 21541
301-387-0111 • 301-387-0111 • Fax: 301-387-0190
relax@deepcreekinns.com

Member Since 2000

Maryland

Deep Creek Lake

Innkeeper
Ed Spak

The Lake Pointe Inn decorated in the Arts & Crafts style, embraces you with an exceptionally warm welcome when you enter the chestnut paneled Great Room with its Mission Style furnishings. Nestled in the Lake Pointe Community in Western Maryland, the Inn is perched just 13 feet from water's edge. The wraparound porch invites you to relax in a rocking chair, read or watch the waterfowl frolic. It is easy to enjoy Garrett County's 4 season activities while staying at the Inn. Golf, skiing and snowboarding await you at the Wisp Resort, adjacent to the Lake Pointe Community. Tour the area using our complimentary canoes, kayaks and bicycles or hike in the 5 nearby State Parks. The outdoor fireplace, herb garden and hammock provide a perfect haven for private conversation or stargazing. Frank Lloyd Wright's Fallingwater and Kentuck Knob are nearby. Lake Pointe Inn is a perfect getaway in any season for any reason!

Rates
$212/$292; All have gas fireplaces, TV/DVD. Some rooms have: Spa Tub, Steam Shower, Balcony. Number of Rooms: 10

Cuisine
Full breakfast and light hors d'oeuvres included in daily rate; dinners served to Inn guests on 3-day holiday weekends.

Nearest Airport
Pittsburgh International PA Washington DC Baltimore MD

SelectRegistry.com

Sandaway Waterfront Lodging

www.sandaway.com
Close to St. Michaels, 103 W. Strand Rd., Oxford, MD USA 21654
888-726-3292 • 888-SANDAWAY
sandaway@live.com

Member Since 1970

Maryland Oxford

Innkeeper/Active Owners
Ben Gibson/Ken & Wendy Gibson

Sandaway is a Chesapeake Bay getaway with eighteen bed and breakfast style accommodations on 2.5 acres of waterfront property with a private sandy beach. Our waterfront location in the colonial village of Oxford, Maryland makes us a unique destination. Guests can walk to restaurants, marinas, our museum, and some shops along brick sidewalks past charming homes with white picket fences. Overnight guests can choose between suites in the circa 1875 Sandaway Lodge, or Sandaway's more modern Deluxe Waterfront rooms. Most guestrooms on the property have water views or porches, overlooking the Tred Avon River, Choptank River, and Chesapeake Bay beyond. Sandaway guests can take the car ferry across the river for a short-cut to St. Michaels, and also drive to the nearby towns of Easton, Tilghman, and Cambridge. At the end of the day, find yourself a beachfront seat at Sandaway. Sailboats entering the harbor at sunset and osprey flying by will create lasting memories. We are indeed "The Land of Pleasant Living."

Rates
Sandaway's rates range from $179 to $299. Most guestrooms and suites are waterfront with private porches. Wedding and Group Rates Available. Not Recommended for Children. Non-Smoking Accommodations. Number of Rooms: 18

Cuisine
24 hour coffee, tea, and snacks. At breakfast time a "Lite Fare Breakfast" is delivered to your door in a basket. Walk to famous Oxford restaurants, or dine close by in St. Michaels, Trappe, Easton & Cambridge. Enjoy Eastern Shore of Maryland cuisine.

Nearest Airport
BWI & National - 1.5 hours. Dulles - 2 hrs. 15 min. Recommended directions at sandaway.com

♿ 🍽 🍽 🍽 ♀

Savage River Lodge

www.savageriverlodge.com
1600 Mt. Aetna Road, Frostburg, MD USA 21532
301-689-3200 • Fax: (301) 689-2746
info@savageriverlodge.com

Member Since 2010

Innkeepers/Owners
Jan Russell and Mike Dreisbach

The Savage River Lodge is situated on 42 acres in the center of a 750-acre state forest in Western Maryland. We offer 18 individual luxury cabins and eight glamorous camping (glamping) yurts, a gourmet restaurant, fully-stocked bar and superior hospitality. Our outdoor recreation includes xc skiing, snowshoeing, biking, fly fishing, geocaching and 14 miles of hiking trails. Other attractions in the area include Frank Lloyd Wright's Fallingwater, downhill skiing, golf and more. Our restaurant offers some of the most interesting food in the area such as wild game, vegetarian/vegan and gluten free options. We specialize in American classics, such as steak, and seafood and have in-cabin dining available for those who want a more private experience. Complimentary homemade muffins and juice are delivered to the cabins each morning. We are annually awarded the Wine Spectator Award of Excellence for our 185+ variety wine list. We are a certified Maryland Green Travel Partner. SRL has many green practices and strives to be as sustainable as possible.

Rates
Our cabin and yurt rates begin at $225 per night for a double occupancy Standard cabin, which includes a complimentary morning muffin basket with freshly made muffins and orange juice. The cabins are pet friendly. Number of Rooms: 26

Cuisine
The Savage River Lodge is where wild game meets tempeh. Our seasonally changing menus have a variety of American classics and serve all palates, including vegetarian/vegan and gluten free. Open daily for lunch and dinner and breakfast on the weekends.

Nearest Airport
2 1/2 hours from Pittsburgh, Baltimore Washington International and Dulles Airports.

SelectRegistry.com

Stoney Creek Farm

www.stoneycreekfarm.com
19223 Manor Church Road, Boonsboro, MD USA 21713
301-432-6272
innkeeper@stoneycreekfarm.com

Member Since 2007

Innkeepers/Owners
Denise Lawhead and David Kempton

Get away from the hustle and bustle, unwind at Stoney Creek Farm! Lovingly restored, our bed & breakfast spares no comfort and affords every modern amenity to eclectic travelers from near and far. Guests at the inn enjoy our beautifully accommodated rooms, wonderful gardens and grounds, five miles of wooded trails for hiking, as well as our delicious hot breakfast in the mornings. Delicious upscale dining and unique shopping, including many antique shops, are all around. We're just minutes from the beautiful C&O canal & Antietam Battlefield, a twenty minute drive from historic Shepherdstown, and a half hour from historic Gettysburg. Stoney Creek Farm is also a unique location for your special event including wedding ceremonies, receptions, civil unions or even your company retreat. Get away from the hustle and bustle, visit Stoney Creek Farm. Situated in the rolling hills of beautiful Washington County, Maryland, Stoney Creek Farm awaits your arrival and welcomes you home to our historic inn.

Rates
King Rooms $240 (Monday through Thursday) $265 (Friday through Sunday) Queen Rooms $220 (Monday through Thursday) $250 (Friday through Sunday) Number of Rooms: 4

Cuisine
Delicious coursed gourmet breakfast served each morning.

Nearest Airport
Baltimore, Washington Dulles

Wayside Inn Bed & Breakfast

www.waysideinnmd.com
4344 Columbia Road, Ellicott City, MD USA 21042-5910
410-461-4636
bnbboy@verizon.net

Member Since 2008

Maryland

Ellicott City

Innkeepers/Owners
David & Susan Balderson

Step back in time to a gentler way of living. Two hundred years of history await you at the Wayside Inn. Conveniently located in historic Ellicott City, Maryland, and within a short drive of either Baltimore, Annapolis or Washington, D.C., the Wayside Inn is the perfect place for you to escape into the past. Guests of the Inn enjoy outstanding, home-away-from-home hospitality. Your Room or Suite is filled with fine antiques or reproductions, the finest linens, and too many amenities to list here. Your comfortable night's sleep in one of our exquisite rooms is followed by a full, gourmet breakfast, created fresh that morning by the innkeepers. Then spend the day exploring the area: shopping in Historic Ellicott City, antiquing in Frederick, touring our nation's capital, meandering through Annapolis, cruising on the Chesapeake Bay, or experiencing Baltimore's famous Inner Harbor. In the evening, treat yourself to a fabulous dinner at one of our area's many restaurants, wine bars or micro-breweries. Five of Baltimore Magazine's Top 50 restaurants are within a five mile radius.

Rates
$159-$219. Number of Rooms: 6

Cuisine
A full, upscale breakfast is served each morning between 7:30 AM and 9:30 AM. This includes the freshest fruit, breads, and either sweet or savory breakfast entrees. All care is given to assure that each guest is served something they will LOVE!

Nearest Airport
Baltimore/Washington International. Travelers also come into National and Dulles Airports.

SelectRegistry.com

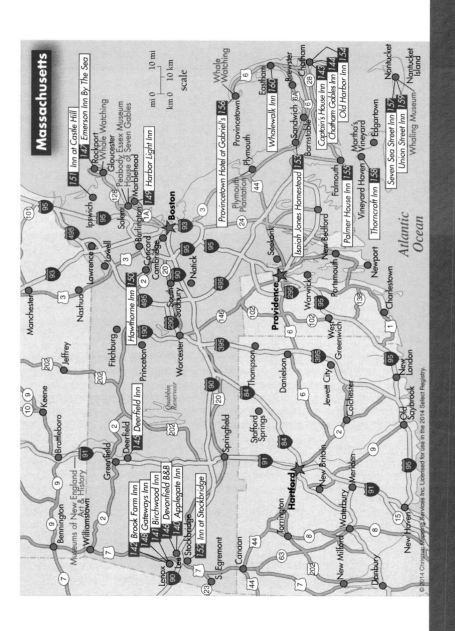

Massachusetts

Massachusetts

151 Inn at Castle Hill
147 Emerson Inn By The Sea
Rockport
Whale Watching
Gloucester
Peabody Essex Museum
House of Seven Gables
Marblehead
149 Harbor Light Inn
Ipswich
Salem
Boston
Burlington
Concord
Cambridge
Natick
South Sudbury
150 Hawthorne Inn
Princeton
Worcester
Fitchburg
Manchester
Nashua
Lawrence
Lowell
Jeffrey
Keene
Brattleboro
Bennington
Williamstown
Museums of New England Art & History
Deerfield
145 Deerfield Inn
Greenfield
Quabbin Reservoir
Springfield
Stafford Springs
142 Brook Farm Inn
148 Gateways Inn
141 Birchwood Inn
146 Devonfield B&B
140 Applegate Inn
Stockbridge
152 Inn at Stockbridge
Lenox
Lee
Egremont
S. Egremont
Canaan
New Milford
Waterbury
Torrington
Hartford
New Britain
Meriden
Danbury
New Haven
Thompson
Danielson
Jewett City
Colchester
West Greenwich
Warwick
Providence
Seekonk
Portsmouth
Newport
Charlestown
New London
Old Saybrook
Whale Watching
Provincetown
Provincetown Hotel at Gabriel's 156
Plymouth
Plymouth Plantation
Eastham
160 Whalewalk Inn
Brewster
Chatham
144 Chatham Gables Inn
154 Old Harbor Inn
Sandwich
Barnstable
153 Isaiah Jones Homestead
Falmouth
155 Palmer House Inn
New Bedford
Martha's Vineyard
Edgartown
Vineyard Haven
158 Thorncroft Inn
Nantucket
Nantucket Island
Nantucket Whaling Museum
157 Seven Sea Street Inn
159 Union Street Inn

Atlantic Ocean

mi 0   10 mi
km 0   10 km
scale

© 2014 Christmas Mapping Services Inc. Licensed for use in the 2014 Select Registry.

♿ 🍴   🍷

Applegate Inn

www.applegateinn.com
279 West Park Street, Lee, MA USA 01238
800-691-9012 • 413-243-4451 • Fax: 413-243-9832
info@applegateinn.com

Member Since 2002

Owners/Innkeepers
Len & Gloria Friedman

Once inside the iron gate, the circular drive lined with lilac bushes reveals this elegant 1920s white-pillared Georgian mansion. It is situated on a 6 acre country estate across the road from a golf and tennis club, half a mile from the historic town of Lee and 3 miles from Stockbridge. The 11 upscale guest accommodations are uniquely decorated and luxuriously appointed. For your comfort, the inn is air conditioned and heated with individual room controls and provides WiFi Internet. From the screened porch look beyond the heated swimming pool to the lawns, towering trees and gardens. This is tranquility itself; a relaxing place to rejuvenate while pampered with attentive service, candlelit breakfasts, and wine and cheese served each afternoon. Explore Tanglewood, Jacob's Pillow Dance Festival, theatre, Norman Rockwell Museum, golf, tennis, hiking, swimming, boating, skiing, antiquing, shopping and other natural and cultural wonders of the Berkshires. Or linger at the inn by a roaring fire, rest in a hammock for two under an old apple tree and stroll the perennial gardens.

Rates
Rooms $160/$285; Suites $295/$395; "Cottage" $295/$395. AC, TV, VCR/DVD, CD, Wi-Fi, some with fireplace, jacuzzi, mini-fridge, balcony, patio and steam shower for two. All have robes, hair dryer, brandy & chocolate. Number of Rooms: 11

Cuisine
Multi-course gourmet candlelit breakfast served on china & crystal. Gluten-free friendly. Wine & cheese served every afternoon. Fruit bowl, cookie jar & guest pantry always available. Breakfast is also served on the screened porch in the summer.

Nearest Airport
Albany & Bradley Airports

f 🐦

Birchwood Inn

www.birchwood-inn.com
7 Hubbard Street, P.O. Box 2020, Lenox, MA USA 01240
800-524-1646 • 413-637-2600 • Fax: 413-637-4604
innkeeper@birchwood-inn.com   *Member Since 2003*

Innkeeper/Owner
Ellen Gutman Chenaux

We welcome you to our romantic Colonial Revival 1766 inn in Lenox, MA, in the heart of the Berkshires, with the wag of a friendly tail, hot-from-the-oven chocolate chip cookies, the wake-up aroma of freshly baked bread and our special coffee blend. Our award-winning breakfasts are created by one of the "Eight Broads in the Kitchen." New England stone-fenced gardens. Enjoy afternoon tea and the Berkshire breezes on our tranquil front porch, curl up next to a crackling hearth with a good read and a steaming mug of mulled cider, relax in a hammock and enjoy the spring blossoms, fireflies in the summer twilight, autumn's vibrant foliage, or firesides and snow angels when snowflakes fall. Hiking, biking or snowshoeing on neighboring Kennedy Park's trails. A short walk to the shops, restaurants, and galleries of historic Lenox. Picnicking at Tanglewood, exploring historic homes, indulging your passion for food with a "Fun for Foodies" experience, de-stressing in a yoga class, luxuriating in a spa day... are all at our doorstep.

Rates
$199/$379. Rates and minimum stays change seasonally. Comfortably elegant guestrooms, six with fireplaces. Number of Rooms: 11

Cuisine
Our award-winning breakfasts feature fruit dishes, local produce, homemade breads, and creative entrees, served fireside at individual tables. Afternoon Tea and Sweet Dreams feature homemade pastries, ice creams, and sorbets.

Nearest Airport
1 hour from Albany and Hartford (Bradley) airports. 2 1/2 hours from Boston (Logan) and 3 hours from NYC airports.

♿ 🍽️

Brook Farm Inn

www.brookfarm.com
15 Hawthorne Street, Lenox, MA USA 01240
800-285-7638 • 413-637-3013 • Fax: 413-637-4751
innkeeper@brookfarm.com   *Member Since 2001*

Phil & Linda Halpern/Owners
Robert Pelliciotti/Innkeeper

There is poetry here... This Victorian Berkshires treasure is nestled in a wooded glen,
surrounded by gardens. Brook Farm Inn is just a short walk to historic Lenox village.
Furnished with antiques, the inn features a library filled with poetry, history and literature,
where the sounds of classical music can be heard. The main building has 12 guest
rooms, and the carriage house has luxury accommodations. Brook Farm Inn is close to
Tanglewood and all cultural and outdoor attractions. Your friendly hosts offer gracious
hospitality and assistance in planning a memorable Berkshires vacation. The sumptuous
buffet breakfasts are unsurpassed. Afternoon tea and scones are served on weekends. On-site
massages are offered. Seasonal activities are downhill and xc-skiing, hiking, biking, theater,
concerts, antiquing and museum and historic home tours. The foliage season is spectacular,
and special packages are offered. Attractions: Tanglewood, Berkshire Theatre Festival,
Rockwell Museum, Shakespeare & Co., Hancock Shaker Village.

Rates
$159/$429. Antiques, canopy beds. 9 rooms w/fireplaces, some w/whirlpool tubs. WIFI.
Heated outdoor pool. Gardens with picnic area. Open all year. Seasonal package with
restaurant and museum. On-site massage services. Number of Rooms: 15

Cuisine
Full buffet breakfast daily; afternoon tea with homemade scones on weekends.
Well-stocked guest pantry with refrigerators, hot beverages and cookies. Breakfast is
meatless; hot entree, our own granola, fresh fruit, yogurt, fresh breads, homebaked
goods.

Nearest Airport
Albany, NY- 45 mins. Hartford, CT- 1 hour. Boston- 2 hours. NYC area- 3 hours.

The Captain's House Inn

🍽️ 🍽️   🍷

www.captainshouseinn.com
369 Old Harbor Rd, Chatham, MA USA 02633
800-315-0728 • 508-945-0127 • Fax: 508-945-0866
info@captainshouseinn.com   *Member Since 1989*

Innkeepers/Owners
James and Jill Meyer

Perhaps Cape Cod's finest small inn, this historic 1839 sea captain's estate on two acres is the perfect choice for a romantic getaway or elegant retreat. Gourmet breakfasts, English afternoon teas, beautifully decorated rooms with king and queen size beds, fireplaces, seating areas, telephones, WiFi capability, iPod docking stations and TVs with DVD players; some with whirlpool tubs. Enjoy uncompromising service from an enthusiastic international staff, take pleasure in the inn's many gardens and fountains, heated outdoor pool, fitness center, and savor the scenic beauty of the historic seafaring village of Chatham with its 70 miles of spectacular shoreline. The Captain's House Inn of Chatham has been a AAA Four Diamond award winner since 1987.

Rates
12 Rooms, $275 to $480 in Summer, $185 to $325 in Winter; 4 Suites, $275 to $480 in Summer, $185 to $325 Winter. Open year-round. Rates are per night, based upon double occupancy. Tax is not included. Number of Rooms: 16

Cuisine
Breakfast, poolside lunches, afternoon tea, evening snacks. Carefully selected wine and craft beer list.

Nearest Airport
Providence or Boston

Chatham Gables Inn

www.chathamgablesinn.com
364 Old Harbor Road, Chatham, MA USA 02633
508-945-5859
info@chathamgablesinn.com

Member Since 2013

Owners
David and Andrea Smith

Leave the real world behind and escape to Chatham Gables Inn–a romantic Chatham, MA bed and breakfast, just minutes from the National Seashore, with some of New England's most beautiful beaches, and of course, world class shopping. After a day of sightseeing, beach time, shopping–or just a day of touring the beautiful Cape Cod area–return to the inn for a peaceful rest. Then, after a respite in your cozy room, come down to our intimate sitting rooms to savor a glass of wine and local cheeses, offered each evening before dinner during high season. After an aromatherapy bath using our delicate Zents amenities, a peaceful rest, wrapped in your luxurious CGI robe and Kashwere blanket and a perfect night's sleep, tucked into your Comphy sheets. A full country breakfast will be made to order just for you, complete with specialty teas, locally roasted Art-of-Roasting coffee, freshly baked Nantucket Tri-berry muffins, Chatham jams and jellies, fruit pancakes, French toast and a special omelette of the day with Vermont sausage or bacon.

Rates
$180-$355. Number of Rooms: 8

Cuisine
Your stay with us includes a delicious bountiful breakfast for two in our sunlit Garden Room. After a night in one of our spacious and beautifully restored guestrooms, join us for a sumptuous morning meal between 8:00 am-9:30 am.

Nearest Airport
Logan International Airport, Boston, MA; Providence Airport, Providence, RI

Deerfield Inn

www.deerfieldinn.com
81 Old Main Street, Deerfield, MA 01342
413-774-5587 • Fax: 413-775-7221
frontdesk@deerfieldinn.com

Member Since 1996

Massachusetts

Deerfield

Innkeepers
Karl Sabo & Jane Howard

A traditional, original country inn, guests were first welcomed here in July 1884. Still standing as the centerpiece of a mile-long National Historic Landmark village, we have eleven lovely, comfortable guest rooms in the main inn and thirteen in the carriage house. Our rooms are all light and inviting with pleasing amenities, AC, and WiFi. We have two cozy living rooms for reading and relaxing; a porch and outdoor terrace for dining when the weather is fair; a Relaxing Room for therapeutic massages; and a fireplace tavern for a coffee or a cocktail. Champney's Restaurant & Tavern has market-driven menus that reflect our philosophy of eating the view. An 18-seat mahogany bar, fireplace dining, a full bar, 12 draught beers, and many wines by the glass complement your lunch or dinner. Deerfield is a perfect destination for those looking for an authentic, unspoiled New England experience. Enjoy Deerfield's museums, farms, area attractions, country walks, eclectic, interesting area shops, and the beautiful, bucolic scenery. We look forward to welcoming you here!

Rates
$160/$270. Kings, queens, double queens, and a suite with a gas fireplace. Afternoon tea and cookies and a country inn breakfast included. Number of Rooms: 24

Cuisine
Champney's Restaurant & Tavern at the Deerfield Inn is open all day, seven days a week, for breakfast, lunch, and dinner, with brunch on Sunday. Come and gather at our New England table for farm to fork fare.

Nearest Airport
Bradley Field, CT is 55 minutes away, and an easy drive up I-91N to exit 24

Devonfield Bed & Breakfast

🍽️ 🍷

www.devonfield.com
85 Stockbridge Road., Lee, MA USA 01238
800-664-0880 • 413-243-3298 • Fax: 413-243-1360
innkeeper@devonfield.com

Member Since 2003

Massachusetts

Lee

Innkeepers/Owners
Bruce & Ronnie Singer

Centrally located, yet a world apart, Devonfield is set on a 32 acre pastoral meadow shaded by graceful birch trees, with the rolling tapestry of the Berkshire Hills beyond. This 200 year old historic estate home has been graciously updated and is filled with fine antiques. It is sophisticated, yet comfortable and inviting. Devonfield's upscale suites and bedrooms are all beautifully appointed, spacious and offer modern private baths. Quilts, down comforters, plush sheets, towels, CD players and TV/DVDs enhance every room along with handmade chocolates and bottled water. Many have wood-burning fireplaces, Jacuzzis and fine terry robes. For your comfort, the Inn is completely air conditioned and provides wireless Internet. The guest pantry is always open and stocked with treats. There is a refrigerator and microwave as well. Follow breakfast with a stroll through the flower-filled gardens, play tennis, or take a dip in the heated pool, and then enjoy the best in cultural and recreational activities in all seasons. Or, just relax and enjoy the sights and sounds of nature.

Rates
6 Rooms; 3 Suites; 1 Guest Cottage. Off Season: $180/$325. In Season: $225/$375.
Number of Rooms: 10

Cuisine
A fireside (fall and winter) candlelit gourmet breakfast is served on fine china accompanied by classical music. Breakfast includes a buffet of fresh baked goods, fruits, granola, yogurt, juices and more, followed by a specially selected hot entree.

Nearest Airport
Bradley, CT (63 miles); Albany (45 miles)

 SelectRegistry.com

Emerson Inn By The Sea

www.EmersonInnByTheSea.com
One Cathedral Avenue, Pigeon Cove, Rockport, MA USA 01966
800-964-5550 • 978-546-6321 • Fax: 978-546-7043
info@EmersonInnByTheSea.com

Member Since 1973

Innkeepers/Owners
Bruce and Michele Coates

Ralph Waldo Emerson called the Inn "Thy proper summer home." Today's guests enjoy the relaxed 19th century atmosphere from our broad oceanfront veranda, but can savor the 21st century amenities of a heated outdoor pool, room phones, data ports, high speed wireless Internet, air conditioning, cable television, private baths and spa tubs. Nearby are hiking trails along the oceanfront, tennis, golf, sea kayaking, scuba diving and the always popular whale watches. Halibut Point State Park features the history of the Rockport Quarries and downtown Rockport is famous for shops and art galleries. The historic Emerson is the ideal ocean front location for weddings, retreats and conferences. "Editors Pick," Yankee Travel Guide to New England. Featured in "1000 Places To See in the USA Before You Die" and in Zagat's 2005 and 2006 Top U.S. Hotels, Resorts, and Spas. Historic Hotels of America – National Trust for Historic Preservation. Mobil Three Star, AAA Three Diamond rated.

Rates
$99/$399 B&B; Two Seaside Cottages, each accommodates 8, available for a weekly rental. Open all year. Number of Rooms: 36

Cuisine
Award-winning Restaurant. "Unparalleled ambiance" - The Boston Globe. Outdoor oceanfront dining and elegant turn-of-the-century dining room serving breakfast daily; dinner and live music schedules vary by season. Wine Spectator Award of Excellence.

Nearest Airport
Boston Logan International Airport

🍴🍴🍴 🍷
Gateways Inn

www.gatewaysinn.com
51 Walker Street, Lenox, MA USA 01240
413-637-2532 • Fax: 413-637-1432
innkeeper@gatewaysinn.com

Member Since 2001

Massachusetts   Lenox

Innkeepers/Owners
Michele & Eiran Gazit

Gateways Inn is a stately neoclassical mansion, built in 1912 by Harley Procter of Procter & Gamble as a summer home in the picturesque Berkshire Town of Lenox. The mansion later became an Inn. Today the Innkeepers and staff welcome guests from the world over, providing gracious hospitality in a European Manor Home atmosphere with a Shakespearean theme. The 12 guest rooms are each unique in decor, all with private baths, as well as updated comforts and amenities. The Restaurant showcases a Farm to Table seasonal Mediterranean menu. Our award-winning Piano Bar offers an impressively large collection of Single Malt Scotches and Grappas. Business travelers welcomed. Customized weddings, private parties and meetings are our specialty. Cooking School events are scheduled throughout the year. Shakespeare & Company, The Mount, and Tanglewood, the summer home of the Boston Symphony Orchestra, are all nearby. The Inn is a short stroll to Town Center with many fine shops and galleries. The nearby nature parks offer the best in outdoor activities.

Rates
9 Rooms, 2 Suites, 1 three bedroom house: $200 - $600, depending on season. Peak season minimum stays apply. Open year-round. Corporate Rates and packages available. Number of Rooms: 11

Cuisine
Full scrumptious breakfast served daily. Full bar service. Extensive wine list. Special menus for Holidays. Custom menus for weddings and private parties.

Nearest Airport
Albany, NY- 1 hour drive; Hartford, CT- 1 1/2 hour drive; Boston, MA- 2 hour drive; NYC - 2 1/2 hour drive

SelectRegistry.com

Harbor Light Inn

🍽️ 🍽️ 🍽️ 🍷

www.harborlightinn.com
58 Washington Street, Marblehead, MA USA 01945
781-631-2186 • Fax: 781-631-2216
info@harborlightinn.com

Member Since 1996

Innkeepers/Owners
Peter & Suzanne Conway

Winner of numerous national awards for excellence, including Vacation magazine's "America's Best Romantic Inns." The inn offers first-class accommodations and amenities found in the finest of lodging facilities. Elegant furnishings grace these two connected Federalist mansions. Formal parlors with fireplaces, dining room and bed chambers, double Jacuzzis, large HDTVs, WiFi, sundecks, patio, quiet garden and outdoor heated pool combine to ensure the finest in New England hospitality. Located in the heart of historic Harbor District of fine shops, art galleries and restaurants. Our intimate tavern is open nightly and offers fine wines, beers and cordials along with our bar menu of local favorites.

Rates
20 Rooms, $159/$369; Suites, $199/$369 B&B. Open year-round. Number of Rooms: 20

Cuisine
Breakfast buffet featuring fresh homemade breads, fruit platters, yogurts, bagels, hot casseroles, salmon platter and daily specials. GLUTEN FREE MENU on request. Wine, beer and cordials in new pub. Pub menu is available for lunch and dinner daily.

Nearest Airport
Boston Logan International approximately 15 miles.

Hawthorne Inn

www.ConcordMass.com
462 Lexington Road, Concord, MA USA 01742
978-369-5610 • Fax: 978-287-4949
Inn@ConcordMass.com

Member Since 1980

Innkeepers/Owners
Gregory Burch and Marilyn Mudry

Relaxed Elegance...just 30 minutes from Boston, three rivers wend through a Colonial landscape of Minutemen's fields where moss-covered stonewalls embrace the homes of Hawthorne, Alcott, Thoreau and Emerson. Here you will find an intimate refuge: the Hawthorne Inn. Filled with original artworks to delight your eyes, artifacts that excite imagination, coverlets to snuggle on crisp autumn eves and burnished antiques that speak of home and security. Seven vibrant guestrooms, inspired by a refreshing mix of tradition and artistic expression, offer abundant comforts and modern amenities. Since 1976 the Inn has made welcome business-travelers, lovers, families, seekers and writers to our historic 17th century village. As you amble in the footsteps of Patriots and Poets you will savor the Inn's unique location near the Authors' Homes, Walden Pond, Minuteman National Park and Old North Bridge, where was fired "the shot heard round the world." Many choose the Hawthorne as a base for day-trips to explore Boston, Cambridge, Sturbridge, Salem, Plymouth and the nearby ocean beaches.

Rates
Graciously appointed rooms offering Canopy or Four-poster Bed, Refreshments at Check-in and Multi-course Breakfast. Rates vary by Seasonal Demand and length of stay. Nightly Accommodations from $159-$349. See website for Specials. Number of Rooms: 7

Cuisine
Fine food & good conversation define breakfast at the inn. Daily-changing Innkeeper's Specials may include: Croissant French Toast with berry-infused maple syrup, Award-Winning Pears with Mascarpone, or Egg in Round. Enjoy our table, each other & life.

Nearest Airport
Boston Logan-30 min./ Manchester N.H.-50 min./ Private Planes at Hanscom Field-10 min. See website for directions.

Inn at Castle Hill

www.theinnatcastlehill.com
280 Argilla Road, Ipswich, MA USA 01938
978-412-2555 • Fax: 978-412-2556
theinn@ttor.org

Member Since 2012

Innkeeper
Camilla Eagan

The Inn at Castle Hill on the Crane Estate invites you to return to an age of innocent pursuits. Step into a timeless place of understated elegance and serenity. Located in the heart of the spectacular Crane Estate, enjoy simple, yet luxurious pleasures, and reconnect with what's really important in life. Snug beds, hearty breakfasts, and a warm and generous staff anticipate your arrival. All the rooms at the Inn are uniquely appointed and many feature stunning views over the salt marshes, sand dunes, and Atlantic Ocean. Though no two rooms are alike, all promise a great night's sleep and the excitement of waking up in the magical world that is Castle Hill. Take tea on the veranda and gaze across the spectacular coastline. Read quietly upon a sun-bathed window seat. Stroll along the miles of shoreline. All are part of your stay. Whatever your pleasure, we will help you find it.

Rates
May through October: $235 to $515. April, November & December: $195 to $450. Rates do not include 9.7% tax and 7.5% estate administrative fee. Members of The Trustees of Reservations receive a 10% discount on two nights or more. Number of Rooms: 10

Cuisine
A full breakfast each morning. Home baked muffins or scones. Home made granola. Fresh seasonal fruit. Custom blended Dean's Beans coffee and Harney & Son teas. Special Diets Accommodated, Vegetarian Options. Coffee & tea available 24 hours in pantry.

Nearest Airport
Logan International, Boston

& 🍽 🍷

The Inn at Stockbridge

www.stockbridgeinn.com
30 East Street, Route 7N, Stockbridge, MA USA 01262
888-466-7865 • 413-298-3337 • Fax: 413-298-3406
innkeeper@stockbridgeinn.com

Member Since 1986

Innkeepers/Owners
Jeff Bell & Lisa Morehouse

Enjoy peaceful charm and friendly hospitality in a 1906 Georgian-style mansion on 12 acres in Stockbridge, a town described by Norman Rockwell as "the best of America, the best of New England." Awaken to the aroma of fresh coffee, stroll the beautiful grounds, exercise in the fitness room, and take time away from the cares of the world. In summer, breakfast alfresco on our patio, then take a dip in our heated pool. The inn's three buildings include 7 beautiful rooms in the Main House, 4 spacious rooms in the Cottage House and 4 deluxe suites in the Barn. Some of the available amenities include gas fireplaces, sitting areas and double whirlpool tubs. We are centrally located to all Berkshire cultural attractions including the Norman Rockwell Museum and Tanglewood, theatre, dance, golf, hiking, boating, skiing, antiquing and shopping. Enjoy all the Berkshires has to offer or just relax! Our guest services team will help you plan the perfect getaway!

Rates
Main house rooms $180-$370. Cottage house suites $285-$370 Barn suites $325-$395. Seasonal rates apply, with minimum night stays required for specific dates.
Number of Rooms: 15

Cuisine
Included in your stay: a bountiful full breakfast featuring local and seasonal ingredients, consisting of fresh fruit, a delicious entrée and a variety of freshly baked treats. Wine and cheese reception every afternoon, cookies and treats all day!

Nearest Airport
Albany, NY - Hartford, CT

f 🐦 ◎◎ g+

SelectRegistry.com

Isaiah Jones Homestead

www.isaiahjones.com
165 Main Street, Sandwich, MA USA 02563
800-526-1625 • 508-888-9115 • Fax: 508-888-9648
info@isaiahjones.com

Member Since 1989

Innkeepers/Owners
Don or Katherine Sanderson

Relax in pampered elegance in this 1849 Italianate Victorian inn. The main house has five exquisitely appointed guest rooms with private baths featuring queen beds, antique furnishings, oriental carpets, all with fireplaces or glass-front stoves and two with oversize whirlpool tubs. The unique Carriage House includes two spacious junior suites each with a fireplace and whirlpool bath, one with a king bed. Located in the heart of Sandwich village, the inn is within easy walking distance of the many shops, restaurants and attractions of Cape Cod's oldest town. Unwind by strolling the meandering garden paths around the goldfish pond, by sitting in comfortable Adirondack chairs placed around the well-shaded yard or by relaxing by the original antique-tiled fireplace in the gathering room. A full breakfast sets a warm tone to start your day. Chosen Editors Choice, Cape Cod Travel Guide. Selected as "Insider Pick" for Romantic Getaways by Destination Insider. Featured in "Checking In," Boston Sunday Globe and The Wall Street Journal's "Take Monday Off" on Cape Cod.

Rates
Seven rooms: $179/$300, including a full, three-course breakfast. Air conditioned. Open year-round. Complimentary parking and WiFi. Number of Rooms: 7

Cuisine
Breakfast is served in our sunny, cherry paneled dining room or on the deck overlooking the garden. Enjoy a full three-course breakfast of fresh fruit, juices, creative hot entrees, home-baked scones and muffins, and our special blend of gourmet coffee.

Nearest Airport
Logan Airport, Boston, MA; TF Green, Providence, RI

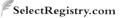

Old Harbor Inn

www.chathamoldharborinn.com
22 Old Harbor Road, Chatham, MA USA 02633
800-942-4434 • 508 945-4434 • Fax: 508 945-7665
info@chathamoldharborinn.com

Member Since 2004

Massachusetts
Chatham

Approved

Innkeepers/Owners
Ray & Judy Braz

Originally built by the local doctor in 1932, The Old Harbor Inn is now entering its fourth decade of providing distinctive lodging to the discriminating traveler. The Inn is ideally located just steps from the center of the historic seaside village of Chatham. Designer appointed rooms with king or queen beds are just the start of a luxurious experience. The most extensive renovations were completed in the spring of 2014 making the inn a truly outstanding property. The professionally designed and meticulously maintained gardens and Koi ponds are sure to please. Judy, Ray, Tanya and their knowledgeable international staff are always available to help plan your days. Chatham serves as a centralized base for exploring all of Cape Cod and the Islands. Provincetown, Falmouth, Martha's Vineyard and Nantucket are all easily accessible. Whether you are planning a romantic getaway or an elegant retreat, every day you get our best.

Rates
Spring $189-$299, Summer $259-$399, Fall $199-$319, Winter $169-$249. Peak season minimum stays apply. Number of Rooms: 12

Cuisine
The full breakfast includes fresh juices, gourmet teas and coffees, seasonal fresh fruit, assorted breads and cereals, plus a fresh prepared entree and a fresh bakery specialty.

Nearest Airport
Boston or Providence

SelectRegistry.com

Palmer House Inn.

www.palmerhouseinn.com
81 Palmer Avenue, Falmouth, MA USA 02540
800-472-2632 • 508-548-1230 • Fax: 508-540-1878
innkeepers@palmerhouseinn.com

Member Since 2001

Innkeepers/Owners
Bill & Pat O'Connell

On a quiet tree-lined street in the heart of Falmouth's Historic District sits the Palmer House Inn, an elegant Victorian home. Beautiful beaches, quaint shops, ferry shuttles, and excellent restaurants are only a short stroll away. The innkeepers pamper you with fresh flowers, extra pillows, fluffy robes, fine linens and meticulous housekeeping. Stained glass windows, rich woodwork, gleaming hardwood floors and antique furnishings create an overall sense of warmth and harmony. The Palmer House Inn is the perfect place to stay, in splendid comfort and gracious care. Local activities include: golf, swimming, cycling on the Shining Sea Bike Path on one of the Palmer House's bicycles, fishing, charter sailing, kayaking, hiking, bird watching, whale watching and more.

Rates
16 Rooms, $169/$329; 1 Cottage Suite, $269/$329. Many rooms w/ whirlpool tubs and fireplaces. All rooms have 600 thread count sheets, TV, phones, hair dryers, irons & boards, ice buckets, AC and WiFi. Open year-round Number of Rooms: 17

Cuisine
Full two to three course Cape Cod gourmet breakfasts are served with candlelight and classical music. Afternoon and evening refreshments. Early morning coffee.

Nearest Airport
Logan (Boston), TF Green (Providence)

The Provincetown Hotel at Gabriel's

www.provincetownhotel.com
102 Bradford Street, Provincetown, MA United States 02657
508-487-3232
info@provincetownhotel.com

Member Since 2011

Massachusetts

Provincetown

Innkeepers/Owners
Elizabeth & Elizabeth Brooke

Enjoy affordable luxury in the heart of Provincetown! Our downtown Provincetown hotel offers luxurious rooms, suites, and spacious apartment units in four historic buildings circling a garden courtyard with multi-tiered decks, barbecue areas, and an inviting outdoor fire pit. The Provincetown Hotel at Gabriel's thoughtful in-room amenities include tempurpedic mattresses, private balconies, fireplaces, Jacuzzi tubs, steam baths, free WiFi, TVs, DVD players, wet bar, and Keurig coffee makers.

Guests delight in our complimentary made to order breakfast, served daily in the Great Room or our lush garden courtyard patio. Enjoy homemade cookies and refreshments every afternoon. Children and pets are always welcome for an additional charge. Private nearby parking is available for $10 daily and we offer a free shuttle service from the Provincetown Airport or the Pier. Come experience our first class property, 24 hour front desk, and personal service today!

Rates
Rates for our Provincetown lodging ranges from $125 to $400 depending on the room and the season. We are open year round. Off season specials and packages are often available. Number of Rooms: 16

Cuisine
You will love our made to order breakfast served each morning in our Great Room or the lovely garden courtyard at our Provincetown, MA hotel. Our famous home baked cookies, tea, coffee, and organic drinks are available anytime.

Nearest Airport
Provincetown Airport (PVC), Boston Logan Airport (BOS), Providence T.F. Green Airport (PVD)

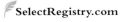

Seven Sea Street Inn

www.sevenseastreetinn.com
7 Sea Street, Nantucket, MA USA 02554
800-651-9262 • 508-228-3577 • Fax: 508-228-3578
innkeeper@sevenseastreetinn.com

Member Since 1996

Approved

Innkeeper/Owner
Matthew Parker

Enjoy Seven Sea Street Inn, a truly charming Nantucket bed and breakfast Inn, where we pride ourselves on the attentive service and elegant accommodations that will make your stay with us a fond memory. Our Inn is distinguished by its beautiful red oak post and beam style, designed and constructed with an authentic Nantucket ambiance in mind. In addition to providing exceptional comfort and hospitality, we offer a stunning view of Nantucket Harbor from our Widow's Walk deck. All of our guest rooms are furnished with luxurious Stearns and Foster queen or king mattresses, the world's finest bedding. Each Main house guest room and suite is furnished with rainshower showerheads, ACs, high definition TV, high speed wireless connectivity and a bow box of Nantucket's famous chocolate covered cranberries. Our location, nestled on a quiet tree-lined side street and less than a five-minute walk from Main Street shopping, restaurants, museums and the beach, couldn't be better. Indulge yourself at our lovely Inn this year.

Rates
13 Guest Rooms, $99/$349 B&B; 2 Suites, $159/$449 B&B. Seasonal rates. Number of Rooms: 15

Cuisine
Expanded Buffet Continental Breakfast served daily. Two seatings, 8 a.m. and 9 a.m. Gourmet coffee, tea, soda, bottled water and homemade cookies available anytime.

Nearest Airport
Nantucket Memorial Airport

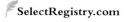

Thorncroft Inn

www.thorncroft.com
460 Main St., P.O. Box 1022, Martha's Vineyard, MA USA 02568
800-332-1236 • 508-693-3333 • Fax: 508-693-5419
innkeeper@thorncroft.com

Member Since 1994

Proprietors/Innkeepers
Karl & Lynn Buder

Thorncroft Inn is situated in three restored buildings on 1 1/2 acres of quiet, treed grounds on the Island of Martha's Vineyard. It is a secluded, adult and couples-oriented bed & breakfast. All rooms have phone, TV, high-speed wireless and wired Internet access, air-conditioning, deluxe bathrobes and an array of amenities. Most rooms have working, wood-burning, match-ready fireplaces and canopied beds. Some have two-person whirlpool bathtubs or private 250-gallon hot tubs. Some offer private exterior entrances or furnished private porches or balconies. Full country breakfast is served in our two dining rooms or a continental breakfast is delivered to the room. Our concierge service is renowned and focuses on the specific needs of each couple. Thorncroft Inn is an ideal setting for honeymoons, anniversaries, engagements, birthdays or any romantic getaway for couples.

Rates
Nine antique appointed rooms, $195 to $495 B&B per evening with seasonal variations. Number of Rooms: 9

Cuisine
Full country breakfast served in two dining rooms at individual tables for two or an ample continental breakfast delivered to room; Traditional or healthful entrees.

Nearest Airport
Martha's Vineyard Airport-5 miles; Logan Airport, Boston-77 miles; Green Airport, Providence-79 miles

SelectRegistry.com

Union Street Inn

www.UnionInn.com
7 Union Street, Nantucket, MA USA 02554
888-517-0707 • 508-228-9222 • Fax: 508-325-0848
info@UnionInn.com

Member Since 2005

Innkeepers/Owners
Ken & Deborah Withrow

"Best Nantucket Boutique Hotel"—BEST OF BOSTON MAGAZINE. "This mint 1770 house in the middle of town has more style than most—not a surprise, given the previous careers of proprietors Ken (ex-GM of the Royalton in New York City) and Deborah (a display manager at Henri Bendel). They've decorated the 12 rooms in impeccable New England-by-way-of-France style—Pierre Deux wallpaper, high-poster beds, polished original floorboards, and a few non-fusty antiques. Six also have fireplaces. Add to the mix delicious breakfasts served on the outside patio (try the challah-bread French toast with fresh berries), a concierge to score hard-to-get dinner reservations, and just-baked cookies served every afternoon, and you'll see why this place has return guests every summer."— CONDE NAST TRAVELER. Rooms have private baths, A/C, flat screen TVs, Frette and Matouk bedding, bath amenities by (MALIN+GOETZ), and complimentary WiFi. Restaurants, shops, galleries, museums, and ferries are a short stroll. Walk or bicycle to Nantucket's beautiful beaches.

Rates
12 Rooms. High Season: $299-$689; Shoulder Seasons: $149-$589. Closed November through March. Number of Rooms: 12

Cuisine
We are the only Nantucket B&B serving a Full Cooked-To-Order Breakfast. Available in the Dining Room, Garden Patio or In Bed. Afternoon Treats include Home-Baked Cookies, Carrot Cake and Brownies. Coffee, Tea, and Bottled Spring Water always available.

Nearest Airport
Nantucket Memorial Airport-10 minute taxi ride.

The Whalewalk Inn and Spa

www.whalewalkinn.com
220 Bridge Road, Eastham, Cape Cod, MA USA 02642
800-440-1281 • 508-255-0617 • Fax: 508-240-0017
reservations@whalewalkinn.com

Member Since 1993

Innkeepers/Owners
Kevin & Elaine Conlin

Abandon every day life. Rekindle your romance and rejuvenate your body and mind. Relax at Cape Cod's most romantic country Inn and Spa. Secluded, but centrally located to all attractions which make Cape Cod so special. After a gourmet breakfast, walk the "Outer Cape" beaches while listening to the soothing sound of the waves lapping on Cape Cod Bay or crashing at the National Seashore. At the end of a day on the beach, riding the Rail Trail, kayaking, shopping or museum hopping, restore your inner balance and harmony at The Spa, a special place with your comfort and exercise regime in mind. Forget the weather; pamper your mind and body with a massage or facial; feel the heat of the dry sauna or workout in the indoor resistance pool or on cardiovascular machines. Have fun with Wii Sports and Fit. Stay in the luxurious Spa Penthouse or in one of 16 other beautiful accommodations. All are individually decorated having amenities such as air-conditioning, TV/DVD/CD, fireplace, refrigerator, and high speed WiFi. Come and enjoy our impeccable service and heartfelt hospitality.

Rates
$220/$420. Call for off-season rates. Open April to November 30. Number of Rooms: 17

Cuisine
Full-service gourmet breakfast with fresh home-baked delights and entrees: Waffle Sundaes, Eggs Benedict, Corn Pancakes with Dill Shallot Sauce and Salmon Rosettes, Grand Marnier Oatmeal Pie, Baked Omelet, and Granola Pizza. After dinner cordials.

Nearest Airport
Boston, MA; Providence, RI

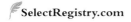
SelectRegistry.com

Michigan

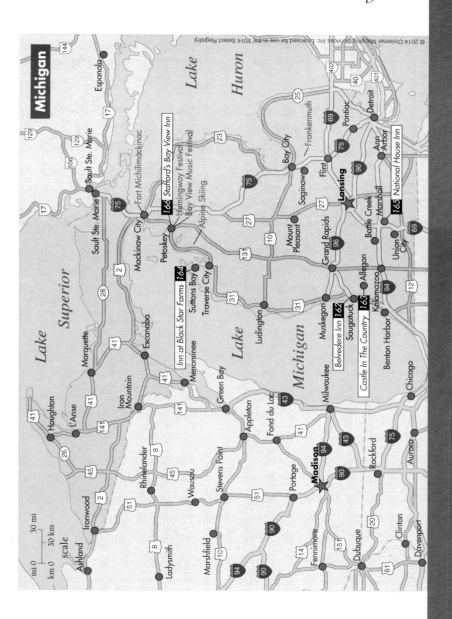

Michigan

© 2014 Chrismar Mapping Services Inc. Licensed for use in the 2014 Select Registry.

Lake Huron

Lake Superior

Lake Michigan

Espanola

Sault Ste. Marie

Fort Michilimackinac

Mackinaw City

Petoskey

166 Stafford's Bay View Inn

Hemingway Festival
Bay View Music Festival
Alpine Skiing

Traverse City

Suttons Bay

164 Inn at Black Star Farms

Ludington

Menominee

Green Bay

Marquette

Escanaba

Iron Mountain

Houghton

L'Anse

Ironwood

Ashland

Rhinelander

Wausau

Stevens Point

Marshfield

Ladysmith

Appleton

Fond du Lac

Portage

Fennimore

Dubuque

Clinton

Davenport

Madison

Rockford

Aurora

Milwaukee

Muskegon

Grand Rapids

Allegan

163 Castle In The Country

162 Belvedere Inn

Saugatuck

Kalamazoo

Benton Harbor

Chicago

Union City

165 National House Inn

Marshall

Battle Creek

Lansing

Ann Arbor

Flint

Saginaw

Bay City

Mount Pleasant

Frankenmuth

Pontiac

Detroit

scale
mi 0   30 mi
km 0   30 km

🍴 🍴 🍴 🍷
Belvedere Inn

www.thebelvedereinn.com
3656 63rd Street, Saugatuck, MI USA 49453
877-858-5777 • 269-857-5777 • Fax: 269-857-7557
info@thebelvedereinn.com   *Member Since 2012*

Michigan

Saugatuck

Innkeepers/Owners
Shaun Glynn & Pete Ta

Often referred to as Mini Versailles, The Belvedere Inn, which translates to "Beautiful View," is a peaceful country estate and is one of the few European-style B&Bs in Michigan. The Inn's success relies on one main ingredient – Excellence – a single minded belief based on good taste, quality service, gourmet food and an exquisitely restored mansion. Built in 1913 & designed by Dwight Perkins, a colleague of Frank Lloyd Wright, the Inn sits on 5 acres of manicured gardens just 1.5 miles from downtown Saugatuck. The Inn's history is perpetuated through skillful restoration, gleaming hardwoods and the patina of fine antiques while discrete modernization offers the highest standard of guest comforts. The award winning restaurant is renowned for its fine food & wine. Chef Shaun Glynn of Galway, Ireland offers eclectic classical dishes made from local ingredients, served in an intimate setting. The magnificent grounds make a picture perfect backdrop for a wedding or any special occasion. The unique setting also satisfies the demands of a successful business meeting or retreat.

Rates
Rooms & Suites $145-$345. All with fireplaces & deluxe amenities. Luxury suites feature plush memory foam top beds & two person whirlpools. Offering Bed Breakfast & Dinner packages year round. Come for Dinner, Stay for Breakfast! Number of Rooms: 10

Cuisine
Full breakfast at private tables in dining room or terrace & delicious treats throughout the day. Restaurant has seasonal hours for dinner. Guests enjoy complimentary 4 course dinner for two at various times during the year. Full bar service.

Nearest Airport
Tulip City (Holland 15 mins), Gerald Ford (Grand Rapids 45 mins), Midway (Chicago 2.5 hrs), O'Hare (Chicago 3 hrs).

Castle in the Country

www.castleinthecountry.com
340 M-40 South, Allegan, MI USA 49010
888-673-8054 • 269-673-8054
info@castleinthecountry.com

Member Since 2008

Michigan

Allegan

Innkeepers/Owners
Herb & Ruth Boven

Escape the ordinary at Castle in the Country. Walk hand in hand through our wooded forest trails, sip a glass of wine in the screened porch beside our private lake or close the door to your own romantic suite with a whirlpool tub for two, fireplace and gourmet breakfast. Schedule a side-by-side couple's massage in our secluded Royal Retreat Spa Area. Awarded "Most Romantic Hideaway in North America!" and "Best Getaway in the Great Lakes." When you choose Castle in the Country, you choose a Michigan getaway with extraordinary decor, amenities, and service! Scenic countryside provides a peaceful pastoral and wooded setting for your getaway. We offer 10 individually decorated Rooms/Suites within the timeless beauty of our century-old Victorian Castle and in our contemporary country manor house, the Castle Keep. Whether you're looking for a romantic getaway for two to celebrate a birthday, anniversary or honeymoon or, the perfect venue for an elopement or a Destination Wedding and Reception, our Innkeepers will help you create an experience that will exceed every expectation.

Rates
8 whirlpool/fireplace suites $219-$309; 2 fireplace rooms $149-$199; Midweek discounts; Spa & Dinner Packages; Wedding Packages;1 Barrier Free Suite. Number of Rooms: 10

Cuisine
Full breakfasts are artfully presented and served daily at your own individual table for two in our dining rooms overlooking the pond. Picnic baskets filled with fresh baked bread, and creative Dinner Packages may be added by advanced reservation.

Nearest Airport
Kalamazoo/Battle Creek International

& 🍽️ 🍽️ 🍽️ 🍷

Inn at Black Star Farms

www.blackstarfarms.com
10844 E. Revold Rd., Suttons Bay, MI USA 49682
877-466-9463 • 231-944-1251 • Fax: 231-944-1259
innkeeper@blackstarfarms.com   *Member Since 2003*

Michigan

Suttons Bay

Proprietor
Don Coe

Expect consistently exceptional experiences at our year-round inn, nestled below a hillside of vineyards in the heart of Leelanau Peninsula wine country. Our ten contemporary guestrooms, each with private bath and some with fireplaces and spa tubs, have fine furniture, luxurious linens, and Aveda toiletries. Amenities include complimentary WiFi, flat screen televisions, a bottle of our House wine, cozy robes, evening hospitality hour and complimentary tasting of our award-winning wines and fruit brandies at our on-site tasting room. Our wine making team produces a full range of regionally expressive and seasonally dynamic table and dessert wines. Private massage and sauna are available. A gourmet breakfast is prepared daily using ingredients from the farm and region. Casual and upscale farmstead cuisine, wines and spirits are seasonally available at Hearth and Vine and the inn. We are happy to direct you to local must-see destinations, including Sleeping Bear Dunes National Lakeshore, voted the Most Beautiful Place in America. Meetings, reunions, and weddings welcomed.

Rates
High season May 24, 2014-October 25, 2014: $225-$415/night. Low season October 26, 2014-May 21, 2015: $150-$310/night. Rates subject to 6% sales tax and 5% destination fee. Number of Rooms: 10

Cuisine
Start your day with fruit, house made baked goods and granola, and a seasonal farmstead entree served at your private table. We are committed to locally sourced ingredients as the seasons allow. Picnic baskets, wine, and cocktails available on request.

Nearest Airport
Cherry Capitol Airport (TVC)

National House Inn

www.nationalhouseinn.com
102 S. Parkview, Marshall, MI USA 49068
269-781-7374
frontdesk@nationalhouseinn.com

Member Since 1978

Michigan Marshall

Innkeeper/Owner
Barbara Bradley

Historic Marshall, Michigan is a quintessential American small town that sits along the Interstate roughly equidistant between Chicago and Detroit. Every fall, visitors come to the city's Historic Home Tour, which features a selection of restored homes within its National Historic Landmark District boundaries. Marshall's nickname is "The City of Hospitality," which is appropriate since it is home to The National House Inn Bed and Breakfast, Michigan's oldest operating bed and breakfast inn. The inn overlooks the city's historic Fountain Circle and is just steps from shopping, museums, galleries, ghost tours, carriage rides, walking tours, Schuler's Restaurant & Pub, and more. Read a good book on the porch, warm by a crackling fire, relax with afternoon tea, savor a delicious breakfast, or treasure some quiet time in one of three parlors. Experience the same gracious hospitality first enjoyed by stagecoach travelers some 170 years ago, paired with modern conveniences and comfort. Do you ever wonder where the fast lane ends? You've found it…at the National House Inn!

Rates
$110-$170. Number of Rooms: 15

Cuisine
Breakfast, afternoon tea, catered dinners for receptions.

Nearest Airport
Kalamazoo (AZO), 40 minute drive & Detroit (DTW), 90 minute drive

¶○¶ ¶○¶ ¶○¶ ℗

Stafford's Bay View Inn

www.staffords.com
2011 Woodland Ave., Petoskey, MI USA 49770
800-258-1886 • 231-347-2771 • Fax: 231-347-3413
bayview@staffords.com   *Member Since 1972*

Michigan

Petoskey

Proprietor
Stafford Smith

Stafford's Bay View Inn was purchased by Stafford and Janice Smith in 1961. Stafford and his family have owned, operated, and lovingly restored this grand Victorian Country Inn on the shores of Lake Michigan's Little Traverse Bay. Built as a rooming house in 1886 in the Historic Landmark District of Bay View, this inn sets the standard in country inn dining and gracious service. Each beautifully appointed guest room features a private bath and individual climate controls. Visitors to the area enjoy summer Chautauqua programs, championship golf, paved bike paths just out our front door, fall color tours, winter ski packages, and sleigh rides around the Bay View cottage grounds. Petoskey's Historic Gaslight Shopping District and marina are located nearby. Our inn is an exquisite place to hold weddings, rehearsal dinners, receptions and reunions. Many quiet corners offer a wonderful environment for company meetings and conferences. Voted "Michigan's Best Brunch" by Michigan Living. This Inn is the flagship property of Stafford's Hospitality.

Rates
21 Victorian rooms $99/$269, 10 spa and fireplace Suites $159/$329. Number of Rooms: 31

Cuisine
Breakfast and Dinner: May-October and winter weekends. Lunch: Late May-October. Sunday Brunch: June-October and Holidays. Visit www.staffords.com for menus, dining schedules and info on full-service, year-round, innkeeper-owned properties nearby.

Nearest Airport
Pellston (PLN) - 17 miles, Traverse (TVC) - 65 miles

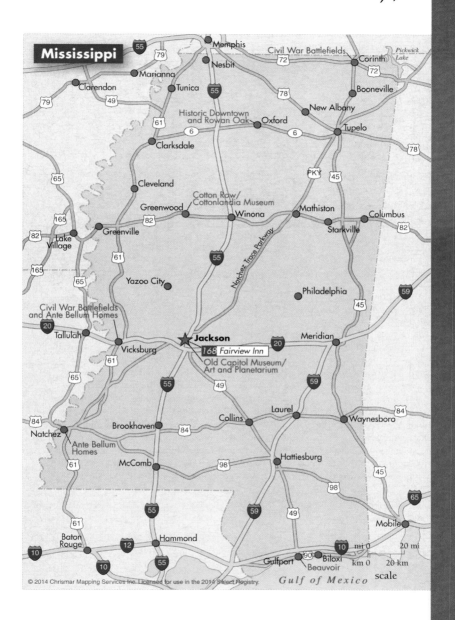

🍽️ 🍽️ 🍽️ 🍷
Fairview Inn

www.fairviewinn.com
734 Fairview Street, Jackson, MS USA 39202
888-948-1908 • 601-948-3429 • Fax: 601-948-1203
innkeeper@fairviewinn.com

Member Since 1994

Mississippi Jackson

Proprietors
Peter and Tamar Sharp

The Fairview Inn, Jackson's only AAA four-diamond small luxury hotel, invites you to experience this unique historic 1908 Colonial Revival mansion. This bed and breakfast Inn is one of the few architecturally designed homes of that period remaining, which exudes the rich history of Jackson, Mississippi. On the National Register of Historic Places and conveniently located in the Belhaven historic neighborhood, the Fairview Inn is minutes away from downtown Jackson's arts, theater, museums and shopping. Antique and boutique shops are also close by in the nearby Fondren District. More than a bed & breakfast, the Inn boasts 18 luxurious guest rooms, 1908 Provisions restaurant serving lunch, dinner and Sunday brunch, nomiSpa for relaxation and rejuvenation, a game room and private guest lounge. The Fairview Inn is popular not only for leisure travelers seeking the history and culture of the South, but also with business travelers looking for unique, comfortable accommodations where they can entertain clients in a luxury and discreet setting.

Rates
5 Rooms and 13 Suites, $149/$319 Luxury Inn. Open year-round. Rates Include Full Breakfast. Number of Rooms: 18

Cuisine
Full breakfast each morning for Inn guests. Fine Dining: Lunch Monday-Friday 11:00 a.m to 2:00 p.m. Dinner Monday-Friday 5:00 p.m. to 9:30 p.m. Sunday Brunch 11:00 a.m. to 2:00 p.m. Full Bar and extensive wine list available.

Nearest Airport
Jackson-Evers International Airport

SelectRegistry.com

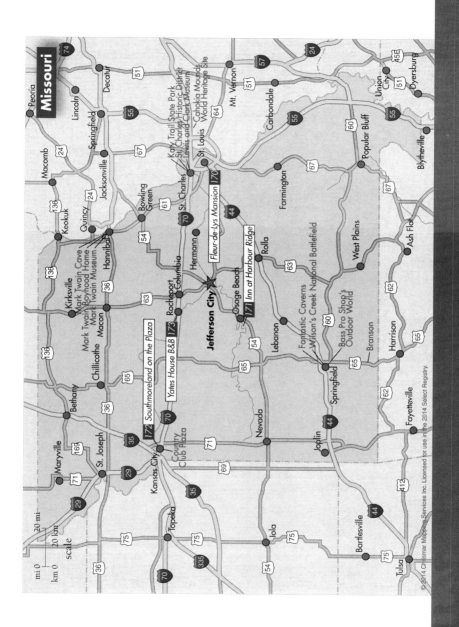

Missouri

Peoria

74

Decatur

51

Lincoln

Springfield

55

24

Macomb

Jacksonville

24

Quincy

136

Keokuk

136

Kirksville

Mark Twain Cave
Mark Twain Boyhood Home
Mark Twain Museum

Hannibal

Bowling Green

Katy Trail State Park
St. Charles Historic District
Lewis and Clark Museum
Cahokia Mounds
World Heritage Site

St. Louis

St. Charles

61

Mt. Vernon

51

57

24

45E

Dyersburg

Union City

51

Carbondale

55

Popular Bluff

60

55

Blytheville

67

Ash Flat

67

Farmington

64

Fleur-de-Lys Mansion 170

44

Hermann

70

54

Columbia

Rochport

63

Macon

36

Chillicothe

Bethany

65

36

St. Joseph

Maryville

169

71

29

29

Topeka

35

75

335

70

Jefferson City

Osage Beach

Inn at Harbour Ridge 171

Rolla

63

West Plains

62

65

Harrison

Branson

Fantastic Caverns
Wilson's Creek National Battlefield
Bass Pro Shop's
Outdoor World

60

Springfield

65

Lebanon

54

65

Nevada

71

69

44

Joplin

Iola

54

75

Bartlesville

44

75

Tulsa

112

Fayetteville

62

Southmoreland on the Plaza 172

Yates House B&B 173

70

Kansas City

Country Club Plaza

35

scale

mi 0 ___ 20 mi
km 0 ___ 20 km

©2014 Chrismar Mapping Services Inc. Licensed for use in the 2014 Select Registry.

Fleur-de-Lys Mansion

www.thefleurdelys.com
3500 Russell Blvd, St. Louis, MO United States 63104
314-773-3500 • 1-888-693-3500
fdlminfo@thefleurdelys.com

Member Since 2011

Missouri St. Louis

Owners
Jerilyn & Gary Sadler

Circa 1913. Overlooking Compton Hill Reservoir Park and the majestic Compton Hill Water Tower in the Compton Heights Historic District, the Fleur-de-Lys Mansion has received numerous awards including the iLoveInns.com Top 10 Romantic Inn of 2009, TripAdvisor Traveler's Choice Award Winner 2010, rated #7 Best in the World and #5 Best in the U.S. by TripAdvisor, and among Midwest Living's "Best of the Midwest" in 2011. The Fleur-de-Lys is a meticulously restored Tudor Revival mansion. The atmosphere exudes a comfortable elegance and luxury amenities that make it perfect for business or leisure. Stay in a Parkside Room or Jacuzzi Suite with antiques, period reproductions, towel warmers and free wireless Internet. Guests have said our beds are like "sleeping on a cloud" with down comforters and ironed, lavender-scented linens. Relax in a terry-lined robe, take a private dip in our hot tub, or enjoy the beauty of our urban garden. Awaken to the aromas of the gourmet breakfast that is waiting for you in our Parkside Dining Room. Enjoy the TLC while we serve you!

Rates
King Rooms: $235 (Sunday-Thursday) $305 (Friday-Saturday). Queen Rooms:$160 (Sunday-Thursday) $205 (Friday-Saturday). Number of Rooms: 4

Cuisine
A gourmet breakfast is included in your room rate. Our menu changes daily and includes imaginative uses of fresh fruits, yogurt, homemade granola, sweet and savory crepes, and a variety of luscious baked eggs and decadent French toasts.

Nearest Airport
Lambert St. Louis International Airport

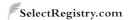
SelectRegistry.com

Inn at Harbour Ridge

www.HarbourRidgeInn.com
6334 Red Barn Road, Osage Beach, MO USA 65065
573-302-0411 • 573-216-6021
stay@harbourridgeinn.com

Member Since 2012

Innkeepers/Owners
Sue & Ron Westenhaver

Rest, relaxation and romance are waiting just for you at the award winning Inn at Harbour Ridge. Located at Lake of the Ozarks in Central Missouri, we're less than a day's drive from anywhere in the central United States. Our private decks and patios, gazebo or the Inn's dock are great places to escape the world and listen to the quiet. The Missouri Ozarks offer 1150 miles of lake shoreline, rolling hills, dramatic bluffs and quiet coves to explore. Enjoy boating, fishing, para-sailing or a lazy afternoon float. Play championship golf on one of fourteen golf courses. Hike at nearby state parks. Visit our wineries and eateries both on and off the water. Retail therapy is available at over 100 stores at the Osage Beach Premium Outlets, at local boutiques, or nearby Mennonite markets. This "built as" contemporary Lake of the Ozarks Bed and Breakfast has received four Certificates of Excellence from Trip Advisor, and top awards from BedandBreakfast.com. Proud member of Bed and Breakfast Inns of Missouri.

Rates
$149-$199 Our guestrooms offer luxurious linens, flicker fireplaces, Cable TV and DVD players, as well as complimentary Wi-Fi. Choose a private starlit hot tub, twosome tubby, or innside hot tub for your romantic getaway. Number of Rooms: 5

Cuisine
Fun and fabulous breakfast parties at the Inn at Harbour Ridge feature comfort gourmet foods, including strawberry fruitinis and egg puffs. Fresh herbs from our own herb garden are used; every lady is served a flower on her breakfast plate.

Nearest Airport
Kansas City International, Lambert-Saint Louis International

Southmoreland on the Plaza

www.southmoreland.com
116 East 46th St., Kansas City, MO USA 64112
816-531-7979 • Fax: 816-531-2407
innkeeper@southmoreland.com

Member Since 1992

Missouri

Kansas City

Innkeepers/Owners
Mark Reichle and Nancy Miller Reichle

Southmoreland on the Plaza - an Urban Inn sets the standard for B&B hospitality and comfort. Located just one and one-half blocks off of the Country Club Plaza and two blocks from the Nelson Atkins Museum of Art, the inn blends classic New England Bed and Breakfast ambiance with small hotel amenities. Twelve guestrooms and the Carriage House suite offer private baths, telephones, and off-street parking. Guests enjoy individually decorated rooms featuring decks, fireplaces or Jacuzzi baths. Business travelers find respite at Southmoreland. We are pleased to offer corporate rates and a rare mix of services conducive to business travel: in-room phones, WiFi, fax, copier, voice mail, 24-hour access and switchboard, and guest privileges at a local full-service fitness center. Southmoreland on the Plaza is an inn of national reputation, worthy of its Plaza locale; warm and accommodating like Kansas City itself. Featured on the Food Network's "Barbecue with Bobby Flay." Visit us at www.southmoreland.com.

Rates
12 Rooms in Main House; $135/$200 Summer, $130/$215 Winter. Carriage House $250 (less $20 SGL.). Number of Rooms: 13

Cuisine
Gourmet breakfast served daily. Complimentary afternoon wine and hors d'oeuvres, with hot beverages and sweets served in the evening. Courtyard breakfast BBQ served Saturdays, Apr 15-Oct 15.

Nearest Airport
Kansas City International

SelectRegistry.com

Yates House Bed & Breakfast

www.yateshouse.com
305 Second Street, Rocheport, MO USA 65279
573-698-2129
info@yateshouse.com

Member Since 2005

Missouri Rocheport

Innkeepers/Owners
Dixie & Conrad Yates

Located in "One of America's Top Ten Coolest Small Towns" Frommers Budget Travel Guide. Everything you'll need for luxurious and relaxing lodging is provided. Rooms are large, beautifully furnished, and well equipped. King beds, jetted tubs, and fireplace are available. Wireless Internet and other business services are provided. Twenty-six seat dining/meeting room available and catering for small groups. Individual table or in-room breakfast provided. Famous for seasonal, gourmet breakfast menu and cooking classes. "Dixie can flat cook," observed Southern Living magazine. Within a block of most scenic section of Katy Trail State Park. Photogenic trails, bluffs, tunnels, and Missouri River within short walking distance. Vineyards, winery, shops and restaurants nearby. Voted "Favorite Day Trip" by readers of the Kansas City Star. Fortunately located midway between Kansas City and St. Louis and fifteen minutes from University of Missouri town of Columbia.

Rates
Five Rooms:$189-$289 One Suite:$279-$309. Number of Rooms: 6

Cuisine
Locally sourced, seasonally changing, full gourmet breakfast with individual table or in-room service (Some rooms). Afternoon cookies fresh daily.

Nearest Airport
Columbia Regional Airport, 30 min. American Airlines nonstop connections to Chicago O'Hare and Dallas/Fort Worth.

New Hampshire

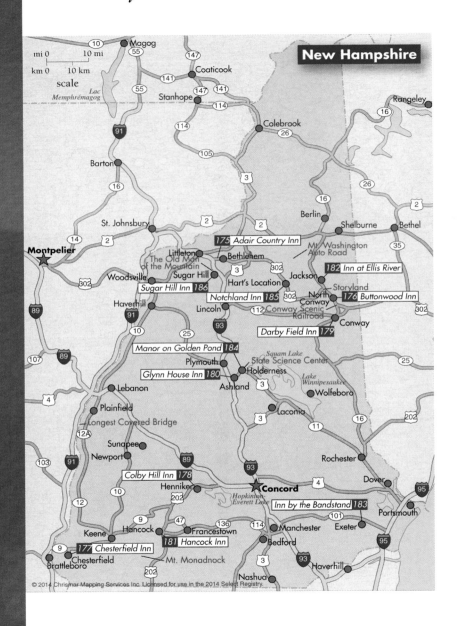

New Hampshire

mi 0   10 mi

km 0   10 km

scale

Lac Memphrémagog

Magog

Coaticook

Stanhope

Colebrook

Barton

St. Johnsbury

Rangeley

Berlin

Shelburne

Bethel

Montpelier

175 Adair Country Inn

Mt. Washington Auto Road

Littleton

Bethlehem

The Old Man of the Mountain

Sugar Hill

Woodsville

Sugar Hill Inn 186

Jackson

182 Inn at Ellis River

Hart's Location

Storyland

176 Buttonwood Inn

Haverhill

Notchland Inn 185

North Conway

Conway Scenic Railroad

Lincoln

Conway

Darby Field Inn 179

Manor on Golden Pond 184

Squam Lake State Science Center

Plymouth

Glynn House Inn 180

Holderness

Ashland

Lake Winnipesaukee

Lebanon

Wolfeboro

Plainfield

Longest Covered Bridge

Laconia

Sunapee

Newport

Rochester

Colby Hill Inn 178

Henniker

Concord

Dover

Inn by the Bandstand 183

Portsmouth

Hopkinton-Everett Lake

Keene

Hancock

Francestown

Manchester

Exeter

177 Chesterfield Inn

181 Hancock Inn

Bedford

Chesterfield

Brattleboro

Mt. Monadnock

Haverhill

Nashua

© 2014 Chrismar Mapping Services Inc. Licensed for use in the 2014 Select Registry.

SelectRegistry.com

Adair Country Inn & Restaurant

www.adairinn.com
80 Guider Lane, Bethlehem, NH USA 03574
888-444-2600 • 603-444-2600 • Fax: 603-444-4823
innkeeper@adairinn.com

Member Since 1995

Approved

Owners/Innkeepers
Betsy and Nick Young/Kimberly and Barry Hunter

"Adair Country Inn & Restaurant is everything you dreamed a New England country inn would be." - USA Today. Get away from it all and unwind at this peaceful country inn. Enter a woodland oasis via a long winding drive surrounded by stone walls, stately pines, ponds, gardens all on 200 acres of private forest. The inn's scenic grounds were originally created by the Olmsted Brothers. This elegant inn sits atop a knoll and enjoys magnificent views of the Presidential Range and comfortably appointed guest rooms with fireplaces, antiques, reproductions and air conditioning. Adair serves as an intimate, romantic retreat for adults who enjoy observing wildlife, hiking, golfing, skiing and more in the nearby White Mountains. The inn's relaxing ambiance and casual dress belie uncompromising attention to detail, highly personalized, warm service and award-winning New England style cuisine. Adair is within a short drive of Franconia Notch, Mt. Washington, Mt. Lafayette, Flume Gorge, superb hiking, numerous cross-country venues and major ski areas. Deliberately small...naturally quiet!

Rates
$195/$325 B&B. Spacious rooms with views and private baths, 7 with fireplaces, 3 with 2-person tubs, Queen or King feather beds. Complimentary wireless Internet. Number of Rooms: 9

Cuisine
Breakfast features fresh fruit, homemade granola, steaming popovers and a hot entree. Afternoon tea with homemade goodies. New England style cuisine Thursday thru Monday in a cozy fireside restaurant with seasonal patio seating. Full beverage service.

Nearest Airport
Manchester NH 95 miles, Boston MA 155 miles, Montreal 180 miles

♿ 🍽️

The Buttonwood Inn on Mt. Surprise

www.buttonwoodinn.com
P.O. Box 1817, 64 Mount Surprise Road, North Conway, NH USA 03860
800-258-2625 • 603-356-2625 • Fax: 603-356-3140
innkeeper@buttonwoodinn.com   *Member Since 1999*

New Hampshire

North Conway

Innkeepers/Owners
Bill and Paula Petrone

"The Daily Meal" nominated The Buttonwood Inn "The Top 50 US Bed-and-Breakfasts for Food" in May 2013. Winner of 2010-2011 "Best of New England" and 2009-2010 "Best Food" on BedandBreakfast.com. TravelChannel.com named Buttonwood Inn one of "Top 10 New England Bed and Breakfasts" in October 2010. Free WiFi, gourmet breakfasts, TV/DVD and Smartphone docking stations, central AC, swimming pool, outdoor hot tub, and more. Our inn is situated on more than five secluded acres of field and forests near the villages of North Conway and Jackson. Offering a peaceful, rural setting, and the convenience of being close to area activities, the Inn was originally an 1820s farmhouse with wide pine floors, antiques, murals, and stenciling. Unwind with afternoon tea and home baked treats in front of one of our wood burning fireplaces in either the spacious living room or the Mt. Surprise Room media and game room when days are cool. During summer, take a dip in our heated pool, or soak in our open air hot tub with a view of the mountains and forest by day and stars by night.

Rates
QUIET Season (April to mid-June & Nov to mid-Dec): Week: $109-$199, Weekends: $119-$209. INN Season (mid-Dec to March & mid-June to mid-Sept): Week: $119-$209 Weekends: $129-$219. PEAK Season (mid-Sept to Oct): $169-$249.
Number of Rooms: 10

Cuisine
A full gourmet breakfast with delicious starters and entrees is prepared with fresh ingredients by Paula alternating savory one morning and sweet the next day. An afternoon beverage service with English teas and homemade baked treats is provided.

Nearest Airport
Portland, ME - 65 miles; Manchester, NH - 100 miles; Boston, MA - 139 miles

         *SelectRegistry.com*

Chesterfield Inn

www.chesterfieldinn.com
20 Cross Road, Chesterfield, NH USA 03466
800-365-5515 • 603-256-3211 • Fax: 603-256-6131
info@chesterfieldinn.com

Member Since 1990

New Hampshire

Chesterfield

Innkeepers/Owners
Phil and Judy Hueber

The Chesterfield Inn is a unique blend of new and old New Hampshire. The inn rests on a hill overlooking the Vermont Green Mountains and Connecticut River Valley. Originally built in 1787 as a farm, this luxurious country hotel is today a showpiece of elegance, style, and comfort. The inn has comfortable guest rooms, stunning dining rooms, and beautifully landscaped grounds. Come and relax awhile at this elegant yet comfortable renovated farmhouse with its cathedral ceilings and rambling views of the Connecticut River Valley. Feel the stress of every day life disappear as you sit in front of the fire in the parlor of this small country hotel. Spend the day reading in one of the Adirondack chairs in the back yard or explore local villages and the countryside. Return at dusk to a sumptuous dinner in our candlelit dining room. Privacy, delicious cuisine, personal service, and relaxation are yours at one of the most unique and accommodating inns in New England. This is a perfect place for a romantic getaway in the country!

Rates
15 Rooms, $149/$344; 2 Suites, $269/$294. Open year-round except Christmas Eve and Christmas Day. Number of Rooms: 15

Cuisine
Full Country Breakfast is cooked to order and served daily. Dinner is served Monday through Saturday in our candlelit dining room with sweeping views of the Green Mountains. Room service is available for breakfast and dinner. Wine list and full bar.

Nearest Airport
Hartford/Bradley Airport- 1.5 hour drive; Boston/Logan Airport 2.5 hour drive.

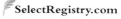

Colby Hill Inn

www.colbyhillinn.com
33 The Oaks, P.O. Box 779, Henniker, NH USA 03242
800-531-0330 • 603-428-3281 • Fax: 603-428-9218
innkeeper@colbyhillinn.com

Member Since 1993

New Hampshire

Henniker

Innkeepers/Owners
Cyndi and Mason Cobb

Intimate and romantic country inn located in the charming unspoiled village of Henniker, NH, just 90 minutes North of Boston. Enjoy romantic touches including down comforters, plush bathrobes, two-person whirlpools, crackling fireplaces and luxurious linens. 14 individually decorated guest rooms including two intimate suites with two-person whirlpools and fireplaces. All guest rooms include gourmet breakfast and have private baths, phones and complimentary WiFi access. Award winning dining nightly overlooking lush gardens, antique barns and gazebo. "Exquisite and Romantic Dining..." says Getaways for Gourmets. Bountiful breakfasts and candlelight dinners. Genuine hospitality and central New England location make this an ideal getaway spot. Enjoy cooking classes and theme weekends including "Chocolate Lovers Weekend" and "WineFest Weekends." Outdoor pool, cross country and downhill skiing , hiking, biking, and tennis all nearby. Yankee Magazine Editor's Pick. Featured in The Boston Globe, More Magazine & Ski Magazine. Voted "Best Gourmet Getaway" by Yankee Magazine.

Rates
$144/$285 (Double Occupancy) depending on season. Additional person sharing room $25 per person, per night. Some guest rooms have two-person whirlpools/fireplaces. Bountiful breakfast included. Number of Rooms: 14

Cuisine
Bountiful breakfast including specialties like pumpkin pancakes with warm maple cream. Afternoon cookies, coffee & tea. Award-winning romantic dining with full service bar, fine wines and spirits. Dinner available nightly for inn guests and public.

Nearest Airport
Manchester

SelectRegistry.com

The Darby Field Inn

www.darbyfield.com
185 Chase Hill Road, Albany, NH USA 03818
800-426-4147 • 603-447-2181
marc@darbyfield.com

Member Since 1981

Innkeepers/Owners
Marc & Maria Donaldson

Wander off the beaten path and discover the Darby Field Inn, an historic country inn featuring a panoramic view of the Presidential Mountains. The inn is much more than a little bed and breakfast. It is a romantic escape, offering deluxe rooms/suites with fireplaces and Jacuzzi tubs, soothing massage services, and special packages to celebrate any occasion. It is an escape from the ordinary, with a restaurant, cozy tavern, Christmas Cookie and Spring Herb Tour weekends, and local activities for every season and interest. It is a relaxing retreat that invites you to wander through perennial flower gardens, curl up with a book or game in front of a crackling fire in the living room, swim in the summertime heated pool, or commune with nature on our wooded trails. The inn is located only a few miles from local shopping, area attractions, and scenic trails for all abilities. No matter what initially brings you to the White Mountains and the Darby Field Inn, our friendly, knowledgeable staff look forward to offering you an experience that brings you back, year after year!

Rates
7 standard rooms ranging from $165-$210 per night. 6 deluxe rooms/suites ranging from $220-$280 per night. All rooms include private bath and WiFi. Rates are before 9% tax. Peak rates apply during fall foliage and some holidays Number of Rooms: 13

Cuisine
Full country breakfast is included each morning. Casual evening dining is offered on a seasonal basis...please inquire about availability at time of booking.

Nearest Airport
(1) Portland, ME: 60 Mi. (2) Manchester, NH: 100 Mi. (3) Logan Airport (Boston), MA: 135 Mi.

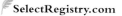

Glynn House Inn

www.glynnhouse.com
59 Highland Street, Ashland, NH USA 03217
603-968-3775
innkeeper@glynnhouse.com

Member Since 2005

Innkeepers/Owners
Pamela, Ingrid & Glenn Heidenreich

This historic circa 1896 Victorian is the perfect choice for romance, recreation and relaxation. Delicious breakfasts are served at individual tables in the elegant Victorian dining room. A full gluten-free breakfast menu is always available. Afternoon refreshments and complimentary wine & hors d'oeuvres are offered in the sitting room or outside on the wraparound porches. Tastefully decorated guest rooms include WiFi, private bathrooms, fireplaces, A/C, satellite TV, DVD players and iPod radios. In-room massage is available. Seven suites, many with separate sitting rooms, also have double whirlpool baths.

Venture away from the inn and experience New Hampshire's spectacular White Mountains and Lakes Region. Enjoy antiquing, art galleries, boating, fine dining, fishing, golf, hiking, historic sites, skiing, sleigh rides, snowmobiling and 'tax-free' shopping. The innkeepers will make your visit an experience to remember by providing genuine hospitality and uncompromising service. Bring your favorite four-footed canine pal and reserve one of five pet friendly rooms.

Rates
Low season: $149-$279; High season: $159-$289; Peak season: $169-$299; Number of Rooms: 12

Cuisine
Gourmet breakfasts, with a choice of entrees, are served each morning. Afternoon refreshments are offered daily. Guests love our delicious cookies. In the evening, join other guests and the innkeepers for complimentary wine & appetizing hors d'oeuvres.

Nearest Airport
Manchester - 50 miles; Boston - 78 miles

SelectRegistry.com

The Hancock Inn

www.hancockinn.com
33 Main Street , P.O. Box 96, Hancock, NH USA 03449
800-525-1789 • 603-525-3318
innkeeper@hancockinn.com

Member Since 1971

Innkeepers/Owners
Jarvis & Marcia Coffin

CELEBRATE THE SEASONS AT NEW HAMPSHIRE'S OLDEST INN, circa 1789.

In New England it's all about the weather. From warm summer nights to crisp autumn days & snowy winter woods to babbling spring brooks ~ there's something to enjoy each season at the historic Hancock Inn. Named New England's Best Historic Inn by YANKEE MAGAZINE in 2014, the inn maintains authentic colonial charm combined with familial warmth and modern amenities.

The Inn is located in the town of Hancock at the heart of the beautiful Monadnock Region in Southern New Hampshire. Come enjoy our wooded hills, trails, lakes & streams, antiques & arts, music and theatre and experience the pleasures of what many regard as one of the prettiest villages in New England.

Rates
Rates: $140 ~ $300. 12 rooms & 1 suite. 1 room is handicap-accessible and dog friendly. All rooms have private baths, air conditioning, hairdryers and robes, free WiFi and phone . Some rooms have jetted tubs and fireplaces. Number of Rooms: 13

Cuisine
Room rate includes full cooked-to-order breakfast. Fine New England cuisine and tavern specialties are served Monday-Saturday 5:30-8 pm (Weds-Sat only Nov-May). On Sunday night enjoy a simple Innkeepers' 1-dish-menu; check weekly for the bill of fare.

Nearest Airport
Manchester, NH - 50 miles ~ Boston Logan - 90 miles

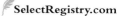

Inn at Ellis River

www.innatellisriver.com
P.O. Box 656, 17 Harriman Road, Jackson, NH USA 03846
800-233-8309 • 603-383-9339 • Fax: 603-383-4142
stay@innatellisriver.com

Member Since 2009

New Hampshire

Jackson

Innkeepers/Owners
Lyn Norris-Baker and Frank Baker

Nestled by a sparkling stream on several acres at the edge of picturesque Jackson Village in the heart of the White Mountains, the inn's rooms and rustic cottage for two are appointed with period furnishings, many with two-person whirlpool tubs and/or balconies and most with fireplaces. Let the river's soothing sounds lull you to sleep, and awaken to clear mountain air and a bountiful homemade breakfast. Spend your days exploring waterfalls or enjoy scenic drives, hiking, golf, canoeing, fishing, mountain biking, or tax-free shopping. In summer, scale Mount Washington by road or cog railway, take a moose tour, or relax by our heated pool. In winter, cross-country ski, snowshoe, take a sleigh ride, or choose from one of five Alpine Ski Centers nearby. Return each day to enjoy afternoon refreshments, a game of darts or billiards in our cozy gameroom/pub, the challenge of a Stave puzzle or board game in our sitting room, or the relaxing view of the river as you soak in our atrium-enclosed hot tub. Recipient of multiple Best of BedandBreakfast.com Awards.

Rates
Classic rooms $129/$199; Fireplace rooms $159/$239; 7 rooms & one cottage w/whirlpool tubs & fireplaces $229/$349. Number of Rooms: 21

Cuisine
Gourmet country breakfast with menu changing daily. Afternoon refreshments include home-baked sweets and seasonal beverages. Several restaurants within walking distance.

Nearest Airport
Portland, ME ~ 75 miles; Manchester, NH ~ 110 miles; Boston (Logan) ~ 140 miles.

🌲 **SelectRegistry.com**

Inn by the Bandstand

www.innbythebandstand.com
6 Front Street, Exeter, NH USA 03833
603-772-6352 • 877-239-3837
info@innbythebandstand.com

Member Since 2006

New Hampshire   Exeter

Owner/Innkeeper
Jaime Lopez

The award-winning Inn by the Bandstand is the premier lodging establishment in Exeter, New Hampshire. The inn is an 1809 historic Federal house; located only 2 blocks from the prestigious Phillips Exeter Academy, 8 miles to the seacoast and beaches, 20 minutes from Portsmouth and 1 hour from Boston. The charming boutique inn offers 9 antique-furnished guest rooms and suites, all with private baths. The inn is surrounded by quaint shops, museums and fine restaurants. Explore the downtown bookstore plus many fine gift and apparel boutiques. Stroll around the river walk near the Academy boat house. Visit the American Independence Museum and enjoy the historical self-guided tours to broaden your knowledge and interest of this area and its importance in our nation's founding history. Our accommodations are spacious, each with complimentary port wine, luxurious robes and slippers, WiFi, cozy sitting areas, and most with gracious fireplaces. Our beds are made with luxurious linens, and our bathrooms feature soft, plush towels. Two of our suites feature Jacuzzi tubs.

Rates
5 guest rooms, 4 suites from $179 to $259 per night based on double occupancy. Suites can accommodate up to 6. Limited handicap accessible and pet friendly accommodations. Some weekends require a two-or-three-night minimum stay. Number of Rooms: 9

Cuisine
Full gourmet breakfast featuring local seasonal ingredients. Menu adapted from the Culinary Institute of America, changes daily. Afternoon tea, evening wine and hors d' oeuvres. 24-hour coffee and tea bar. Dietary restrictions accommodated with notice.

Nearest Airport
Manchester-Boston Regional Airport, New Hampshire
Boston Logan International Airport, Massachusetts

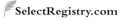

ᵗ�O┤ ᵗO┤ ᵗO┤ ♀

The Manor on Golden Pond

www.manorongoldenpond.com
P.O. Box T Route 3, 31 Manor Drive, Holderness, NH USA 03245
800-545-2141 • 603-968-3348 • Fax: 603-968-2116
info@manorongoldenpond.com   *Member Since 1995*

New Hampshire

Holderness

Innkeepers/Owners
Brian and Mary Ellen Shields

It was the sheer romantic beauty of its mountain and lake view setting that inspired the building of The Manor on Golden Pond. And while the view still inspires, so does the hotel's cuisine and leisure facilities. The romantic story behind the resort began in 1904, when a wealthy Englishman fell in love with the mountain and lake view setting and built the Manor for his bride. In many senses, the idyll continues, inspiring the Oscar-winning Hepburn and Fonda film 'On Golden Pond.' Enjoy tea and dreamy end-of-day reveries in the library or alternatively retreat to the excellent restaurant. Guests awaken to our delectable gourmet breakfasts each morning. The cuisine is the finest in the region, complemented by a celebrated cellar. Seasons Spa offers New Hampshire indigenous spa treatments to relax and soothe the most seasoned spa goers. Perhaps the best way to enjoy The Manor On Golden Pond is fireside after dinner, with a large Port and entertaining company. Fodor's 2012 Choice Hotel, Andrew Harper's "Hideaway Report" recommended. Zagat's Recommended. AAA Four Diamond rated.

Rates
22 rooms, 2 Suites $220/$550 B&B for 2 ppl/ night. Open year-round. Log-burning fireplaces, oversized jacuzzis & flat screen TV. Keurig coffee makers. Heated outdoor pool, clay tennis court & lawn games. Number of Rooms: 24

Cuisine
Our chef's innovative creations showcase his wide-ranging culinary training and award-winning New England cuisine using the freshest local products. Experience our Van Horn Dining Room or "M" Bistro. Full gourmet breakfast each morning.

Nearest Airport
Laconia, NH (LCI) .5 hours; Manchester, NH (MHT) 1 hour; Portland, ME (PWM) 1.5 hour; Boston, MA (BOS) 2 hours

ℱ **SelectRegistry.com**

The Notchland Inn

www.notchland.com
2 Morey Road, Hart's Location, NH USA 03812-4105
800-866-6131 • 603-374-6131
innkeepers@notchland.com

Member Since 1996

New Hampshire

Hart's Location

Innkeepers/Owners
Les Schoof and Ed Butler

Get away from it all, relax and rejuvenate at our comfortable granite manor house, completed in 1862, on a 100 acre estate within the White Mountain National Forest. Settle into one of 8 spacious, romantic guest rooms, five luxurious suites or two pet-friendly cottages which offer couples or families a bit more independence. Our guest spaces are individually appointed and each has a working wood burning fireplace. Here in Crawford Notch, where outdoor activities abound in every season, we are spared both television and cell phone signals; however, you are only a click away from complimentary Wi-Fi throughout the main inn building. A wonderful 5-course dinner and full country breakfast are served in a fireplaced dining room overlooking the pond and gardens. Visit with Gypsy, our Bernese Mountain Dog. Secluded, yet near to all the Mt. Washington Valley has to offer. Notchland...a magical location.

Rates
8 Deluxe Rooms, 5 Suites, 2 Cottages $199/$385, B&B. Open year-round. Number of Rooms: 15

Cuisine
5-course distinctive dinners Weds-Sun, hearty country breakfast daily. Fully licensed: wine/spirits/beer. Dinner is a leisurely affair, taking about 2 hours. $42 per person for in-house guests. $45 Wed, Thurs, Sun; $50 Fri, Sat & Holidays for others.

Nearest Airport
Manchester, NH, approx. 125 miles; Burlington, VT, approx. 130 miles

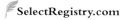

185

Sugar Hill Inn

www.sugarhillinn.com
116 Route 117, Sugar Hill, NH USA 03586
800-548-4748 • 603-823-5621
info@sugarhillinn.com

Member Since 2001

DiRōNA

AWARD OF EXCELLENCE 2013

Owners/Innkeepers
Karen and Steven Allen

Nestled in New Hampshire's White Mountains, Sugar Hill Inn is a romantic getaway known for fine dining, original art and stylish guest rooms and cottages. You'll be immersed in country inn ambiance, New England hospitality and all the recreation of the Franconia region. Impeccably restored, this country inn ranges from charming and cozy to sophisticated and distinctive. This 1789 farmhouse is perched on a hillside on acres of woodlands, rolling lawns and gardens, and is enhanced by a White Mountains view. All rooms have a/c, and many have fireplaces, whirlpool tubs, and private decks. The Dream Cottage with a cathedral ceiling, stone fireplace, whirlpool and sauna has been featured in "Everyday with Rachael Ray" magazine. Whether you seek a convenient base for the attractions and outdoor activities of Franconia Notch and the White Mountains or a special private hideaway to snuggle in front of a fireplace...come share the good life at the Sugar Hill Inn...your destination of choice. Yankee Magazine Editors' Choice. Best of New Hampshire.

Rates
Classic Rooms: $175/$305; Standard Rooms: $190/$340; Cottage Rooms: $190/$340; Luxury Rooms: $240/$440. Dream Cottage: $370/$505; Open year-round. All rooms have Nespresso Espresso Makers and Robes. Swimming Pool. Number of Rooms: 14

Cuisine
Full breakfast, afternoon small bites and cocktails. Dinner Thurs.-Mon. by reservation. Relax in the Tavern with your favorite drink before dinner. Over 100 wines from around the world. Distinguished Restaurants of North America (DiRōNA) award.

Nearest Airport
Manchester NH - 100 miles; Lebanon NH - 67; Burlington Vt - 108; Portland Me - 107; Boston Logan - 149

New Jersey

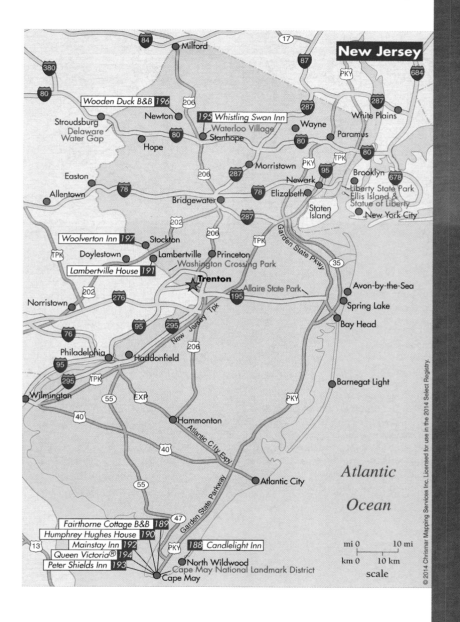

New Jersey

- 84 Milford
- 17
- 87
- 380
- PKY
- 684
- 80
- Wooden Duck B&B 196
- 206
- Newton
- 195 Whistling Swan Inn
- Wayne
- 287
- 287
- White Plains
- Stroudsburg
- Delaware Water Gap
- Waterloo Village
- Stanhope
- 80
- PKY
- TPK
- 80
- Hope
- 80
- Paramus
- Easton
- 206
- 287
- Morristown
- PKY
- 95
- Newark
- Brooklyn
- 678
- Allentown
- 78
- Bridgewater
- 78
- Elizabeth
- Liberty State Park
- Ellis Island & Statue of Liberty
- Staten Island
- New York City
- 202
- 287
- Woolverton Inn 197 Stockton
- 206
- Garden State Pkwy
- TPK
- Doylestown
- Lambertville
- Princeton
- 35
- TPK
- Lambertville House 191
- Washington Crossing Park
- **Trenton**
- 202
- 276
- 95
- 295
- 195
- Allaire State Park
- Avon-by-the-Sea
- Norristown
- New Jersey Tpk
- Spring Lake
- 76
- 206
- Bay Head
- Philadelphia
- 95
- Haddonfield
- 295
- TPK
- Wilmington
- 55
- EXP
- Barnegat Light
- 40
- PKY
- Hammonton
- 40
- Atlantic City Expy.
- 55
- Atlantic City
- **Atlantic Ocean**
- 47
- Garden State Parkway
- Fairthorne Cottage B&B 189
- Humphrey Hughes House 190
- 13
- Mainstay Inn 192
- PKY
- 188 Candlelight Inn
- Queen Victoria® 194
- Peter Shields Inn 193
- North Wildwood
- Cape May National Landmark District
- Cape May

mi 0   10 mi

km 0   10 km

scale

© 2014 Chrismar Mapping Services Inc. Licensed for use in the 2014 Select Registry.

Candlelight Inn

www.candlelight-inn.com
2310 Central Avenue, North Wildwood, NJ USA 08260
800-992-2632 • 609-522-6200 • Fax: 609-522-6125
info@candlelight-inn.com

Member Since 2001

Innkeepers/Owners
Bill and Nancy Moncrief and Eileen Burchsted

Let the SR Innkeepers of the Year 2011 be your hosts. Enjoy the quiet elegance reminiscent of another era. The Candlelight Inn is a beautifully restored Queen Anne Victorian home, offering rooms and suites with TV/DVD players, a decanter for a night-cap & specialty chocolates, fireplaces, private baths, some with double whirlpool tubs. Sit on our spacious veranda where cool ocean breezes delight you and watch fireworks Friday nights in the summer. Relax anytime of the year enjoying a starlit night in our outdoor hot tub, or during cool nights warm yourself by a fire in our inglenook. Minutes away are spacious, award winning beaches, water sports, lighthouses, antiquing, fine dining, nature activities, golfing, shopping, history, and a fun-filled boardwalk... something for everyone. Cape May County has islands with great Atlantic Ocean beaches, a Naval Air Station Museum, Historic Cold Spring Village, and Leaming's Gardens - the country's largest garden of annuals. Our inn is a small piece of the New Jersey Coast that we would like to share with you and your special someone.

Rates
7 Rooms, $125/$219; 3 Suites, $145/$289. Some have double whirlpool tubs. All rooms have either queen or king beds, private baths, air conditioning, gas or electric fire places, plus many other amenities. Open year-round. Number of Rooms: 10

Cuisine
A 3-course, sit-down breakfast with a choice of entrees, afternoon refreshments, and complimentary soft-drinks, coffee & teas all day.

Nearest Airport
Atlantic City (ACY) - 40 minutes; Philadelphia Intern'l (PHL) - 90 minutes; Newark 'Liberty' Intern'l - 2 hours

SelectRegistry.com

The Fairthorne Cottage Bed & Breakfast

www.fairthorne.com
115 Ocean Street, Cape May, NJ USA 08204
800-438-8742 • 609-884-8791 • Fax: 609-898-6129
fairthornebnb@aol.com

Member Since 2001

Innkeepers/Owners
Ed & Diane Hutchinson

Diane and Ed welcome you to their intimate seaside inn. The Fairthorne's four rooms feature King Sleep Number Beds complimented by cool luxury linens. All rooms have complimentary on site parking, flat screen TVs, iPod, iPhone docking stations and WiFi access. Each bathroom is a haven to relax with rain shower heads or perhaps one of our two person air tub rooms. Fireplaces to take the chill off while you sip some sherry. Bicycles and beach chairs and towels are available for your use. You won't be disappointed in your choice to stay at The Fairthorne. Within walking distance to shopping, fun restaurants and white beaches.

Rates
Rooms, $175/$295, Shoulder season specials. Number of Rooms: 4

Cuisine
Full breakfast and afternoon cookies. Make yourself a hot cup of cocoa, tea or coffee from our 24 hour Flavia Service. Also a fully stocked fridge with complimentary soft drinks.

Nearest Airport
Philadelphia and Atlantic City

The Humphrey Hughes House

www.humphreyhugheshouse.com
29 Ocean Street, Cape May, NJ USA 08204
609-884-4428
TheHumphreyHughes@comcast.net

Member Since 1999

New Jersey

Cape May

Innkeepers/Owners
Terry & Lorraine Schmidt

The Humphrey Hughes House, which is nestled in the heart of Cape May's Primary Historic District, offers superior accommodations in a picturesque setting. The Owners/ Innkeepers of The Humphrey Hughes House take great pride in adhering to the strict and high standards of Select Registry – Distinguished Inns of North America. Beautiful antique filled and expansive common rooms are both gracious and comfortable. Relax on the large wraparound veranda filled with rockers and enjoy the ocean view and colorful gardens. Our large, welcoming guest rooms offer pleasant, clean accommodations. All rooms are air-conditioned with cable TV and free wireless Internet. Our prime downtown Cape May location offers visitors the opportunity to walk to the beach, restaurants, shops, theatre, concerts, and nature trails. A full breakfast is served to all guests at 9 am each day. Consider joining other "Ladies and Gentlemen on Seaside Holiday" at this impecably restored and maintained inn...one of the best in Cape May.

Rates
$175/$350 per night, dbl. Weekday discounts Fall and Spring. All rooms and suites with queen or king. Last minute calls for reservations may find a "last minute special."
Number of Rooms: 10

Cuisine
A delicious and beautifully presented hot breakfast is served, depending on the weather, in our dining room or at individual tables for two on the large Ocean view Veranda. Refreshments are available 24/7 on the bright and beautiful sunporch.

Nearest Airport
Atlantic City International

 SelectRegistry.com

Lambertville House

www.lambertvillehouse.com
32 Bridge Street, Lambertville, NJ USA 08530
888-867-8859 • 609-397-0200 • Fax: 609-397-0511
innkeeper@lambertvillehouse.com

Member Since 2009

Proprietors
Edric & Mary Ellen Mason

The Lambertville House has been a landmark in the Delaware Valley area since 1812 providing gracious hospitality to American presidents, business leaders, dignitaries and discriminating guests from around the world. Proud recipients of the AAA Four Diamond Award for the past 15 years and listed on National Historic Register. Centrally located, yet a world apart, this sophisticated boutique hotel offers amenities and attention to detail found only in the finest upscale properties. Each guest room features a private bath with whirlpool tub, fireplace, iPod docking radio, flat screen TV, Wireless Internet and exquisite ambiance. We offer complimentary health club priviledges and a complimentary Continental breakfast. A cozy hotel bar and restaurant serves lunch and dinner every day. Uncompromising service and an experienced and knowledgeable staff always available to assist you. An ideal choice for a romantic getaway, a business meeting designed to refresh people and ideas or, an all-inclusive event venue for a wedding, rehearsal dinner or special celebration.

Rates
Rates: 26 Rooms/Suites $180/$350. Beautifully appointed baths with large whirlpool tubs, complimentary bathrobes, exclusive Aveda amenities, Evening turndown service, daily paper, complimentary bottled water, coffee and tea. Number of Rooms: 26

Cuisine
Lambertville House Lounge features imaginative and fresh dining options in a handsome setting. Lunch and dinner is served daily. Classic cocktails, an impressive wine list and the "best martini in town" is offered in the bar. Outdoor patio seating.

Nearest Airport
Philadelphia International, Newark International

The Mainstay Inn

www.mainstayinn.com
635 Columbia Ave., Cape May, NJ USA 08204
609-884-8690 • Fax: 609-884-1498
mainstayinn@comcast.net

Member Since 1976

Innkeeper/Owners
Diane Clark / Pete & Esther Scalone

The Mainstay is a Landmark within a National Historic Town surrounded by restaurants, shops, theater, nature trails and beautiful fine sand beaches. The Mansion & adjoining Cottage were built in the early 1870s and designed by famous Philadelphia architect Stephen Decatur Button. The Inn offers a glimpse into Cape May's past when the Mansion operated as Jackson's Clubhouse, a 19th century pleasure palace, where gentlemen gathered in an elegant setting for gambling and other amusements. The Mansion features 14 ft. ceilings and floor to ceiling walk-through windows that open out to the most iconic porch in town where you can enjoy an assortment of swings and rocking chairs that surrounds the house. The Inn is like stepping back in time, but all rooms offer private baths, air conditioning, cable TV and Internet. We also have an Apartment for up to 4 guests. Beach chairs and towels are provided as well as a shower room for after checkout use. The Inn is listed in the book "1000 Places to See Before You Die" so please come and enjoy Cape May soon. Call or check web for specials.

Rates
Cottage Rooms $175 to $325 / Mansion Rooms $235 to $345 Mid-Oct/Mid-May weekday rates as low as $122.50 per night w/"Buy One Get One Special" or stay "The Long Weekend" by adding a third weekend night for an extra $100 (Fri-Sat-Sun). Number of Rooms: 13

Cuisine
Full hot breakfast featuring fresh baked cakes and fresh seasonal fruits. Relax in the dining room or enjoy the wide porch that surrounds the house. The refreshments continue with a Tea service afternoons at 4 pm with additional baked items and savories

Nearest Airport
Atlantic City (ACY) 40 min; Philadelphia (PHL) 90 min. Drive or Ferry from Wash. DC (DCA or IAD) or Baltimore (BWI)

SelectRegistry.com

Peter Shields Inn

www.petershieldsinn.com
1301 Beach Avenue, Cape May, NJ USA 08204
609-884-9090
psi@petershieldsinn.com

Member Since 2008

New Jersey
Cape May

Proprietor/ Co-Proprietor
Jeff & Maria Gernitis

This 1907 Georgian revival mansion is an architectural masterpiece, directly across from the Atlantic Ocean in Cape May, New Jersey with golfing, fishing and Atlantic City all within reach. The Peter Shields Inn is the ideal choice for a relaxing getaway. Just a short stroll from Cape May's historic district, the inn offers a charming sanctuary. Enjoy easy access to our beautiful beaches in the summer season or sip a glass of wine next to a cozy fireplace in the fall and winter. We provide the perfect setting any time of year. Each of our nine guest rooms offers individual ambiance with private baths, most have Jacuzzi tubs and fireplaces, flat screen cable television, plush bedding, exclusive bath amenities, nightly turn down service, individual climate control for heat and air conditioning.

The inn also specializes in both casual and elegant ocean front weddings and special events.

With our inviting guest rooms, fine dining restaurant, beautiful location and an attentive and caring staff, your visit to the Peter Shields Inn is sure to be a memorable one.

Rates
$150-$425 Includes full breakfast daily, afternoon wine & cheese, 24 hour hospitality suite with complimentary soft drinks, and snacks, concierge service, free WiFi, private parking, beach chairs, towels, umbrellas and bicycles. Number of Rooms: 9

Cuisine
Whether you're in the mood to dine indoors next to a warm fireplace or on our porch overlooking the sea, our award-winning, Zagat-rated restaurant offers Cape May's finest dining. The chef serves creative cuisine using the freshest local ingredients.

Nearest Airport
Atlantic City or Philadelphia International

The Queen Victoria

www.queenvictoria.com
102 Ocean Street, Cape May, NJ USA 08204
609-884-8702
reservations@queenvictoria.com

Member Since 1992

Innkeepers/Owners
Doug and Anna Marie McMain

A Cape May tradition since 1980, The Queen Victoria is one of America's most renowned bed & breakfast inns. Four impeccably restored 1880s homes are filled with fine antiques, beautiful quilts, and many thoughtful extras. The hospitality is warm and the atmosphere is social. Choose from thirty-five inviting and spacious rooms and suites, all with private bath, AC, mini-refrigerator, safe, robes and TV with DVD. Pamper yourself with a whirlpool tub or gas-log fireplace.

For your Victorian enjoyment, rocking chairs fill porches and gardens. Wicker swings carry you back to a quieter time. Bicycles are provided free of charge, as are beach chairs and beach towels. The Queen Victoria is open all year and is located in the heart of the historic district, one block from the Atlantic Ocean, tours, shopping, and fine restaurants. Victorian Cape May offers tours, special events, and activities all year including the Spring Music Festival, Victorian Weekend, the Food & Wine Festival and Christmas in Cape May.

Rates
25 Rooms: $130/$290. 10 Suites: $180/$430. Seasonal and Weekday discounts Fall, Winter and Spring. Always open. Complimentary WiFi. Number of Rooms: 35

Cuisine
Rates include generous buffet breakfast and afternoon tea with sweets and savories. Complimentary juices, soft drinks, bottled water, coffee and teas. Baked treats and fresh fruit always available. Casual and fine dining within walking distance.

Nearest Airport
Atlantic City (ACY), Philadelphia (PHL)

SelectRegistry.com

Whistling Swan Inn

www.whistlingswaninn.com
110 Main St., Stanhope, NJ USA 07874
888-507-2337 • 973-347-6369 • Fax: 973-347-6379
info@whistlingswaninn.com

Member Since 1992

Innkeepers
Tom and Rosalind Bruno

Set amidst a spectacular garden on a quiet, tree-lined street, the Whistling Swan Inn exudes romance and warmth. This elegant 1905 Queen Anne Victorian features a gracious wraparound veranda where leisurely breakfasts are served on pleasant mornings. Each room embraces you with comfort and warmth with period antiques and modern conveniences; TV/VCR/DVD, airconditioning, wireless Internet, plus refrigerators, gas fireplaces and Jacuzzis in our suites. Whatever the season, a myriad of activities awaits you. After a busy day of hiking, biking, shopping or antiquing, relax in a hammock or share pleasant conversations with new-found friends. Enjoy fine dining at one of the area gourmet restaurants, some within walking distance. At day's end, snuggle up with your special someone next to the fireplace. Sink into your featherbed and fall asleep to a movie from our DVD library. The Whistling Swan Inn is where modern luxury meets Victorian elegance.

Rates
5 Rooms (all with private bath), $135-$179; 4 Suites (Jacuzzi, fireplace), $195-$279. Corporate/Government/Single rates available. Number of Rooms: 9

Cuisine
Full country buffet breakfast, 24-hour complimentary guest snack bar, including our signature chocolate chip cookies. Special diets accommodated.

Nearest Airport
Newark - 45 minutes; Allentown, PA - 1 hour

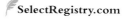

&. ᶠ⦾ᶠ

The Wooden Duck B&B

www.woodenduckinn.com
140 Goodale Road, Newton, NJ USA 07860
973-300-0395
woodenduckinn@aol.com

Member Since 2003

New Jersey

Newton

Innkeepers/Owners
Karl & Beth Krummel

An oasis of country pleasures! This beautiful mini-estate is nestled on 10 wooded acres adjacent to the 1600-acre Kittatinny Valley State Park, abounding with wildlife and hiking trails. Our in-ground pool is open all summer. One guest room has a king bed; all other guestrooms have queen beds. All have a private bath, clock radio, satellite TV/VCR, telephone, hair dryer, iron/ironing board, comfortable sitting area and a desk. Complimentary wireless Internet is available throughout. Some rooms have soaking tub for two, 2-sided gas fireplace, DVD player and private balcony. Guests are welcome to use the game room with fireplace, TV/VCR, board games, and video library. The Guest Pantry with complimentary snacks, homemade cookies, soda, coffee, and tea is available 24/7. Nearby are many antique and craft shops, fine dining, winter and summer sports, horseback riding, hiking and fishing, mineral and mining museums, and numerous golf courses. Less than an hour to the Crossings Outlet Mall in PA and only 55 miles to Times Square in Manhattan.

Rates
$129-$299 per night/double. Corporate rates Sunday through Thursday. Open all year. Number of Rooms: 10

Cuisine
Full country breakfast featuring a rotating menu of delicious baked French toast or egg casseroles, meat and fruit, with homebaked bread or coffee cake, juice, tea, and coffee. Trail mix, cookies, snacks, hot and cold beverages available 24/7.

Nearest Airport
Newark Airport, 45 Miles. Aeroflex private airport within walking distance.

SelectRegistry.com

Woolverton Inn

www.woolvertoninn.com
6 Woolverton Road, Stockton, NJ USA 08559
888-264-6648 • 609-397-0802 • Fax: 609-397-0987
sheep@woolvertoninn.com

Member Since 2002

Innkeepers/Owners
Carolyn McGavin and Bob Haas

Perched high above the Delaware River, surrounded by 300 acres of rolling farmland and forest, The Woolverton Inn provides the seclusion of a grand country estate, yet the activities of New Hope and Lambertville are just five minutes away. Enjoy the glorious setting and relaxed elegance of this 1792 stone manor, while feeling as comfortable as you would at your own home in the country. All guestrooms are unique and thoughtfully decorated; they feature bucolic views, fireplaces, whirlpool tubs and showers for two, private outdoor sitting areas, stocked refrigerators, and Bose CD Wave radios. Dogs are permitted in the Garden Cottage. As recommended by "1000 Places to See Before You Die in the USA and Canada" and National Geographic Traveler, among others.

Rates
6 Rooms $150/$345; 2 Suites $285/$365; 5 Cottages $305/$435. Rooms offer featherbeds, fresh flowers, robes, luxury linens, CD Players, two person whirlpool tubs, two person showers, fireplaces. Number of Rooms: 13

Cuisine
Full gourmet breakfast served in our dining room, gardens or in bed. Signature dishes include: homemade apple-cranberry turkey sausage, lemon-ricotta hotcakes, pina colada scones and fabulous cookies.

Nearest Airport
Philadelphia International and Newark

New Mexico

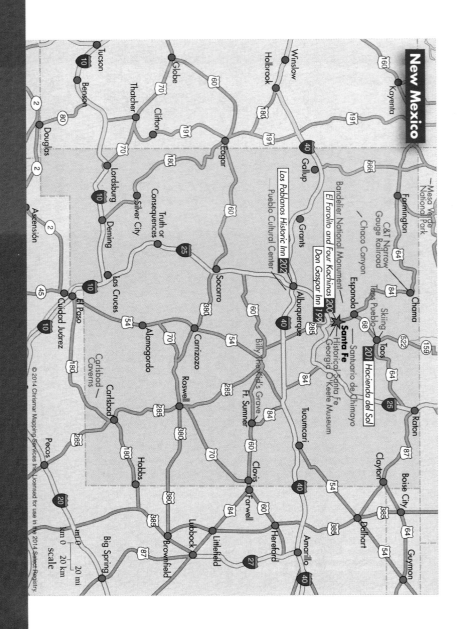

New Mexico

Kayenta
160
Mesa Verde National Park
Farmington
64
Chama
84
Raton
87
C&T Narrow Gauge Railroad
Chaco Canyon
Española
Taos Pueblo
Skiing
Taos
201 Hacienda del Sol
25
522
159
64
385
Boise City
Clayton
Guymon
64
Dalhart
54
Bandelier National Monument
El Farolito and Four Kachinas 200
Don Gaspar Inn 199
Santa Fe
Historical Santa Fe
Georgia O'Keefe Museum
Santuario de Chimayo
68
Los Poblanos Historic Inn 202
Pueblo Cultural Center
Grants
Gallup
Holbrook
Winslow
Tucson
Globe
Thatcher
Clifton
Eagar
Benson
Douglas
Lordsburg
Silver City
Deming
Ascension
Las Cruces
El Paso
Ciudad Juárez
Truth or Consequences
Socorro
Albuquerque
Tucumcari
84
285
Carrizozo
Alamogordo
Billy the Kid's Grave
Ft. Summer
Roswell
Carlsbad Caverns
Carlsbad
Hobbs
Clovis
Farwell
Hereford
Amarillo
Pecos
Brownfield
Littlefield
Lubbock
Big Spring

160
10
180
60
191
666
666
40
60
25
380
60
40
285
54
70
54
70
54
380
380
380
285
285
180
180
180
45
2
2
2
80
70
70
191
285
84
84
60
385
27
87
20

© 2014 Christmas Mapping Services Inc. Licensed for use in the 2014 Select Registry

km 0   20 km
mi 0   20 mi
scale

SelectRegistry.com

Don Gaspar Inn

www.dongaspar.com
623 Don Gasper Ave, Sante Fe, NM USA 87505
505-986-8664 • 888-986-8664 • Fax: 505-986-0696
info@dongaspar.com

Member Since 2013

Owners
Shirley and David Alford

More than a traditional bed and breakfast, the Don Gaspar Inn offers guests a selection of impressive, Santa Fe, New Mexico accommodations. Visitors may choose between 7 large private suites, 2 one-bedroom casitas, and a 3-bedroom home. Each offer a private bath, private entrance and patio seating.

Often referred to as "the best kept secret in Santa Fe," the offerings here are unsurpassed. The trademark gardens and courtyards that surround the Inn add to the ambiance of this wonderful property.

Nestled in the historic Don Gaspar neighborhood, we are just a 7-minute walk to local attractions and activities, such as the Plaza, galleries, spas, unique shops, and wonderful restaurants. Enjoy our daily delicious breakfast consisting of Northern New Mexican favorites and traditional entrees in the dining room, your private suite, or on our garden patio.

Rates
$149-$389. 10 Rooms, Suites, and a 3 Bedroom Home. Each unit has a romantic fireplace, hand crafted furniture and decor, original Native American and Southwest inspired art. Enjoy the lush gardens from your private deck. Number of Rooms: 10

Cuisine
Full breakfast daily. Start the day with our famous Southwest inspired breakfast buffet. Freshly brewed coffee, seasonal fresh fruit, house made granola, fresh pastries, with rotating hot items including Challah French Toast and Migas with Papitas.

Nearest Airport
Santa Fe Municipal Airport (SAF) is just 15 min. from the Don Gaspar Inn. Albuquerque Airport (ABQ) is 1 hr. away.

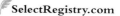

El Farolito and Four Kachinas Inns

www.farolito.com and www.fourkachinas.com
514 Galisteo St (ELF), 512 Webber St (4K), Santa Fe, NM 87501
888-634-8782 • 505-988-1631 • Fax: 505-989-1323
innkeeper@farolito.com

Member Since 2001

Innkeepers/Owners
Walt Wyss and Wayne Mainus

Enjoy the richness of Santa Fe's art, culture and history in two beautiful downtown properties - El Farolito Bed and Breakfast Inn (ELF) and the Four Kachinas Inn (4K). These inns, under the same ownership and management, offer you award-winning accommodations, showcasing exquisite original Southwestern art and handcrafted furnishings. The rooms are decorated in styles relevant to Santa Fe's rich cultural heritage of native American, Spanish and Anglo inhabitants. Modern amenities also abound including fine linens, rich fabrics, AC, private entrances, flat panel TVs and free Internet access. The two inns are conveniently located in the downtown historic district, a short pleasant walk to numerous galleries, shops, museums, world-class fine dining, and the central Plaza. Savor a leisurely breakfast on the back portal and relax on your garden patio. At ELF, enjoy a fireside breakfast in the brightly decorated dining room and the coziness of a fireplace in your room. At the 4K Inn, enjoy anytime access to the cozy lounge/breakfast room or relax on one of our garden patios.

Rates
13 Rooms, $130/$240; 1 Suite, $210/$275. 7 rooms/1 suite at El Farolito and 6 rooms at Four Kachinas. Features: flat panel TV, fine linens, AC, free WiFi, garden patios. Fireplaces, in-room coffee and refrigerators at ELF. Number of Rooms: 14

Cuisine
Complete healthy breakfast buffet with quality home-baked goods, hot entree, fresh fruit, yogurts, and ample accompaniment. Complimentary afternoon light refreshments. Walking distance to numerous world-class fine dining restaurants.

Nearest Airport
Santa Fe - direct to/from Dallas, Denver, LA and Phoenix.
Albuquerque - 60 miles away with extensive service.

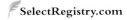

Hacienda del Sol

www.taoshaciendadelsol.com
P.O. Box 177, 109 Mabel Dodge Lane, Taos, NM USA 87571
866-333-4459 • 575-758-0287 • Fax: 575-758-5895
stay@taoshaciendadelsol.com

Member Since 2003

Innkeepers/Owners
Gerd and Luellen Hertel

Taos Mountain provides a magnificent backdrop to our Hacienda, which borders thousands of acres of panoramic and peaceful Indian Pueblo land. Enjoy a serene and beautiful view from the tranquil gardens or steaming Jacuzzi as you stargaze in the stillness of our many clear nights. The original 1804 adobe once belonged to legendary art patroness Mabel Dodge Luhan. This historic inn has hosted guests such as D.H. Lawrence, Georgia O'Keefe, Frank Waters and Ansel Adams. Southwestern rooms enchant our guests with kiva fireplaces, viga and latilla ceilings, and handcrafted furniture. In the heat of summer, Taos elevation combined with the shade of towering cottonwoods, elms, willows and blue spruce on the property provide blissful conditions. Experience the culinary talents of award winning chef/owner Gerd Hertel every Thursday night for a fun cooking demonstration followed by a 4 course meal including wine. We also offer gourmet theme dinners for holidays and special occasions. Weddings can be arranged in either of our garden courtyards with full catering services provided.

Rates
7 Rooms, $135/$325 B&B. 4 Suites, $190/$540 B&B. Open year round. Number of Rooms: 11

Cuisine
2-course breakfast with hot entree. Gourmet Coffees and tea and hot cocoa available all day. Afternoon homemade snacks and sweets are available in the Dining room. Breakfast served on the patio in summer or by the open kiva fireplace in winter.

Nearest Airport
Santa Fe and Albuquerque Airport

Los Poblanos Historic Inn & Organic Farm

🍽 🍽 ♀

www.lospoblanos.com
4803 Rio Grande Blvd. NW, Los Ranchos de Albuquerque, NM USA 87107
866-344-9297 • 505-344-9297 • Fax: 505-342-1302
info@lospoblanos.com

Member Since 2005

New Mexico

Los Ranchos de Albuquerque

Innkeepers/Owners
The Rembe Family

Set amongst 25 acres of lavender fields and lush gardens, the award-winning Los Poblanos Inn is one of the most prestigious historic properties in the Southwest. Designed in 1932 by famed architect John Gaw Meem, the "Father of Santa Fe Style," the buildings feature agricultural-themed artwork by important New Mexico artists of the period. The "Field to Fork" dining at Los Poblanos is rooted in the organic ingredients from its own farm as well as from the region. The elegant guest rooms feature wood burning fireplaces, hardwood floors, original artwork, and antique New Mexican furnishings. Guests can relax around the salt water pool, explore the property's extensive gardens, take an architecture tour, or attend a class. As Los Poblanos wanders the line between refined and rugged, guests can also experience a real working farm, complete with animals, crops and barns. Awarded one of the Top 100 hotels in the world by Fodors, Los Poblanos has also been featured in New Mexico Magazine, The New York Times, and as a "Top Foodie Destination" by Zagat.

Rates
20 Guest Rooms and Suites, seasonal rates from $155 to $300. Fireplaces, salt water pool, complimentary bikes, spa services upon request, WiFi, flatscreen TVs, fitness center, free onsite parking and Farm Shop. Open year-round. Number of Rooms: 20

Cuisine
Complimentary gourmet breakfast with fresh organic ingredients from our farm, including honey, eggs, produce and pork. With advanced reservations, guests can add an in-room charcuterie, Field to Fork dinners, cooking classes and workshops.

Nearest Airport
Albuquerque International Sunport

SelectRegistry.com

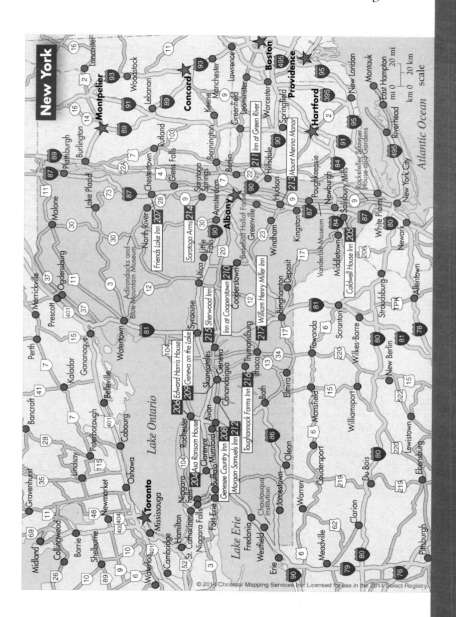

New York

& ‖ଠ‖ ‖ଠ‖ ‖ଠ‖ ♀

Asa Ransom House

www.asaransom.com
10529 Main St. Rt. 5, Clarence, NY USA 14031
800-841-2340 • 716-759-2315
innfo@asaransom.com

Member Since 1976

New York

Clarence

Approved
❦ ❦ ❦

Innkeeper
Robert Lenz

On the site of the first gristmill built in Erie County (1803), where guests are romanced in the winter by the glowing fireplaces and spacious grounds full of herbs and flowers in the summer. Many rooms have porches or balconies to view the grounds or just relax. Experience world-class cuisine and full country breakfasts with delicious regional accents. Voted best food, service, hospitality, romantic setting and historical charm in Buffalo News readers survey. Often upon arrival you will find the aroma of fresh pies and breads lingering in the air! Clarence is known throughout the east for its antiques and treasures, along with unusual shops full of gifts, art and crafts. Explore the hiking/bike trails or visit the nearby Opera House, Erie Canal Cruises, Albright-Knox Art Gallery and Frank Lloyd Wright's Martin House Complex. Also Niagara wineries, Fort Niagara, Letchworth State Park and much more. Only 28 miles from Niagara Falls.

Rates
$129/$198 B&B; $198/$295 MAP. Single rates available. All private baths. Full country breakfast included, queen or king beds, 9 with fireplace, 2 with whirlpool. Complimentary wireless Internet. Refrigerators in all rooms. Number of Rooms: 10

Cuisine
Fine country dining with regional specialties. Fully licensed - New York State Wine award and voted "Best Place to Take Out-of-Town Guests"
Menu changes with each season, using many local products.

Nearest Airport
Buffalo/Niagara 9 miles, Amtrak 11 miles

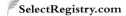
SelectRegistry.com

Caldwell House Bed and Breakfast

www.caldwellhouse.com
25 Orrs Mills Road, Salisbury Mills, NY USA 12577
845-496-2954 • 8454962954
info@caldwellhouse.com

Member Since 2014

New York

Salisbury Mills

Owners/Innkeepers
John and Dena Finneran

The inn, located in the heart of New York's Hudson Valley and 60 minutes from New York City, was built while Thomas Jefferson was President and opened the same year as the United States Military Academy at West Point. It offers the architectural splendor of that era while tastefully and discreetly incorporating all the modern conveniences that today's traveler seeks.

Our guests will find the original wide-planked wooden floors, high ceilings with crown molding, and large, beautifully designed fireplaces that the first owners of the home used and enjoyed. Over the years, the Inn has been meticulously cared for and updated to add all the comforts of a modern home, without doing anything to harm its original charm and majesty.

Our multi-award winning Bed and Breakfast awaits you and its owners, Dena and John, look forward to providing you, with a stay you will remember for a long time to come.

Rates
$185-$375. Number of Rooms: 10

Cuisine
Awake to the smell of Dena's delicious three-course breakfast. The menu changes daily and all special requests are honored.
Coffee/Tea/Soda and snacks available 24/7.
Large wine selection is available for on-site consumption.

Nearest Airport
SWF - 5 miles; NYC airports 60 miles

The Edward Harris House B&B Inn

www.edwardharrishouse.com
35 Argyle Street, Rochester, NY USA 14607
585-473-9752 • 800-419-1213 • Fax: 585-486-1491
innkeeper@edwardharrishouse.com

Member Since 2013

Innkeepers/Owners
Susan and Manny Alvarez

On the National Register of Historic Places, enjoy the quiet ambiance of our award winning 1896 inn. This urban bed and breakfast offers business and pleasure travelers alike the quiet relaxation of neighborhood living with the convenience of a central city location. Nestled in the historic Arts and Cultural District of Park/East Avenues, walk tree lined streets (one block) to area cafes, shops, fine dining, galleries and museums. Our guest rooms, suites and cottages are as individual as the guests who enjoy them. Our guest suites are well appointed, comfortable, and beautiful, most rooms have fireplaces for added ambiance. Furnishings blend the charm of old world and antiques together with the modern conveniences you desire. Relax with a drink on the terraces, front porch or by waterside at one of the cottages. While we strive to anticipate your needs, we describe our innkeeping style as one of unobtrusive comfort, warmth and informatility. Making for a restful environment in which to spend quiet time together after a long day of work or play. Rest, relax, renew.

Rates
3 King Suites, 1 Queen Room in the main Inn, 2-2brm pet friendly Cottages. $169-$275. Special event and college weekends, special rates may apply. All rooms have private baths, heat/ac, flat screen TV/Cable, and complimentary WIFI. Number of Rooms: 8

Cuisine
A full breakfast includes: fresh seasonal fruit or berries, hot southern biscuits, warm croissants or baked goods, chef's choice of entree using local produce and farm fresh eggs when available. Complimentary refreshments available throughout the day.

Nearest Airport
Rochester Int'l Airport (ROC) Just 20 minutes from the airport.

Friends Lake Inn

iOi iOi iOi ♀

www.friendslake.com
963 Friends Lake Road, Chestertown, NY USA 12817
518-494-4751 • Fax: 518-494-4616
friends@friendslake.com

Member Since 1998

Innkeepers/Owners
John and Trudy Phillips

Experience the romance and intimate ambiance of this elegantly restored inn surrounded by the natural beauty of the Adirondacks. The Friends Lake Inn is the perfect getaway to reconnect, celebrate that special occasion or just to relax and enjoy each others company. This charming and intimate inn offers 17 guest rooms, many with Jacuzzi tubs, lake views and fireplaces. Four Adirondack rooms highlight the special quality of the outdoors; "Great Camp" style furniture, real-wood burning stone fireplaces, steam showers, Jacuzzi tubs and private porches overlooking our gardens. The highly acclaimed restaurant tantalizes with innovative New-American cuisine complemented by a superior wine collection, served in the rustic elegance and warmth of a 19th century dining room. We have a variety of packages built specifically with a couple's enjoyment in mind, and the Adirondack's offers plenty to do for every season of the year. Please come and enjoy luxurious accommodations and dining at Friends Lake Inn, one of the most beautiful places in the world!

Rates
Choose from 17 luxurious guest rooms, all with private baths. Rooms with Jacuzzis or Adirondack Rooms with fireplaces available. Rooms range from $359-$550 per couple. (MAP, full country breakfast and three course dinner included). Number of Rooms: 17

Cuisine
Full country breakfast and candlelit dinner served daily. Bistro open at 2 pm on weekends, 4 pm weekdays. Inquire about conferences, rehearsal dinners, and weddings. Lighter Wine Bar Menu available. Extensive wine collection.

Nearest Airport
Albany International

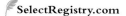

Genesee Country Inn Bed and Breakfast

www.geneseecountryinn.com
948 George Street, P.O. Box 226, Mumford-Rochester, NY USA 14511
585-538-2500 • 800-697-8297 • Fax: 585-538-9867
stay@geneseecountryinn.com   *Member Since 1988*

New York

Mumford-Rochester

Innkeepers/Owners
Deborah & Richard Stankevich

Enjoy the simple elegance, fine hospitality, and natural beauty the of Genesee Valley. This historic bed and breakfast/country inn, an 1833 plaster-paper mill, is situated on eight acres along Spring Creek with mill ponds and a waterfall to enthrall any traveler. Hike the grounds, MacKay Wildlife Preserve, and Genesee Country Village & Museum Nature Center. Enjoy the art of fly-fishing on our private Spring Creek, fish the famed Oatka Creek, and visit the historic NYS Fish Hatchery. The inn's idyllic country ambiance is perfect for a secluded, romantic getaway, yet it is close to the arts, entertainment, Finger Lakes wineries, antique shops, and over 70 golf courses. The inn is a wonderful location for family reunions, birthday parties, corporate events, bridal or baby showers, and intimate weddings or elopements. Romance, spa, and fly-fishing packages are available! The inn has wireless Internet, TVs with DVD players, an extensive DVD collection, fax, and meeting facilities. Check our web site for additional special packages and getaway weekends. See you at the inn!

Rates
Six Old Mill Rooms (one on the first floor - $160 and five on the second floor - $130-$150); Three Garden Rooms - $185; and One King Suite - $200. Number of Rooms: 10

Cuisine
A full hot country breakfast is offered daily, which includes fresh fruit, yogurt, homemade granola, sweet breads, muffins, and scones with plenty of locally blended coffee. Homemade chocolate chip cookies are available throughout the day.

Nearest Airport
Rochester International Airport (13 miles east); Buffalo International Airport (41 miles west)

 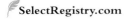

Geneva On The Lake

www.genevaonthelake.com
1001 Lochland Road, Route 14, Geneva, NY USA 14456
315-789-7190 • Fax: 315-789-0322
info@genevaonthelake.com

Member Since 2003

General Manager
William J. Schickel

Experience European elegance and friendly hospitality in the heart of the Finger Lakes Wine Country. Amidst an ambiance of Italian Renaissance architecture, classical sculptures, luxurious suites, and Stickley furnishings, guests from around the world enjoy vacation getaways, family reunions, weddings and executive retreats. Rest, relax, and surrender yourself to gracious service and breathtaking surroundings. Candlelight dining with live music. A complimentary bottle of wine and flowers are in your suite on arrival. The New York Times or Wall Street Journal are available. Complimentary high-speed wireless Internet. Glorious formal gardens for lawn games, a 70' outdoor pool, and boat-house with dock and moorings. Adjacent are Geneva's charming Historic District and the campus of Hobart and William Smith Colleges, both complete with architectural gems. Enjoy magnificent scenic beauty on the Seneca Lake Wine Trail. Golf and antiques are nearby. "The food is extraordinarily good." – Bon Appetit. "One of the 10 most romantic inns in the United States." – American Historic Inns.

Rates
29 guest accommodations (13 one-bedroom suites, 10 two-bedroom suites and 6 studios). Room rates from $173 to $835 per night. Many packages with candlelight dinner and full breakfast from $347 to $1009 per night. Number of Rooms: 29

Cuisine
Gourmet dinner is served with a smile in the warmth of candlelight and live music. Breakfast daily and Sunday brunch. Lunch on The Terrace in summer. The kitchen uses much local produce and the wine list includes over 70 Finger Lakes wines.

Nearest Airport
Rochester International

♿ 🍽️

The Inn at Cooperstown

www.innatcooperstown.com
16 Chestnut Street, Cooperstown, NY USA 13326
607–547–5756 • Fax: 607-547-8779
info@innatcooperstown.com

Member Since 1998

Innkeepers/Owners
Marc and Sherrie Kingsley

A warm welcome awaits you at The Inn at Cooperstown! This award-winning historic hotel was built in 1874, fully restored in 1985, and is thoughtfully improved upon each year. Spotless guest rooms are individually decorated with many charming touches. The hotel is ideally situated in the heart of the village creating a "park and walk" experience. It is just a short stroll to the National Baseball Hall of Fame, Main Street shops and restaurants, as well as Otsego Lake. After exploring Cooperstown, visitors can unwind in a rocking chair on the hotel's sweeping veranda or enjoy the fireplace in a cozy sitting room. Check out the one-of-a-kind packages that are offered with the National Baseball Hall of Fame, Brewery Ommegang, The Farmers' Museum, Fenimore Art Museum, and Cooperstown Bat Company. Don't just "visit" Cooperstown, "experience" Cooperstown with one of these unique packages! The owners are bicycle enthusiasts and have created a very special bicycle clubhouse available to all guests. Bring your bike for some of the finest cycling in the northeast!

Rates
All guest rooms have private bath, A/C, CD/clock radio, hair dryer, iron, wireless internet, and flat panel television. Off-street parking. Standard: $115/$195, Classic: $140/$240, Suites: $195/$325, $285/$498. Open year-round. Number of Rooms: 18

Cuisine
Expanded continental breakfast with hot entree, afternoon refreshments, and fine restaurants within walking distance.

Nearest Airport
Albany, NY (ALB) or Syracuse, NY (SYR)

🖋 SelectRegistry.com

Inn at Green River

www.innatgreenriver.com
9 Nobletown Road, Hillsdale, NY USA 12529
518-325-7248
stay@innatgreenriver.com

Member Since 2014

Owner/Innkeeper
Deborah Bowen

Known for its beautiful, serene setting in the upper Hudson Valley, in the foothills of the Berkshires, a romantic getaway to this bed & breakfast will leave you feeling refreshed and renewed. "The Travelers Guide to the Hudson River Valley" noted: "You will feel like a weekend guest rather than a paying customer" and "The setting is sylvan and relaxing." The Federal style c. 1830 inn sits on an acre of lawn and gardens. The hammock, the Adirondack chairs and the screened porch by the fish pool will entice you to spend the day relaxing at the inn, but the central location is perfect, both for outdoors activities – hiking, biking, skiing – & cultural/historic sites – Tanglewood, summer home of the Boston Symphony; modern dance at Jacob's Pillow; theater at Barrington Stage, the Berkshire Theater Group, Shakespeare & Co.; museums & historic houses like the Norman Rockwell, Hancock Shaker Village, Hudson River Valley School painter Frederic Church's Olana. Close to antiques & auctions in Hudson, great farm to table restaurants, & retail therapy in the many locally owned shops.

Rates
$139-$295 depending on room/season. Corporate rates midweek. 5 rooms have gas fireplaces, 2 have outdoor seating areas, 2 have whirlpool tubs, 2 have showers for two, 4 have cable TV, all have AC, WiFi, spa robes and hair dryers. Number of Rooms: 7

Cuisine
Breakfast is served any time you like from 8:30-10:00 am in the sun room and dining room and features freshly baked scones, local jams, a fruit course and a hot entree. Homemade ginger molasses cookies and tea, coffee or hot chocolate in the afternoon.

Nearest Airport
Albany 1 hr; Hartford, CT (Bradley) 1.5 hrs; Boston (Logan) 2.5 hrs; Kennedy/LaGuardia (New York) 2.5 hrs

Morgan-Samuels Inn

www.morgansamuelsinn.com
2920 Smith Rd., Canandaigua, NY USA 14424
585-394-9232 • 585-704-3399
MorSamBB@aol.com

Member Since 1992

New York

Canandaigua

Innkeepers/Owners
Julie & John Sullivan

Travel the tree-lined 2000 ft. drive to the exquisite 1810 European stone mansion. She sits on a tree-covered rise on 46 private acres, only 1.5 miles north of the lake in Finger Lakes Wine Country. You would expect wood or coal grate fireplaces in each room (11), double spa-tubs, a library with a game table and TV, beamed ceilings, grand gardens, baby grand piano, soothing music in all common areas, finest amenities, complimentary beverages. What sets us apart from other outstanding properties is the sophisticated dinner cuisine, enjoyed in candlelight private areas or with other guests, if desired. All dining areas have panoramic views. Guest reviews confirm that the dining experience is worth motoring hundreds of miles. Personal pampering by the owners. One staff member for every two guests. Warmth and comfort of the common areas. Massage studio complete with field stone trimmed with mahogany. Five acres with six outdoor patios. Miles long adjacent walking trail. Some rooms are pet friendly.

Rates
Five rooms, $179/$279 B&B; the suite, $299/$325 B&B. Number of Rooms: 6

Cuisine
Innkeeper dinner by reservation and breakfast served privately, if desired. The signature fruit tray with a variety of 24 seasonal fruits starts the day, followed by a verbalized menu which includes our renowned open-faced omelets.

Nearest Airport
Canandaigua Airport and Hopewell Airpark
Rochester International Airport (ROC)
Syracuse International Airport (SYR)

SelectRegistry.com

Mount Merino Manor

www.mountmerinomanor.com
4317 Route 23, Hudson, NY USA 12534
518-828-5583 • Fax: 518-828-4292
info@mountmerinomanor.com

Member Since 2009

New York

Hudson

Innkeepers/Owners
Rita and Patrick Birmingham

Enjoy the comforts of a luxury Bed and Breakfast in the historic Hudson Valley. Sitting on a lush hilltop surrounded by 100 acres of shaded woodlands, this stately Victorian has magnificent views of the Catskill Mountains and Hudson River. Decorated with an eclectic mix of treasured furniture, period pieces and fine fabrics, each guest room is spacious and romantic. Many have mountain views, candle-lit fireplaces, whirlpool tubs, spa showers and king beds. Special amenities such as thick Egyptian cotton towels, luxury bed linens, spa robes, aromatherapy bath products, fresh flowers and artisanal chocolates pamper every guest. With modern conveniences such as complimentary WiFi, TV/DVD and in-room climate control, Mount Merino Manor provides the luxury of a small boutique hotel with the personal service of a Bed and Breakfast. Just outside the city of Hudson and a neighbor to Olana State Historic site, there is never a shortage of things to see and do. Fine dining, shopping, art, antiques hiking, biking, skiing and other outdoor activities are just minutes from the manor.

Rates
$195-$425. All private baths. Mid-week rates/packages. 1 Room ADA compliant. Number of Rooms: 7

Cuisine
Breakfast is served in our light-filled dining room at individual tables. Farm fresh fruit, daily baked breads and muffins and a hot entree including gourmet coffee and teas. A guest kitchen provides hot and cold beverages and snacks anytime.

Nearest Airport
Albany International Airport 45 miles. Columbia County Airport 10 miles.

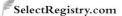

♿ 🍽 🍷

Saratoga Arms

www.SaratogaArms.com
497 Broadway, Saratoga Springs, NY USA 12866
518-584-1775 • Fax: 518-581-4064
info@SaratogaArms.com

Member Since 2008

New York

Saratoga Springs

Innkeepers/Owners
The Smith Family

This award winning luxurious concierge hotel is in the heart of downtown Saratoga Springs. Step off its jewel of a wraparound porch to acclaimed restaurants, museums, shopping and colleges. Individually decorated rooms are designed with the guest's needs and comfort foremost, including 24-hour concierge service, individually controlled air and heat, free WiFi, luxurious bathrobes, bath amenities, high ceilings, fireplaces, double whirlpool tubs and in-room safes. The chef utilizes locally grown ingredients and changes the menu daily -- from breakfast to small plates and farm fresh eggs to tasty vegan. Saratoga Arms is perfect for executive conferences and meetings with state-of-the-art equipment and support. Custom décor in the 31 rooms and common areas, from traditional to contemporary, are updated yearly by a professional designer. Enjoy a full breakfast in the formal dining room or gather with guests for a glass of wine on the porch. The hotel offers on-site massages, facials, a 24-hour complimentary stocked snack pantry, business center and a fitness room.

Rates
$199-$379, Racing Season $379-$649. Cable TV, Individually controlled heat and air-conditioning, WiFi. Complimentary full breakfast. Open year round. Number of Rooms: 31

Cuisine
A full breakfast prepared by the on-site Culinary Institute of America chef utilizing farm fresh ingredients. Small plates are available in the afternoon as are wine, beer and champagne served on the porch, Walton Room by the fire, or in guest rooms.

Nearest Airport
Albany, NY (ALB) 28 miles; Saratoga (private) 3 miles.

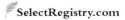
SelectRegistry.com

The Sherwood Inn

🍽️ 🍽️ 🍽️ 🍷

www.thesherwoodinn.com
26 West Genesee Street, Skaneateles, NY USA 13152
800-374-3796 • 315-685-3405 • Fax: 315-685-8983
info@thesherwoodinn.com

Member Since 1979

Owner
William B. Eberhardt

Built as a stagecoach stop in 1807, the Sherwood Inn has been a favorite resting place for travelers for over two centuries. The inn has been meticulously restored to the beauty of a bygone era with three wood burning fireplaces, antique furniture and fine wood detailing to create a relaxing harmony away from everyday cares. Our dining rooms, banquet rooms and many of our 25 guest rooms overlook beautiful Skaneateles Lake, creating an idyllic setting for any occasion. Guests of the Sherwood Inn enjoy casual lakeside dining and a menu rooted in classic American fare featuring local and regional ingredients. The restaurant also offers an impressive wine list featuring New York State wines. Recognized by the New York Times, Bon Appetit, Country Living, Harper's Bazaar, New Yorker and Wine Spectator magazines, the Sherwood Inn is one of the premiere destinations in New York's Finger Lakes Region.

Rates
$175/$295. Many rooms have fireplaces/whirlpool baths. Complimentary continental breakfast buffet is served daily. We are open year-round. Number of Rooms: 25

Cuisine
Casual, lakeside dining with a seasonally changing menu featuring the freshest seafood, finest steaks and chops, and the freshest locally grown produce is offered in the Sherwood Inn Tavern, Lakeview Porch and Main Dining Room. Serving Daily.

Nearest Airport
Syracuse (Hancock International)

ら |O| |O| ?

Taughannock Farms Inn

www.t-farms.com
2030 Gorge Road, Trumansburg, NY USA 14886
888-387-7711 • 607-387-7711 • Fax: 607-387-7721

Member Since 2002

Innkeepers/Owners
Tom & Susan Sheridan

Relax and enjoy a bygone era at this Victorian country inn. Majestically situated above Cayuga's waters, the inn offers commanding views of the lake. This Finger Lake's wine region landmark, built in 1873, is known for its gracious hospitality, abundant American cuisine, and charming accommodations. In addition to the five rooms in the Main inn that are furnished with antiques, we also have four guesthouses for a total of 23 rooms. Our newest guesthouse, Edgewood, has 10 rooms with either covered balconies or patios that have outstanding views of Cayuga Lake, and 4 king units featuring Jacuzzis. Savor a romantic dinner in the 150-seat fine dining restaurant overlooking the lake. The four-course meal features American cuisine and is complemented by wonderful Finger Lakes wines.

Rates
Main Inn rooms $115/$225. 3 Guesthouses $130/$235 per room. Full cottage $414/$584. Seasonal rates. Number of Rooms: 23

Cuisine
Expanded Continental breakfast of juice, coffee, fruit, breakfast pastries, cereal, yogurt and at least one hot item. Dinner includes appetizer, salad or sorbet, entree, and dessert. Banquets available.

Nearest Airport
Tompkins County Airport

F **SelectRegistry.com**

William Henry Miller Inn

www.MillerInn.com
303 North Aurora Street, At the corner of East Buffalo Street, Ithaca,
NY USA 14850
877-256-4553 • 607-256-4553 • Fax: 607-256-0092
millerinn@aol.com

Member Since 2003

New York Ithaca

Innkeeper/Owner
Lynnette Scofield

We would love for you to be our guest! There is so much to see and do in America's number one College Town and The William Henry Miller Inn is right in the heart of downtown Ithaca—close to Cornell University; Ithaca College; The Cayuga Wine Trail; The Finger Lakes and 150 waterfalls!

The inn, known as the centerpiece of downtown Ithaca, exhibits the best of a beautiful 1880 home with all the modern amenities. Tiffany stained glass amazes and chestnut woodwork is spectacular.

We proudly offer a full breakfast and all of our breads, English Muffins, bagels and jams are homemade. Guests love to linger over homemade desserts each evening and coffee and tea are always available.

Your comfortable bed will feature lovely linens that are all hand pressed. We do hope that will help to bring you a wonderful night's sleep.

Our Business Center will provide a comfortable and complete work center and our Guest Pantry is always available.

Whether traveling for business or pleasure, you'll quickly learn why "Ithaca is Gorges"!

Rates
$185/night to $280/night plus tax. Full breakfast, evening dessert, always available beverages, wireless and on site parking included. Our Aurora room is fully accessible and The Garner Suite is dog friendly. Number of Rooms: 9

Cuisine
Breakfast -- a choice of two main dishes is served during a two hour period. Homemade evening desserts and always available coffee and tea. Wonderful restaurants nearby including the world famous Moosewood. We gladly accommodate dietary requests.

Nearest Airport
Tompkins County (Ithaca) Airport is just ten minutes away. Syracuse is sixty-five minutes north.

North Carolina

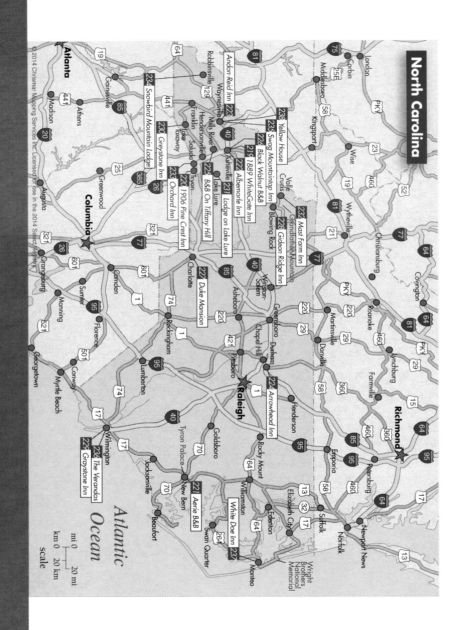

© 2014 Chrismar Mapping Services Inc. Licensed for use in the 2014 Select Registry

Map Labels

234 Snowbird Mountain Lodge
225 Andon-Reid Inn
238 Yellow House
235 Swag Mountaintop Inn
226 Black Walnut B&B
215 1889 WhiteGate Inn
222 Albemarle Inn
230 Greystone Inn
223 Orchard Inn
220 1906 Pine Crest Inn
231 Lodge on Lake Lure
228 B&B On Tiffany Hill
233 Mast Farm Inn
227 Gideon Ridge Inn
222 Duke Mansion
222 Arrowhead Inn
223 The Verandas
229 Graystone Inn
222 Aerie B&B
White Doe Inn 237

Cities and places

Atlanta
Atens
Madison
Gainesville
Corbin
London
Middlesboro
Kingsport
Robbinsville
Waynesville
Valle Crucis
Wise
Greenwood
Franklin
Saluda
Tryon
Asheville
Blowing Rock
Wytheville
Christiansburg
Augusta
Columbia
Greenwood
Lake Toxaway
Hendersonville
Winston-Salem
Asheboro
Greensboro
Chapel Hill
Durham
Martinsville
Danville
Roanoke
Covington
Orangeburg
Camden
Charlotte
Rockingham
Pittsboro
Henderson
Lynchburg
Farmville
Sumter
Lumberton
Raleigh
Rocky Mount
Emporia
Richmond
Manning
Florence
Goldsboro
Williamston
Edenton
Petersburg
Georgetown
Conway
Tyron Palace
New Bern
Elizabeth City
Suffolk
Norfolk
Newport News
Myrtle Beach
Wilmington
Jacksonville
Beaufort
Swan Quarter
Manteo
Wright Brothers National Memorial

Atlantic Ocean

scale
mi 0   20 mi
km 0   20 km

218

1889 WhiteGate Inn & Cottage

www.whitegate.net
173 East Chestnut Street, Asheville, NC USA 28801
800-485-3045 • 828-253-2553 • Fax: 828-281-1883
innkeeper@whitegate.net

Member Since 2005

North Carolina

Asheville

Owners/Innkeepers
Ralph Coffey and Frank Salvo

The historic 1889 WhiteGate Inn & Cottage is a AAA 4 Diamond property that tempts travelers with the delightful charm of an historic Asheville Bed and Breakfast and the luxurious amenities of a boutique hotel. For couples craving a romantic Asheville getaway or those seeking serenity in a long weekend, our inn offers a respite from the distractions of everyday life. A sumptuous 3 course breakfast begins each day. Wander the stunning award winning gardens or stroll through the downtown shops, galleries and restaurants. Enjoy hors d'oeuvres and beverages served every evening in the garden or the solarium. Treat yourself, or you and a loved one, to the ultimate in luxury when staying in one of our Carriage House suites. Complete handicapped accessible suite available. 1 & 2 bedroom Bungalow suites offer ultimate privacy including a full kitchen. In-room couples massage and spa treatments available by appointment. Our fitness room offers workout equipment and a dry sauna. Pet friendly units are available.

Rates
$159/$379. Separate cottages with full kitchens, on site orchid greenhouse, gym, dry sauna. Some Pet Friendly rooms, complete ADA suite available. No Smoking on property or guests under 18 years old. Number of Rooms: 11

Cuisine
3 Course Gourmet Breakfast, complimentary hors d'oeuvres and wine served each evening in the garden, weather permitting, 24 hour cakes, cookies, pastries made fresh in house, fresh fruit, and hot and cold beverages.
Picnic baskets by order.

Nearest Airport
Asheville

 ♿ 🍽 🍽 🍽 🍷

1906 Pine Crest Inn & Restaurant

www.pinecrestinn.com
85 Pine Crest Lane, Tryon, NC USA 28782
800-633-3001 • 828-859-9135 • Fax: 828-859-9136
select@pinecrestinn.com

Member Since 1991

Innkeeper/Owner
Carl Caudle

Imagine 250-year old cabins so captivating that they inspired literary greats F. Scott Fitzgerald and Ernest Hemingway. Or pamper yourself with a Jacuzzi tub, a massage, artisan cheese and a bottle of wine with a dozen roses. Tranquility and relaxation await you in any of our 32 romantic rooms, suites or private cottages on our beautifully landscaped 10-acre property. Art and antique shopping, golf, waterfall hikes and winery tours, white water rafting, drives along the Blue Ridge Parkway, The Biltmore Estate...these experiences and more can be found at our distinctive retreat just south of Asheville.

Renowned for our "Best Breakfast in the Southeast," exceptional fine dining, and celebrity wine dinners. Recognized in Southern Living, Fodor's, Our State Magazine, and on the National Register of Historic Places. Romance packages, destination weddings, reunions, or executive retreats in our conference center can all be managed with ease by our professional staff. Our guests create memories that will last a lifetime.

Rates
20 Rooms $99-$229; 8 Suites $179-$279; 4 Cottages $189-$599. Seasonal specials and packages are available. Number of Rooms: 32

Cuisine
Sumptuous, made-to-order 3-course breakfast... that can be served in bed! Distinctive a la carte dinner menu with regional accents, organic ingredients & fresh herbs from our gardens. Afternoon tea, award-winning wine list, & evening port and sherry.

Nearest Airport
Asheville, NC (AVL), Greenville, SC (GSP), Charlotte, NC (CLT)

The Aerie Bed & Breakfast

www.aeriebedandbreakfast.com
509 Pollock Street, New Bern, NC USA 28562
800-849-5553 • 252-636-5553 • Fax: 252-514-2157
info@aeriebedandbreakfast.com

Member Since 2008

North Carolina New Bern

Innkeepers/Owners
Michael and Marty Gunhus

Two Beautiful Buildings...One Bed & Breakfast...The historic Street-Ward residence, circa 1882, is home to New Bern's premiere B&B. An inviting welcome pervades the inn as staff surrounds guests with detailed service, striking the perfect balance between personal attention and individual freedom. Nine delightfully distinctive guest rooms are ready to pamper with private baths, luxurious linens and exquisite furnishings. We offer a variety of packages to include romantic getaways, relaxing spa services, fun water activities on our twin rivers, and our "Walk To Remember" package focused on local author, Nicholas Sparks.

Period antiques complement modern amenities such as cable TV/DVD/CD players, highspeed WiFi, and a state-of-the-art conference center with reception area. Consider The Aerie Guest House & Conference Center when planning business meetings, special events, weddings or receptions. The Aerie can accommodate every need. Since 2003, The Aerie has the distinction of being awarded "Simply The Best" more times than any other bed and breakfast in the region.

Rates
Nine rooms/suites, some including jetted tubs and spa showers. Sunday-Thursday $129-$209/night, Friday-Saturday $149-$229/night. 2-night minimums on weekends, holidays, and special events. Please call for special corporate rates. Number of Rooms: 9

Cuisine
A gourmet breakfast features a menu that changes daily, and guests may choose between three delicious hot-entree selections. Evening social hour with wine, hors d'oeuvres. Complimentary coffee, soft drinks, bottled water, and ice are available 24/7.

Nearest Airport
New Bern (EWN), Raleigh (RDU)

♿ 🍽 ♟
Albemarle Inn

www.albemarleinn.com
86 Edgemont Road, Asheville, NC USA 28801
800-621-7435 • 828-255-0027 • Fax: 828-575-9313
info@albemarleinn.com

Member Since 2002

North Carolina

Asheville

AAA
Four Diamond
♦♦♦ ♦♦♦ ♦♦♦
Award

Innkeepers/Owners
Fabrizio & Rosemary Chiariello

The Albemarle Inn is a quiet, romantic mansion located in the Grove Park district of Asheville. Built in 1907 for one of Asheville's prominent families, the Reynolds, the inn is listed on the National Register of Historic Places. Enjoy gracious hospitality and romantic timeless appeal during your stay. The Albemarle offers 11 unique and elegant guest rooms. Our first floor rooms, with original wide oak pocket doors, offer modern spa-like bathrooms. The sweeping grand staircase with ornate woodwork leads to the upper floor guestrooms, with romantic canopy or sleigh beds, some with fireplaces and jetted tubs, all with fine linens and duvets. In evenings guests enjoy relaxing on the grand stone veranda with its impressive Corinthian columns overlooking our gardens. Just minutes away are Asheville's vibrant downtown, the Biltmore Estate & the Blue Ridge Parkway. Guests can indulge & relax with our mini-spa treatment packages. Our Italian cooking class weekends offer food & fun! A 3-course breakfast is served daily. Ideal for meetings, private parties, elopements & weddings.

Rates
$175/$395. Rates vary with season and depend on room types and amenities. Some rooms have spa-like showers, some period claw-foot tubs, some jetted tubs. Specials and seasonal and holiday packages offered. Corporate and group rates. Number of Rooms: 11

Cuisine
A 3-course seasonal, fresh & creative breakfast served daily. Weekend Social Hour. Dietary requests gladly accommodated. 24 hour guest pantry. Picnic meals available. Luncheons, teas, showers & parties can be arranged. Italian cooking class weekends.

Nearest Airport
Asheville/Hendersonvillle Airport (AVL) - 16 miles

SelectRegistry.com

Andon-Reid Inn Bed & Breakfast

www.andonreidinn.com
92 Daisy Avenue, Waynesville, NC USA 28786
828-452-3089 • 800-293-6190
info@andonreidinn.com

Member Since 2011

North Carolina   Waynesville

Innkeeper
Mark Barbar

Experience Southern hospitality in our meticulously restored turn-of-the-century bed and breakfast, originally constructed in 1902. Welcome to a special place where you can lose yourself in our mountain views and find some much needed relaxation. We are an excellent choice for your romantic getaway, outdoor fun or just an escape to the mountains.

Our award winning bed and breakfast has six beautifully appointed guest rooms, all with private baths, fireplaces, glorious views and many distinctive features that will contribute to your comfort, relaxation, and romance. Take advantage of our complete fitness studio, recreation room and sauna. Relax on our wraparound porch or enjoy a glass of wine while sitting under the stars around our fire pit and new patio.

Situated in a residential area, we are surrounded by the Great Smoky Mountains, Blue Ridge Parkway and Pisgah National Forest. The quaint town of Waynesville is only a short walk from our bed and breakfast and is filled with an array of art studios, galleries, outstanding restaurants and antique shops.

Rates
Rooms range from $145-$155 and our luxurious suites are $185-$195. This includes breakfast, complimentary hot and cold beverages, snacks and freshly baked afternoon desserts. It also includes the use of the fun recreation room. Number of Rooms: 6

Cuisine
Our relaxing breakfast is not to be missed! We have a special blend juice and a first course like poached pears to get started. Menus change daily with entrees such as a mushroom and ham frittata, lemon ricotta pancakes or deliciously filled crepes.

Nearest Airport
Asheville Regional (AVL)

Arrowhead Inn

www.arrowheadinn.com
106 Mason Road, Durham, NC USA 27712
919-477-8430 • 800-528-2207 • Fax: 919-471-9538
info@arrowheadinn.com

Member Since 2003

North Carolina
Durham

Innkeepers/Owners
Phil & Gloria Teber

Relax in the quiet comfort of our 18th Century plantation home. The inn rests on six acres of stunning gardens and lawns amid venerable magnolia and pecan trees. Each of our elegant guest rooms, Carolina Log Cabin and Garden Cottage provide a serene respite with the amenities of a fine hotel. The Arrowhead Inn, circa 1775, has been carefully renovated retaining original moldings, mantelpieces, and heart-of-pine floors. Watch hummingbirds flutter on flowering hibiscus while relaxing with friends on our sun-warmed patio. Drift off for an afternoon nap next to your cozy fireplace. Unwind in your private whirlpool tub while enjoying fine wine & delicacies. Slip into your luxurious soft terry robe after refreshing yourself in a soothing steam shower. Awake to the delight of our abundant breakfast. Savor the cuisine of our fine inn dining, along with Durham's nationally famous chefs and restaurants. The Arrowhead Inn welcomes you for peaceful and romantic getaways, family & friend gatherings, and business retreats. Our Tiffany Gazebo provides a lovely setting for small weddings.

Rates
Rooms & Suites in Manor House $159-$269. Cottage & Log Cabin $269-$329. Rates include full breakfast & afternoon refreshments. Seasonal specials & packages available. Working fireplaces, whirlpool tubs, steam showers and free WiFi. Number of Rooms: 9

Cuisine
Delicious gourmet breakfast: puffed soufflé, ricotta pancakes, fresh vegetable quiche, glazed scones, & fresh fruit. Chef/Owner prepares mouth-watering tasting dinners served in romantic setting or in the privacy of your suite. Fine wine & beer cellar.

Nearest Airport
Raleigh/Durham International Airport (RDU). Thirty-minute drive to the inn.

SelectRegistry.com

Bed & Breakfast on Tiffany Hill

♿ 🍽

www.BBonTiffanyHill.com
400 Ray Hill Rd, Mills River, NC USA 28759
828-290-6080
vacation@BBonTiffanyHill.com

Member Since 2010

North Carolina

Mills River

Innkeeper/Proprietor
Selena Einwechter

Casual Elegance filled with Southern Hospitality is what we have created at the Bed & Breakfast on Tiffany Hill. Newly constructed in 2009, Tiffany Hill is situated on 6 acres of beautiful gardens nestled in the mountains of Western NC. Conveniently located just south of Asheville & the Biltmore Estate, we are 5 minutes to the new Sierra Nevada Brewery, 10 minutes to the Asheville Regional Airport, 15 minutes to either Brevard or Hendersonville and minutes from Dupont State Forest as well as the Pisgah National Forest.

On Tiffany Hill, each suite is specifically designed from one of our favorite southern towns. Suites include private baths, 7 layer beds, flat Screen TV/DVD players, wireless hi-speed Internet access, piped-in music, luxurious robes, writing desks, keyless entry and 24 hour access to complimentary beverages and snacks. Second floor suites & Carriage House have individual temperature controls. Your stay comes with breakfast for 2 each morning and lots of southern hospitality. Come do as much or as little as you like on Tiffany Hill!

Rates
Tiffany Hill is open year round. Rates range from $185 to $275 per night before taxes. Madison - $185; Natchez - $195; Beaufort - $215; Seaside - $225; Charlottesville - $245; Mountain Brook Suite - $255; Lexington Suite - $275 Number of Rooms: 7

Cuisine
Join us for breakfast at Tiffany's and experience a seasonal 3 course gourmet breakfast. Let us know if it is your anniversary & we will make it candlelit. Happy to accommodate individual breakfast dietary requests. Breakfast to go is also available.

Nearest Airport
Asheville Regional - 10 minutes; Greenville, South Carolina - 45 minutes Charlotte, North Carolina - 2 hours

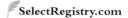

♿ 🍽 Black Walnut Bed & Breakfast

www.blackwalnut.com
288 Montford Avenue, Asheville, NC USA 28801
800-381-3878 • 828-254-3878
info@blackwalnut.com

Member Since 2007

North Carolina

Asheville

Innkeepers/Owners
Peter & Lori White

The perfect in-town location in the heart of the Historic District of Montford. Within walking distance to the shops, restaurants and galleries of the city. Surrounded by manicured gardens and waterfall Koi ponds. Relax in the rockers on the porch, or the terrace when the weather is fair, or enjoy a fire in one of the 11 fireplaces. All guest rooms are complete with private bath en-suite and King or Queen luxury kingsdown mattresses, most with working fireplaces. Fresh flowers, chocolates and luxury bedding compliment the antiques. Indulge in a gourmet 3-course breakfast with homemade pastries, fruit and hot entree. Your innkeepers have more than 50 years of experience as professional bakers and chefs! In the late afternoon, relax with complimentary fine wines and hors d'oeuvres with your hosts. We are always happy to help with suggestions, recommendations and reservations!

Rates
6 rooms in the main house, 2 pet-friendly suites located in the carriage house.
$185/$325. Full breakfast, complimentary beverages, WiFi, computer station,
afternoon tea included. Off season rates available. Open all Year. Number of Rooms: 8

Cuisine
Decadent 3 course breakfasts. Afternoon tea with selection of fine wines and hot and
cold hors d'oeuvres, homemade pastries. 24 hour complimentary beverages.

Nearest Airport
Asheville (AVL)

SelectRegistry.com

The Duke Mansion

www.dukemansion.com
400 Hermitage Road, Charlotte, NC USA 28207
888-202-1009 • 704-714-4400 • Fax: 704-714-4435
frontdesk@dukemansion.org

Member Since 2005

North Carolina Charlotte

General Manager
Becky Farris

The Duke Mansion, built in 1915 and listed on the National Register of Historic Places, offers 20 unique guest rooms in true Southern splendor with a full breakfast. The rooms are residential in their decor, and appointed with beautiful artwork and furnishings, giving you a breathtaking image of what it was like to be a member of the prestigious Duke family who made The Mansion their home. All rooms have queen or king sized beds, private baths, exquisite linens, luxurious robes, and a gourmet goodnight treat. The Mansion is an integral part of Charlotte's most prestigious and beautiful neighborhood, and is situated on four and a half acres of beautiful grounds, just two miles south of Center City Charlotte. Its professional culinary staff and beautiful public rooms can accommodate family or business celebrations of 10-300 guests. When you select The Duke Mansion, you are supporting a nonprofit where all of the proceeds are used to preserve and protect it.

Rates
$187-$279, including breakfast, plus tax. Special seasonal rates also available.
Number of Rooms: 20

Cuisine
Full-time onsite professional culinary staff featuring New South cuisine. A deluxe made to order breakfast is included with every guest room.

Nearest Airport
Charlotte-Douglas International Airport, 20 minutes

Gideon Ridge Inn

www.gideonridge.com
202 Gideon Ridge Rd., P.O. Box 1929, Blowing Rock, NC USA 28605
888-889-4036 • 828-295-3644 • Fax: 828-295-4586
Innkeeper@gideonridge.com

Member Since 1990

North Carolina

Blowing Rock

Innkeepers/Owners
Cindy & Cobb Milner

Gideon Ridge Inn is ten delightful guest rooms with mountain breezes, French doors and stone terraces. Ceiling fans and wicker chairs. Antiques and good books. Bedrooms with warm fireplaces and comfortable sitting areas. Crisp cotton bed linens and well-appointed bathrooms. Suites with whirlpool tubs and king beds. Fine breakfasts to linger over. Afternoon tea with fresh-baked shortbread to savor. Evening dining at the Restaurant, where guests and local residents enjoy farm to table fresh ingredients prepared by Chef Michael Foreman in the classic style. And in the library, a piano with a breathtaking view of the mountains. Really.....

Guests enjoy hiking and walking the Blue Ridge Parkway. Golf at nearby clubs. Shopping and dining at Blowing Rock Village shops & restaurants. Biking in summer and skiing in winter. Or just sitting on our beautiful stone terrace and enjoying the cool mountain air.

Rates
3 Deluxe Suites with king bed and separate sitting area. 3 Terrace Rooms with private stone terrace. 9 rooms have fireplaces. 4 have whirlpools. All rooms B&B. A/C
$155/$375. Open year-round. Number of Rooms: 10

Cuisine
Full breakfast included, featuring our apple cornmeal pancakes, blueberry-stuffed French toast or other signature entrees. Afternoon tea with fresh-made shortbread cookies or scones. Dinner served Tues.-Sat. Cocktails and full wine list.

Nearest Airport
Charlotte, NC, 1.5 hours, (CLT); Greensboro, NC, 2 hours, (GSO)

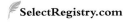
SelectRegistry.com

Graystone Inn

www.graystoneinn.com
100 South 3rd Street, Wilmington, NC USA 28401
888-763-4773 • 910-763-2000 • Fax: 910-763-5555
contactus@graystoneinn.com

Member Since 2005

North Carolina

Wilmington

Innkeepers/Owners
Rich & Marcia Moore

The Graystone Inn, one of the most elegant historical structures in Wilmington, is located in the heart of the historic district and just three blocks from shopping, fine dining and the River Walk. The Graystone, originally the "Bridgers Mansion," was built as a private residence in 1905 by Elizabeth Haywood Bridgers and is an excellent representation of the neo-classical revival style. Each elegantly decorated bedroom has its own private bath, telephones with voice-mail and data port, WiFi and cable TV. All rooms contain period furnishings, exquisite draperies and fine pima cotton linens, towels and robes. Intricately carved fireplaces grace seven of the nine bedrooms. The Graystone has frequently been used as a set for motion pictures and television and lists many notable personalities among its guests.

Rates
6 rooms $159/$269. 3 Jr. suites $209/$369. Two night weekends. Open year round.
Number of Rooms: 9

Cuisine
Full gourmet breakfast prepared by chef-owner. Early morning coffee bar.
Complimentary beverages. Evening wine.

Nearest Airport
Wilmington International

& 🍽️ 🍽️ 🍽️ 🍷

The Greystone Inn

www.greystoneinn.com
220 Greystone Lane, Lake Toxaway, NC USA 28747
800-587-5351 • 828-966-4700 • Fax: 828-862-5689
info@greystoneinn.com

Member Since 1991

North Carolina

Lake Toxaway

Owner
Reg Heinitsh, Jr.

All of the intimacies of a charming & historic inn are combined with the luxurious amenities of a full service resort at The Greystone Inn. Our AAA Four Diamond rated property is situated on the shores of North Carolina's largest private lake in the heart of the Blue Ridge Mountains, and is an ideal setting for those looking to truly get away from it all. Highlights include a pampering spa, lake activities, a new Kris Spence designed golf course, tennis, croquet, a fitness center, and more. Of course, our signature amenity is our daily Champagne cruise aboard our 26-passenger mahogany launch "Miss Lucy". Each guestroom is unique with amenities that include gas and wood fireplaces, private porches, lake views, Jacuzzi bathtubs, wet bars and more. We pride ourselves on attentive and personal service – our goal is to make folks feel like guests in our home. We hope to see you soon!

Rates
Rooms & Suites ranging from $350-$600. Rate includes MAP meals, tennis, croquet, canoe/kayaks, fitness center, our daily Champagne cruise, and more. Spa, Golf, Romance, and Hiking Packages are available. Number of Rooms: 31

Cuisine
A full breakfast, afternoon tea & treats, hors d'oeuvres, and a six-course dinner are included in our Modified American Plan (MAP) rates. A la carte lunch is available at the adjacent country club. We have a full bar and an extensive wine list.

Nearest Airport
Asheville (AVL)

SelectRegistry.com

Lodge on Lake Lure

www.lodgeonlakelure.com
361 Charlotte Dr., Lake Lure, NC USA 28746
828-625-2789
info@lodgeonlakelure.com

Member Since 2003

Innkeeper
Susie Zimmerman

Situated between Charlotte, Asheville and Greenville at the entrance of Hickory Nut
Gorge lies the historic 1930s Lodge, the only Waterfront B&B on the Lake. It offers
sweeping views and complete tranquility on a secluded peninsula at the center of the lake.
Guests often tell us why they love to return here. Each room with its own personality and
thoughtful décor makes them feel like they are coming home. Enjoy the Lake from the top
of our boathouse, canoe to explore the quiet coves and breathtaking views, a late afternoon
pontoon ride or hike one of the well marked trails. Biltmore, Du Pont Forest and Chimney
Rock Park are easy drives away. Let us pack you a delicious sandwich for your excursion
and return for a glass of wine at mingling hour before joining us in The Tree Tops Dining
Room during sunset for a mouth watering dinner to end a perfect day. For your next
seminar, intimate wedding, business meeting or family reunion, we offer meeting rooms
in a relaxed setting and free WiFi. Our Spa facilities include a hot tub and our specialized
therapists await your call.

Rates
$135 to $310 Most rooms with private balconies and lakeviews; 11 w/fireplace;
Superior Rooms with relaxing panaramic lake views from the bath tub as well;
complimentaty high-speed WiFi. Number of Rooms: 17

Cuisine
Dedicated to the pleasures of good food, we combine our passion for SOUTHERN
CUISINE with Continental flair.

Nearest Airport
Greenville SC, Asheville NC, Charlotte NC.

& 🍽 🍽 ⚲

The Mast Farm Inn

www.MastFarmInn.com
2543 Broadstone Road, P.O. Box 704, Valle Crucis, NC USA 28691
888-963-5857 • 828-963-5857 • Fax: 828-963-6404
stay@mastfarminn.com   *Member Since 1988*

Innkeepers/Owners
Sandra Siano and Danielle Deschamps

The Mast Farm Inn is more than a bed and breakfast, with inn rooms, private getaway
cottages, fine dining and great wines, organic gardens, and unique gifts that complete our
historic country appeal. The key to the Inn's success, however, lies in the exceptionally
friendly and caring service offered to lodging and dinner guests alike. With inspired
restoration and continuing care, the inn continues to welcome guests, as it did over 100
years ago. Choose from eight guest rooms in our 1880s farmhouse and seven cottages,
some restored from original farm buildings. Cottages range in size from cozy ones suitable
for a couple to large ones for up to six guests. All are unique spaces. The Inn's restaurant
is celebrated, enjoyed by lodging guests and locals. The service is attentive, yet relaxed and
friendly. Enjoy fireside or terrace dining, depending on the season. The current innkeepers
place special emphasis on the environment, creating a "green" inn where recycling,
reducing waste, and buying organic produce locally are taken seriously.

Rates
8 guest rooms: $145/$250. 7 private cottages: $225/$450. Number of Rooms: 15

Cuisine
Full 2-course gourmet breakfast included with lodging. Dinner features fresh, organic
delightfully creative cuisine. Dining schedule varies seasonally. Fine wines and beer
available. Private parties.

Nearest Airport
Greensboro (GSO) or Charlotte (CLT)

The Orchard Inn

www.orchardinn.com
100 Orchard Inn Lane, on Rt 176, Saluda, NC USA 28773
800-581-3800 • 828-749-5471
innkeeper@orchardinn.com

Member Since 1985

North Carolina Saluda

Innkeepers/Owners
Marc & Marianne Blazar

Located just 30 miles south of Asheville in the foothills of the Blue Ridge Mountains, the rest of the world melts away the moment you enter the long winding driveway and approach our elegant mountain top escape, comfortably nestled on 12 peaceful acres. All rooms have private bathrooms and are furnished with period pieces and antiques. Cozy cottages feature fireplaces, whirlpools and private decks. Our ultra luxurious linens and cool fresh mountain air are a perfect recipe for a great night's sleep. Enjoy award-winning cuisine in our fine dining restaurant which overlooks the organic garden, vineyard, orchard and surrounding mountains. Hike nearby trails and waterfalls; fly fish native trout streams; paddle the nationally acclaimed Green River; schedule a massage or yoga class; play golf on a private course; zip line the amazing Gorge canopy adventure; visit the Biltmore Estate, Carl Sandburg home or local craft galleries in historic Saluda; then experience the peace & tranquility of this gracious historic, romantic inn. An ideal setting for weddings and corporate retreats.

Rates
9 Rooms, $145/$245 B&B; 5 Cottages, $210/$595 B&B. All rooms have private baths, some w/ gas fireplaces, whirlpool & steam shower. Ultra luxurious linens and towels. Many rooms have spectacular mountain views. Number of Rooms: 14

Cuisine
Full gourmet breakfast included in room rate. Award-winning European inspired cuisine served Thurs-Sat evenings, featuring farm to table fresh local produce. Fine wine & beer. Listed as a "Food Find" by Southern Living. Member Chaîne des Rôtisseurs.

Nearest Airport
Asheville (AVL) 25 min, Greenville (GSP) 45 min, Charlotte (CLT) 90 min.

Snowbird Mountain Lodge

🍽️ 🍽️ 🍽️ 🍷

www.snowbirdlodge.com
4633 Santeetlah Rd., Robbinsville, NC USA 28771
800-941-9290 • 828-479-3433 • Fax: 828-479-3473
innkeeper@snowbirdlodge.com

Member Since 1973

North Carolina

Robbinsville

Innkeeper/Owner
Robert Rankin

High up in Santeetlah Gap, on the Southern border of the Great Smoky Mountains National Park, lies this secluded, rustic yet elegant, historic lodge built of stone and huge chestnut logs. Offering the finest in modern convenience and traditional comfort, Snowbird is the perfect retreat from the pressures of a busy world. The view from the lovely mountaintop terrace is one of the best in the Smokies. An excellent library, huge stone fireplaces, tennis courts and hiking trails on 100 acres of forest with numerous "quiet getaway" spots, offer guests a rare chance to relax. Award-winning gourmet cuisine and a lovely fireside bar with an exceptionally well-stocked wine cellar will have you looking forward to your next meal. Whether it's fly-fishing, hiking, biking, or just relaxing in front of the fire, we can make your next trip to the mountains picture-perfect. It's no wonder that guests have been coming to Snowbird to relax and renew themselves for over 60 years.

Rates
$275-$385 FAP. In-room fireplaces, air conditioning, whirlpool tubs, steam showers and private hot tubs available. Number of Rooms: 23

Cuisine
Full gourmet breakfast, packed picnic lunch and four course gourmet dinner.

Nearest Airport
Knoxville, Atlanta

The Swag Mountaintop Inn

🍴 🍴 🍴

www.theswag.com
2300 Swag Road, Waynesville, NC USA 28785
800-789-7672 • 828-926-0430 • Fax: 828-926-2036
brooks@theswag.com

Member Since 1991

North Carolina

Waynesville

General Manager
Brooks Bradbury

The place where stress disappears has an address...30 miles west of Asheville, North Carolina. The Swag Mountaintop Inn is an intimate hideaway that invites you to discover the wonders of nature just steps from your bedroom. The Swag is where nature meets the luxury getaway. An old split rail fence boundary with the Great Smoky Mountains National Park borders the inn's property and stretches for more than a mile. The spectacular beauty of the Appalachian high country is captured architecturally in our historic hand-hewn logs and local field stone design. The construction was inspired by the past while built for the future. This hidden and secluded mountaintop setting at 5,000 feet in elevation reveals to you well-marked nature trails that crowds have yet to find. It begins to unfold at the bottom of our driveway where the pavement ends, and the gate opens...your romantic adventure begins. The Swag -- an award-winning luxury mountaintop inn -- capturing the Appalachians as they used to be.

Rates
8 Rooms $495/$750; 6 Cabins/Suites $760/$875. All inclusive. Open mid-April through November. Number of Rooms: 14

Cuisine
A not-to-be-missed hors d'oeuvre hour precedes our superb four-course meal nightly. All three meals are included for two guests in the room rate. The Swag does not sell wine and spirits, guests are welcome to bring their own.

Nearest Airport
Asheville, NC (AVL)

The Verandas

www.verandas.com
202 Nun Street, Wilmington, NC USA 28401
910-251-2212 • Fax: 910-251-8932
verandas4@aol.com

Member Since 2001

Owners
Dennis Madsen and Chuck Pennington

Towering above a quiet tree-lined street in the historic district stands this grand antebellum mansion. Built in 1854, the 13 year award-winning Inn is a blend of history, luxury, charm and hospitality. Guest space abounds with wonderful colors, original art, French and English antiques. Four verandas, garden terrace and cupola offer hideaways. Professionally decorated guestrooms have sitting areas, telephone, cable TV. Hand-ironed linens dress comfortable beds. Baths have soaking tubs, showers, marble floors, luxury amenities and robes. French pressed coffee with a gourmet breakfast. Complimentary beverages and snacks and social wine hour. Walking distance to the Riverwalk and restaurants and shopping. High speed wireless Internet. Enjoy The Verandas - "An Inn Second to Nun!"

Rates
All Corner Rooms $169/$269. Two-nights minimum on weekends Dec., Jan., Feb., special: 3 nights for two. Number of Rooms: 8

Cuisine
Included with the room rate is a full gourmet breakfast with French pressed coffee served in our beautiful dining room. Complimentary beverages and snacks are available and white wine is served in the evening.

Nearest Airport
Wilmington International

White Doe Inn

www.whitedoeinn.com
319 Sir Walter Raleigh Street, P.O. Box 1029, Manteo, NC USA 27954
800-473-6091 • 252-473-9851 • Fax: 252-473-4708
whitedoe@whitedoeinn.com   *Member Since 2005*

Proprietors
Robert & Bebe Woody

The White Doe Inn is situated in the quaint coastal waterfront village of Manteo on Roanoke Island, which we believe is the best part of the Outer Banks of North Carolina. Luxury lodging, quality service, and a piece of the island life await you here. Centrally located, it's the perfect place to take advantage of all that the Outer Banks has to offer. Guests come from near and far to experience gracious hospitality in this lovely historic Victorian home. The inn offers a four course complimentary breakfast each morning, afternoon & evening refreshments, bicycles for our guests, concierge services, WiFi and much more. The Inn's staff is available to make reservations or to arrange the purchase of advance tickets to events and activities. The White Doe Inn is listed on the National Register of Historic Places and is noted for its historic and architectural significance. The inn is also a member of the North Carolina Bed & Breakfast Inns and the Professional Association of Innkeepers International.

Rates
Off: $210/$315, Mid: $225/$335, In: $275/$380. All rooms have fireplaces. 1 Suite with king bed, sitting area, wet bar; 4 balcony rooms, 5 rooms with whirlpools/ soaking tubs. Number of Rooms: 8

Cuisine
Join us as we serve a four course breakfast daily in our dining room. Weather permitting we serve outside on the veranda. Glad to accommodate individual breakfast dietary requests. Continental to go is also available.

Nearest Airport
Norfolk Int'l Airport (ORF) 2 Hours, Raleigh/Durham Int'l Airport (RDU) 3 Hours

The Yellow House on Plott Creek Road

www.theyellowhouse.com
89 Oakview Drive, Waynesville, NC USA 28786
800-563-1236 • 828-452-0991
info@theyellowhouse.com

Member Since 1998

North Carolina

Waynesville

General Managers
Don Cerise/Shawn Bresnahan

A European-style inn of casual elegance, the 19th century Yellow House accents
fine service in a romantic, intimate setting. Located a mile from the lovely mountain
community of Waynesville, NC, the inn sits atop a knoll 3,000 feet above sea level.
Five beautifully landscaped acres of lawns and gardens feature two ponds, a waterfall, a
footbridge and a deck. The inn offers three rooms and seven suites, each with luxury linens,
private bath, gas fireplace, coffee service, refrigerator and bathrobes; suites also have wet
bar and 2-person jetted tub. Most rooms include private balcony or patio. The Inn offers a
quiet rural setting with exceptional views, soothing music, and free wireless Internet service
for guests. Minutes from the Blue Ridge Parkway, Smoky Mountains National Park, Pisgah
Forest, Cherokee Reservation, horseback riding and ski area, and Maggie Valley. Close to 4
mountain golf courses, Asheville and the Biltmore Estate. Voted by Lanierbb.com as BEST
INN for changing of leaves for 2011. A "place you must see" by North Carolina's "Our
State Magazine" 10/2012.

Rates
3 Rooms, 7 Suites, $165-$265. Weekly specials, week day rates, Seasonal Rates and
Packages Available. Entire Inn can be rented for weddings, reunions and business
retreats. Number of Rooms: 10

Cuisine
Gourmet breakfast each morning served en suite, on private balcony, veranda or
dining room depending on accommodation; sweets always and appetizers each
evening. Picnic lunches and Chocolate covered strawberries can be arranged with
prior notice.

Nearest Airport
Asheville (AVL), Greenville/Spartanburg (GSP), Knoxville (TYS)

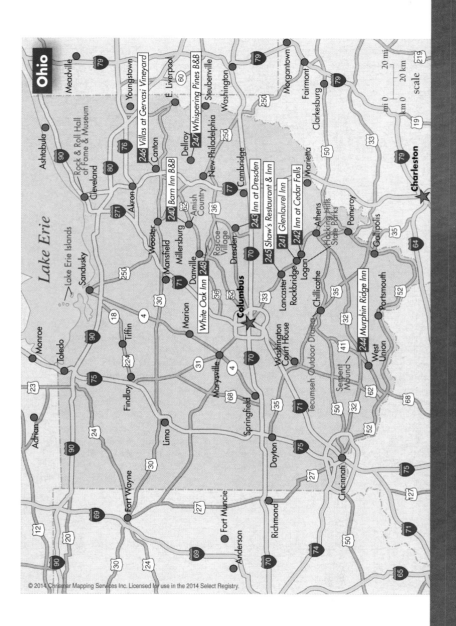

Ohio

Lake Erie

Lake Erie Islands

246 *Villas at Gervasi Vineyard*

247 *Whispering Pines B&B*

240 *Barn Inn B&B*

243 *Inn at Dresden*

245 *Shaw's Restaurant & Inn*

241 *Glenlaurel Inn*

242 *Inn at Cedar Falls*

248 *White Oak Inn*

244 *Murphin Ridge Inn*

Columbus

20 mi
20 km
scale

© 2014 Chrismar Mapping Services Inc. Licensed for use in the 2014 Select Registry.

♿ 🍽 🍷

The Barn Inn Bed and Breakfast

www.thebarninn.com
6838 County Road 203, Millersburg, OH USA 44654
330-674-7600 • Fax: 330-674-0761
reservations@thebarninn.com

Member Since 2013

Innkeepers/Owners
Paul & Loretta Coblentz

Recipient of numerous national and state awards for excellence in hospitality, which include Top 10 Worldwide and Best Innkeeper by bedandbreakfast.com, The Barn Inn offers fine accommodations, spa packages, hot country breakfasts, and authentic hospitality in unspoiled Ohio Amish country, a region rich in old-world traditions. Make this home base as you tour the area's unique businesses and attractions, where a people group have maintained their distinct European origins and where days of touring and shopping opportunities abound. Enjoy the sights and sounds of horse and carriage travel, and the tapestry of harvest fields and rolling hills. Return to the comfort and privacy of the inn where modern-day appointments await you; fireplaces, whirlpool tubs, balconies, free WiFi, satellite TV, DVD library, climate control, and complimentary evening snacks. Make it a memorable stay with a couples massage or any other spa service available.

Rates
The inn has several types of rooms and accommodations ranging from $119 to $219. Number of Rooms: 11

Cuisine
Each morning's complimentary breakfast always includes fresh fruit cups, several hot entrees, homemade breads, locally-made sausage, juices, and other options. We are pleased to cook for dietary restrictions with prior notice.

Nearest Airport
Akron Canton airport is approximately one hour away. Millersburg Airport, 7 miles, can accommodate smaller planes.

Glenlaurel, A Scottish Country Inn

🍽️ 🍽️ 🍽️ 🍷

www.glenlaurel.com
14940 Mount Olive Road, Rockbridge, OH USA 43149
740-385-4070 • Fax: 740-385-9669
info@glenlaurel.com

Member Since 1998

Innkeeper
Sabrina McCartt

Sometimes at dinner, the story is told of how Glenlaurel was first imagined- 300 years ago in the heart of the Scottish Highlands. Today, the heavily wooded 140-acre estate has the look of the old world, a veil of romance, and a pace of times gone by. Whether in the stately Manor House, the nearby Carriage House, or one of the crofts or cottages, luxury abounds with sumptuous fine dining, hot tub frolics, intimate fireside secrets, hiking through our Camusfearna Gorge, and a round of golf on our Scottish Links course- as it was played 100 years ago! The old-world elegance of the Inn and the secluded, peaceful setting are ideal for romantic nights for two, peaceful getaways for one, intimate weddings, and small group events. Our Anniversary Club honors a successful marriage, year after year; so make Glenlaurel your anniversary destination. You will undoubtedly enjoy an extra level of comfort while admiring our refined decor & spaciousness.

Rates
3 Rooms $189/$239, 3 Suites $219/$289, 7 Crofts $249/$319, 6 Cottages $299/$369. Open year-round. Number of Rooms: 19

Cuisine
Dinner is "a private invitation to dine at an estate house in the country" with social time, greetings from your host, and a candlelit culinary adventure-in the European tradition.

Nearest Airport
Port Columbus Airport (CMH) - 55 minutes. Onsite helipad.

ᕕ ᕮᕤᕥ ᕮᕤᕥ ᕮᕤᕥ ᖴ

Inn & Spa At Cedar Falls

http://innatcedarfalls.com
21190 State Route 374, Logan, OH USA 43138
800-653-2557 • 740-385-7489 • Fax: 740-385-0820
info@innatcedarfalls.com

Member Since 1989

Ohio

Logan

Innkeepers/Owners
Ellen Grinsfelder & Terry Lingo

The rugged and beautiful Hocking Hills State Parks with glorious caves and waterfalls flanks the inn's 75 acres on three sides. Comfortable B&B rooms in a barn-like structure have refrigerators, several with electric fireplaces and all offer sweeping views of meadows and wildlife. Quaint cottages are ideal for two, or secluded, fully-equipped 19th century log cabins accommodate up to six. A select few are dog friendly. Our restored & comfortably rustic 1840 log houses are an open kitchen-dining room serving the most refined of American cuisine. Weather permitting, enjoy casual fine dining on the patio for breakfast, lunch, or dinner. Enjoy spirits in the tavern, fireside lounge, or firepit. Discover a new degree of relaxation as you escape into a sanctuary of natural beauty at the Spa at Cedar Falls. The Gathering Place, a state-of-the-art green meeting/wedding location is a perfect fit for meetings and events. Casual and avid hikers will enjoy Old Man's Cave, Cedar Falls and Ash Cave. A variety of cooking classes and beer/wine tastings are scheduled year round.

Rates
9 Rooms, $149/$245 B&B; 12 Cottages, $199/$309 B&B; 5 Cabins, $209/$365 B&B and based on two people occupancy. A full, hot breakfast awaits you. Number of Rooms: 26

Cuisine
Watch meals being created in the open kitchen. Hearty country breakfasts, delectable lunches, sumptuous dinners. Picnic baskets for romantic dinners in your room. Brown bag lunches to take hiking. Patio dining in the warm months. Seasonal menus.

Nearest Airport
Columbus which is 50 miles.

🔥 SelectRegistry.com

The Inn at Dresden

www.theinnatdresden.com
209 Ames Drive, Dresden, OH USA 43821
800-373-7336 • 740-754-1122 • Fax: 740-754-9856
info@theinnatdresden.com

Member Since 2000

Ohio Dresden

Owner/Innkeeper
Thomas Lyall/James Madigan

Tucked away among the rolling hills of Southeastern Ohio, The Inn at Dresden provides the perfect setting for a relaxing getaway with family and friends, or a quiet weekend with someone special. Originally built by Dave Longaberger, founder of Longaberger Baskets, this elegant Tudor home offers guests a panoramic view of Dresden and the surrounding countryside. Guests at the inn enjoy a full gourmet breakfast, an evening social hour and optional fine dining. Individually decorated rooms feature CD/DVD players (350 movies available) and special amenities such as wraparound private decks, single and two person Jacuzzi tubs and gas-log fireplaces. In season there is access to a 10,000 sq.ft. pavilion for guest enjoyment.

Rates
$115/$190 per night. Each room is individually decorated to depict the area. Number of Rooms: 10

Cuisine
The Inn provides a full breakfast, an evening social hour of wine and cheese, followed by optional evening fine dining, by reservation for guests and their guests only.

Nearest Airport
Columbus Airport-60 min./ Akron Canton Airport-90 min.

Murphin Ridge Inn

www.murphinridgeinn.com
750 Murphin Ridge Rd., West Union, OH USA 45693
877-687-7446 • 937-544-2263 • Fax: 937-544-8442
murphinn@bright.net

Member Since 1992

Innkeepers/Owners
Paula & Jerry Schutt

One of National Geographic Traveler's top 54 inns in the U.S. and awarded a prestigious 5-Star TripAdvisor Certificate of Excellence, this prize-winning inn welcomes you to 142 acres of beauty. The Guest House has spacious rooms, some with fireplaces or porches, and romantic cabins with fireplace, two person whirlpool, luxurious shower and porch; all decorated with David T. Smith furniture. The1828 farmhouse features dining rooms with original fireplaces and a gift shop. Dining is more than an amenity. Chef takes seriously the mandate to use the freshest, healthiest, regional and seasonal ingredients skillfully prepared to keep our award-winning reputation. Our full breakfast is the dessert of your stay. Fine wine, beer and liquors available everyday but Sunday. By night, view the Appalachian foothills by the firepit. By day, visit Amish Shops and the Great Serpent Mound, or be pampered by an in-room massage. Murphin boasts an in-season pool, hiking, birding, tennis, and lawn games. Wi-fi makes us perfect for conferences. At Murphin Ridge, innkeeping is in the details.

Rates
10 Rooms - $130/$155. 9 Cabins - $215/$265. Call for business rates. Our from-scratch Country Breakfast for Two is included in all Room/Cabin rates. Special rates available Sunday through Thursday. Number of Rooms: 19

Cuisine
Chef Josh uses both our and our Amish neighbors' gardens, sourcing only the best for "farm to table" cuisine. Bountiful breakfast daily. Boxed Lunches available. Seasonal Patio Dining. Pleasing our guests' palettes is our mission. No Sunday alcohol.

Nearest Airport
Cincinnati/Northern Kentucky International

Shaw's Restaurant & Inn

🍴 🍴 🍴 🍷

www.shawsinn.com
123 North Broad St., Lancaster, OH USA 43130
800-654-2477 • 740-654-1842 • Fax: 740-654-7032
shaws@greenapple.com

Member Since 2005

AWARD OF EXCELLENCE 2013

Innkeepers/Owners
Nancy Cork, Susie Cork

Located on a tree-shaded square in historic downtown Lancaster, Shaw's has been described as "a unique blend of country freshness and well traveled sophistication." Just minutes from Hocking Hills, Shaw's Inn offers 25 individually decorated theme rooms. Nine have large in-room whirlpool tubs, in which some are called the Napa Valley, The Savannah, Casablanca and Louis XIV. Full breakfast in the restaurant is included with all rooms. Shaw's Restaurant has a reputation for New York Strip, Filet Mignon, Prime Rib, Fresh Seafood and innovative Vegetarian and Gluten-Free items. The Chef creates a daily changing menu with seasonal items--Spring Lamb, Soft Shell Crab, Fresh Walleye, 4-pound Lobster, and many others. Add to your Holiday Festivities with four weeks of Christmas Dinners. There are Cooking Classes on Saturdays. Cork's Bar, serving every day, has a warm setting of dark wood and brass. Free High-Speed Wireless Internet access throughout. Nearby attractions include: The Sherman House, The Decorative Arts Center of Ohio, The Georgian, and The Ohio Glass Museum.

Rates
Whirlpool Rooms $152/$218, Deluxe Rooms $125/$145, Corporate Rooms $97 for Double Occupancy. Full Breakfast is Included in the Restaurant from the current seasonal menu. Number of Rooms: 25

Cuisine
Known for Steaks, Prime Rib, Seafood and innovative Vegetarian, Gluten-Free and FIT menu offerings. Wine Spectator Award of Excellence continuously since 1996. Ever-changing and extensive microbrew beer list as well.

Nearest Airport
Port Columbus Airport

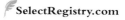

♿ 🍽 🍽 🍽 ♀

The Villas at Gervasi Vineyard

www.gervasivineyard.com
1700 55th Street NE, Canton, OH USA 44721
330-497-1000 • Fax: 330-497-1008
susan@gervasivineyard.com

Member Since 2012

Ohio
Canton

Villa Operations Manager
Susan Monteleone

As you drive through the welcoming arches at Gervasi's entrance, it's as if you are being transported into Tuscany! The Villas at Gervasi Vineyard offer a premier, upscale overnight destination with a Tuscan village atmosphere. Six villas, each with 4 individual suites (24 total), give guests the option of reserving an individual suite or entire villa.

This Tuscan-inspired inn is a luxurious retreat for those seeking to get away and relax. Nestled around the lake, this boutique inn offers luxurious suites with old world charm. Just across the spring-fed lake you can visit the beautiful grounds, vineyard, bistro, and marketplace for the ultimate Tuscan experience.

Delight in the luxury of the spacious suites which feature plush linens, feather pillows and duvets, bathrobes, slippers, and special room amenities; the ultimate in comfort. The cozy fireplace, heated Travertine limestone floors, refrigerator, flat screen television, and Blu-Ray DVD player will leave you feeling relaxed, pampered and refreshed.

New for 2014 The Farmhouse (built in 1830) sleeps 7-8 guests.

Rates
6 Double Queens, 6 Two-Level Kings, 12 King suites. All suites include fireplaces, walk-in showers, heated tile floors, and shared Villa Lobby. Off Season Rates $189-$309, Peak Season Rates $209-$349. Farmhouse $459-$1166. Number of Rooms: 25

Cuisine
Italian-style continental breakfast included, delivered to Villa along with fresh coffee. Lunch and Dinner: Gervasi's Italian Bistro & Crush House both feature authentic Italian menus. The Piazza for casual outdoor dining during the summer months.

Nearest Airport
Akron/Canton Airport - 15 minutes
Cleveland Hopkins International Airport - 60 minutes

SelectRegistry.com

Whispering Pines Bed & Breakfast

www.atwoodlake.com
1268 Magnolia Road SW, Dellroy, OH USA 44620
330-735-2824 • 266-452-5388 • Fax: 330-735-7006
whisperingpines@atwoodlake.com

Member Since 2006

Innkeepers/Owners
Bill & Linda Horn

Whispering Pines is located in gently rolling hills overlooking beautiful Atwood Lake and its picturesque lush landscape. The lake views will take your breath away and the surroundings are indescribably tranquil. Enjoy a quiet conversation in an outdoor space on the hillside or decks, and gather around the fire pit in the evening roasting s'mores. Nine guest rooms with 2-person whirlpool tubs, wonderful views, Bose music system, all-season fireplace, private balcony and upscale amenities. Breakfast is served in our large glass enclosed sun-room overlooking the lake where the view is spectacular. We offer additional services such as an in-room massage, girlfriend getaways and other gift packages. We can also accommodate small weddings and meetings. Endless activities with 28 miles of shoreline - walk/hike in the park, kayak, pontoon, swimming, fishing, golf, horse back riding, museums, wineries, motorcycles, the Amish area and many things to do in the Canton, OH area. Whispering Pines is the perfect place for celebrating a special occasion or a brief getaway.

Rates
Seasonal rates: Inn-Season: $199-$239, Mid-Season: $169-$219, Quiet-Season: $149-$189. Open year round. Number of Rooms: 9

Cuisine
A delicious breakfast of seasonal fruit or cobblers, scones, cakes or muffins & a variety of hot entrees served between 9-10 am. Morning coffee delivered to your room. House made chocolate chip cookies. Grill your own burger or steak in the summer.

Nearest Airport
Akron/Canton - 40 minutes

The White Oak Inn

 ♿ 🍽️   🍽️

www.whiteoakinn.com
29683 Walhonding Rd (SR715), Danville, OH USA 43014
740-599-6107
info@whiteoakinn.com

Member Since 1989

Innkeepers/Owners
Ian & Yvonne Martin

Come and stay where a warm welcome awaits, the cookie jar is full of homemade treats and the resident black Labrador greets you with a wagging tail. Located in Ohio's Amish area, an hour from Columbus and close to Kenyon College, The White Oak Inn has ten comfortable guest rooms and two luxury log cabin cottages. It's the perfect location to explore Amish Country, enjoy outdoor activities including the nearby zip line, take a wine tour, or just sit on the front porch and watch the hummingbirds. Let us entertain you at a Murder Mystery, or just enjoy a pampering weekend with in-room massages and dinner delivered to your room. Innkeeper Yvonne, one of the Eight Broads in the Kitchen, creates delicious breakfasts and dinners daily, using fresh local ingredients and herbs from the inn's gardens. Whether your visit is to celebrate something special or just recharge your batteries, The White Oak Inn has the perfect recipes for romance and relaxation. See our website for more information about our packages, including elopements, honeymoons and girlfriends' getaways.

Rates
Traditional queen or king rooms from $155 to $175 a night, fireplace rooms from $175 to $185, Whirlpool/fireplace rooms $185 to $205 and luxury cottages from $215 to $250 a night. See our website for package rates and specials. Number of Rooms: 12

Cuisine
Generous country breakfast daily. Evening meals available for inn guests, either as a delicious 4-course dinner in the dining room or a romantic dinner basket delivered to the room. Advance reservations requested. Lunches available for groups. BYOB

Nearest Airport
Port Columbus - 55 miles

🎿 **SelectRegistry.com**

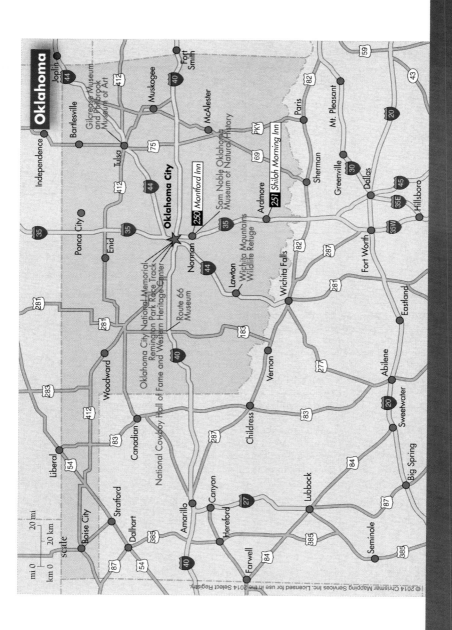

Oklahoma

Oklahoma

Joplin
44
Independence
Bartlesville
Gilcrease Museum and Philbrook Museum of Art
112
Muskogee
Fort Smith
40
McAlester
Tulsa
75
44
112
250 *Montford Inn*
Oklahoma City
Sam Noble Oklahoma Museum of Natural History
PKY
69
251 *Shiloh Morning Inn*
Ponca City
Norman
35
Enid
35
35
Ardmore
44
Lawton
Wichita Mountains Wildlife Refuge
82
Oklahoma City National Memorial
Remington Park Race Track
National Cowboy Hall of Fame and Western Heritage Center
Route 66 Museum
Wichita Falls
287
281
183
281
40
Vernon
277
Woodward
285
412
Canadian
83
Childress
287
83
Liberal
54
Stratford
Boise City
Dalhart
385
Amarillo
Canyon
Hereford
Farwell
27
Lubbock
385
84
40
87
54
Paris
Mt. Pleasant
82
20
Sherman
Greenville
30
Dallas
45
35E
Hillsboro
35W
Fort Worth
82
287
28
Eastland
Abilene
20
Sweetwater
Big Spring
84
Seminole
87
385
59
43

scale
20 mi
20 km
mi 0
km 0

© 2014 Christma Mapping Services Inc. Licensed for use in the 2014 Select Registry.

♿ 🍽 ☭

Montford Inn & Cottages

www.montfordinn.com
322 W. Tonhawa, Norman, OK USA 73069
800-321-8969 • 405-321-2200 • Fax: 405-321-8347
innkeeper@montfordinn.com

Member Since 1997

Oklahoma

Norman

Innkeepers/Owners
William Murray, Phyllis & Ron Murray

Designed and built in 1994, the Murrays welcome you to the award-winning Montford Inn and Cottages. With its ten uniquely decorated rooms in the main house, and six incredible cottage suites, the Montford Inn has everything the discriminating inngoer is looking for in lodging. Located in the heart of Norman's Historic District, this Prairie-style inn envelops travelers in a relaxing atmosphere. Antiques, family heirlooms and Native American art accent the individually decorated guest rooms and suites. Awaken to rich coffees and a gourmet country breakfast served in the beautifully appointed dining room or in the more intimate setting of the suites. Relax in private hot tubs. Escape in luxurious whirlpool bathtubs. Unwind in elegant cottage suites. Stroll through beautiful gardens. Find your heart...at the Montford Inn and Cottages! Featured in Southern Living, Country, Holiday, Fodor's, and Oklahoma Today.

Rates
10 Rooms, $119/$169; 6 Cottage Suites, $209/$239. Open year-round, possible restrictions for Christmas. Number of Rooms: 16

Cuisine
Full breakfast served in cottages and dining room. Complimentary wine and refreshments served early evening.

Nearest Airport
Will Rogers World Airport in Oklahoma City

Shiloh Morning Inn & Cottages

www.shilohmorning.com
2179 Ponderosa Road, Ardmore, OK USA 73401
888-554-7674 • 580-223-9500
innkeepers@shilohmorning.com

Member Since 2004

Oklahoma

Ardmore

Innkeepers/Owners
David & Jessica Pfau

Shiloh Morning Inn is located on 73 wooded acres, just minutes off I-35, conveniently located half-way between Dallas and Oklahoma City. The suites and cottages offer large luxurious baths, king-size beds, fireplaces, TV/DVD, private hot tubs or jetted tubs for two, and a private balcony, patio, or deck. Guests choose from an extensive library of movies and books. The 73 acres include a pond perfect for a picnic and/or fishing. Walking trails are dotted with hammocks and park benches. Wildlife abounds. With luxury and privacy as priorities, Shiloh Morning Inn is the perfect romantic getaway for couples seeking the quiet seclusion of a rural countryside.

Rates
5 suites and 4 cottages; $165 to $300. Full breakfast included. Number of Rooms: 9

Cuisine
Three-course, gourmet breakfast in the dining room at tables for two. Dinner available by reservation for intimate, room-service dining.

Nearest Airport
Dallas (DFW); Oklahoma City (OKC)

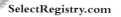

Oregon

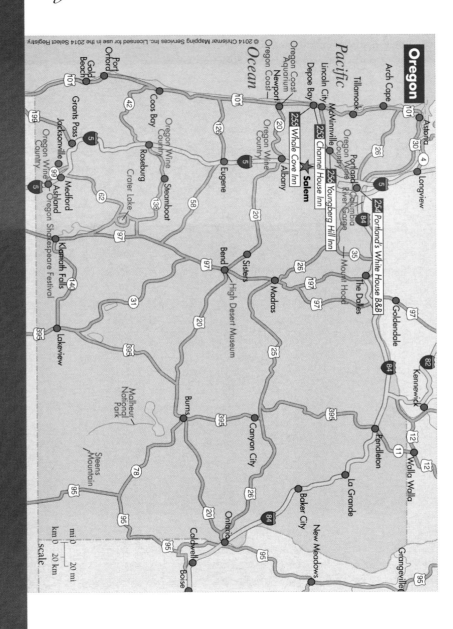

© 2014 Chrismar Mapping Services Inc. Licensed for use in the 2014 Select Registry.

Pacific

Ocean

Gold Beach
Port Orford
101

Grants Pass
199
Jacksonville
5
Oregon Wine Country
Medford
99
Ashland
5
Oregon Shakespeare Festival

Oregon Wine Country
Coos Bay
42
126
Roseburg
Steamboat
138
Crater Lake
62
Klamath Falls
140
97
31
395
Lakeview
58
Eugene

Oregon Wine Country
Albany
20
★ Salem
20

Coos Bay
Depoe Bay
Lincoln City
McMinnville
Tillamook
Arch Cape
Astoria
101
30
4
Longview
26
5
Newport
Oregon Coast—Aquarium
Oregon Coast—

255 Whale Cove Inn
253 Channel House Inn
256 Youngberg Hill Inn
Oregon Wine Country
Portland
Columbia River Gorge
254 Portland's White House B&B
84
35
Mount Hood
The Dalles
Goldendale
97
84
82
Kennewick
12
Pendleton
11
12
Walla Walla
Grangeville

Bend
97
Sisters
High Desert Museum
Madras
26
197
97
25

Burns
395
Canyon City
26
Baker City
84
La Grande
New Meadows
95
Grangeville
Ontario
20
Caldwell
95
Boise
95

Malheur National Park
Steens Mountain
78
95

mi 0   20 mi
km 0   20 km
scale

252

SelectRegistry.com

Channel House Inn

www.channelhouse.com
35 Ellingson Street, P.O. Box 56, Depoe Bay, OR USA 97341
800-447-2140 • 541-765-2140 • Fax: 541-765-2191
info@channelhouse.com

Member Since 1997

General Manager/Proprietors
Sarah Jincks/Carl & Vicki Finseth

Nestled in the Oregon Coast's magnificent scenery, Channel House combines the comforts of a first-class hotel with the congeniality of a small country inn. Imagine fresh ocean breezes, sweeping panoramic views, powerful surf, truly unbelievable sunsets and whales within a stone's throw. Perched on an oceanfront bluff, guestrooms have an understated natural elegance and contemporary decor, including whirlpools on oceanfront decks and gas fireplaces. The friendly staff will attend to your every need. One of the West Coast's most renowned and romantic inns, it has been listed by Harry Shattuck among "a baker's dozen of world's (sic) most delectible hotels" and by Sunset Magazine as one of the 20 best Seaside Getaways on the West Coast.

Rates
3 Oceanfront Rooms $230/$265; 14 Oceanfront Suites, $245/$330. Number of Rooms: 16

Cuisine
Buffet-style breakfast featuring fresh-baked goods is served in our oceanfront dining room. Enjoy a morning repast while having one of the best views on the coast. We have a significant wine selection available with many fine restaurants nearby.

Nearest Airport
Portland International (PDX) - 2.5 Hours

Portland's White House Bed and Breakfast

www.portlandswhitehouse.com
1914 NE 22nd Avenue, Portland, OR USA 97212
800-272-7131 • 503-287-7131 • Fax: 503-249-1641
pdxwhi@portlandswhitehouse.com

Member Since 2004

Oregon Portland

Owner
Lanning Blanks

Situated in Portland's North East Historic Irvington District, Portland's White House was built as a summer home in 1911 by Robert Lytle, a wealthy lumber baron. The house was billed as the most expensive home built in the district for the period. This Greek Revival Mansion boasts a lifestyle of past years with 14 massive columns, circular drive and fountain to greet you. Summer days show impressive hanging baskets and wonderful flowers to warm your senses. Restored to its original splendor by Lanning with sparkling European Chandeliers, formal linened dining room, large parlor, grand staircase, magnificent leaded glass windows, gilt-gold ceilings, Trompe loeil and Grande Ballroom. Extensive collections of European and Continental Porcelains, 18th and 19th Century oil paintings. Guest rooms are perfectly appointed with period antiques, paintings, king or queen size feather beds, exquisite linens. Fresh local breakfast, utilizing SLOW FOODS when possible, served in the Main Dining room by candlelight. Romantic weddings & events offered. "Top 10 City Inns" - Sunset Magazine.

Rates
$135/$250. Molton Brown amenities in all rooms, Complimentary secured wireless, and each room has a flat screen cable TV. Climate control. Number of Rooms: 8

Cuisine
Candlelight gourmet breakfast, always vegetarian, breakfast meat offered on the side. Housemade Bread Pudding French Toast, Crab Cake Eggs Benedict, Balsamic Vegetable Fritatta, Oregon Blueberry Muffins, Pear Ginger Scones. Full Espresso bar.

Nearest Airport
Portland International Airport, 15 minutes. Located 2 blocks from public transportation.

Whale Cove Inn

www.whalecoveinn.com
2345 S. Highway 101, P.O. Box 56, Depoe Bay, OR USA 97341
800-628-3409 • 541-765-4300 • Fax: 541-765-3409
info@whalecoveinn.com

Member Since 2009

Oregon Depoe Bay

General Manager/Proprietors
Sarah Jincks/Carl & Vicki Finseth

The Whale Cove Inn has eight luxury hotel suites perched above the pristine Whale Cove marine refuge on the Central Oregon Coast. Every amenity guarantees your stay will be the ultimate luxury experience - from king-sized Tempur-Pedic beds with down comforters to Jacuzzis on private decks. Each luxury suite is spacious, with cozy gas fireplaces, artisan-tiled showers with European water features, wet bars and flat-screen HDTVs. Every luxury suite offers panoramic views of Whale Cove and the Pacific Ocean - highlighted by orca whales in migration, bald eagles, and a front row seat for storm-watching, when the surf pounds the rocks at the mouth of the cove below. And there is no finer place to be for spectacular evening sunsets. As a quaint fishing village, Depoe Bay is home to many fine restaurants and a host of beach activities - from charter fishing for Chinook and Coho Salmon, Halibut, Albacore Tuna, Dungeness Crab, Rockfish and Ling Cod -- to exploring tide pools, shopping or flying kites. Grey Whales can be seen 10 months of the year.

Rates
7 Signature Suites $425; 1 Owner's Suite $825. Other rates may apply for off season/ holidays. Number of Rooms: 8

Cuisine
Breakfast is included, Oven-baked pastries, Fresh seasonal fruit, Quiches, Fresh roasted coffee and more. Dinner is served in the oceanfront dining room with progressive new American cuisine of Restaurant Beck. www.restaurantbeck.com

Nearest Airport
Portland International Airport (PDX) 2.5 Hours

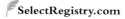

♿ 🍽 ♂ ⚵

Youngberg Hill Vineyards & Inn

www.youngberghill.com
10660 SW Youngberg Hill Road, McMinnville, OR USA 97128
888-657-8668 • 503-472-2727 • Fax: 503-472-1313
info@youngberghill.com   *Member Since 2008*

Oregon
McMinnville

GRAND
AWARD
2013

Innkeeper/Owner
Nicolette Bailey

Oregon's premier wine country estate and one of Wine Spectator's favorite locations; set on a 50 acre hilltop surrounded by a vineyard. We have an amazing 22 year old vineyard that is farmed organically. We are well known for producing award winning Pinot Noir and Pinot Gris wines. As passionate farmers and winemakers we are thrilled to share, educate, and talk wine. We respect the environment and believe that we can make a difference in how we treat the land and each other every day. We care for our wine and guests with this same respect and philosophy.

Youngberg Hill will take your breath away with the most beautiful views, warm luxurious Inn, personal and impeccable service and exceptional estate wines. Youngberg Hill provides the perfect location for those seeking a quiet, romantic getaway and a great base for touring Oregon wine country. We are centrally located in the Willamette Valley and have over 100 wineries and tasting rooms within 20 minute drive.

Rates
$200-$350. Number of Rooms: 8

Cuisine
We create a 2 course gourmet breakfast each morning focusing on regional food and products. Our menu changes because of this regularly. Some of our guest favorites are sure to be around. *Cornished baked eggs * Salmon Hash * Pinot Poached Pears

Nearest Airport
Portland International (PDX)

🎣 **SelectRegistry.com**

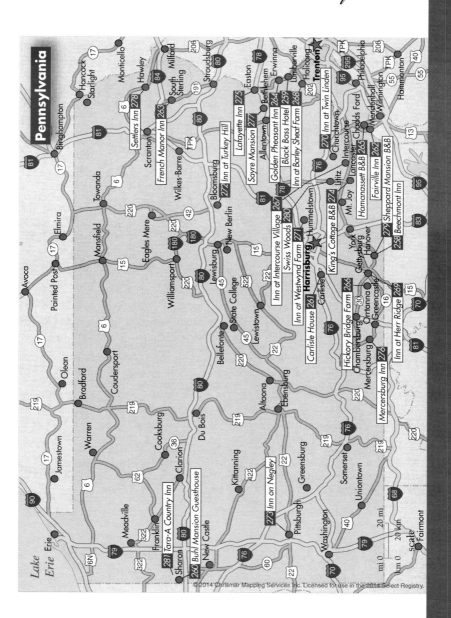

Pennsylvania

Pennsylvania

Lake Erie

Settlers Inn 278
French Manor Inn 263
Inn at Turkey Hill
Inn at Intercourse Village 267
Swiss Woods 280
Inn at Westwynd Farm 271
Carlisle House 261
King's Cottage B&B
Hickory Bridge Farm 266
Mercersburg Inn 276
Inn at Negley 273
Tara-A Country Inn 281
Buhl Mansion Guesthouse 260
Lafayette Inn 275
Sayre Mansion 277
Golden Pheasant Inn 264
Black Bass Hotel 259
Inn at Barley Sheaf Farm 268
Inn at Twin Linden 270
Hamanassett B&B 265
Fairville Inn 262
Sheppard Mansion B&B 279
Beechmont Inn 258
Inn at Herr Ridge 269

© 2014 Chrismar Mapping Services Inc. Licensed for use in the 2014 Select Registry.

SelectRegistry.com

257

♿ 🍽️

The Beechmont Inn Bed and Breakfast

www.thebeechmont.com
315 Broadway, Hanover, PA USA 17331
800-553-7009 • 717-632-3013 • Fax: 717-632-2769
innkeeper@thebeechmont.com   *Member Since 2003*

Innkeepers/Owners
Thomas & Kathryn White

Recognized as Pennsylvania's 2009 Innkeeper of the Year, the Whites consider hospitality one of The Beechmont's most important offerings. Breakfast is a close second, as Kathryn is part of Eight Broads in the Kitchen, a group of imaginative innkeepers who share recipes and local insights (www.eightbroads.com). Located on a tree-lined street of stately historic homes in a town just 14 miles east of Gettysburg, The Beechmont welcomes travelers with thoughtful extras that exceed one's expectations. A well-stocked library, lovely gardens and patio offer a backdrop for relaxed conversation, while well-appointed guest rooms assure a comfortable stay and sweet dreams. Gain insight into the Civil War at the Gettysburg Battlefield and Museum. Explore President Eisenhower's farm. Search for bargains in antique malls, tour wineries and ale trails, bicycle back country roads, savor fresh vegetables and fruits from farm markets, dine at great restaurants, and get married in The Beechmont garden. Come for the history, stay for the hospitality, return for the experience all over again!

Rates
$159-$189. Corporate rates Mon-Thur. A/C, WiFi throughout, guest Internet station, cable TV, fireplaces, all baths with custom jetted showers. Four 2-room suites. Winter specials noted online. Number of Rooms: 6

Cuisine
Sumptuous breakfast served at the time you select. Start with freshly brewed coffee from Mukilteo Coffee roasters, then a made-from-scratch breakfast with locally grown produce and goods. Afternoon sweet treat. We gladly accommodate dietary requests.

Nearest Airport
75 min Baltimore Washington International (BWI) and Harrisburg (MDT); 90 min from Dulles; 2 hrs Philadelphia (PHL).

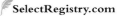 **SelectRegistry.com**

Black Bass Hotel

www.blackbasshotel.com
3774 River Road, Lumberville, PA USA 18933
215-297-9260 • Fax: 215-297-9261
info@blackbasshotel.com

Member Since 2014

Pennsylvania Lumberville

General Manager
Grant Ross

Nestled in the heart of scenic Bucks County, The Black Bass Hotel boasts a breathtaking river view with all the exceptional features expected of a historic local inn. Enjoy fine dining to more casual fare, private dining to banquet facilities, and of course, our luxury guest suites. Each has been meticulously renovated to maintain its historic charm while providing modern conveniences like computer access and flat screen TVs. All rooms have deluxe private baths, most with private decks facing the Delaware River.

No matter the occasion, any affair at The Black Bass Hotel is guaranteed to be uniquely elegant. Our charming restaurant and inn - which is part of the National Register of Historic Places - captures a distinctive spirit that can't be replicated. Experience the Jewel of the Delaware and create memories to cherish for a lifetime.

Visit our website for details about The Black Bass Hotel, including menus, upcoming events and special offers.

Rates
Rooms range from $225-$395; based on double occupancy. Breakfast included. A minimum of two nights is required for weekends May 1 to October 31. Number of Rooms: 9

Cuisine
For an experience unlike any other, The Black Bass Hotel offers incredible ambiance with a breathtaking view of the Delaware River and eclectic menus featuring fine dining or casual fare. Weather permitting, guests can dine al fresco on the River Deck.

Nearest Airport
Philadelphia

Buhl Mansion Guesthouse & Spa

www.BuhlMansion.com
422 East State Street, Sharon, PA USA 16146
866-345-2845 • 724-346-3046 • Fax: 724-346-3156
Info@BuhlMansion.com

Member Since 2002

Owner/General Manager
Donna Winner/Laura Ackley

Buhl Mansion Guesthouse & Spa, rated one of America's Top 10 Most Romantic Inns, offers the ultimate in luxury, pampering and unsurpassed hospitality. Listed on the National Register of Historic Places, this1890 Romanesque castle is steeped in history and romance. After years of neglect and abuse, the opulent home of Steel Baron Frank Buhl is now lovingly restored and offers grand memories of a lifetime as guests experience the life of America's royalty in our lavishly appointed guestrooms with fireplaces and Jacuzzis. The full-service spa offers the epitome of indulgence with over 100 options of services from which to choose. The Spa Romance Package is the most popular, offering couples massages, facials, manicures, lunch and a bottle of champagne. Guests have complimentary access to the spa's sauna, steam room and monsoon showers. Indulge each morning with breakfast in bed or dine in the picturesque sunroom. The limo takes guests to Tara for gourmet or casual dining. Perfect for romantic getaways, indulgent spa escapes, exclusive executive retreats and castle weddings.

Rates
Castle Escape Packages: $350 King & Queen Rooms; $450 Royal Grand Rooms; $50 off 2nd night. "Castle for a Day" packages available for weddings, spa, golf or executive retreats. Number of Rooms: 10

Cuisine
Champagne & Welcome Tray in each room. Afternoon Tea served daily, Champagne Reception served Fri & Sat. Rates include 25% discount at Ashley's Gourmet Dining Room or Stonewall's Tavern, both at Tara-A Country Inn (Limo shuttle provided on weekends).

Nearest Airport
Pittsburgh, PA; Cleveland, OH

 SelectRegistry.com

Carlisle House

www.thecarlislehouse.com
148 South Hanover Street, Carlisle, PA USA 17013
717-249-0350 • Fax: 717-249-0458
maryd@thecarlislehouse.com

Member Since 2011

Innkeepers/Owners
Alan and Mary Faller Duxbury

Located a ½ mile from I-81 and 3 miles from I-76 (the Pa Turnpike) in Downtown Carlisle's National Register Historic District, the Carlisle House is in the heart of the most exciting restaurant area in South Central PA. You will find an extraordinary combination of gourmet restaurants featuring Spanish Tapas, Crepes and Chocolate, Belgian, Thai, Japanese, Vietnamese, English, Chinese, Italian, or American cuisine.

Relax in your room with amenities such as wired and wireless Internet access at the writing desk, long-distance phone service, Flat-screen TVs, a DVD library, and in-room fridge with complimentary beverages.

Start your day with breakfast featuring our renowned international-themed quiches, then embark on a day of antiquing, shopping, golfing, hiking the Appalachian Trail, or fly-fish on two of the world's top streams (the Letort and the Yellow Breeches).

Schedule your visit to include a class at the Kitchen Shoppe's culinary school, exhibits at historical museums, or one of Carlisle's world-famous auto shows. Come enjoy hospitality with history!

Rates
Open year round featuring well-appointed rooms and suites from $159 to $299. Private baths, several with whirlpools, soaking tubs, or jetted showers, individual A/C, HDTVs, WiFi, luxurious linens, spa robes, and custom amenities. Number of Rooms: 10

Cuisine
Breakfasts are a social affair featuring our signature savory quiches, house-baked muffins or cake, fruit, cereals and juices, with freshly ground coffee and a selection of Twinings teas. Special needs accommodated. Walk to more than 20 restaurants.

Nearest Airport
Harrisburg 37 min; Balt/Washington 2 hr; Philadelphia 2 hr. 20 min; Washington Dulles 2 hr; Washington Reagan 2 hr. 15 min

Fairville Inn

www.fairvilleinn.com
506 Kennett Pike (Rte. 52), Chadds Ford, PA USA 19317
877-285-7772 • 610-388-5900 • Fax: 610-388-5902
info@fairvilleinn.com
Member Since 1995

Pennsylvania

Chadds Ford

Innkeepers/Owners
Laura and Rick Carro

The Fairville Inn, located in the heart of the historic Brandywine Valley and listed on the National Register of Historic Places, echoes the pastoral scenes of Wyeth Family paintings. The allure of the Brandywine Valley comes from the enchanting landscape. World-class venues, including Longwood Gardens, the Winterthur Estate, the Hagley Museum, and the Brandywine River ("Wyeth") Museum are just minutes away. Leisurely travel the Brandywine Valley Wine Trail and sample the latest vintages of local wineries. Accented with barn wood, beams, and the occasional cathedral ceiling, the Fairville Inn is the embodiment of elegant country comfort. Most rooms feature decks overlooking the gardens or the meadow rolling toward a serene pond. Each room in the Main House (ca. 1826), Carriage House, and Springhouse has a private bath, satellite TV, telephone (with voice mail and complimentary local and long-distance service), free high-speed wireless Internet, and individually controlled heating/air conditioning. Most rooms have a canopy bed and many have fireplaces (seasonal).

Rates
11 Rooms ($175-$230), 2 Deluxe Rooms ($275), and 2 Spacious Suites ($305). Open every day. (Rates are subject to change modestly.) Please visit our website for seasonal and other specials. Number of Rooms: 15

Cuisine
Full breakfast (Mon-Fri 7-9 am; weekends and holidays 8-10 am) of refreshing beverages, cereal, fresh fruit, yogurt, Inn-baked goods and a choice of three hot entrees. Afternoon tea served daily with cheese, crackers, fresh fruit, and Inn-baked goods.

Nearest Airport
Philadelphia International, about 28 miles.

The French Manor Inn and Spa

www.thefrenchmanor.com
50 Huntingdon Drive, South Sterling, PA USA 18445
877-720-6090 • 570-676-3244
info@thefrenchmanor.com

Member Since 1991

Four Diamond Award

Innkeepers/Owners
The Logan Family

An enchanting storybook stone chateau, the French Manor Inn and Spa is nestled on 45 acres overlooking the beautiful Pocono Mountains. Old world charm and elegant furnishings are seamlessly joined with all the modern conveniences. Le Spa Forêt at the French Manor is a Green Spa with indoor salt water pool, hot tub, fitness room, and offers fireside massages, spa facials, body wraps and nail services. Guests can enjoy luxurious suites with fireplace, Jacuzzi, and private balconies. Every guest is welcomed with complimentary sherry, cheese and fruit plate, and pampered with turndown service with Godiva chocolates. The four diamond award winning restaurant features authentic & Nouvelle French cuisine served in the "Great Hall" where a 40-foot vaulted ceiling & magnificent twin fireplaces create a romantic setting. An excellent wine list compliments the dining experience. Travelers can also enjoy a cocktail or a causal meal in Hanna's Cafe or on the veranda in nicer weather. Enjoy miles of trails for hiking, mountain biking, picnicking, and snowshoeing. AAA Four Diamond.

Rates
5 Rooms, $190/$285 B&B; 14 Suites, $265/$375 B&B. All suites FP, most with whirlpool tub & balcony view. Girlfriend getaways, Wine Lover's Weekends and Couples Spa Retreat packages available. Number of Rooms: 19

Cuisine
Gourmet breakfast. Room service available. Nouvelle and authentic French cuisine for dinner. Spa Cuisine Lunch and picnic basket lunches available upon request. Cafe and Bar onsite. An extensive wine list is available and top-shelf liquors.

Nearest Airport
Scranton/Wilkes-Barre (AVP), Lehigh Valley International Airport (LVIA)

Golden Pheasant Inn

www.goldenpheasant.com
763 River Road, Erwinna, PA USA 18920
610-294-9595 • Fax: 610-294-9882
brittany@goldenpheasant.com

Member Since 2012

Innkeepers
Brittany Faure Booz

Perfect for a relaxed country meal, a weekend getaway or a glass of wine by the fire, it is hard to imagine a more picturesque setting than the Golden Pheasant Inn. The atmosphere is magical with exposed stone walls, beamed ceilings and the beautiful Bucks County countryside all around. Located between the Delaware River and Canal in a historic fieldstone inn, we are the longest continuously operating restaurant/hotel along the Canal and recognized on the National Register of Historic Places. The Inn has been family-owned and operated for over 27 years. Guests can enjoy the beauty and history of Bucks County from the comfort of our newly restored, luxurious property. Each gracious guest room is decorated with a blend of antique and updated furnishings, with water views from every room. Enjoy the property from a rocking chair on the front porch, at a bench in our garden or strolling along the towpath which is directly out our back door. We look forward to welcoming you to the Golden Pheasant Inn and sharing the best of Bucks County. Please come visit us!

Rates
Our guest rooms range in price from $195-$340 with special weekday rates available.
Number of Rooms: Four

Cuisine
Chefs Blake Faure and Jon Ramsay offer the best local food to our guests. The emphasis is on fresh, natural ingredients with a menu that changes seasonally. Voted "best ambiance" and "most romantic" in the Philadelphia/NJ area by Open Table diners.

Nearest Airport
We are approximately one hour and fifteen minutes from Newark Airport and one hour and a half from Philadelphia.

Hamanassett Bed & Breakfast

www.hamanassett.com
115 Indian Springs Drive, P.O. Box 366, Chadds Ford, PA USA 19017
877-836-8212 • 610-459-3000
Hamanassett@aol.com

Member Since 2005

Innkeepers/Owners
Glenn & Ashley Mon

A worthy destination in the Brandywine Valley, Hamanassett Bed & Breakfast is a grand 1856 English country house on 7 acres where Southern hospitality and personal service is emphasized. Seven spacious bedrooms and suites, featuring en suite baths, hardwood floors, antique furniture, FPs, Q or K beds, TV/DVD with free movies, WiFi, guest computer, in room coffee makers and robes. Enjoy the billiards room, living room, and light-filled sun room, terrace or porch overlooking the koi pond with waterfall. Two private, two-story 2 bedroom cottages for those traveling with small children, dogs, or for those who just want extra privacy. Cooking classes. Convenient to Longwood Gardens, Winterthur, Wyeth Museum, Nemours, Hagley and Philadelphia. Only 20 minutes to Wilmington, DE, and one hour from Amish Country. Recommended by major publications including The New York Times; "The elaborate breakfasts are a highlight." "Sets the standard for luxury in the Brandywine area" – David Langlieb from his book "Philadelphia, Brandywine Valley & Bucks Co." Enjoy our user friendly front porch!

Rates
Rooms: $170/$269. $50 extra person in rooms sleeping 3. Carriage House and Meadow Cottage: $350 based on two people. $25 per night per dog fee up to max of $100. Number of Rooms: 9

Cuisine
Full gourmet candlelight breakfast. Special diets accommodated if notified in advance. 24 hour guest pantry stocked with complimentary soft drinks, juice and snacks, microwave oven, ice maker, refrigerator and cookies baked fresh daily.

Nearest Airport
Philadelphia International 17 miles, Baltimore Washington International 94 miles. See web site for directions.

Hickory Bridge Farm

www.hickorybridgefarm.com
96 Hickory Bridge Road, Orrtanna, PA USA 17353
717-642-5261 • Fax: 717-642-6419
info@hickorybridgefarm.com

Member Since 1976

Pennsylvania

Orrtanna

Innkeepers/Owners
Robert and Mary Lynn Martin

A quaint country retreat offering 5-bedroom farmhouse (circa 1750s) accommodations (some with whirlpool baths), and two duplex cottages with wood burning fireplaces along a mountain stream. Dinner is served on weekends, and some weeknights, in a beautiful restored Pennsylvania barn decorated with hundreds of antiques. All meals are prepared from scratch and are served family style at your own private table. Dinner is prepared with local ingredients enhanced with local wine and beer. Full breakfast is offered to guests at the farmhouse except on Sunday, when a basket breakfast is delivered to your room. The farm is located nine miles west of Gettysburg, Pennsylvania, on 75 beautiful acres-a wonderful place to relax while visiting Gettysburg, antiquing, or biking in the nearby area. Featured in Taste of Home magazine and National Geographic Traveler. Family owned and operated since 1977.

Rates
9 Rooms, Cottages and Farmhouse; $125/$175 B&B. Open year-round. Number of Rooms: 9

Cuisine
Fine family-style dining in a beautiful restored Pennsylvania barn. All meals are prepared from scratch. Friday, Saturday, and Sunday, some weeknights. Banquets and parties are served daily. You may bring your own spirits. Reservations suggested!

Nearest Airport
Harrisburg, 54 miles (1 hour & 20 minutes)
Washington BWI, 70 miles (1 hour & 45 minutes)

The Inn & Spa at Intercourse Village

www.inn-spa.com
P.O. Box 598, 3542 Old Philadelphia Pike, Intercourse, PA USA 17534
800-664-0949 • 717-768-2626
info@inn-spa.com

Member Since 2005

Innkeepers
Kurt & Char Thomas

Winner of the "Top Ten Romantic Inns" Award. Enjoy elegance and luxury in the heart of Amish Country. Stay in the Historic 1909 Inn with rooms filled with period treasures without compromising on modern amenities. If upscale country is more your style, then reserve one of our Homestead suites having a private entrance and over 400 sq. ft. of living space. Our suites offer pillow top beds, private bath, luxury linens, separate sitting area, gas-log fireplace, flat panel TV/DVD, a wet bar with Keurig & refrigerator. Our most popular and spacious Grand Jacuzzi suites feature all of the homestead amenities and more, each boasting a unique style and Jacuzzi for two. Lose yourself in sumptuous grandeur as you experience the ultimate in romance and relaxation as you slip on plush robes after a soaking Jacuzzi bath and curl up near the fireplace feeling refreshed and rejuvenated in these exquisite Grand suites. Arise to a five course candlelit breakfast, indulge yourself in a delightful diversion at our onsite Spa, all before embarking on sightseeing beautiful Lancaster County.

Rates
Grand Suites w/King bed, flat panel TV/DVD, fireplace, Jacuzzi, $269-$399,
Homestead Suites w/Queen or King bed, flat panel TV/DVD, fireplace, $169-$239,
Historic Main House Rooms w/Queen bed, flat panel TV/DVD, fireplace $149-$199.
Number of Rooms: 9

Cuisine
Enjoy a nice 5 course candlelit breakfast, prepared by our chef and served on fine English china in our Victorian dining room. Walk to the village for lunch. Enjoy sodas, coffee, fruit, pretzels or a homemade snack provided daily by our chef.

Nearest Airport
Harrisburg International 1 hr, Philadelphia International 1 1/2 hrs, Baltimore 1 1/2 hrs.

Pennsylvania Intercourse

The Inn at Barley Sheaf Farm

www.barleysheaf.com
5281 York Road (Rte 202), Holicong, Bucks County, PA USA 18928
215-794-5104 • Fax: 215-794-5332
info@barleysheaf.com   *Member Since 1982*

Pennsylvania

Holicong, Bucks County

Innkeeper/Owner
Christine Figueroa

Recommended by National Geographic Traveler and Fodor's Travel Guide, The Inn at Barley Sheaf Farm is the only historic Select Registry property in Buck's County. One of the most important historic properties in the region, thanks to its native American, colonial, and Alogonquin Round Table histories, the grand estate dates back to 1740 and includes The Manor House, Guest Cottage, and Stone Bank Barn. Complimentary wine and cheese served everyday, extensive brunch and full afternoon high tea are all included in your stay. All rooms feature flat screen TVs, Bose Stereos, Pratesi linens, Frette towels, robes, and featherbeds. Many offer fireplaces, whirlpool tubs, steam showers with body sprays, wet bars, sunrooms and private terraces. Two hundred acre views, fire pit, junior size olympic swiming pool, putting green, spa, work out facility. Croquet, volleyball, walking trails, miniature horses on property. 24 hour room service and laundry/dry cleaning services. Available for weddings and conferences with event planners on site.

Rates
$275/$525 Open year round. Activities: Spa, New Hope shops, antiquing, museums, art galleries, Delaware River outdoor activities. Number of Rooms: 16

Cuisine
Full gourmet brunch, afternoon snack, dinners Friday and Saturday evenings, other nights by request. Wine and cheese in our Conservatory Dining Room from 4-6 PM.

Nearest Airport
Philadelphia Airport (PA) and Newark Airport (NJ)

Inn at Herr Ridge

🍴🍴🍴 🍷

www.herrtavern.com
900 Chambersburg Rd., Gettysburg, PA USA 17325
800-362-9849 • 717-334-4332 • Fax: 717-334-3332
info@herrtavern.com

Member Since 2004

Innkeeper/Owner
Steven Wolf

The enchanting atmosphere of the Inn at Herr Ridge is unforgettable. Built in 1815 and nestled between the historic battlefields of Gettysburg and one of Pennsylvania's wooded treasures, Caledonia State Park on historic Rt 30. The Inn offers a rare experience to every guest who crosses the threshold, and is only minutes from town. Tastefully decorated, charmingly unique rooms await. Enjoy our roof top patio overlooking Seminary Ridge or step into your private Jacuzzi bath. Hungry? Relax while our chef creates a fabulous meal soon not to be forgotten. And don't forget the wine. Our Wine Spectator award winning wine list offers over 1000 selections, many of which are stored in our exquisite, windowed wine cellar. Our full-service bar also offers premium spirits. The main house of the Inn became the first Confederate hospital during the battle of Gettysburg. It is beautifully restored and listed in the National Register of Historic Places. If you are searching for a relaxing and romantic getaway, look no further. The fireplace is glowing & the wine is chilled. Come visit us!

Rates
$169-$359. Open year-round. All rooms have private baths, spa robes, pillow top featherbeds, and gas fireplaces. Most rooms with two person jacuzzi tubs. Corporate rates available for groups. Number of Rooms: 17

Cuisine
Bountiful breakfast consisting of daily baked muffins & cinnamon buns. House made granola and a hot breakfast created by the chefs. Fabulous innovative and seasonal influenced lunch and dinner menus. Private Dining and Banquet facilities.

Nearest Airport
Harrisburg (MDT), Baltimore (BWI), Washington DC (IAD)

Pennsylvania
Gettysburg

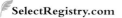

Inn at Twin Linden

www.InnAtTwinLinden.com
2092 Main St. , Historic Village of Churchtown, Narvon, PA USA 17555
866-445-7614 • 717-445-7619
info@InnAtTwinLinden.com

Member Since 2011

Innkeeper/Owner
Sue Kuestner

Imagine the ambience of a restored 1840's country estate - a gracious manor surrounded by 2 acres of beautiful gardens and stately trees. Farm-dotted valleys stretch as far as the eye can see while the "clip-clop" of horse-drawn buggies is heard echoing down the main street. These pleasures await you where discriminating guests are welcomed to relax and rejuvenate with exceptional accommodations and the finest cuisine. Guest rooms feature pillow-topped canopy beds, fireplaces and whirlpool tubs. Deluxe rooms offer the ultimate in privacy with a refined contemporary decor. Menus are created using seasonal, local farm produce and meats. The inn overlooks scenic Amish and Mennonite farm valleys, yet is conveniently located to a wide range of activities from Amish farm tours, country auctions, and antiquing to wineries, museums, theatre, historic sites, state parks, and lots of shopping. Relax at day's end by wandering through moonlit gardens or sit for a spell on the porch swing and just enjoy the garden view - then retire to a comfy, cozy room for a night's rest.

Rates
6 tastefully appointed rooms $130-$199, 2 deluxe rooms with private entrances and grand view of scenic countryside $245-$275. Private Baths, Fireplaces, Whirlpool Tubs, Bath Robes, Cable TV, Free WiFi. Number of Rooms: 8

Cuisine
A full-course breakfast served in our garden-view dining room by candlelight. Refreshments available 24/7. Fine dining offered on Saturday evenings by reservation - prix-fix menu, BYOB. Dietary restrictions are accommodated with advance notice.

Nearest Airport
Lancaster (LNS) 18 mi., Philadelphia (PHL) 41 mi., Harrisburg (MDT) 43 mi., Lehigh Valley (ABE) 46 mi.

SelectRegistry.com

The Inn at Westwynd Farm

www.westwyndfarminn.com
1620 Sand Beach Rd., Hummelstown, PA USA 17036
717-533-6764 • 877-937-8996
innkeeper@westwyndfarminn.com

Member Since 2011

Innkeeper/Owner
Carolyn Troxell

The Inn at Westwynd Farm invites you to step into a world of casual elegance and relaxation. Tucked away on our horse farm overlooking Hershey, enjoy beautiful gardens, lovely views, gourmet breakfasts and refreshments. Let us pamper you with comforting amenities accented by antiques, fireplaces, Jacuzzis, and luxurious linens.

The nuzzle of a horse, the soft purr of a sweet barn cat or perhaps a quiet glass of wine by the waterfall ensures any hint of care will drift away. Surrounded by flowering gardens, our Hershey bed and breakfast offers the perfect escape, while just moments away from all that Central Pennsylvania has to offer.

Hersheypark, Chocolate World and the Giant Center, Hershey Theatre, Convention Center and Medical Center are minutes away. Amish Country, Civil War sites, antiquing, biking, canoeing, or shopping - whatever brings you here, the inn is situated to be the perfect base for your activities.

Rates
Rates change seasonally and range from $60 to $275 reflecting room amenities. Off season specials are often available. Number of Rooms: 11

Cuisine
American Gourmet featuring locally produced and farm fresh ingredients whenever possible. In addition to a full breakfast, complimentary beverages and refreshments are available throughout the day.

Nearest Airport
Harrisburg International - 15 miles away

The Inn, Farmhouse & Brewing Co. at Turkey Hill

www.innatturkeyhill.com
991 Central Road, Bloomsburg, PA USA 17815
570-387-1500 • Fax: 570-784-3718
info@innatturkeyhill.com

Member Since 2002

Pennsylvania

Bloomsburg

Innkeeper/Owner
Andrew B. Pruden

The inn is a destination stop and lodging experience for all travelers. Nestled just seconds off Interstate 80 Exit 236, it is considered "an oasis along the interstate." Guests are treated to a casually elegant and comfortably appointed escape of charm and class located among the rolling hills and farmlands of northeastern PA. Rejuvenate yourself in one of our guest rooms attractively furnished with period pieces or give in to the allure of a whirlpool bath and fireplace. Enjoy award winning fine dining at The Farmhouse, featuring creative, world class cuisine & acclaimed wine list. Indulge in a fresh, craft beer from a renovated 1839 bank barn turned brewpub, that offers guests a casual dining alternative. Turkey Hill Brewing Company features craft beer brewed on-site and local, organic cuisine paired with weekly entertainment. Sample one or a few of our beers at the Pub before walking just seconds across the grounds to a delicious dinner at The Farmhouse. Whether business, pleasure, passing through or no reason at all, make a habit of staying in Bloomsburg at the inn.

Rates
14 Traditional Rooms $139/$153; 2 Main House Rooms $144/$158; 5 Stable Rooms $172/$206; Deluxe King $188/$228; King Supreme $205/$248. Lodging/Fine Dining & Brewery Packages Available. Number of Rooms: 23

Cuisine
The Farmhouse opens at 5:30 & The Brewing Co. at 4:00. Both serving seven days a week. Deluxe Continental Breakfast daily in the main house.
Pastry Chef - Jeff Yemola
Executive Chef Farmhouse - Matthew Revak
Head Chef Brewing Co. - Steve Tloczynski

Nearest Airport
Wilkes-Barre, Williamsport, Harrisburg, Allentown

The Inn on Negley

www.innonnegley.com
703 South Negley, Pittsburgh, PA USA 15232
412-661-0631 • Fax: 412-661-7525
info@innonnegly.com

Member Since 2006

Pennsylvania Pittsburgh

Proprietor
Elizabeth Sullivan

The Inn on Negley is a beautifully restored Italianate Victorian house located in the heart of Pittsburgh's historic Shadyside area. This distinguished inn offers elegant accommodations with the highest level of personalized attention paid to details. Each of the eight spacious guest rooms feature private baths, period furnishings, quality linens and L'Occitane bath products, plus all of the modern amenities you would expect from a luxury hotel. Warm fireplaces, a garden patio, tranquil music and a friendly dedicated staff welcome you to indulge in pure comfort. Additionally, our lovely Fernwood Tea Room serves afternoon English High Tea, by appointment. The inn is located within walking distance to some of the finest and most unique shopping and dining experiences in the city. Whether you are planning a romantic getaway or relaxing retreat, visiting a nearby university or traveling for business, you will find that the charming setting and considerate staff of The Inn on Negley will meet your every need.

Rates
King Suites: $205/$260. Queen Suites: $180/$214. Beautifully appointed with private baths, luxurious linens, fireplaces, jacuzzi tubs, robes, slippers, air conditioning, Wi-Fi, cable television & private phones w/ voicemail. Number of Rooms: 8

Cuisine
Full service gourmet breakfast prepared by our professional chefs, including scratch made pastries, fresh fruit and a variety of hot entrees. Also, complimentary afternoon sweets, beverages and evening wine. High tea and Cocoa services available.

Nearest Airport
Pittsburgh International (20 miles)

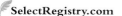

King's Cottage Bed & Breakfast

www.kingscottagebb.com
1049 East King Street, Lancaster, PA USA 17602
800-747-8717 • 717-397-1017 • Fax: 717-397-3447
info@kingscottagebb.com

Member Since 1995

Innkeepers/Owners
Janis Kutterer and Ann Willets

Feel yourself unwind as you travel through Lancaster County's tranquil back roads in Amish Country. Enjoy world-class entertainment, savor Pennsylvania Dutch cooking, visit historic sites, stroll art galleries, enjoy intimate gourmet restaurants – all within minutes of the King's Cottage - your home away from home. Come enjoy our wonderful Lancaster Bed and Breakfast. Elegant, luxurious guest rooms with cozy fireplaces enhance relaxation and romance! Let us pamper you with our gourmet breakfast, afternoon goodies and even a couples massage that melts your cares away. Or immerse yourself in a decadent rose petal bath while you nibble on chocolate-covered strawberries. The possibilities for celebrating a special occasion or just plain spoiling yourself are endless at the King's Cottage. Our location offers the best of both worlds - being a mile and a half away from a buzzing art scene and fabulous restaurants, while just a few minutes from the Amish farmland! We have not forgotten our business traveler with 24-hour check-in, early breakfast, fax service & complimentary WiFi.

Rates
$175-$289 Kg/Qn/Tw (2 with whirlpool tub), Carriage House w/ whirlpool tub. Central Air Conditioning, Fireplaces, High Def TVs, DVD Players, DVD Library, Free WiFi, on-site Massage room, Gift Shop. Business rates available. Number of Rooms: 8

Cuisine
Multi-course Gourmet breakfast, afternoon refreshments. Dietary restrictions accommodated with advance notice. Close to casual and fine dining. Guest kitchen with ice, bottled water, snacks, hot beverages, Microwave & Small Refrigerator.

Nearest Airport
Harrisburg (MDT) 40 min, Philadelphia (PHL) 90 min, Baltimore (BWI) 120 min

SelectRegistry.com

♿ 🍽️

The Lafayette Inn

www.lafayetteinn.com
525 W. Monroe St., Easton, PA USA 18042
610-253-4500 • 800-509-6990 • Fax: 610-253-4635
info@lafayetteinn.com

Member Since 2000

Innkeepers/Owners
Paul and Laura Di Liello

Our elegant mansion, built in 1895, is situated in a beautiful historic neighborhood near Lafayette College. Eighteen antique filled guest rooms welcome travelers visiting the Lehigh Valley's many attractions. The suites feature fireplaces and whirlpool tubs for that special getaway. The inviting parlor, wrap-around porch and tiered patio with fountain/waterfall call out to those longing to relax with a cup of coffee and a good book. A bountiful, freshly prepared breakfast is served at individual tables in our bright sunroom or on the porch. Complimentary soft drinks, coffee, fresh baked goods and fruit are available all day. The entire inn has free wireless high-speed Internet access and a loaner laptop is available. Whether visiting the colors of the Crayola Experience with the kids, riding the historic, mule-drawn canal boats, hot air ballooning above the countryside, exploring underwater diving excitement, visiting area colleges or just lounging and rejuvenating, The Lafayette Inn makes a great base for your getaway. Welcome to our inn!

Rates
18 Rooms (5 Suites) $139/$250. Antique-filled rooms with all the modern amenities, including TV/DVD, phones, and WiFi. All have private baths. Number of Rooms: 18

Cuisine
Full American breakfast daily. Complimentary soft drinks, coffee, fruit, and pastries available all day. Excellent restaurants within walking distance. No liquor license.

Nearest Airport
20 minutes from Lehigh Valley International (ABE), 60 minutes from Newark (EWR) or Philadelphia (PHL)

Mercersburg Inn

www.mercersburginn.com
405 South Main St., Mercersburg, PA USA 17236
717-328-5231 • 866-MBURG-01 • Fax: 717-328-3403
Lisa@mercersburginn.com   *Member Since 1998*

Pennsylvania

Mercersburg

Owners
Jim & Lisa McCoy

In 1909, Ione and Harry Byron had a magnificent dream; to build a home that brought comfort and entertainment to those that entered. From that dream, the 24,000 sq. ft. Prospect, with 11 ft. ceilings throughout, was born. The mahogany-paneled dining room and the sun-filled enclosed porch invite our guests to a culinary experience that will not be soon forgotten. Large enough to ensure your privacy but still able to maintain the intimacy and service of a country inn. The double-curving staircases lead you to our luxuriously appointed guest rooms. Draw yourself a nice warm bath in one of our antique soaking tubs, dry off with the softest of towels, slip on a fine robe, and drift away to sleep on your feather-bed. Awake in the morning to the smell of fresh baked morning goods, and our delicious 3-course breakfast. If the season permits, stroll through the flower and herb gardens that appoint the 5.5 acre property. If golfing, hiking, swimming, fly-fishing, or skiing are on your to-do-list, let our staff make the arrangements for you. We look forward to having you in our home.

Rates
$140/$395; 3 w/fireplaces, 1 w/clawfoot whirlpool tub, 2 w/Jacuzzi and TV, 3 w/ antique baths. Kings and Queens. Open year round except Christmas Eve and Christmas Day. Number of Rooms: 17

Cuisine
Enjoy our full gourmet breakfast. Fine dining and wines at Byron's, our fine dining restaurant. Seating 5:30 pm till 8:30 pm, Thurs-Sun. Reservations are recommended. Full bar service. Join us for a French Cooking Class or Wine Tasting/Pairing Dinner.

Nearest Airport
BWI, Dulles, Hagerstown Regional

Sayre Mansion

www.sayremansion.com
250 Wyandotte Street, Bethlehem, PA USA 18015
877-345-9019 • 610-882-2100 • Fax: 610-882-1223
innkeeper@sayremansion.com

Member Since 2003

Proprietors
Grant & Jeanne Genzlinger and Carrie Ohlandt

Timeless Elegance in a Distinguished Gothic Revival Mansion. The Inn offers luxury and comfort in nineteen guest rooms each preserving the architectural details of the Main House. In addition to the Main House, our classically restored Carriage House offers guests a home-away-from-home atmosphere in their choice of three suites. Each suite provides a separate living room and bedroom allowing guests ultimate privacy. Amenities include: fine linens, private baths, high-speed wireless Internet access, featherbeds, Jacuzzi bathtubs, and flat screen TVs. Robert Sayre's Wine Cellar offers guests an opportunity to sample a selection of wine. Personal Service is the cornerstone of the guest experience. The Asa Packer Room, our unique conference center, is ideal for business meetings. Gatherings and special events are held in a pair of elegant parlors, each with its own fireplace. Century old trees adorn the two acres of picturesque grounds which provide a beautiful setting for weddings or large gatherings under our 30' × 60' tent.

Rates
Rooms and Suites, $139/$295 B&B. Open Year-Round. Number of Rooms: 22

Cuisine
Breakfast highlights artisan breads, home made pastries, house specialties including belgian waffles, quiche, and omelets. Excellent restaurants serving lunch and dinner are located within one mile of the Inn.

Nearest Airport
Lehigh Valley International Airport is a five minute drive.

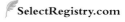

❛❍❜ ❛❍❜ ❛❍❜ ♀
The Settlers Inn at Bingham Park

www.thesettlersinn.com
4 Main Avenue, Hawley, PA USA 18428
800-833-8527 • 570-226-2993 • Fax: 570-226-1874
settler@thesettlersinn.com

Member Since 1992

Innkeepers/Owners
Grant & Jeanne Genzlinger

The Settlers Inn is a place to gather, relax, play and rejuvenate at this carefully restored arts and crafts inn. Stroll the extensive grounds and discover colorful flower and herb gardens, a quiet reflecting pond, or sit along the banks of the meandering Lackawaxen River. Guestrooms are thoughtfully and simply appointed with your comfort in mind. Luxurious European linens, featherbeds, whirlpool tubs and fireplaces invite travelers to pamper themselves. High speed wireless Internet, available at no additional cost, provides the flexibility to stay connected. The cornerstone of the inn is the award winning farm-to-table restaurant highlighting artisan breads and menus influenced by the seasons. The Dining Room and Chestnut Tavern reflect the style of William Morris which is carried throughout the building. After a day of hiking or cross-country skiing, bask in the warmth of the bluestone fireplace. Summer offers dining alfresco on the terrace overlooking the grounds as well as the Potting Shed, a gift shop in the garden.

Rates
21 Rooms and Suites, $165/$260 B&B. Open year-round. Number of Rooms: 21

Cuisine
Our award winning restaurant, rated AAA 4 Diamond, has a 20+ year tradition of working with local farmers and producers. It offers a comfortable and casual atmosphere for a romantic dinner for two or gathering place for friends and family.

Nearest Airport
Scranton (AVP), Allentown (ABE)

Sheppard Mansion

www.sheppardmansion.com
117 Frederick St., Hanover, PA USA 17331
877-762-6746 • 717-633-8075 • Fax: 717-633-8074
reservations@sheppardmansion.com

Member Since 2002

Innkeeper/Owner
Kathryn Sheppard Hoar

Nestled in the heart of Hanover's Historic District stands a grand 3-story brick and marble Mansion surrounded by lush gardens. Built in 1913 by Mr. and Mrs. H.D. Sheppard, co-founder of The Hanover Shoe, the Mansion now operates as an elegant full service inn and event facility. Full of the original furnishings and restored with modern amenities, the Mansion features bedrooms and suites with over-sized soaking tubs in the private marble baths--all for our guests' enjoyment. Days can be spent exploring nearby Gettysburg, antique hunting or touring Lancaster, Baltimore, Washington, DC. Want to relax instead? Have a massage and lounge around the house. Complete your pampered experience with an exquisite meal in our Dining Room, serving seasonal refined American cuisine Wednesday through Saturday nights. Check our website for lodging and dining packages. Our entire staff eagerly awaits the opportunity to be of service; whether for business or pleasure, the Sheppard Mansion is sure to be an unforgettable experience.

Rates
6 rooms and suites, King, Queen Beds, $140/$350 per night. 2 BR Guest Cottage on property available weekly. Corporate rates available. All rooms have private baths, A/C, WiFi, TV, Telephones and in-room coffee. Number of Rooms: 6

Cuisine
Full gourmet breakfast included. Fine dining offered Wed. thru Sat. nights features local produce in an ever-changing seasonal menu of refined American cuisine.

Nearest Airport
BWI - 1 hour, MDT - 1 hour

Swiss Woods

www.swisswoods.com
500 Blantz Road, Lititz, PA USA 17543
800-594-8018 • 717-627-3358 • Fax: 717-627-3483
innkeeper@swisswoods.com

Member Since 1993

Innkeepers/Owners
Werner and Debrah Mosimann

Surrounded by meadows, gardens and woods, Swiss Woods is a quiet retreat on 35 acres in Lancaster's Amish country. Perfect for those who love quiet and all things nature. Our rooms feature patios or balconies, bordering on the gardens and are decorated with the natural wood furnishings typical of Switzerland. Fabulous breakfasts, complemented by our own blend of coffee and a wide assortment of quality teas, are served in a sunlit common room. Convenient to Lancaster's Amish community, the small town of Lititz with its wonderful shops and restaurants, and Hershey is also just a short drive. After a day of antiquing, shopping or touring enjoy views of extraordinary gardens, landscaped with a wide variety of annuals and perennials. Take a relaxing hike through the woods, watch the huge variety of birds, or enjoy a drink on the garden swing with a good book and a sweet treat from our kitchen. Enjoy the evening around the outdoor chimenea in spring, summer and fall. In winter settle in to read next to the Inn's handsome sandstone fireplace. German spoken.

Rates
6 Rooms (2 with Jacuzzi, balconies, and high open beamed ceilings), all with patios or balconies. $175-$225 1 suite $205/$255. Additional guests in the Suite, $30 per person. Number of Rooms: 7

Cuisine
Inn breakfast specialties may include garden fritatta, freshly-baked breads from old world recipes, all created by Debbie, one of the 8 Broads in the Kitchen. The afternoon boasts sweets on the sideboard such as caramel apple cake or fresh fig cake.

Nearest Airport
Harrisburg and Philadelphia. Lancaster Airport is close for those with private planes.

SelectRegistry.com

Tara – A Country Inn

www.Tara-Inn.com
2844 Lake Road, Clark, PA USA 16113
800-782-2803 • 724-962-3535 • Fax: 724-962-3250
Info@Tara-Inn.com

Member Since 1986

Owner/General Manager
Donna Winner/Deborah DeCapua

Inspired by the great movie, Gone With the Wind, Tara is in essence an embodiment of the Old South. Tara, although located in the "North," offers you a lasting impression of Southern Hospitality and a chance to enjoy the luxuries of days gone by. Tara is a virtual museum of Civil War and Gone With the Wind memorabilia and antiques. Indulge in our magnificent guest rooms complete with fireplaces and Jacuzzis and enjoy the finest in gourmet or casual dining. Tara offers an extensive wine list and an expertly stocked lounge. Afternoon Tea is a daily opportunity for houseguests to mingle and enjoy. Take a leisurely swim in either our indoor or outdoor heated pools, or stroll through formal gardens overlooking the beautiful 450-acre Shenango Lake. Guests may enjoy massages in-house or pamper themselves at nearby Buhl Mansion Spa. Award-winning dining and overnight accommodations since 1986. Tara is the ultimate in World Class Country Inns, devoted to guests who expect the exceptional and appreciate the best.

Rates
Gone With The Wind Getaway Packages (MAP) $350-$425. (B&B) $200-$350.
Corporate rates available. Number of Rooms: 27

Cuisine
Ashley's Gourmet Dining Room offers the finest in 7-course white-glove and candlelight service while Stonewall's Tavern boasts a casual atmosphere with a wide array of hearty dinner selections.

Nearest Airport
Pittsburgh, PA; Cleveland, OH

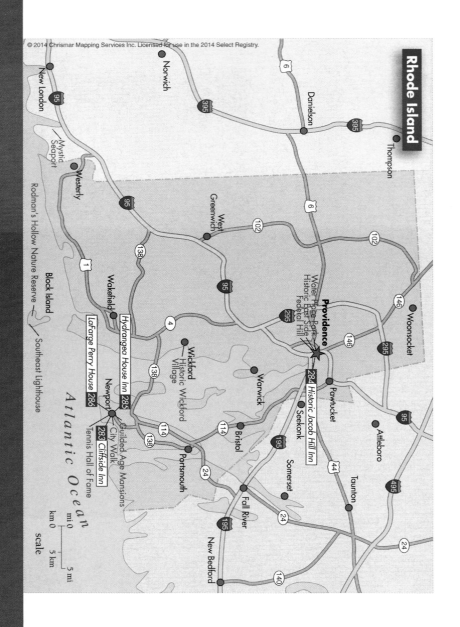

© 2014 Chrismar Mapping Services Inc. Licensed for use in the 2014 Select Registry.

Rhode Island

New London
Norwich
Danielson
Thompson
6
95
395
395
6
Mystic Seaport
Westerly
West Greenwich
102
102
Rodman's Hollow Nature Reserve
95
138
95
146
Woonsocket
Black Island
1
Wakefield
4
Wickford Historic Wickford Village
295
Providence
Water Place Park
Historic East Side
Federal Hill
146
146
295
Southeast Lighthouse
Hydrangea House Inn 285
Newport
Warwick
284 Historic Jacob Hill Inn
Pawtucket
Seekonk
95
LaForge Perry House 286
City Walk
Guilded Age Mansions
138
114
114
Bristol
195
Attleboro
283 Cliffside Inn
Tennis Hall of Fame
Portsmouth
138
24
Somerset
44
Taunton
Atlantic Ocean
24
Fall River
495
195
New Bedford
24
140
scale
km 0   5 km
mi 0   5 mi

Cliffside Inn

www.cliffsideinn.com
2 Seaview Avenue, Newport, RI USA 02840
800-845-1811 • 401-847-1811 • Fax: 401-847-1865
reservations@cliffsideinn.com

Member Since 1997

Owners
Nancy and Bill Bagwill

The celebrated Cliffside Inn, the former home of legendary artist Beatrice Turner and the original location of St. George's Prep School, has earned a worldwide reputation as one of New England's most distinguished luxury inns. Known for seamlessly blending today's finest amenities - deluxe bathrooms (many with whirlpool baths), fireplaces, grand beds, fine Italian linens, and iPod sound systems – with Victorian elegance and antiques, refined design, and stunning artwork. The Cliffside Inn is a magical hideaway. The grand Victorian Manor House and "coastal chic" Seaview Cottage are peacefully perched about the Atlantic Ocean and Newport's dramatic Cliff Walk. Whether you are looking for a relaxing vacation or romantic getaway, guests enjoy Cliffside's warm hospitality, epicurean delights, attentive service, and the Cliffside Inn special touches. Our wine cellar features the best of many local and select international vineyards. We also offer signature in-room spa services for our guests.

Rates
Rates vary by season; with our Deluxe Suites/State Rooms offered between $265-$510; our Deluxe Rooms offered between $200-$435; and our Classic Rooms available between $160-$410. Number of Rooms: 16

Cuisine
Guests enjoy a delicious multi-course breakfast, and are welcomed back to an afternoon wine and hors d'oeuvres reception. Afternoon tea, featuring traditional and contemporary accompaniments, is offered seasonally. Our signature Fondelés at turndown.

Nearest Airport
Providence, RI: 45 mins, Boston's Logan Airport: 1 hour and 30 mins.

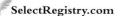

Historic Jacob Hill Inn, A Providence Luxury Hotel

www.Jacobhill.com
Providence, RI USA 02940
401-527-3629 • 508-336-9165
JacobHillInn@msn.com

Member Since 2000

Rhode Island   Providence

Innkeepers/Owners
Bill & Eleonora Rezek

Located on a peaceful country estate, just a 10 minute drive from downtown Providence, the Rhode Island Convention Center, Brown University and the Historic East Side. Built in 1722, Jacob Hill has a long history of hosting America's most prominent families, including the Vanderbilts. Recently updated rooms are spacious, all with private bathrooms; most have Jacuzzi tubs. King-and queen-sized beds blend with hand-picked antiques and Oriental rugs. The gleaming wood floors mirror the romantic flames from the original fireplaces. The elegant surroundings are complemented by the genuine warm hospitality that will make you feel at home. Awarded AAA Four Diamonds, "Top 10 Most Romantic Inns," ZAGAT "Top U.S. Hotels, Resorts & Spas," TripAdvisor.com "Travelers' Choice Award," Inn Traveler "Best Guest accommodations," "Ten best Urban Inns" Forbes.com, "Room of the Year" Inns Magazine. Featured by the New York Times, Country Living Magazine, USA Today and many others. Centrally located to visit: Boston, Cape Cod, Plymouth, MA, Newport, RI or Mystic, CT all will make great day trips.

Rates
Unique guestrooms, w/private bathrooms in Two Buildings $199/$459. Open year round. In ground pool, tennis, ping pong, billiard room, meeting room & gazebo to view the beautiful sunsets. Spa services near by. Number of Rooms: 12

Cuisine
Award-winning four course breakfast, complimentary beverages, chocolate chip cookies afternoon cheese plate. Many fine restaurants nearby for lunch and dinner.

Nearest Airport
Providence T F Green 20 minutes, Boston Logan 1 hour
Physical address: 120 Jacob Street, Seekonk, MA 02771

Hydrangea House Inn

www.hydrangeahouse.com
16 Bellevue Avenue, Newport, RI USA 02840
800-945-4667 • 401-846-4435 • Fax: 401-846-6602
hydrangeahouseinn@cox.net

Member Since 2005

Innkeepers/Owners
Grant Edmondson & Dennis Blair

Enter a world of grace, elegance and style where the intimate charm of Hydrangea House is complemented by its prestigious Bellevue Avenue address where once lived the Vanderbilts, the Astors and the Dukes. Its proximity to the magical gilded mansions, recreational harbor, historic sites, fine dining, and extraordinary shopping means you can walk to almost everything right from our front door. All ten rooms and suites are individually decorated with a dramatic use of color, sumptuous fabrics, trims and elegant furnishings. Suites have the added luxury of a two-person spa tub, a marble shower, steam bath and flat screen "mirror" television. All rooms offer plush robes, triple sheeting, complimentary high speed Internet, long distance and local calling, CD players or iPod hook-ups. Complimentary wine and cheese is served daily in the parlor or on one of Hydrangea House Inn's expansive porches. To make your night complete, don't miss our home-made chocolate chip cookies at turn-down. AAA Four Diamond award (8th year). Travel Channel's Top 10 New England Bed and Breakfast.

Rates
Rates: $295/$475. "Stay More - Pay Less!" The more nights you stay with us the less per night you will pay. Available in our luxury suites (all year) and standard rooms (winter). Massage service and special packages available. Number of Rooms: 10

Cuisine
Expect to find more than the usual continental breakfast. We will serve you our own special blend of fresh ground House Coffee, home-baked breads & granola--as well as our incredible raspberry pancakes perhaps or seasoned scrambled eggs in puff pastry.

Nearest Airport
Providence Airport (PVD) 30 minutes.

La Farge Perry House

www.lafargeperry.com
24 Kay Street, Newport, RI USA 02840
877-736-1100 • 401-847-2223 • Fax: 401-847-3620
reservations@lafargeperry.com

Member Since 2006

Innkeeper
Jennifer Balch

La Farge Perry House is a Victorian-era luxury inn located on a quiet street within walking distance to major attractions in Newport. The inn is named after the famed artist John La Farge, who lived in the house in the 1860s. Each of the inn's six distinctive rooms honor La Farge, his family, and ancestors. Four guestrooms feature queen-size beds and two feature king beds. All rooms are adorned with luxurious private bathrooms, luxury bedding and amenities, and feature fresh flowers from the award winning gardens. Many rooms also feature Jacuzzi tubs, fireplaces, and large sitting areas. Common areas include a formal living room, French Provencal kitchen with sitting area and a fireplace, dining room with hand-painted panoramic murals of Newport, secluded balcony on the third floor, front porch with white wicker furniture, and Adirondack chairs in the award-winning backyard gardens.

Rates
Summer Rates range from $249 to $349 on weekdays and from $289 to $499 on weekends. Winter Rates range from $139 to $169 on weekdays and from $189 to $289 on weekends. Number of Rooms: 6

Cuisine
Breakfasts are cooked to order by our innkeeper with many choices, including Eggs Benedict on Sundays. The table is set daily with homemade jams, pastries, fresh fruit, and more. Seasonal afternoon refreshments are also offered.

Nearest Airport
Providence/TF Green, RI

SelectRegistry.com

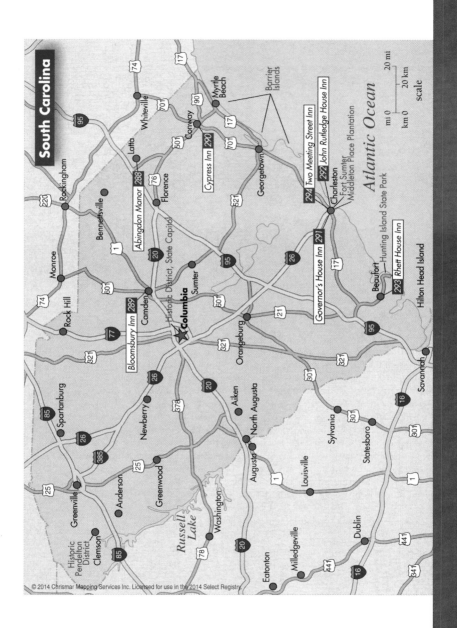

South Carolina

South Carolina

Atlantic Ocean

scale
mi 0   20 mi
km 0   20 km

Barrier Islands

74
17
Whiteville
701
Latta
Rockingham
220
95
Bennettsville
Monroe
74
Rock Hill
77
321
Spartanburg
85
26
385
25
Greenville
Anderson
Historic Pendleton District
Clemson
85

1
Camden
Bloomsbury Inn 289
26
Newberry
378
Greenwood
25
Russell Lake
Washington
78
20
Eatonton

74
701
Conway
90
Myrtle Beach
17
501
Florence
76
Abingdon Manor 288
288
20
95
321
Cypress Inn 290
290
701
Georgetown
17
294 Two Meeting Street Inn
292 John Rutledge House Inn
Charleston
Fort Sumter
Middleton Place Plantation
Historic District, State Capitol
★ Columbia
Sumter
501
321
95
26
Governor's House Inn 291
291
21
Hunting Island State Park
17
Beaufort
293 Rhett House Inn
Hilton Head Island
Aiken
North Augusta
Augusta
1
Louisville
Sylvania
301
Statesboro
Savannah
16
301
Orangeburg
321
30
321
95
1
Dublin
441
16
Milledgeville
441
341

© 2014 Chrismar Mapping Services Inc. Licensed for use in the 2014 Select Registry.

Abingdon Manor

www.abingdonmanor.com
307 Church Street, Latta, SC USA 29565
888-752-5090 • 843-752-5090
abingdon@bellsouth.net

Member Since 2005

Innkeepers/Owners
Chef Patty & Michael Griffey

The only establishment offering both luxury accommodations and fine dining in the Carolinas and Georgia close to I-95, Abingdon Manor is the overnight destination for travelers on the East Coast. Halfway between NYC and Palm Beach, the inn provides superior lodging, extraordinary cuisine and impeccable service. One of only a select few properties in SC to be awarded a AAA 4-diamond rating annually for both the inn and restaurant, Abingdon Manor offers the amenities of a small luxury hotel in an opulent National Register mansion. Located in a quaint village, the inn features 3 acres of landscaped grounds. For destination travelers, the inn offers a variety of activities including cooking school weekends, historic touring, nature-based activities and private country club golf. Food writers and critics consistently rank "The Dining Room at Abingdon Manor" as one of the best restaurants in the Carolinas. An English Country House offering a refined, yet comfortable, atmosphere for the discriminating traveler, Abingdon Manor is the recipient of TripAdvisor's Award of Excellence.

Rates
$185/$215. All guestrooms offer ensuite bathrooms, cable TV, working fireplaces, individual temperature controls and wifi. Number of Rooms: 7

Cuisine
The award winning restaurant offers exceptional fine dining nightly. The one seating, pre-fixe meal is crafted daily using the freshest ingredients available and begins with cocktails at 7:00. A full breakfast is offered from 7:45 to 9:00 am.

Nearest Airport
Florence, Myrtle Beach

F SelectRegistry.com

Bloomsbury Inn

www.bloomsburyinn.com
1707 Lyttleton Street, Camden, SC USA 29020
803-432-5858 • Fax: 803-432-5858
info@bloomsburyinn.com

Member Since 2010

Innkeepers/Owners
Bruce A. and Katherine L. Brown

Sensational in Every Season! Bloomsbury, 2014 Travelers' Choice award-winner, is known for Southern hospitality, gourmet breakfasts and complimentary socials which include a walk through history. Located in the historic district, 3 miles off I-20, near fine shops/arts and great restaurants, Bloomsbury Inn, circa 1850, awaits you. Significant notoriety is derived from the writings of the famous diarist, Mary Boykin Chesnut, author of A Diary from Dixie. From the outside in, this beautifully appointed property offers old world charm with all the modern comforts. On two acres of manicured grounds, several garden sitting areas and the veranda offer peace and tranquility from the everyday stresses of life. Inside this lovingly restored antebellum home, with uncompromising attention to detail, we have created a warm, welcoming environment for all who traverse the leaded glass doorway. With large bed chambers and luxurious amenities, Bloomsbury will well-surpass your expectations. Recommended by Southern Living and Fodor's. We have everything ready for your arrival; safe travels!

Rates
Enjoy gracious, oversized guest bed chambers, king and queen, with Italian tile private baths, featuring luxury amenities. $169 - $215 (inclusive rate: full gourmet breakfast, 5:30 pm social, wifi, top amenities, all taxes). Number of Rooms: 4

Cuisine
Delicious gourmet breakfasts, using local products...farm fresh eggs, homemade breads/jams, real butter, aged cheeses, custom-blended coffee. Dining room or veranda; diet restrictions honored. Complimentary social: tea/wine and light hors d'oeuvres.

Nearest Airport
Columbia SC (CAE) or Charlotte NC (CLT) are easy drives. I-20, exit 98, Hwy 521 N, R@ Chesnut St, L@ Lyttleton St

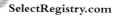

The Cypress Inn

www.acypressinn.com
16 Elm Street, Conway, SC USA 29526
800-575-5307 • 843-248-8199 • Fax: 843-248-0329
info@acypressinn.com

Member Since 2001

Innkeepers/Owners
Hugh & Carol Archer, George & Anne Bullock

Overlooking the Waccamaw River, tucked away in the historic town of Conway, this luxury inn is near, but distinctly apart from, the golf mecca of Myrtle Beach. Located 2 blocks from the downtown area of Conway, the inn is within walking distance of charming shops, restaurants, art galleries and stately live oak trees. Twelve unique guestrooms offer comforts such as en-suite private baths with Jacuzzis, plush robes, individual heat/air, and high speed Internet (WiFi). We also have an on-site massage therapist. The inn offers the privacy of a hotel with the personal service of a bed and breakfast. Enjoy the pristine beaches of the South Carolina coast, the peacefulness of an ancient river, an outstanding sculpture garden or live theater shows. Many extras such as fresh flowers, chocolates and strawberries and a selection of fine wines are available. In addition to being a charming destination, the inn is great for those traveling north or south along the east coast and for the business traveler seeking a relaxing atmosphere. Meeting and banquet facilities are also available.

Rates
$145-$245 B&B. Open year-round. Corporate Rates. Number of Rooms: 12

Cuisine
A wonderful hot breakfast is served each morning. There are fine restaurants within walking distance. A small guest refrigerator is stocked with lemonade, sodas, bottled water. Complimentary wine and beer, cookies and other treats.

Nearest Airport
Myrtle Beach

 **SelectRegistry.com**

Governor's House Inn

www.governorshouse.com
117 Broad Street, Charleston, SC USA 29401
800-720-9812 • 843-720-2070 • Fax: 843-805-6549
governorshouse@aol.com

Member Since 2000

General Manager/Owners
Angela Ward/Janice Gardner, Sue & Kevin Shibilski

Governor's House is a magnificent National Historic Landmark (circa 1760) reflecting the Old South's civility and grandeur. Praised by one national publication as "Charleston's most glamorous and sophisticated inn," the former Governor's mansion is the perfect blend of historic splendor and romantic elegance. The mansion's original living rooms, dining room, nine fireplaces, Irish crystal chandeliers, and sweeping southern porches delight guests from around the globe. Harmonize these aristocratic pleasures with luxuries like whirlpool baths, wetbars, high speed Internet and individually controlled room environments, and the result is refined gentility. During the American Revolution, Governor's House was the home of Edward Rutledge, youngest signer of the Declaration of Independence. Today, the Inn has been acclaimed as "a flawless urban hideaway" by Southern Living. Visit us online at: www. governorshouse.com.

Rates
The Inn has 11 guest rooms and suites with private baths, luxury robes, hairdryers, irons and ironing boards. Rates are $185-$545. Concierge services, bicycles, WiFi, and private parking are a complimentary addition to your stay. Number of Rooms: 11

Cuisine
Gourmet breakfast, Low-country afternoon tea with wine and cheese, and Evening Sherry. Delicious peach iced tea and other beverages always available. Premiere restaurants just a short, pleasant stroll.

Nearest Airport
Charleston International Airport

John Rutledge House Inn

www.johnrutledgehouseinn.com
116 Broad Street, Charleston, SC USA 29401
800-476-9741 • 843-723-7999 • Fax: 843-720-2615
kleslie@charminginns.com

Member Since 1992

Owner/Innkeeper
Richard Widman/Kathy Leslie

John Rutledge, one of the 55 signers of the U.S. Constitution, built his home in 1763. Now exquisitely restored, it is one of only fifteen homes belonging to those signers to survive and the only one to now accommodate overnight guests. One may choose between the classic elegance of rooms and spacious suites in the grand residence or its two carriage houses. The inn is located in the heart of the Historic District where you are just a few steps away from the famed "South of Broad" neighborhood. Antique and boutique shopping, museums and many other local attractions are just around the corner. Spa services and dinner reservations at acclaimed Circa 1886 Restaurant are available nearby to our guests. Afternoon tea and evening port, sherry and brandy are offered in the Signers Ballroom where patriots, statesmen and presidents have met. Wireless Internet access, nightly turn-down service and breakfast are included with your room. A charter member of Historic Hotels of America, designated a National Historic Landmark. AAA Four Diamond.

Rates
16 Rooms, $219/$385 and 3 Suites, $320/$455. Open year-round. Daily parking fee.
Number of Rooms: 19

Cuisine
Breakfast served with daily hot item and expanded continental included. Afternoon tea and refreshments. Guests have a choice of having breakfast served in their room, in the courtyard or the Signers Ballroom.

Nearest Airport
Charleston International Airport- 12 miles.

SelectRegistry.com

The Rhett House Inn

www.rhetthouseinn.com
1009 Craven St., GPS: 32.4329453,-80.6737595, Beaufort, SC 29902
888-480-9530 • 843-524-9030 • Fax: 843-524-1310
info@rhetthouseinn.com

Member Since 1991

South Carolina Beaufort

Owners
Steve & Marianne Harrison

The Rhett House Inn consists of the Thomas Rhett House, built ca. 1820 as a summer home for one of S.C.'s wealthiest planters and statesmen; The Cottage, built ca. 1864 as a combination school/store for freedmen; and The Suites at Newcastle Cottage, a beautiful 2-suite house adjacent to the inn, perfect for two couples, wedding family members, special occasions, etc. Listed in the National Register of Historic Places, the Rhett House contains 10 rooms; in 1996 the Cottage was renovated and transformed into 7 additional charming and historic rooms, with fireplaces, whirlpool baths, and individual decks/patios. Newcastle Cottage contains 2 beautiful suites, with a large living/dining area, gourmet kitchen, and screened veranda. The house and many of the rooms are decorated with English and American antiques, oriental rugs, fresh orchids, and spacious verandas. Situated in Beaufort's 300 year-old National Historic Landmark District, the Inn, Cottage, and Newcastle Cottage are the perfect base for your trip to the southern jewel that is Beaufort. AAA Four Diamond rated.

Rates
9 rooms with fireplaces, 8 rooms with whirlpool baths. Open 365 days/year.
$180-$300. Number of Rooms: 19

Cuisine
A stay at The Rhett House Inn includes a Full Southern Breakfast; afternoon teas, lemonade, and pastries; evening hors d'oeuvres and cocktail gathering; nightly homemade desserts; and picnic baskets to order.

Nearest Airport
Savannah/Hilton Head International Airport

Two Meeting Street Inn

www.twomeetingstreet.com
2 Meeting Street, Charleston, SC USA 29401
888-723-7322 • 843-723-7322
innkeeper2meetst@bellsouth.net

Member Since 1992

Innkeepers/Owners
Pete and Jean Spell, Karen Spell Shaw

No other place is like Charleston, and in Charleston, no place is quite like Two Meeting Street Inn- the jewel in the crown of the city's historic inns. From the Inn's gracious Southern veranda- one of the most photographed porches in the South- guests enjoy layers of natural beauty. The Queen Anne Mansion was given as a wedding gift by a bride's loving father in 1890. The inn features a carved English oak stairwell and Tiffany windows, as well as the Spells' collection of antiques and silver. Immediately surrounded by century-old live oaks amid lush gardens with a finely manicured lawn and cherry red azaleas, the inn overlooks Charleston's historic harbor, tip of the Battery; a few blocks away, world-class dining, modern boutiques, antique shops, art galleries, and historic museum houses await. Guests enjoy a hot Southern breakfast in the oval dining room and gracious afternoon tea on the veranda. Here, the pace slows and the mind rests. The inn invites you to discard your stress and relish the exquisite civility and romance of Charleston. We await your arrival.

Rates
9 Unique guest rooms with private baths. Tariffs $235 to $519. Besides breakfast and afternoon tea, our complimentary package includes concierge services, daily newspapers, hi-def cable television, wireless Internet and parking. Number of Rooms: 9

Cuisine
Begin your day with Southern pecan coffee and a full, hot breakfast. Be rejuvenated with Lowcountry afternoon tea. Indulge in an enticing array of Key Lime Pound Cake, Plantation Brownies and Benne Wafers. An evening cream sherry ends your day.

Nearest Airport
Charleston International Airport 12 miles from downtown.

SelectRegistry.com

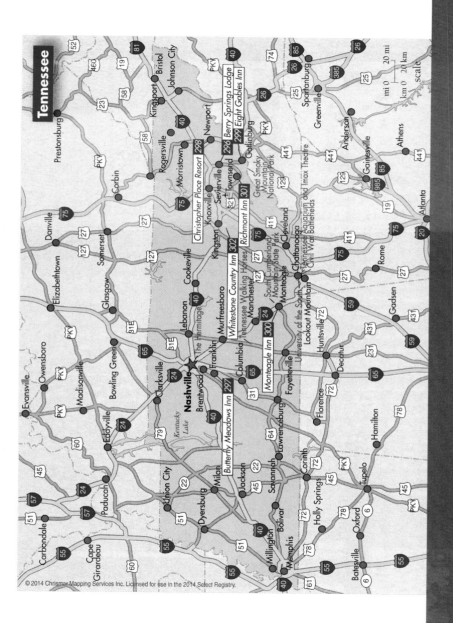

Tennessee

Christopher Place Resort 298
Berry Springs Lodge 296
Eight Gables Inn 292
Richmont Inn 301
Whitestone Country Inn 302
Tennessee Walking Horses
Monteagle Inn 300
Butterfly Meadows Inn 297

© 2014 Chrismar Mapping Services Inc. Licensed for use in the 2014 Select Registry.

Berry Springs Lodge

www.berrysprings.com
2149 Seaton Springs Road, Sevierville, TN USA 37862
888-760-8297 • 865-908-7935
stay@berrysprings.com

Member Since 2005

Sevierville

Innkeepers/Owners
Patrick & Sue Eisert

Perched on a 33 acre secluded scenic ridge top in the Great Smoky Mountains, this lodge offers the perfect picture of solitude and romance. Take a leisurely walk down to the bass or catfish ponds and try your luck. Ride bikes, play horseshoes, relax in a hammock or just sit back and enjoy the beautiful views of the Smoky Mountains from your rocking chair on the main deck of the lodge. With this remote setting, one would not guess the lodge is within a 15-minute drive of most area destinations, including Gatlinburg, Pigeon Forge, Sevierville and the "Great Smoky Mountain National Park." Awards and Accolades: 2013 Top 20 Inn in USA on TripAdvisor, 2012 Trip Advisor: "#1 Rated B&B in TN," 2006 USA Today: "10 great places to settle into for fall viewing," 2005 Blue Ridge Country: "Tennessee's Berry Springs Lodge Gives the Gift of Trees," 2004 Arrington's Inn Traveler: "Best Scenic Mount View," 2003 Arrington's Inn Traveler: "Best Inn for Rest and Relaxation," 2001 Better Bed and Breakfasts: "Enjoy the Best of Both Worlds at Berry Springs Lodge."

Rates
9 rooms. $145/$225, 2 Suites $205/$245. Includes breakfast and evening desserts. Open year-round. Number of Rooms: 11

Cuisine
Country gourmet breakfast. Lunch and dinner picnic baskets are available upon advanced request. Local restaurants within 15 minutes. Nightly signature desserts.

Nearest Airport
Knoxville

SelectRegistry.com

Butterfly Meadows Inn & Farm

🍽️ 🍽️ 🍽️

www.butterflymeadowsinn.com
6775 Bethesda Arno Road, Franklin, TN 37179
877-671-4594 • 615-671-4594
relax@butterflymeadowsinn.com

Member Since 2012

Tennessee

Franklin

Innkeepers/Owners
Darlene & Norman Bobo

Nestled atop a ridge and surrounded by 40 acres of woods and meadows, Butterfly Meadows Inn & Farm offers the perfect backdrop for stories to begin and to continue. The Inn is a new farmhouse reflecting a strong devotion to the culture and heritage of the area's history while incorporating modern amenities. Breathtaking panoramic views and bountiful nature are paralleled by exceptional personalized service & attention to detail. A cozy library is home to thousands of volumes and hundreds of movies. The rocking chair porch offers a peaceful place to enjoy an early morning cup of coffee, view amazing sunsets, or end an evening under a blanket of stars. Choose Butterfly Meadows Inn & Farm for a romantic getaway for two, as a rejuvenating group retreat, an inspiring business retreat, or a spectacular event site for a wedding or celebration. You're just minutes to historic Franklin & Nashville. This is an inviting place where the best of yesterday and today seamlessly intertwine for an experience like no other. Come visit and discover why our motto is Relax ~ Breathe ~ Create!

Rates
Range seasonally: $169-$279/night double. Accommodations wrap you in comfort & luxurious amenities: most w/ king beds, private baths, fresh baked cookies, robes, fresh flowers, Wi-Fi, Apple TV, fine bath products, turndowns & more. Number of Rooms: 7

Cuisine
A delectable gourmet breakfast will await you each morning. Our skilled culinary team can offer additional meal options for your entire stay. Our menus change seasonally and feature farm fresh produce and herbs from our kitchen garden.

Nearest Airport
Nashville International Airport-36 miles; Huntsville International Airport-98 miles

Christopher Place an Intimate Resort

www.christopherplace.com
1500 Pinnacles Way, Newport, TN USA 37821
800-595-9441 • 423-623-6555
stay@christopherplace.com

Member Since 2000

Tennessee

Newport

Innkeeper/Owner
Marston Price

Secluded in the scenic Smoky Mountains on a 200-acre private estate, Christopher Place, an Intimate Resort, is the ideal inn for a romantic, relaxing getaway. An elegant setting is coupled with friendly, unpretentious service and unspoiled, panoramic views. The hosts know your name and greet you with a warm smile. You can fill your days with activities, or with none at all, as the inn is centrally located to most of the sights and attractions of the Smokies and offers many resort amenities of its own. Rooms and Suites are spacious and romantically appointed. Casual fine dining with an extensive wine list completes your romantic retreat. Special requests are encouraged. A AAA Four Diamond Award winner for 20 years. Voted the area's Best B&B. Named one of the 10 most romantic inns in America; one of the 12 best locations for a fantasy B&B wedding; and a winner of BedandBreakfast.com's Best of the South! We invite you to sit back, enjoy, and overlook nothing but the Smokies.

Rates
6 Rooms, $150-$185; 4 Suites, $295-$330. Each room has unique offerings which may include double whirlpools, wood-burning fireplaces, private dining, cable TV, and scenic views. All rooms feature complimentary WiFi. Number of Rooms: 10

Cuisine
Hearty mountain breakfast served at your leisure. Picnics and back-pack lunches. Intimate four course candlelit dinners served to Tuesday through Saturday by reservation at tables set for two in our exquisite dining room overlooking the mountains.

Nearest Airport
Knoxville

 SelectRegistry.com

Eight Gables Inn

www.eightgables.com
219 North Mountain Trail, Gatlinburg, TN USA 37738
800-279-5716 • 865-430-3344 • Fax: 865-430-8767
Gm@eightgables.com

Member Since 2002

General Manager
Anthony Flatt

Eight Gables Inn, The Smoky Mountains' Premier Country Inn, offers 21 luxurious rooms and suites. All rooms have private baths, cable TV, feather top beds, plush bathrobes, telephones, personal amenities and several feature the warmth of fireplaces and whirlpool tubs. Our rates include a full served breakfast, and evening dessert. Conveniently located on the drive between Gatlinburg and Pigeon Forge, our peaceful setting lends itself to a casual elegance and relaxing charm. Eight Gables is easily accessible to all the area attractions including the Smoky Mountain National Park. Knoxville and the airport is just 30 miles away. We are also on the trolley route. AAA Four Diamond rated.

Rates
10 Rooms $159-209; 9 Deluxe Suites $179-229. Diamond Suites $199-249, TV/VCR/CD, complementary designer coffees, teas, and bottled water, bath robes, most with King beds, fireplaces, Jacuzzi. Number of Rooms: 21

Cuisine
Full seated service breakfast, and evening dessert.

Nearest Airport
Knoxville TN, McGee Tyson
TYS

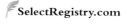

Monteagle Inn & Retreat Center

www.monteagleinn.com
204 West Main Street, P.O. Box 39, Monteagle, TN USA 37356
888-480-3245 • 931-924-3869 • Fax: 931-924-3867
suites@monteagleinn.com

Member Since 2006

Tennessee

Monteagle

Innkeeper/Owner
Jim & Lee Harmon

Monteagle Inn is located atop the Cumberland Plateau just minutes away from The
University of the South, with hiking trails, antique shops and superb restaurants. The Living
areas are outfitted with overstuffed furnishings graced with special antiques, which invite
you to relax and experience the mountaintop. The inn's large living room with 4 distinct
sitting areas encourages you to curl up on one of the oversized sofas with a good book.
A welcoming fire in the cool months adds to the total relaxation. Picturesque balconies, a
spacious front porch and garden courtyards provide private outdoor relaxation hide-a-ways.
Crisp white linens welcome you to relax and enjoy your bedroom with hot cookies and
flavored teas. The spacious dining room is filled with light and color from windows on 3
sides while Provencal linens grace the windows and tables. Brightly-patterned Italian urns,
bowls and dishes serve as a backdrop for your gourmet breakfast specialties. Monteagle
Inn is the perfect place for your getaway and business retreats, family reunions and
wedding functions.

Rates
All of the rooms have spacious private baths and are furnished with luxurious white bed
and bath linens. Wireless DSL is provided throughout the Inn. $165/$275. The Cottage
has 2 Queen Bedrooms for $385. Mountain Gourmet Breakfast. Number of Rooms: 15

Cuisine
Extensive herb & vegetable gardens help create acclaimed "mountain gourmet" breakfast.
New Orleans Praline French Toast, Mays Eggs Bearnaise, Garden Fresh Frittatas & Herb
Roasted Sweet Potato Fries are just a few bountiful items prepared each morning.

Nearest Airport
Chattanooga-45 miles
Nashville-85 miles-shuttle available
Winchester -20 miles

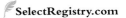 **SelectRegistry.com**

The Richmont Inn of the Great Smokies

&♿ 🍽️   🍽️ 🍴

www.richmontinn.com
220 Winterberry Lane, Townsend, TN USA 37882
866-267-7086 • 865-448-6751 • Fax: 865-448-6480
richmontinn@comcast.net

Member Since 1997

Innkeepers/Owners
Jim & Susan Hind

Escape to the Great Smoky Mountains and refresh your body and soul. Relax in our secluded mountain top setting with breathtaking views, privacy and quietness, 18th century English antiques and French paintings, amenities such as spa tubs, private balconies, wood-burning fireplaces, candlelight desserts, and a gourmet breakfast. Main lodge is styled as an Appalachian cantilevered barn, an icon of the Smokies. New Chalet with luxurious suites, ideally suited for small business groups, family socials or a romantic rendezvous. Open air Chapel-in-the-Woods and wedding services for small groups, private and memorable. Special Weekend Rendezvous and three night Rose and Romance Packages available. Ten minutes to National Park and Cades Cove. Rated "Top Inn" by Country Inns and awarded grand prize by Gourmet Magazine for our signature dessert. "...may be the most romantic place in the Smokies" -Southern Living. "A wonderful place to recharge your batteries" -Country Magazine "Romantic getaway" -HGTV

Rates
3 rooms, $180/$220 Queen - 3 rooms $190/$220 King - 3 rooms $205-$225 King - 1 Luxury Suite $220/$250 King.
Chalet Luxury Suites $275/$375, King beds - spa tubs - fireplaces - balconies - fridge - piped in music Number of Rooms: 14

Cuisine
Full French and Swiss style breakfasts. Complimentary gourmet desserts and flavored coffees by candlelight. Classic four course authentic Swiss fondue dinners by reservation. Fine Champagnes, wines, and imported beers. Tea and coffee in your room.

Nearest Airport
Only 30 mins. from McGhee Tyson (Metro Knoxville) airport.
10 mins. to National Park \ Cades Cove.

Whitestone Country Inn

www.whitestoneinn.com
1200 Paint Rock Rd., Kingston, TN USA 37763
888-247-2464 • 865-376-0113 • Fax: 865-376-4454
info@whitestoneinn.com

Member Since 2000

Innkeepers/Owners
Paul & Jean Cowell

A spectacular 360 acre Country Estate with views of the Smoky Mountains provides you with a serene combination of natural woods and landscaped gardens. Whitestone's rolling hillsides and peaceful surroundings are guaranteed to soothe your soul and calm your spirit. We serve three lavish meals a day, and you can nibble on home baked cookies and other delectable treats anytime. Many of our rooms are equipped with the sensuous delight of waterfall-spa showers and private decks. You will be surrounded by 5,400 acres of wildlife-waterfowl refuge and 39,000 acre Watts Bar Lake with opportunities for birding, fishing, kayaking, canoeing, paddle-boating or just rocking on our many porches and swinging in our hammocks. This is the perfect place for vacations, retreats, meetings, weddings or honeymoons. Whitestone Country Inn is one of only seven AAA Four Diamond properties in Tennessee, and was named one of the "10 Most Romantic Inns in America!" Discover a Sanctuary for your Soul.

Rates
Rooms/Suites, $165/$325 per night. Each room and suite has fireplace, king bed, spa tub, TV/DVD, free WiFi, and refrigerator. Number of Rooms: 22

Cuisine
The very best classic cuisine. Enjoy elegant meals in one of our three dining rooms, two overlooking the lake. For between-meal snacks, sample from the cookie jars in our kitchen.

Nearest Airport
Knoxville, Mcghee/Tyson airport

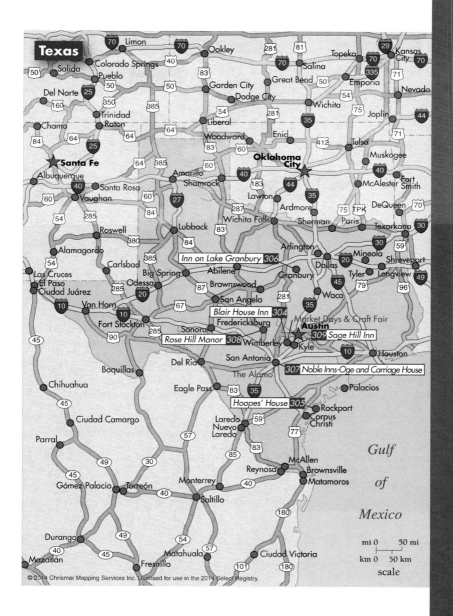

Texas

Texas

Limon · Oakley · Topeka · Kansas City

Colorado Springs · Salina · Great Bend · Emporia · Nevada

Salida · Pueblo · Garden City · Dodge City · Wichita · Joplin

Del Norte · Trinidad · Liberal · Woodward · Enid · Tulsa · Muskogee

Chama · Raton

Santa Fe · Amarillo · Oklahoma City · McAlester · Fort Smith

Albuquerque · Santa Rosa · Shamrock · Lawton · Ardmore · DeQueen

Vaughan · Lubbock · Wichita Falls · Sherman · Paris · Texarkana

Roswell · Arlington · Mineola · Shreveport

Alamagordo · Carlsbad · Big Spring · *Inn on Lake Granbury* 306 · Dallas · Tyler · Longview

Las Cruces · El Paso · Ciudad Juárez · Odessa · Abilene · Granbury · Waco

Van Horn · Fort Stockton · San Angelo · *Blair House Inn* 304 · Market Days & Craft Fair

Sonora · Fredericksburg · Austin · 309 *Sage Hill Inn*

Rose Hill Manor 308 · Wimberley · Kyle · Houston

Boquillas · Del Rio · San Antonio · The Alamo · 307 *Noble Inns-Oge and Carriage House*

Chihuahua · Eagle Pass · *Hoopes' House* 305 · Rockport · Palacios

Ciudad Camargo · Laredo · Nuevo Laredo · Corpus Christi

Parral · McAllen · Brownsville

Reynosa · Matamoros

Gómez Palacio · Torreón · Monterrey · Saltillo

Gulf

of

Mexico

Durango · Matahuala · Ciudad Victoria

Mazatlán · Fresnillo

mi 0   50 mi
km 0   50 km
scale

© 2014 Chrismar Mapping Services Inc. Licensed for use in the 2014 Select Registry.

Blair House Inn

www.blairhouseinn.com
100 W. Spoke Hill Drive, Wimberley, TX USA 78676
877-549-5450 • 512-847-1111
info@blairhouseinn.com

Member Since 1998

Texas

Wimberley

Innkeepers/Owners
Mike and Vickie Schneider

Conveniently located just minutes from the Wimberley Square, Blair House Inn is situated on 22 peaceful acres featuring breathtaking hill country vistas. Meticulous service, warm hospitality, delectable food and luxury amenities provide the ultimate in comfort. This inviting inn is light and airy and features one of the best art galleries in Wimberley. A pool and whirlpool spa set in the hillside allows for spectacular views while relaxing. Blair House also provides spacious and attractive common areas including a living room with a fireplace, television/game room, library, and a front porch with beautiful sunset views and patio by the herb garden. Guests can enjoy a massage in the day spa, relax in the sauna, hike the grounds, venture out on one of the bicycles or just nap in a hammock. Rated third nationwide as "Best Evening Cuisine" and "Best B&B for Relaxing and Unwinding," by Inn Traveler™ Magazine and the "Best Breakfast in Texas" – Southern Living.™ Winner – TripAdvisor Certificate of Excellence 2011 & 2012.

Rates
3 Rooms, Main House, $160/$176. 5 Suites, $235/$260. 4 Individual Cottages, $299/$348. Open year-round. Number of Rooms: 12

Cuisine
Full 3-course gourmet breakfast, evening dessert, 5-course fixed menu gourmet dinner on Saturday evenings. Complimentary beverages.

Nearest Airport
Austin/San Antonio

Hoopes' House

www.hoopeshouse.com
417 N. Broadway, Rockport, TX USA 78382
800-924-1008 • Fax: 361-790-9288
hoopeshouse@sbcglobal.net

Member Since 2010

Texas Rockport

General Manager
Paula Sargent

Built in the 1890s, the historic Hoopes' House in Rockport, Texas has been meticulously renovated and restored to its original splendor. The sunny yellow inn commands a panoramic view of Rockport Harbor and is within walking distance of museums, shops, galleries and restaurants. The main house consists of four charming guest rooms, each with a private bath. For those wanting a more private experience, a new wing houses four additional guest rooms, each beautifully appointed. The grounds feature a pool, a hot tub and a gazebo. Elegant but casual, the Hoopes' House combines modern luxury with old world charm. Hardwood floors, 12 foot ceilings, intricately carved fireplaces, crown molding, fine art and antiques recall another time... another era. Relax with a good book in the parlor. Enjoy the Gulf breeze under the gazebo. Linger over morning coffee in the sun-room. Listen to the call of the gulls on the porch. Delight in the pleasures of a slower time.

Rates
Range from $110 to $175 per night. Check web site for each room rate, full facility available for $1,400/night. Closed Christmas week. No pets allowed. Children 12 years and older. Number of Rooms: 8

Cuisine
Breakfast is served each morning from 9 am to 10 am in either the formal dining room, gazebo or sun-room. Breakfast fare includes pineapple casserole, fresh fruit, blueberry pancakes and cream cheese bread pudding for starters.

Nearest Airport
Located 35 miles north of Corpus Christi

♿ 🍽   ♀

Inn on Lake Granbury

www.innonlakegranbury.com
205 West Doyle Street, Granbury, TX USA 76048
877-573-0046 • 817-573-0046
info@innonlakegranbury.com

Member Since 2006

Innkeepers/Owners
Cathy Casey and Jim Leitch

The Inn on Lake Granbury offers upscale guestrooms, suites, and private houses on three landscaped acres directly on beautiful Lake Granbury. There are 15 total luxury accommodations, either single or double occupancy. Each luxurious room, suite or house has an oversized king or queen bed, fabulously comfortable guest robes, private two person showers (some with steam showers and heated bathroom floors), some with jetted tubs, some with lake views, and all with wireless Internet access. Our newest addition to the Inn is a wonderfully spacious contemporary lake house comprising approximately 2000 square feet, in the southwest corner of the property with floor to ceiling glass doors and windows overlooking the lake. Experience our flagstone encased saltwater pool with large deck, tanning ledge and waterfall. Sit on the swing under 200 year old oak trees for a spectacular view of the lake. Walk less than three blocks to the historic square for shopping and fine dining. Complimentary appetizers and beverages are served every afternoon along with a full breakfast each morning.

Rates
$195/$325 per night Sunday-Thursday and $235/$595 per night Friday and Saturday. Group rates available for corporate/business retreats. Wedding package pricing also available upon request. Number of Rooms: 15

Cuisine
Rates include a full gourmet breakfast and appetizers and complimentary beverages including wine each afternoon. Lunch and dinner for overnight group stays upon request.

Nearest Airport
Dallas Fort Worth Airport

 SelectRegistry.com

Noble Inns – Oge and Carriage Houses

www.nobleinns.com
209 Washington Street, San Antonio, TX USA 78204
800-242-2770 • 210-223-2353 • Fax: 210-225-4045
stay@nobleinns.com

Member Since 1994

Owners
Don & Liesl Noble

Don and Liesl Noble, sixth-generation San Antonians, invite guests to experience the rich history and ambiance of San Antonio. These 2 properties are located across the street from each other in the King William Historic District. AAA 4-Diamond Oge House, an 1857 Antebellum Mansion that is one of Texas' historic architectural gems, boasts large verandas and 1.5 acres of gardens directly on the famous RiverWalk. The Aaron Pancoast Carriage House features rooms w/living/dining room, full kitchen, gas fireplace and garden w/ outdoor pool and heated spa. All rooms include king or queen bed, private bath, antique furnishings and elegant fabrics, free WiFi, flat-panel TV w/cable and DVD player, DVD library access, private phone w/voice mail, custom guest robes, air conditioning and refrigerator. Spacious suites have luxurious marble/granite bath w/2-person whirlpool tub. Near all downtown sites, including the Alamo, convention center, Alamodome, shopping, dining and entertainment. Complete your experience by booking a ride to dinner in our classic 1960 Rolls Royce Silver Cloud II.

Rates
9 Rooms, $159/$289; 4 Suites, $239/$399. Inquire about special advance purchase, group and corporate rates, and last minute specials. Get best rates and book online at www.nobleinns.com. Number of Rooms: 13

Cuisine
The Oge House features a delicious full breakfast, afternoon refreshments, evening sherry and port. Aaron Pancoast Carriage House features full breakfast for adult groups at the Oge House and expanded continental breakfast in room for groups w/children

Nearest Airport
San Antonio International - 9 miles/13 minutes via expressway to downtown.

Rose Hill Manor

www.rose-hill.com
2614 Upper Albert Road, Near Fredericksburg, TX USA 78671
877-767-3445 • 830-644-2247
rosehill@ktc.com

Member Since 2006

Innkeepers/Owners
Robert & Patricia VanderLyn

Rose Hill Manor is the only place in Texas where you can stay at a AAA Four Diamond inn with a fine dining restaurant and walk to a winery and tasting room. Our graciously appointed and spacious accommodations offer all the amenities required by the Four Diamond standard. Enjoy the celebrated cuisine of the on-site gourmet restaurant, where great meals are creatively prepared and wines are poured from a thoughtfully chosen cellar highlighted by fine vintages from around the world and premium liquor. Nestled in the heart of the Texas wine country, Rose Hill is located only fifteen minutes from the historical town of Fredericksburg, Texas, and serves as an excellent base for exploring the region's best wineries, historical architecture, shopping and museums. Rose Hill has received critical acclaim for both the lodging and restaurant in Gourmet Magazine, Wine Spectator, Victoria Magazine, The Dallas Morning News, and Texas Highways. Come escape to an oasis of tranquility, Texas hill country style!

Rates
1 Queen Suite, $155/$249. 3 King Suites, $155/$249. 8 King Cottages, $155/$249.
Number of Rooms: 12

Cuisine
Complimentary multiple-course breakfast to overnite guests at private tables. On-Site upscale gourmet restaurant with outstanding wine list, each Wednesday through Sunday night - open to both our guests and the general public.

Nearest Airport
Either the San Antonio or Austin airport ~ 1 hour away. Airport for small planes in Fredericksburg - 15 minutes.

Sage Hill Inn Above Onion Creek

 ♿ 🍽 🍽 🍽 ♀

www.sagehill.com
4444 W FM 150, Kyle, TX USA 78640
800-579-7686 • 512-268-1617 • Fax: 512-268-1090
info@sagehill.com

Member Since 2003

Texas Kyle

Innkeeper/Owners
Amy Dolan/Eric Goldreyer and John Banczak

Located 25 minutes from Downtown Austin, the Boutique Inn, Restaurant and Spa sits atop a hill on 88 acres above Onion Creek, with sweeping views of the Hill Country to the West. Built in 1994, Sage Hill has recently completed an enormous renovation including a brand-new larger Spa, huge new pool deck with 14-person hot tub, large outdoor fire pit, new bocce, horseshoe and washer courts, extensive room upgrades and remodels, and an expanded kitchen and restaurant. Our land has miles and miles of hiking trails rich with wildlife including deer, blackbuck antelope, wild turkey, foxes, raccoons and abundant birdlife. We are the top-rated inn near Austin and have been featured recently in publications like Forbes, Austin Monthly, Texas Home and Living, and the Austin-American Statesman. The inn is a perfect place for romantic getaways, small corporate events, and weddings as large as 150 people, ideally situated in the Texas Hill Country near wineries, great shopping, and everything that Austin has to offer.

Rates
15 rooms, including 3 suites, 2 cottages, 3 bedroom house: $249/$599. Rates include Dinner and Breakfast with each night's stay. Each room has fireplace & porch, 7 with whirlpool tubs. Special rates for small meetings and retreats. Number of Rooms: 15

Cuisine
Multi-course dinner served each evening. Gourmet breakfast with freshly squeezed orange juice served from 8:30-10:00 each morning. Dinner and Breakfast with each night's stay. Complimentary coffee, tea, cold drinks, and homemade cookies always!

Nearest Airport
Austin Bergstrom: 35 minutes, San Antonio International: 65 minutes

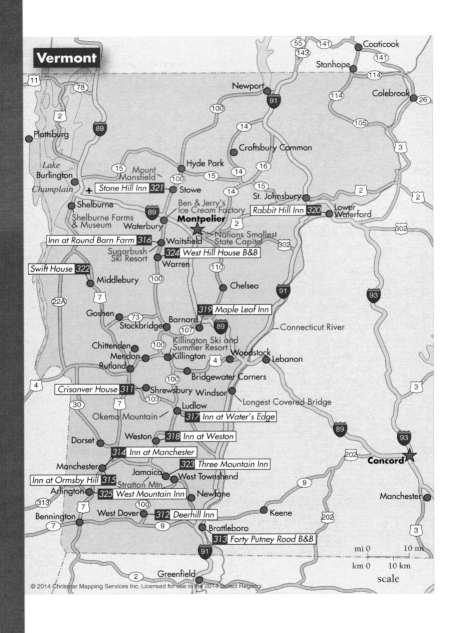

Vermont

55 143 141 Coaticook
Stanhope 141
114
Newport 114 Colebrook
11 78 91 26
2 105
89
Plattsburg 14
Craftsbury Common 3
Lake Hyde Park
Burlington 15 Mount 100 14 16
Champlain Mansfield 15 St. Johnsbury
Stone Hill Inn 321 Stowe 14 15 Lower
Shelburne Ben & Jerry's *Rabbit Hill Inn 320* Waterford
Shelburne Farms Ice Cream Factory 2
& Museum 89 **Montpelier** 802
Waterbury 2
Inn at Round Barn Farm 316 Waitsfield Nations Smallest
Sugarbush *324 West Hill House B&B* State Capitol 802
Ski Resort Warren
Swift House 322 110
Middlebury 100 Chelsea
22A 7 91
Goshen 73 *319 Maple Leaf Inn*
Stockbridge Barnard Connecticut River
107 89 93
Chittenden 100 Killington Ski and
Mendon Summer Resort Woodstock
Rutland Killington 4 Lebanon
100 Bridgewater Corners
4 *Crisanver House 311* Shrewsbury Windsor 3
30 7 103 Ludlow Longest Covered Bridge
Okemo Mountain *317 Inn at Water's Edge* 89 93
Weston *318 Inn at Weston* 202 **Concord**
Dorset *314 Inn at Manchester*
323 Three Mountain Inn Manchester
Manchester Jamaica *325 West Mountain Inn* West Townshend 9
Inn at Ormsby Hill 315 Stratton Mtn. Newfane
Arlington 100 3
313 7 West Dover *312 Deerhill Inn* Keene 202
Bennington 9 Brattleboro 3
7 *313 Forty Putney Road B&B* mi 0 10 mi
91 km 0 10 km
2 Greenfield scale
© 2014 Christmar Mapping Services Inc. Licensed for use in the 2014 Select Registry.

Crisanver House

www.crisanver.com
1434 Crown Point Road, Shrewsbury, VT USA 05738
800-492-8089 • 802-492-3589 • Fax: 802-492-3480
info@crisanver.com

Member Since 2005

Innkeepers/Owners
B. Michael & Carol Calotta

Historic luxury, comfort and rustic elegance nestled in rolling meadows on a country road, a convenient 10 minutes from the highway creating an aura of escape.

A romantic Inn, known for charming innkeepers, beautiful grounds, exceptional accommodations with soundproof walls, warm hospitality, stunning mountain views and fine dining.

At 2000 feet and 120 acres of meadows, woodlands, lawns, gardens, the Inn offers hiking, tennis, bocce, snowshoeing, shuffleboard and swimming to engage you every season. Some of the best skiing at Killington & Okemo, wonderful restaurants and activities of Rutland and Ludlow, great shopping in Manchester, cultural adventures, golf and other outdoor activities are nearby. For Epicureans' the Cheese Trail and Craft Beer Trail delights with Vermont's best.

A getaway you will cherish, See why we are a "1,000 place to see before you die in the US & Canada", awarded Trip Advisor Certificate of Excellence and part of Bed & Breakfast Diamond Collection

Experience the enchantment of the Green Mountains and what makes Crisanver House so special.

Rates
$140 - $425 Varies on room and season. Exceptional accommodations: Main House deluxe 3 suites & 2 guestrooms/Cottages 4 rooms. Free parking, wi-fi, tea/homemade cookies, and freshly prepared breakfast. Special group rates. Number of Rooms: 9

Cuisine
Epicurean dining by candlelight in our glass enclosed conservatory surrounded by the countryside and Green Mountains with fine linens and china. Local fresh and organic food some from the Inn's gardens, prix fixe. 500 bottle wine cellar. Reservations.

Nearest Airport
Rutland Regional - 10 minutes; Albany, Hartford, Burlington International - each 2 hours

Deerhill Inn

www.deerhill.com
14 Valley View Road, P.O. Box 136, West Dover, VT USA 05356
802-464-3100 • 800-993-3379 • Fax: 802-464-5474
innkeeper@deerhill.com

Member Since 1999

Vermont

West Dover

Innkeepers/Owners
Ariane Burgess and Scott Kocher

On a peaceful hillside above the historic village of West Dover, Deerhill Inn gazes across the beautiful Mount Snow Valley to the tranquil Green Mountains. It's a special place with a warm welcome - guests return again and again to explore Southern Vermont or just truly relax. Beautifully-decorated guest rooms with mountain or garden views feature jetted tubs, fireplaces, TV/DVD players, luxury robes, L'Occitane amenities and free WiFi. A pretty pool nestles in flower-filled gardens. Sitting and dining rooms are elegant and welcoming with log fires and wonderful views. All-seasons Southern Vermont offers galleries, craft and antique shops, museums, historic houses, theaters, concerts, quaint farms and villages and fabulous fall foliage driving tours. There's golfing, fishing, hiking, biking, carriage rides, canoeing, kayaking and lake boating in summer; skiing, snowboarding, snowshoeing, husky-mushing, snowmobiling and sleigh-rides in winter – all within easy reach of the Inn. Then home to the Inn, for a restful sleep under Vermont's magical starry skies.

Rates
$145-$325 (Base). $131-$293 (Spring); $145-$335 (Winter); $165-$355 (Foliage & Holidays). For indulgences and extras, celebration and holiday packages and seasonal offers, see our website: www.deerhill.com. Number of Rooms: 13

Cuisine
Made-to-order country breakfast and afternoon tea. Delicious farm-to-table cuisine using fresh local ingredients. Wine Spectator-awarded wine list. Comfortable dining rooms with spectacular views of the Green Mountains and cozy full-service bar.

Nearest Airport
Albany, NY - 1.5 hours; Bradley Hartford, CT - 2 hours; Logan Boston, MA - 3 hours; JFK NYC, NY - 4 hours

SelectRegistry.com

Forty Putney Road Bed & Breakfast

www.fortyputneyroad.com
192 Putney Rd, Brattleboro, VT USA 05301
802-254-6268 • 800-941-2413
innkeepers@fortyputneyroad.com

Member Since 2011

Innkeeper/Owner
Rhonda Calhoun

A comfortable yet elegant 6-room inn overlooking the water and yet just a short walk to vibrant downtown Brattleboro, Vermont boasting great shops, cafes, galleries, restaurants and pubs.

We are not your typical B&B. We have a small pub on site with an array of wine, local craft beers and hard cider. On select Saturday nights, our guests can enjoy a fun and informative craft beer tasting including a variety of locally made craft brews and cheeses while learning about the brewing process and beer styles. Every morning, we serve a full two course gourmet breakfast made with fresh and local ingredients. Relax in the hot tub, or play a game of pool by the fire. Every room has its own private bathroom; several rooms have fireplaces and private entrances. Of course, we have free WiFi; every room has a flat panel TV/DVD player; complimentary snacks and beverages all day, and so much more. We are also your choice for intimate weddings, elopements, civil union ceremonies, and vow renewal celebrations.

Rates
Rates range from around $159 to $319, depending on the particular room and time of year. We occasionally offer specials and last minute deals, so be sure to connect with us on facebook.com/vermontinn or call for more details. Number of Rooms: 6

Cuisine
All of our rates include a Full Two Course Gourmet Breakfast served daily anytime from 8 - 9:30 a.m. From baked peach french toast to souffles to lemon ricotta pancakes to fresh vegetable frittata...every day is different and delicious.

Nearest Airport
Bradley International Airport - Hartford / Springfield (BDL)

The Inn at Manchester

www.innatmanchester.com
3967 Main Street, P.O. Box 41, Manchester, VT USA 05254
802-362-1793 • 800-273-1793 • Fax: 802-362-3218
innkeepers@innatmanchester.com

Member Since 2008

Vermont

Manchester

Innkeepers/Owners
Frank & Julie Hanes

Unforgettable personality and unlimited possibilities await you at one of Vermont's most inviting getaways, The Inn at Manchester. Tucked away in the breathtaking landscape of the Taconic and Green Mountains in Vermont's cultural haven, Manchester - where there's something for everyone year round. Golf, skiing, hiking, fishing, shopping, theatre or art, Manchester and the Mountains has something for every taste. As always, there is no rule you ever have to leave the inn! Unwind beside the hearth in the living room, or over a game of chess in the cozy den. Maybe take a stroll around our beautiful grounds, a dip in the pool, or just relax in a rocker on the porch. Then drop in for a cocktail in the Nineteenth Room, our fully licensed pub - one of the places where guests gather to relax and socialize. We look forward to welcoming you to the Inn at Manchester, a Gem in the Green Mountains.

Rates
Our rates run from $155 to $315. Number of Rooms: 18

Cuisine
We pride ourselves on a full traditional breakfast that is guaranteed to start your day off in the right way! Try our famous cottage cakes with hot apricot sauce or a savory omelet. Also, sneak into our guest pantry and help yourself to refreshments.

Nearest Airport
Albany, New York (Approximate time: 1 1/2 hours)

The Inn at Ormsby Hill

www.ormsbyhill.com
1842 Main Street, Historic Route 7A, Manchester Center, VT USA 05255
802-362-1163 • 800-670-2841 • Fax: 802-362-5176
stay@ormsbyhill.com

Member Since 1996

Innkeepers/Owners
Yoshio and Diane Endo

Step across the massive marble threshold of this beautiful, historic property, drop your bags, and breathe a sigh of relief. Welcome to a house built for happiness and hospitality. Stop first in the heart of our home, the conservatory dining room. With magnificent views of the Green Mountains, an intricately carved mahogany mantle, snacks and beverages day and night, and our amazing three-course breakfast, this room will nourish your body and soul. Our enormous patio and porch beckon with Adirondack rocking chairs, patio tables, porch swings, and views you will never forget. Let yourself dissolve into the surroundings with your book, tablet, wine or favorite beverage. Retreat to your guest oasis, with fireplace, two-person whirlpool tub, and organic bath amenities, for some intimate time. Your room might also have a two-person steam shower, private deck, or cool stereo. Stroll the exquisitely landscaped grounds and expect a few surprises: a labyrinth in the meadow, a cozy gazebo hideaway. The Inn at Ormsby Hill is a world away from cares, where you can be your true self.

Rates
8 Rooms and 2 suites, all with fireplaces and whirlpool tubs for two, $205/$425 B&B.
Open year-round. Number of Rooms: 10

Cuisine
Breakfast will energize you for the day. It features Mocha Joe's local roasted coffee, ground daily, plus three creative and lovingly homemade courses, served in our elegant dining conservatory. Complimentary cookies, snacks, and beverages.

Nearest Airport
Albany, New York (1 hour 15 minutes). Hartford, Connecticut (2 hours 15 minutes).

The Inn at The Round Barn Farm

www.theroundbarn.com
1661 East Warren Road, Waitsfield, VT USA 05673
802-496-2276 • Fax: 802-496-2276
lodging@theroundbarn.com

Member Since 2000

Vermont
Waitsfield

Innkeepers/Owners
Jim and Kim Donahue

We invite you to our elegant, romantic Bed & Breakfast Inn located amidst 245 acres of lush green hills, flower-covered meadows, graceful ponds, and extensive perennial gardens in Vermont's Green Mountains. This four season retreat in the Sugarbush/Mad River Valley has offered an escape for lovers of the arts, history, and the outdoors since 1987. The interior of the inn is memorable; the restoration impeccable. The inn offers wireless Internet access throughout. Our 12 guest rooms are individually decorated featuring refurbished wide-board pine floors covered in oriental rugs, beautiful wallpapers in a palette of rich tones, decorative accents, and attention to the details that matter. In winter, our meadows and woodlands are covered in a blanket of snow. Snowshoe trails and snowshoes are available for our guests to experience the magic of our Vermont winter wonderland. In the summer enjoy concerts, theater, our very own three week opera festival in June, and a variety of outdoor activities. Our innkeepers (and freshly baked cookies) await your arrival.

Rates
Rates $175/$330. Tempur-Pedic beds, down comforters, whirlpool tubs, steam showers, green products, gas fireplaces, individual heat and A/C. Number of Rooms: 12

Cuisine
As founding members of the Vermont Fresh Network and having our own certified organic garden, our breakfasts and hors d'oeuvres are prepared with seasonal and local ingredients. Dinner is enjoyed at one of 15 area restaurants.

Nearest Airport
43 Minutes from the Burlington International Airport (BTV)

316

Inn at Water's Edge

www.innatwatersedge.com
45 Kingdom Road, Ludlow, VT USA 05149
888-706-9736 • 802-228-8143
innatwatersedge@tds.net

Member Since 2003

Innkeepers/Owners
Bruce & Tina Verdrager

Situated on Echo Lake and the Black River, the 150 year old Victorian estate has been thoroughly restored and now boasts all the charm and ambiance of a truly unique Victorian Inn. The Inn exudes the endless enthusiasm of the innkeepers to create the feeling of a bygone era along with the warmth and comfort of being home. Located minutes from skiing and golfing at Okemo and Killington mountains, the Inn is only a short drive to the attractions of Manchester, Weston and Woodstock. Our library, gathering room and English pub all have fireplaces and comfortable seating for guests to enjoy. Each of our 11 guest rooms has a private bath, most with Jacuzzi bathtubs and fireplaces. Whether relaxing in our outdoor hot tub, swimming off our private beach, canoeing or biking, the Inn offers year-round activities. The Inn is also completely air-conditioned and handicapped accessible. The Inn at Water's Edge is a AAA Four Diamond award-winning property and called "A Real Gem" by Connecticut Magazine and "Homier than Home" by the Boston Globe.

Rates
$125-$250 B&B $175-$300MAP. Golf pkgs from $150/ppdo, incl 18 holes, lodging, breakfast & 4-course dinner. Ski pkgs from $100/ppdo.incl lift ticket, lodging, breakfast & 4-course dinner. Reservations can be made 60 days in advance. Number of Rooms: 11

Cuisine
Full country breakfast. Afternoon refreshments. 4-course candlelit dinner. Beer, wine & spirits available in Doc's English Pub & in the Dining room.

Nearest Airport
Bradley International, CT, Manchester, NH

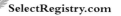

The Inn at Weston

www.innweston.com
630 Main St, PO Box 66, Weston, Vermont USA 05161
802-824-6789
theinnatweston@comcast.net

Member Since 2012

AWARD OF EXCELLENCE 2013

Innkeepers
Robert & Linda Aldrich

Escape to the heart of the Green Mountains where warmth and hospitality greet you at the door! The Inn at Weston is located in the quintessential Southern Vermont Village of Weston. Relax and unwind in one of our 13 graciously appointed guestrooms-some with whirlpools for two and walk-in sauna/steam showers. Several have their own deck, almost all have fireplaces and all have private baths. Stroll to the town green with gazebo, shops, galleries and museum. Sit by the waterfall of the Old Mill, attend services at the Weston Priory or visit our two clapboard New England churches. Visit during Winter and ski one of four local mountains-Magic, Stratton, Bromley and Okemo. All winter sports are nearby. In summer, take in a performance at the award winning Weston Playhouse Theater, bike, hike and picnic in the beautiful Green Mountains. Have a superb dinner in our casually elegant dining room or on our orchid filled deck and gazebo and ask George to play your favorite melody on our grand piano. Tour our onsite orchid greenhouse. We look forward to greeting you!

Rates
Traditional rooms - $185-$205. Luxury rooms - $225-$325. $50 more per night during holidays and foliage. 2 night minimum some weekends. Seasonal packages and specials online. Number of Rooms: 13

Cuisine
Full country breakfast and afternoon tea with home made pastry included. Dinner is Vermont contemporary cuisine using local ingredients. Wine Spectator awarded wine cellar. Large Oregon Pinot Noir selection. Cozy pub with wood burning fireplace.

Nearest Airport
Albany, New York - 1.5 hours. Hartford, Ct - 2 hours. Boston, MA - 3 hours.

The Maple Leaf Inn

www.mapleleafinn.com
5890 VT Rte 12, PO Box 273, Barnard, VT USA 05031
800-516-2753 • 802-234-5342 • Fax: 802-234-6456
innkeeper@mapleleafinn.com

Member Since 2002

Vermont Barnard

Innkeepers/Owners
Mike & Nancy Boyle

We welcome you to refresh your spirit and restore your soul in this pastoral corner of Vermont nestled snugly within sixteen acres of maple and birch trees. Enjoy hiking, biking, golfing, cross-country skiing, and snow-shoeing on the trails nearby, or go fishing, canoeing and kayaking at nearby Silver Lake. Fantastic restaurants are a short drive away. Each luxurious, light-filled guest room has its own personality and charm with crisp linens, comfy duvets and handmade quilts. Individually controlled central heating/air-conditioning, heated bathroom tile floors and a pillow library all add to your personal comfort. Wood-burning fireplaces are set daily for your convenience and a collection of romantic videos awaits your viewing. Snacks, sodas, coffee, tea and bottled water are available at any time. Complimentary wine and beer are served every day. Memorable gourmet breakfasts are prepared fresh each morning and served at candlelit tables for two.

Rates
$150/$290 B&B. Spacious guest rooms with king beds, luxurious private baths w/whirlpools, WiFi. Number of Rooms: 7

Cuisine
A gourmet three-course breakfast is served at candlelit tables. Light afternoon refreshments are served in the parlor at check-in. Complimentary coffee, tea, sodas and snacks available. Complimentary glass of wine or beer each day.

Nearest Airport
Burlington, VT; Manchester, NH; Boston, MA

♿ 🍽️ 🍽️ 🍷

Rabbit Hill Inn

www.rabbithillinn.com
48 Lower Waterford Rd, Lower Waterford, VT USA 05848
802-748-5168 • 800-76-BUNNY • Fax: 802-748-8342
info@rabbithillinn.com

Member Since 1990

Innkeepers/Owners
Brian & Leslie Mulcahy

Even in these fast-paced, continuously connected times, there are still a few places in the world where one can escape to unwind and spend some "adult-only" time with that special someone. Named One of the World's Top 100 Hotels by Travel+Leisure Magazine, Rabbit Hill Inn offers all the luxuries that one would come to expect - fireplaces, double spa tubs, fine bath amenities, and more; yet what sets Rabbit Hill apart from just any nice place to stay is the warmth, comfort, and personal caring provided by its long-time hands-on innkeepers and wonderful staff. Dining at the inn is truly outstanding. Sophisticated, locally sourced food at an intimate, candlelit table adds to a most romantic evening - comfortable and always unpretentious. A myriad of seasonal activities -- everything from adrenaline pumping adventurous pursuits to relaxing in-room massage is available year-round. Zagat Guide said it best: "...this just might be the most romantic place on the planet...!" Free WiFi available; non-smoking.

Rates
Including breakfast, afternoon sweets, turndown service, and gratuity for staff - Classic: $170-$250; Superior w/fireplace: $255-$305; Luxury w/whirlpool & fireplace: $330-$405. Rates vary by season. Check for specials! Number of Rooms: 19

Cuisine
Full country breakfast and afternoon tea and pastries included. Dinner features a frequently changing, modern and innovative menu. Beer, wine, and spirits available in our Snooty Fox Pub.

Nearest Airport
Manchester, NH (MHT)-2 hrs; Burlington, VT (BTV)-2 hrs; Logan Int'l (BOS)-3 hrs

Vermont
Lower Waterford

🎣 **SelectRegistry.com**

Stone Hill Inn

www.stonehillinn.com
89 Houston Farm Road, Stowe, VT USA 05672
802-253-6282 • Fax: 802-253-7415
stay@stonehillinn.com

Member Since 2002

Vermont Stowe

Owners/Innkeepers
Linda and George Fulton

Relax. Quiet, secluded, and barely visible fifty feet above the Mountain Road. Surrounded by woods on 9.5 acres; feels like an island of calm. Here luxury is defined by both the thoughtfulness of your accommodations and opportunities for intimacy — intimacy of life and love. Yet, Stowe, its restaurants, fly fishing among five local streams, spectacular hiking, stand-up paddleboarding, kayaking, canoeing, vista-laden golf and the best skiing in New England are just minutes away. Feel your shoulders unfold as you sink into your bubbling, fireside Jacuzzi for two--every room has one. Fall asleep in your king-size bed warmed by your fireplace and accompanied by a movie from our 300 collection. (Free popcorn!) Massages are available in your room. TripAdvisor 2014 and 2012 Traveler's Choice award winner as one of the top 25 inns/B&Bs in all of the US (#8 & #16 respectively)!

Rates
$285-$425 (varies by season). Visit stonehillinn.com for exact seasonal rates and seasonal packages. Number of Rooms: 9

Cuisine
Like the powdered sugar on your orange-pecan waffle, sun dabbles the two of you during your three-course breakfast within a cathedral of 40 windows. Nine rooms; nine tables. Appetizers and conversation during evening social hours.

Nearest Airport
Burlington, VT (45 min). Morrisville (10 min) has a small airport for private aircraft.

Swift House Inn

www.swifthouseinn.com
25 Stewart Lane, Middlebury, VT USA 05753
866-388-9925 • 802-388-9925 • Fax: 802-388-9927
info@swifthouseinn.com

Member Since 2005

AWARD OF EXCELLENCE
2013

Innkeepers/Owners
Dan & Michele Brown

A historic 20-room former governor's mansion, the Swift House Inn is Middlebury's only in-town Country Inn, and offers the essence of New England warmth. Large, comfortable rooms provide modern amenities in period decor. The Inn's three buildings are on four acres with extensive lawns and gardens. Enjoy a casual dinner in the bar, on the deck, or in Jessica's Restaurant. Relax, sip a glass of wine by the fireplace, or ponder your favorite book. Every window frames a picture of country tranquility, yet shops, museums, and Middlebury College are a short walk away. The Town Hall Theater and College bring numerous world class performing artists to the area with performances most weekends. Enjoy hiking the Trail Around Middlebury or in the nearby Green Mountains. Bike the Champlain Valley, fly fish our numerous rivers and creeks, or participate in water activities on nearby lakes Champlain and Dunmore. Downhill and cross country ski areas are just a short drive. Bring your bike, golf clubs, fly rod or just come to relax. After a busy day enjoy the sauna or steam shower.

Rates
20 Rooms in three buildings. Main House $129-$199, Gate House $129-$169, Carriage House $229-$299, rates vary by season. Many rooms with fireplaces and whirlpool tubs. All rooms have individual heat and A/C controls, satellite TV Number of Rooms: 20

Cuisine
Full Breakfast from 7:30 to 9:30. Dinner in Jessica's is served 4 nights a week winter/spring and 5 nights summer/fall; changing menu prepared with many local Vermont products. Full bar service and extensive wine list, Wine Spectator Award

Nearest Airport
Burlington International Airport, 35 miles Albany Airport 112 miles

Three Mountain Inn

www.threemountaininn.com
3732 VT Routes 30/100, P.O. Box 180, Jamaica, VT USA 05343
802-874-4140
stay@threemtn.com

Member Since 1982

Vermont Jamaica

Innkeepers/Owners
Ed & Jennifer Dorta-Duque

The Three Mountain Inn, located in the small, unspoiled village of Jamaica, Vermont is a perfect choice to spend a few days of rest and relaxation. Peacefully set among Vermont's Green Mountains, the Inn overlooks the woodlands and trails of the Jamaica State Park and is just minutes away from Stratton, Bromley and Magic Mountain Ski areas.

Our individually decorated rooms feature luxurious linens, relaxing robes, period pieces, fabulous queen or king featherbeds, private baths, air conditioning and WiFi. Most have fireplaces while some have private decks, whirlpool tubs and TV/DVDs. With its wide-planked pine walls and multiple fireplaces, the Three Mountain Inn has an abundance of history and a sense of luxury.

Whether you enjoy a romantic dinner in our Dining Room, relax by one of the many fireplaces, indulge in our incredible three-course breakfast, or explore the various outdoor possibilities; the Three Mountain Inn will revive your senses.

Rates
$199 to $360, Seasonal Packages available. Visit www.threemountainn.com. Number of Rooms: 10

Cuisine
Offering an elegant dining experience, showcasing contemporary Vermont Fresh Cuisine.

Nearest Airport
Hartford, CT (1.5 hours); Albany, NY (1.5 hours)

West Hill House B & B

🍴   🍷

www.westhillbb.com
1496 West Hill Road, Warren, VT USA 05674
802-496-7162
innkeepers@westhillbb.com

Member Since 2009

Vermont Warren

Innkeepers/Owners
Peter & Susan MacLaren

Nestled in the serene setting of the Green Mountains, our beautiful 1850s home is on a quiet country road beside Sugarbush's ski resort and its Robert Trent Jones, Sr. golf course. The B&B offers a peaceful retreat at any time of year from the rush of everyday life. In winter enjoy skiing at Sugarbush, Mad River Glen, the Catamount Ski Trail crossing our property, plus Nordic skiing nearby. In the warmer months enjoy our gorgeous perennial gardens and close proximity to golf, hiking the Long Trail, kayaking, biking and many other summer activities. Year round you will enjoy the many attractions and activities of central Vermont. Just minutes away, the shops, artisans and marvelous restaurants of Warren and Waitsfield await you. Our classic Vermont B&B offers comfort, hospitality and delicious breakfasts. The guest rooms have gas fireplaces, HD TVs, A/C, free phone calls and WiFi. Well-appointed ensuite bathrooms all feature Jacuzzis and/or steam showers. An ideal spot for elopements, weddings up to 50 people, business retreats, and most especially a place to come and relax.

Rates
Open year round. $140-$320 per night double occupancy including breakfast. Taxes and fees add 13%. Each room or suite has a king or queen bed and each ensuite has either a Jacuzzi tub, steam shower or both. Number of Rooms: 9

Cuisine
Our sumptuous breakfast starts with juice, home baking and a fruit dish. A tantalizing hot entree gives your taste buds a morning treat, then—dessert! Hot beverages, home-made cookies and honor bar are always available. Single Malt bar in the evening.

Nearest Airport
Burlington International (BTV) is a beautiful 45 mile drive from the B&B.

West Mountain Inn

www.WestMountainInn.com
144 West Mountain Inn Road, Arlington, VT USA 05250
802-375-6516 • Fax: 802-375-6553
info@WestMountainInn.com

Member Since 1984

Vermont Arlington

Innkeepers/Owners
The Carlson Family

A Vermont country retreat you can call your own! Luxurious rooms, splendid meals, refreshing outdoor pursuits, relaxing afternoons and convivial evenings - that is what a visit to the West Mountain Inn is. Set high on a mountainside overlooking the historic village of Arlington and Green Mountains beyond, the century-old West Mountain Inn has welcomed guests for over thirty years. Visitors to the Inn are surrounded by fantastic views and 150 acres of gardens, lawns, woodlands and meadows. Without having to leave the Inn's property, guests can hike or snowshoe on miles of trails, fly fish, swim or canoe in the famous Battenkill River and relax in the Adirondack chairs on the front lawn. The Inn's wood-paneled dining room provides a perfect setting for the lavish country breakfasts and sumptuous 5-course dinners created daily by our award-winning chef. The Inn also offers private dining rooms and a wonderful antique barn for the unique celebration of weddings, birthdays, anniversaries, reunions or business retreats. Fodor's "Choice," Frommers "Highly Recommended".

Rates
12 Rooms, 3 Suites, 3 Townhouses $155/$340 B&B, $255/$420 MAP. Service charges included in all rates. Number of Rooms: 19

Cuisine
A lavish country breakfast and splendid 5-course dinner are prepared daily. Seasonal menus focus on local VT products and organic produce. Weddings and rehearsal dinners a specialty. Full bar, premium beers and exceptional wine list.

Nearest Airport
Albany, NY - 1 Hour. Hartford, CT/Manchester, NH/Burlington, VT - all 2 1/2 hours.

Virginia

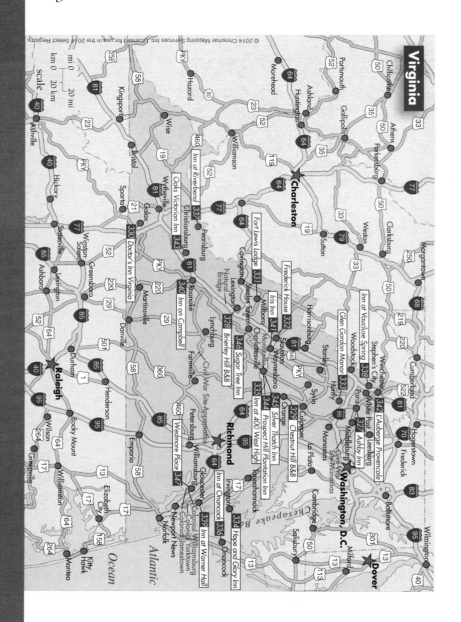

Virginia

scale
mi 0   20 mi
km 0   20 km

Chillicothe
Portsmouth
Morehead
Ashland
Huntington
Gallipolis
Hazard
Athens
Parkersburg
Clarksburg
Morgantown
Cumberland
Hagerstown
Frederick
Baltimore
Wilmington
Dover
Salisbury
Cambridge

Kingsport
Wise
Williamson
Charleston
Weston
Sutton
Ashville
Bristol
Sparta
Galax
Wytheville
Christiansburg
Pearisburg
Covington
Fort Lewis Lodge
Inn of Riverbend 337
Oaks Victorian Inn 343
330 Doctor's Inn Virginia
310 Inn on Campbell
Natural Bridge
Lexington
Roanoke
Frederick House 332
Staunton
Harrisonburg
Winchester
Woodstock
Stanley
Syria
Luray
La Plata
Manassas
Washington, D.C.
Middleburg
Leesburg
Paris
White Post
Ashby Inn 327
Culpeper
Orange
329 Chestnut Hill B&B
344 Prospect Hill Plantation Inn
345 Silver Thatch Inn
335 Inn at 400 West High
346 Sugar Tree Inn
328 Brierley Hill B&B
Iris Inn 341
Glen Gordon Manor 333
Inn of Vaucluse Spring
Stephen's City
L'Auberge Provencale 342
Steeles Tavern
Millboro
Charlottesville
Monticello
Waynesboro

Hickory
Statesville
Winston-Salem
Greensboro
Lexington
Asheboro
Danville
Martinsville
Lynchburg
Farmville
Civil War Site-Appomattox
Raleigh
Durham
Henderson
Rocky Mount
Wilson
Greenville
Williamston
Elizabeth City
Emporia
Petersburg
Richmond
Wedmore Place 347
Williamsburg
Gloucester
Colonial Williamsburg
Yorktown
Colonial Jamestown
Newport News
Norfolk
Inn of Onancock 336
339 Inn at Warner Hall
Irvington
Tappahannock
334 Hope and Glory Inn
Onancock
Chesapeake Bay
Atlantic Ocean
Kitty Hawk
Manteo

326

SelectRegistry.com

The Ashby Inn & Restaurant

www.ashbyinn.com
692 Federal Street, Paris, VA USA 20130
540-592-3900 • 866-336-0099 • Fax: 540-592-3781
info@ashbyinn.com

Member Since 1988

Virginia Paris

AWARD OF EXCELLENCE
2013

Owners/Innkeeper
Jackie and Chuck Leopold/Emily Bettis

This 1829 inn finds its character in the historic village of Paris and its heart in the kitchen. Guests are treated to a meal that offers the creative, progressive, farm to table cuisine of Chef David Dunlap, an award winning wine list featuring Virginia wine and genuine hospitality in a relaxed setting. Four distinct dining rooms feature fireplaces, cozy booths, and an inviting sun porch. Summer dining on the covered terrace overlooking the lawn attracts a wide Washington following. Guest rooms furnished in period pieces, half with fireplaces and balconies, offer bountiful views stretching beyond the formal perennial gardens to the hills of the Blue Ridge. Located in the heart of Virginia's wine country, guests have a variety of activities to choose from. Within just minutes from the inn, one will find over half a dozen wineries, ample hiking at Sky Meadows State Park and boutique shopping in Middleburg. The Ashby was awarded 3 1/2 stars by Washingtonian Magazine in their top 100 restaurants issue and was given the Award of Excellence by Wine Spectator in 2011-2013.

Rates
6 historic guest rooms at the Main Inn, $155-$225 and 4 junior suites with wood-burning fireplaces and private balconies with views of the hillside at the School House, $275-$295, plus tax. Includes a full breakfast and free WiFi. Number of Rooms: 10

Cuisine
A full farmstead breakfast is included for our inn guests. Lunch and Dinner are available Wednesday-Sunday offering modern farm fare with Brunch on Sunday. Wine list and full bar available. Voted "Best Overall" by Open Table Diner's Choice Awards.

Nearest Airport
Winchester Regional Airport (16 miles), Washington/Dulles International Airport (36 miles)

&♿ ⑩ ♟

Brierley Hill Bed & Breakfast

www.brierleyhill.com
985 Borden Road, Lexington, VA USA 24450
800-422-4925 • 540-464-8421 • Fax: 540-464-8925
relax@brierleyhill.com   *Member Since 2007*

Innkeepers/Owners
David & Karen Innocent

Brierley Hill is a Romantic, Peaceful Hillside Retreat with Spectacular Views of the
Shenandoah Valley and the Blue Ridge Mountains. We are minutes away from Historic
downtown Lexington. We have six beautifully decorated rooms, all with private baths,
gas or electric fireplaces, Flat screen TVs and WiFi. Our suites offer whirlpool tubs and
separate sitting areas. One suite is handicap accessible with a oversized shower. The Inn
and cottage suite features central air conditioning/heat for our guest comfort. We have two
common areas where guest can gather. We serve breakfast every morning in the dining
room overlooking the valley, or on the veranda. Our award winning gardens, manicured
grounds and panoramic views are the perfect setting for weddings, retreats, and romantic
getaways. Our guests have garage space to park motorcycles or bicycles while visiting
the Shenandoah Valley and Blue Ridge Parkway. Our pets, Tucker & Deuce (a Golden
Retriever & Bernese Mountain Dog) eagerly await your arrival. Voted Top 10 Romantic
Inns. Brierley Hill , "Where Memories are Made."

Rates
$149/$379 open year round. Number of Rooms: 6

Cuisine
Full 3-course country breakfast, always ending with a dessert. Snacks available in
common area. Coffee and Tea available 24/7. Wine, fruit & cheese trays available at
addition charge. Excellent restaurants and pubs in downtown Lexington.

Nearest Airport
Roanoke (1 hr.)

Chestnut Hill Bed & Breakfast

www.chestnuthillbnb.com
236 Caroline Street, Orange, VA U.S.A. 22960
540-661-0430 • Fax: 540-661-4212
info@chestnuthillbnb.com

Member Since 2010

Virginia, Orange

Owner/Innkeeper
Kathleen Ayers

Built in 1860, the award-winning Chestnut Hill is located in the center of Virginia's wine country and has been skillfully renovated to preserve the master craftsmanship of this renowned historic home. As a result of the extensive six-year renovation combined with being professionally decorated, Chestnut Hill provides guests with an opportunity to appreciate the past while enjoying the luxuries and comforts of the present. Each room offers a private bath with hairdryers, quality toiletries, pillow-top beds dressed in triple-sheeted superior quality cotton linens, lush cozy spa robes, HD flat-screen televisions, and WiFi Internet access. Two guestrooms, Alexander Daley's Master Suite and Ask Anna, feature hot tubs. Extra special touches may include fresh-cut flowers, bottled flat or sparkling water, and homemade tea-time treats and confections. Our savory fusion breakfast, evening wine and cheese tasting, all-day complimentary beverages, access to our outdoor cinema, and unparalleled customer service are always standard offerings during your stay at Chestnut Hill.

Rates
Six luxurious guest rooms with private baths. Fireplaces and hot tubs available. Prices include a full two-course gourmet breakfast served each morning and wine & cheese tasting each afternoon. Prices range from $179-$295. Number of Rooms: 6

Cuisine
Our two-course fusion breakfast varies from sweet one day to savory the next, sometimes a combination of each. We are always prepared to accommodate special dietary needs. Join us for a glass of Virginia wine during our afternoon wine & cheese tasting.

Nearest Airport
Richmond International Airport, Washington Dulles Airport & Reagan National Airport.

The Doctor's Inn Virginia

www.thedoctorsinnvirginia.com
406 W. Stuart Drive, Galax, VA USA 24333
276-238-9998 • 276-237-0144
stay@thedoctorsinnvirginia.com

Member Since 2012

Virginia
Galax

Owner/Innkeeper
Ron Stamey/Margo Crouse

Listed on the National Register of Historic Places: the Doctor's Inn Virginia has achieved a TripAdvisor rating of 5 stars by its guests and therefore has been awarded a Certificate of Excellence for the Year of 2011. The Colonial Revival style house, built in 1913, is located in a small city of Galax, VA and just 10 miles from I-77. We are within walking distance from downtown, the Rex Theater, Chestnut Creek School of the Arts, the New River Trail and Felts Park and only 7 miles from the beautiful Blue Ridge Parkway. Enjoy our elegant simple pleasures: Egyptian cotton linens, luxurious robes, widescreen TV, wireless Internet access, air conditioning, ceiling fans, queen and full rooms with cashmere blankets. Interesting artifacts from around the world mix with elegance from the past. We offer lots of books, periodicals, and games. We provide snacks and beverages for the midnight munchies. Our warm hospitality and relaxing front porch brings our guests back for more. One visit at the inn and you appreciate the "Elegant Simplicity Prescribed by the Doctor."

Rates
In season, June-October $149. Number of Rooms: 4

Cuisine
Gourmet breakfasts served on fine china and linens. Mouthwatering quiche, fruit smoothies, home made scones, made fresh each day and a perfect way to start your morning. Menu changes daily.

Nearest Airport
Greensboro, NC 1.5 hours

Fort Lewis Lodge

& !❍! !❍! !❍! ⍋

www.fortlewislodge.com
603 Old Plantation Way, Millboro, VA USA 24460
540-925-2314 • Fax: 540-925-2352
info@fortlewislodge.com   *Member Since 1990*

Innkeepers/Owners
John and Caryl Cowden

Centuries old, wonderfully wild, uncommonly comfortable. A country inn at the heart of a 3200-acre mountain estate. Outdoor activities abound with miles of river trout and bass fishing, swimming, extensive hiking trails, mountain biking, and magnificent vistas. Fort Lewis is a rare combination of unpretentious elegance and unique architecture offering a variety of lodging choices where every room has a view. Three "in the round" Silo bedrooms, four hand-hewn Log Cabins with stone fireplaces, and Riverside House are perfect for a true country getaway. Evenings are highlighted by contemporary American-style cuisine served in the historic Lewis Gristmill. This is destination dining where the emphasis falls firmly on the cuisine - the kitchen never ceases to impress. Like most country inns, we trade in a change of pace, romance and exceptional fare. But over the years, we've come to understand that Fort Lewis has an asset that very few others have. Our wilderness - the mountains, forests, fields and streams and all the creatures that call this their home.

Rates
13 Rooms, $240/$255 MAP; 3 Family Suites, $255 MAP; 4 Log Cabins, $295/$335 MAP. The Modified American Plan allows you to be our guest for both a memorable dinner and breakfast the next morning. Open April-mid Nov. Number of Rooms: 20

Cuisine
Dinner and breakfast are included in the daily tariff. Evening meals offer a vibrant mix of fresh tastes, just plucked vegetables and interesting menus. The aroma of hickory smoke rising from the grills will leave you yearning to hear the dinner bell.

Nearest Airport
Roanoke, VA (1.5 hrs.); Charlottesville, VA (1.75 hrs.)

🍽️ 🍽️♀ Frederick House

www.frederickhouse.com
28 North New Street, Staunton, VA USA 24401
800-334-5575 • 540-885-4220 • Fax: 540-885-5180
stay@frederickhouse.com   *Member Since 1997*

Virginia **Staunton**

Approved
♦ ♦ ♦

Innkeepers/Owners
Joe and Evy Harman

Frederick House is a small, full service, historic, bed and breakfast hotel in seven separate buildings across from Mary Baldwin College in downtown historic Staunton, the Shenandoah Valley's oldest city. Five historic guest houses contain twenty three guest rooms or suites accommodating up to fifty seven guests and conference facilities for groups up to twenty five. Two furnished apartments are available for overnight or extended stays. Reception and Chumley's, the breakfast room at Frederick House open each morning from 7:30-10:00, are located in a vine covered building adjacent to one of three Frederick House parking lots. Breakfast includes a choice of beverages, hot or cold cereals, homemade granola and yogurt, whole grain waffles with real maple syrup, apple raisin quiche, ham and cheese pie, and strata. Special dietary requests can be met when requested.

The restaurant at Frederick House, Aioli, in an historic building adjacent to reception, serves contemporary Mediterranean cuisine.

Rates
12 Rooms, $109/$189; 11 Suites, $153/$279. Ask about our many packages. Open year-round. Number of Rooms: 25

Cuisine
15 Restaurants available within walking distance; Fine Dining, Seafood, Steaks, Pizza American, Italian, Mexican, Ribs, Gourmet Deli, Southern Home Cooking, Indian, Coffee Shops, Homemade Ice Cream, Homemade Chocolate Candy.

Nearest Airport
Shenandoah Valley Regional Airport or Charlottesville Albemarle Regional Airport

Glen Gordon Manor

www.glengordonmanor.com
1482 Zachary Taylor Hwy, Huntly, VA USA 22640
540–636–6010
info@glengordonmanor.com

Member Since 2012

Virginia Huntly

Owners/Innkeepers
Dayn Smith & Nancy Moon

Over the years, Glen Gordon Manor has hosted members of the British royal family and set the scene for many memorable hunts and balls overlooking Shenandoah National Park from 45 acres of pasture, lawns, and gardens. This captivating retreat glories in views of the Blue Ridge Mountains and neighboring farms and vineyards. Tracing its roots to 1833 as a Wells Fargo stagecoach stop, the main house brims with nostalgic settings: a fire-lit entrance hall, a baronial oak hunt room with minstrel gallery, a stone wine cellar, and a charming country kitchen. Guest rooms echo the warm radiance. Luxuriously appointed Glencroft Cottage suites and spacious Gordon Mews House lend further hospitality, along with a sparkling pool and stables. Enjoy the beauty and activities of the Shenandoah Valley and return to this luxury country estate to experience genuine hospitality and romantic dining. Relax poolside with incredible views or picnic under the largest copper beech tree in Virginia.

Rates
Rooms/Suites $275-$450, Arrival Champagne/Wine included. Gourmet breakfast included. Number of Rooms: 5

Cuisine
Two award winning, classically trained chefs are at the helm of the Manor's kitchen. Breakfast is a multi-course served occasion. Dinner is a five-course seasonal tasting menu, sourced from the garden or the Manor and the many local farms in the area.

Nearest Airport
Dulles International Airport: approx. 50 minute drive, Reagan National approx. 1 hour 10 minute drive

⦿⦿⦿ ⦿⦿ ⦿⦿ ⦿⦿ ☙
Hope and Glory Inn

www.hopeandglory.com
65 Tavern Rd, 170 White Fences Dr (Winery), Irvington, VA USA 22480
800-497-8228 • 804-438-6053 • Fax: 804-438-5362
inquiries@hopeandglory.com   *Member Since 2008*

Virginia

Irvington

Owners
Dudley & Peggy Patteson

"TOP 10 IN THE U.S." - Five times. Frommer's, Fodor's and Moon Travel Guides have awarded the Hope and Glory Inn their highest rating. The only inn in Virginia with this honor. An historic (1890) and very mega stylish schoolhouse, eclectically styled and hopelessly romantic, with quaint Garden Cottages surrounded by flowers rarely seen in Virginia gardens today. Unique in so many ways - a moon garden, which only blooms in the evening; and an outdoor garden shower (Breakers Hotel circa 1940) with a claw foot tub in a most private setting. Additional accommodations can be found within walking distance in the Hope and Glory's Vineyard. Three Carpenter Gothic cottages called "tents" modeled after Oak Bluffs on Martha's Vineyard. Retreats are delightfully held here with today's technology in a creative environment and totally wireless. The inn also offers fine dining in its Dining Hall, cruises aboard its vessel; a hip pool; massage treatments in our special spa space; tennis courts; golf and chic shops in a classy Chesapeake Bay waterfront town.

Rates
Schoolhouse Rooms - $200-$290; Garden Cottages - $250-$355; Vineyard Tents - $320-$695. Number of Rooms: 15

Cuisine
Our dinners are exceptional. The menu changes with the seasons.
We offer America's only Crab Cruise.
We offer wine tastings with local oysters in our vineyard.
We are one of two Virginia hotels that own a vineyard.
The only one with a passenger boat.

Nearest Airport
Newport News / Williamsburg (PHF) 55 min.; Richmond (RIC) 65 min; Norfolk (ORF) 90 min.; Dulles (IAD) 3 hrs

The Inn at 400 West High

www.400westhigh.com
400 West High Street, Charlottesville, VA USA 22902
434-981-0458
merriment@400westhigh.com

Member Since 2014

Owner/Innkeeper
Carolyn Polson McGee

The Inn at 400 West High is an escape from everyday life, a simply sumptuous destination for a getaway right in the heart of Charlottesville's bustling downtown. With three luxurious guest rooms and two suites (one with kitchen and rooftop terrace), there is an intimate atmosphere to the inn. No need to worry about tripping over your fellow guests... each room has a private bath, and all but one have private exterior entrances. Look forward to bright spaces, carefully curated art (much of it by local artists), and tastefully whimsical modern décor. Sit by the fire in the Gathering Room with a glass of Virginia wine, or, in the warmer months, step outside to the flower-filled hidden garden terrace. If you can bring yourself to leave the inn, walk two blocks to Charlottesville's Downtown Mall - a six block pedestrian mall with restaurants, boutique shopping, and performance venues, visit nearby Monticello, Montpelier, or other historic sites, or take a tour of the local vineyards and breweries. Return to the inn at the end of your busy day - the cookie jar will be waiting!

Rates
Central downtown location with three rooms and two suites (one with full kitchen and rooftop terrace). All with private baths. Seasonal rates $175-$350. Complimentary parking, WiFi, and beverages. TV/Blu-Ray in each room. Number of Rooms: 5

Cuisine
Choose your café table in the Gathering Room & eat your fill of crepes, Belgian waffles, omelets, quiches, & other hot breakfast treats made right before your eyes. Don't miss our locally roasted house blend coffee or gluten free granola w/fresh fruit!

Nearest Airport
CHO - Charlottesville Albemarle Airport

Inn at Onancock

www.innatonancock.com
30 North Street, Onancock, Virginia (VA) USA 23417
757-789-7711 • 866-792-7466 • Fax: 757-789-7712
info@innatonancock.com

Member Since 2012

Virginia

Onancock

Innkeepers/Owners
Lisa and Kris LaMontagne

The Inn at Onancock is a gourmet B&B located on Virginia's Eastern Shore just a few steps from the historic downtown and 3 blocks from the deep-water wharf. Enjoy the get-away-from-it-all style in laid back luxury. You may find it difficult to choose from among five spacious guest rooms, each with 10' ceilings and spa-style en suite baths, in settings inspired by favorite worldwide destinations. Antiques and oriental carpets were carefully selected to further create the ambience of these faraway places. You'll be comfortable in all seasons with gas fireplaces in some of the guest rooms and central air and ceiling fans throughout. Sleep in utmost comfort on feather-topped beds dressed with 1,000 thread count luxury linens. Melt away stress in deep soaking air jet tubs surrounded by spa décor. The experience is completed with fluffy white towels, towel warmers, cozy robes and luxury toiletries made especially for The Inn.

Rates
Rates vary by room and season. A minimum stay of two nights is required for weekends beginning May 1 and ending after Labor Day weekend as well as for holidays and special events. Number of Rooms: 5

Cuisine
Breakfasts feature unique entrees, Lisa's famous granola, homemade breads and pastries, locally roasted private blend coffee and an assortment of yogurt, juices and teas. WineDown Hour offers select wines and distinctive handmade hors d'oeuvre.

Nearest Airport
Salisbury Ocean City Wicomico Airport (SBY), Norfolk International (ORF)

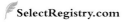

Inn at Riverbend

www.innatriverbend.com
125 River Ridge Drive, Pearisburg, VA USA 24134
540-921-5211 • Fax: 540-921-2720
stay@innatriverbend.com

🍽️ 🍽️ 🍽️ 🍷

Member Since 2005

Innkeepers/Owners
Janet & Jimm Burton

The Inn at Riverbend is an idyllic Pearisburg, VA bed and breakfast set on 14 acres with stunning views of the New River and the Appalachian Mountains. Our bed and breakfast located near Blacksburg, VA provides a unique romantic retreat from the stresses of everyday life in an unspoiled and peaceful setting, where exceptional service is our trademark, our food fresh & delicious, and our guests our number one priority. Each luxurious guestroom provides access to our expansive decks where you can bird watch, spot deer, and listen to the distant sound of trains. Perfect for romantic getaways, outdoor enthusiasts, retreats & family gatherings, and small intimate weddings. All rooms have private baths, luxurious linens & Lather Aromatherapy amenities. Each morning enjoy a sumptuous 3-course breakfast with our Riverbend blend of coffee or Stash tea, and enjoy freshly baked cookies in the afternoon. Let us help plan a guided wine tour, a hike, a trip down the New River, or pack a picnic lunch for the Cascades Waterfall! Complimentary tea, soda & coffee.

Rates
$190/$264. Two night minimum for all weekends and holidays. Corporate and military rates available. Number of Rooms: 7

Cuisine
3 course gourmet full plated breakfast included with Riverbend Blend roasted coffee, assorted Stash teas and juices. Complimentary 24 hour tea, soda & coffee. Monday dinner w/advance reservation.

Nearest Airport
Roanoke (ROA)

The Inn at Vaucluse Spring

www.vauclusespring.com
231 Vaucluse Spring Lane, Stephens City, VA USA 22655
800-869-0525 • 540-869-0200 • Fax: 540-869-9546
mail@vauclusespring.com

Member Since 2000

Virginia

Stephens City

Innkeepers/Owners
Barry & Neil Myers

Come relax in the Shenandoah Valley countryside. Set amidst 100 scenic acres in rolling orchard country, this collection of six guest houses surrounds the beautiful Vaucluse Spring. Experience the elegance of the gracious 200 year old Manor House or the charm of an 1850s log home. For the ultimate in peace and privacy, stay in one of our private cottages. The Mill House Studio sits at the water's edge. The Gallery Guest House enjoys views of the meadow. The Cabin by the Pond overlooks the spring valley. Relax beside Vaucluse Spring's cool, crystal clear waters. Evenings, experience Contemporary American Cuisine in a relaxed atmosphere. Enjoy the pool in summertime or roam the pasture and woods year round. Ideally located between the historic sites of Winchester and the outdoor activities near Front Royal and the Shenandoah National Park's Skyline Drive. Acclaimed by guests for warm hospitality and fabulous food, the inn received TripAdvisor.com's Travelers Choice Award for Top 10 Best Inns and B&Bs in the U.S.

Rates
12 Rooms/Suites: $165/$260 B&B. 3 Private cottages: $280/$320. Beautifully furnished, queen or king beds, all have fireplaces, 14 with Jacuzzis, most have water, mountain, or meadow views. Number of Rooms: 15

Cuisine
Contemporary American Cuisine. Prix fixe dining available Tuesday through Saturday nights by advance reservation only. Wine and beer available. Full 3-course breakfast served daily.

Nearest Airport
Dulles International and Winchester Regional

SelectRegistry.com

Inn at Warner Hall

www.warnerhall.com
4750 Warner Hall Road, Gloucester, VA USA 23061
800-331-2720 • 804-695-9565 • Fax: 804-695-9566
info@warnerhall.com

Member Since 2006

Innkeepers/Owners
Troy & Theresa Stavens

Old world charm and new world amenities create the perfect balance between luxury and history in this beautifully restored romantic waterfront retreat. Established in 1642 by George Washington's great, great grandfather, Warner Hall beckons guests to relax and enjoy. Comfortable elegance, fabulous food and attentive, friendly service are the essence of Warner Hall. Spacious guest rooms combine sumptuous antiques, fabrics and art with modern conveniences. Many rooms offer fireplaces, Jacuzzis or steam showers – all have spectacular views. Experience Chef Eric Garcia's delicious cuisine paired with a bottle of fine wine. Explore the historic triangle of Williamsburg-Jamestown, Yorktown and Gloucester, or simply relax at the Inn's charming boathouse. Ideally situated at the head of the Severn River surrounded by 500 acres of fields and forest, Warner Hall resonates with tranquility and southern hospitality. National Register of Historic Places. Recommended by the Washington Post, Virginia Living, Southern Lady, Travel + Leisure, Hampton Roads Magazine and The Virginian-Pilot.

Rates
$195/$250 Sun-Thurs. $220/$275 Fri-Sat. Number of Rooms: 11

Cuisine
Extraordinary breakfasts included. Chef's Tasting Dinners Fri./ Sat., or by special reservation. Cocktail and wine bar. Gourmet supper baskets Sunday-Thursday. Box lunches daily.

Nearest Airport
Richmond (RIC), Norfolk (ORF)

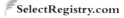

¶❚❘ ¶❚❘ ¶❚❘ ♀
The Inn on Campbell

www.theinnoncampbell.com
118 Campbell Ave. SW, Roanoke, VA. USA 24011
540-400-0183 • 540-537-0657
info@theinnoncampbell.com

Member Since 2012

Virginia

Roanoke

Owners/Innkeepers
Cindy & Keith Hummer

Urban elegance best describes this downtown inn, located within easy walking distance to restaurants, shops, galleries and the famous Roanoke Farmer's Market. Soaring ceilings and wainscotted walls give way to large suites with custom bedding and draperies, oriental rugs, and beautiful furnishings. A large greenhouse style skylight perched thirty feet above the foyer spills sunlight through fixed glass windows in the dining room and the adjoining den. The seating in the den is "overstuffed" and very comfortable- while there, check out the extensive movie and book selections provided for your enjoyment. Sink into a soft leather chair in the kitchen and enjoy reading the morning paper while drinking your coffee. You can have breakfast seated at the large kitchen island or have it served in the antique filled dining room with a lit candelabra gracing the table. Need a dinner reservation, tickets for a show, or copies made for your business meeting? We can arrange that and more. Relax and let The Inn on Campbell pamper you!

Rates
Our rates range from $200 to $375 plus state and local taxes. Additional guests can make use of the sleeper sofa in the Campbell Suite for an additional $25 per person. Number of Rooms: 4

Cuisine
We serve a complimentary wine and cheese "therapy" session for arrriving guests in the kitchen at five. Gourmet breakfast dishes include Cindy's sausage and corn griddle cakes with orange-honey-butter sauce or Keith's Bananas Foster waffles.

Nearest Airport
The Roanoke Regional Airport is just a fifteen minute ride and we can arrange to pick you up or drop you off.

The Iris Inn

www.irisinn.com
191 Chinquapin Drive, Waynesboro, VA USA 22980
888-585-9018 • 540-943-1991 • Fax: 540-942-2093
innkeeper@irisinn.com

Member Since 2013

Virginia Waynesboro

Owners/Innkeepers
Heidi & Dave Lanford

Relax, refresh, and renew yourself in a modern, 1991 purpose-built retreat that overlooks the Shenandoah Valley from a 12-acre Blue Ridge mountain top. Or snuggle together in a new couples cabin and enjoy the bubbling waters of your own hot tub while watching the sun set behind the Appalachian Mountains. Surf the web with free WiFi while unwinding on a deck swing. Relax with your own in-room massage.

Want to explore the local area? Enjoy wine tasting at any of the 28 wineries within 30 minutes of the Iris Inn. Learn from history while visiting the homes of four former U.S. presidents, all within a one-hour drive from our Inn. Do you enjoy the outdoors? Explore hiking trails and overlooks at Skyline Drive and the Blue Ridge Parkway, only 3 miles away. How about theater? Take in a show at one of the many nearby theater productions. Try out delicious cuisine at restaurants that exemplify the farm-to-table revolution in today's dining.

Rates
$149 to $319. All rates include full plated breakfast at individual tables. Evening wine tasting is complimentary. Number of Rooms: 15

Cuisine
From 8 a.m. - 9:30 a.m., join us for the delicious meal that makes a B&B what is it. You can expect to delight in various combinations of fresh fruit, eggs, waffles, French toast, bacon, sausage, and so much more. Cookies and fresh fruit available.

Nearest Airport
Charlottesville VA

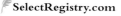

🍴 🍴 🍷
L'Auberge Provencale

www.laubergeprovencale.com
13630 Lord Fairfax Highway, Boyce, VA USA 22620
800-638-1702 • 540-837-1375 • Fax: 540-837-2004
celebrate@laubergeprovencale.com

Member Since 1988

Virginia Boyce

Innkeepers/Owners
Celeste, Alain, or Christian Borel

Enjoy the South of France; no passport required. USA Today rated L'Auberge Provencale as one of the top 100 hotel dining rooms in the country, and Washingtonian Top 100. Indulge yourself in one of the cozy guest rooms or suites at our quintessential French Country Inn. We feature cheerful yet elegant decor with faux walls, French fabrics and antiques to create an atmosphere of a true "Auberge," blending French country comfort with modern luxury. Dine evenings at the main manor house at Mt. Airy (circa 1753) in one of the three intimate dining rooms in our farm to table restaurant La Table Provencale. Orchards, flower, vegetable and herb gardens supply the best and freshest for our cuisine created by Executive Chef Joseph Watters. Area vineyards, antiquing, hiking, biking, horseback riding in the beautiful Shenandoah. Our Villa La Campagnette offers a swimming pool, luxury suites and privacy. The two inns offer a special experience for discerning guests with exquisite food and courteous, attentive service. If you can't go to France, visit L'Auberge Provencale.

Rates
8 Charming Rooms, $175/$295; 6 Romantic Suites, $325/$365. Fireplaces, Aroma Therapy Steam Showers, Flatscreens, WiFi, Jacuzzi , Virginia Garden Tour Gardens & Majestic Views. A touch of France in the Virginia countryside. Number of Rooms: 14

Cuisine
Enjoy elegant, romantic dinners with Provencale flair. Featuring fresh, local produce, meats, fruits and herbs. Dinner served six days, closed Tuesdays. Multi-course breakfast of one's dreams, gourmet picnics. Wine Spectator Award of Excellence.

Nearest Airport
Winchester Regional just 10 mins, Washington Dulles 45 mins, National 1 1/2 hrs

🎯 **SelectRegistry.com**

The Oaks Victorian Inn

www.theoaksvictorianinn.com
311 East Main St., Christiansburg, VA USA 24073
540-381-1500 • 800-336-6257 • Fax: 540-381-3036
stay@theoaksvictorianinn.com

Member Since 1993

Innkeepers/Owners
Linda and Bernie Wurtzburger

The Oaks Victorian Inn welcomes guests to experience a bygone era of romance and elegance. Warm hospitality, beautiful surroundings, luxurious guest rooms, memorable breakfasts and dedication to detail are the hallmark of The Oaks. Each guest room has a private bath, soft bed linens, fluffy towels, elegant plush robes, flat screen TV, DVD player, free WiFi and mini fridge. Our Garden Cottage offers a private hot tub and sauna. Grab some homemade cookies and relax in our cozy library with a good book or friends old and new. The large wrap around porch draws you outside to sit in a rocking chair and enjoy a glass of wine. Discover whimsical sculptures, meandering flower beds and a tranquil fish pond in our backyard's "Secret Garden." Just minutes from Virginia Tech and Radford University, whether you are looking for romance, outdoor adventure, wineries, antique shopping, a drive along the Blue Ridge Parkway, a midway point to meet, or just a place to relax and enjoy the mountains, we invite you to make The Oaks Victorian Inn your home away from home.

Rates
5 Rooms, 1 Cottage; $159-$219. Virginia Tech football and graduation weekend rates slightly higher. Corporate rates Sunday through Thursday for the single business traveler. Open year-round. Number of Rooms: 6

Cuisine
Enjoy a three course candlelit breakfast in our elegant but cozy dining room. Coffee and tea available at 7:30 AM. Homemade cookies, hot beverages and complimentary sherry daily. Special dietary needs happily accommodated. Many fine restaurants nearby.

Nearest Airport
Roanoke, 30 miles

Prospect Hill Plantation Inn

www.prospecthill.com
2887 Poindexter Road, P.O. Box 6909, Charlottesville, VA USA 23093
540-967-0844
stay@prospecthill.com

Member Since 1979

1850 CARRIAGE HOUSE

Virginia

Charlottesville

Innkeepers/Owners
Doc & Paula Findley

Step back in time and experience the romance, the beauty, and the history of Prospect Hill…the oldest continually-operated, frame-house plantation in Virginia, and a founding member of Select Registry. An authentic 18th century plantation, Prospect Hill has since transformed into a majestic country inn. Between the manor house and the nine original slave dependencies (circa 1699–1850), we offer eleven distinctive guest rooms and cottages. By preserving each cottage's original function, our accommodations vary from elegant to rustic. All, however, are packed with character and brimming with history. With private baths, working fireplaces, creaky floors, expansive views, secluded decks, and incomparable charm…each room invites you to linger, and to slow your pace to that of another era. Nature trails, whirlpool tubs (8 rooms), swimming pool, hot tub, and horses, chickens and alpacas (on over 40 acres of beautiful grounds) add to our serenity. All this, and only 15 miles from Charlottesville, Monticello and several excellent wineries.

Rates
We offer 3 charming rooms and 8 historic cottages ($165-$395). All have private baths & fireplaces, air conditioning, gourmet breakfast, and most have whirlpool tubs. Several of our cottages are dog-friendly. Number of Rooms: 11

Cuisine
Three-course, gourmet, hot plated breakfast (in bed, if you wish) included. Elegant 4-course dinner available Friday & Saturday evenings ($125 per couple). Plantation Dinner Baskets available (Sunday-Thursday) by advance reservation.

Nearest Airport
Charlottesville (CHO) - 26 miles; Richmond (RIC) - 65 miles; Washington Dulles (IAD) - 99 miles

SelectRegistry.com

Silver Thatch Inn

www.silverthatch.com
3001 Hollymead Drive, Charlottesville, VA USA 22911
800-261-0720 • 434-978-4686 • Fax: 434-973-6156
info@silverthatch.com

Member Since 1986

Innkeepers/Owners
Jim and Terri Petrovits

An historic Virginia Wine Country inn, Silver Thatch began its life as a barracks built in 1780 by Hessian soldiers captured during the Revolutionary War and marched south to Virginia. This area of Albemarle County was designated by Thomas Jefferson especially for the troops to give them the opportunity to begin their new lives following the war. As wings were added in 1812 and 1937, the Inn served as a boys' school, a tobacco plantation, and a melon farm, and home to BFD Runk, dean of men at University of Virginia. Silver Thatch Inn offers seven comfortable, well-appointed guest rooms, with the community pool available close by. Let us assist with dinner reservations, directions and information for Jefferson's Monticello, the University of Virginia, Monroe's Ashlawn-Highland, Monticello Wine Trail and Brew Ridge Trail to sample Virginia's award winning wines and artisan brews and hard ciders. All within a short drive in the gorgeous Virginia countryside. When you return, gather in our Pub, where we offer beer & wine (and fortified wines, ports, champagnes, and sherrys).

Rates
$180/$220 B&B, excluding taxes and gratuities. Open year-round. Number of Rooms: 7

Cuisine
Start your morning with freshly ground and brewed Greenberry's Coffee, juices, Stash teas, house-baked pastries, fruit, and signature entrée choices, served with Jim's house-made sausage. As much as possible, everything is made in-house, from scratch!

Nearest Airport
Charlottesville/Albemarle Regional Airport, 2 miles.

Sugar Tree Inn

www.sugartreeinn.com
145 Lodge Trail, Vesuvius, VA USA 24483
800-377-2197 • 540-377-2197
innkeeper@sugartreeinn.com

Member Since 1998

Virginia

Vesuvius

Innkeepers/Owners
Jeff & Becky Chanter

Escape your hectic world and come to Virginia's Mountain Inn! Our mountainside lodge is located in the Blue Ridge Mountains between Lexington and Staunton, VA. Less than a mile from Milepost 27 of the Blue Ridge Parkway (yet only 5 miles from I-81/64), you will be surrounded by the George Washington National Forest and, at 2800 feet, have a commanding view over the Shenandoah Valley to the Allegany Mountains. Each of our rooms features a private bath (several with Jacuzzis), wood-burning fireplace, coffee maker, CD player, and a very comfortable bed! We will serve you a full, hearty breakfast each morning in our glass walled dining room and then help you plan your day. We offer nearby hiking or rafting, visiting local wineries, enjoying historic Lexington or Staunton, antiquing, or simply relaxing in a rocker on our front porch. Come enjoy our natural beauty, quiet, and tranquility that persuades you to unwind. On weekend evenings, we offer our guests a great dinner or if you prefer to venture out, there are a lot of good restaurants in nearby Lexington or Staunton.

Rates
Spread out in five buildings (all within a few hundred yards of each other), we have one Luxury Cabin, $248; nine Rooms, $148/$198; two Suites, $178 & $198; and our pet friendly Creek House w/2 bedrooms, bath & full kitchen, $178. Number of Rooms: 13

Cuisine
A hearty country breakfast is served each morning in our glass walled dining room that is tucked into the mountainside. An excellent three course dinner with a varied choice of entrees is available Friday & Saturday. Fine restaurants are not far away.

Nearest Airport
Roanoke, Charlottesville

Wedmore Place

www.wedmoreplace.com
5810 Wessex Hundred, Williamsburg, VA USA 23185
757-941-0310 • 757-941-0310 • Fax: 757-941-0318
info@wedmoreplace.com

Member Since 2007

Virginia Williamsburg

Founders & Managers
The Duffeler Family

Wedmore Place is an elegant European Country Hotel, in the midst of a 300-acre winery farm located just 3 miles from Colonial Williamsburg. Whether for business or pleasure, the hotel offers a highly luxurious and relaxing atmosphere. The decor of each room is inspired by the culture and traditions of 28 different European provinces. Each is furnished and decorated in the style of the province after which it is named; all rooms have wood burning fireplaces, 10' ceilings and king-size beds. Exquisite dining is available in the Cafe Provencal, where fine French inspired Mediterranean cuisine is served daily. The dining room overlooks the pool terrace, offering guests a romantic and relaxed setting. Guests at the hotel can also make use of the massage facilities, fitness room and British Club style Library. No stay is complete without a walk next door to The Williamsburg Winery for a tour and wine tasting and shopping in the retail store. See what our guests are saying on Trip Advisor.

Rates
Traditional Rooms: $165-$210, Classic Rooms: $190-$250, Superior Rooms: $235-$345, 3 Suites from $300-$635. Weekend rates - Friday and Saturday. Holiday Rates may apply. Number of Rooms: 28

Cuisine
Fine French Inspired Mediterranean Cuisine. Chef Tim feels that presentation and atmosphere are as important as the quality and freshness of its ingredients. Having access to the on-site 2 acre garden, local meats and seafood is the key.

Nearest Airport
Newport News/Wmbg Airport (PHF), 26 Miles; Richmond, VA (RIC), 50 Miles; Norfolk, VA (ORF), 65 Miles

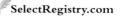

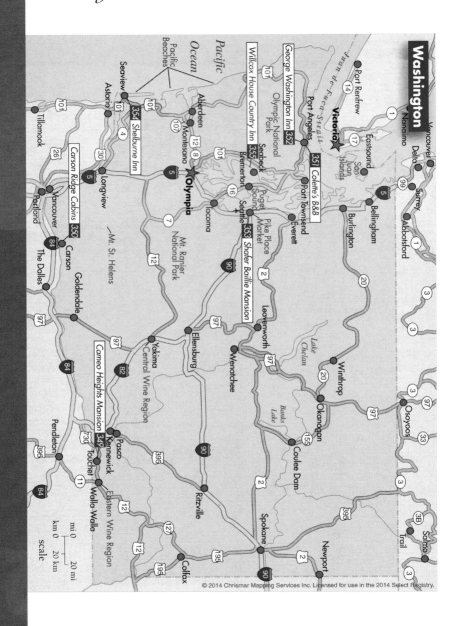

Washington

© 2014 Chrismar Mapping Services Inc. Licensed for use in the 2014 Select Registry.

SelectRegistry.com

Cameo Heights Mansion

🍽️ 🍽️ 🍽️ 🍸

www.cameoheightsmansion.com
PO Box 47, 1072 Oasis Road, Touchet, WA 99360
509-394-0211 • 509-302-0390 • Fax: 509-394-8815
info@cameoheights.com

Member Since 2011

Washington Touchet

Innkeepers/Owners
Alan and Deanne Fielding

Cameo Heights Mansion is a luxury bed and breakfast near Walla Walla, in the heart of Washington wine country. Situated in a quiet country setting, it features seven spacious suites with private baths, air-jetted tubs, gas fireplaces, and sumptuous fine dining. The most common compliment from our guests is: "You have thought of everything." (You imagine it and we surely have it in your suite.) The common area includes a large hospitality room with snacks, ping pong, games, and an adjacent theatre room with a world class sound system and over 200 DVDs and Blu-rays. Spectacular describes the view of the Walla Walla river valley with the rolling Tuscan hills in the background. Stargazing from the hot tub, swimming or sun tanning poolside in the desert heat, roasting s'mores, tetherball, horseshoes, hiking, and veranda dining at sunset are just a few of the recreational pleasures of the Mansion! In 2012, ranked Top 10 in US by BedandBreakfast.com. In 2013, recipients of the 2013 Travelers' Choice from TripAdvisor.com for Top 25 inns in America.

Rates
6 River view and Orchard view rooms $229-$269; 1 limited view room $199. Winter discounts available. All rooms have the same amenities--everything imaginable.
Number of Rooms: 7

Cuisine
Morning begins with "Wake-Up-Service" of coffee and danish at 8AM followed by a full country breakfast at 9 AM. For your ultimate pleasure and convenience, we also offer the option of exquisite evening dining at our on-site restaurant, "The Vine."

Nearest Airport
Pasco (PSC), Walla Walla (ALW)

Carson Ridge Luxury Cabins

& 🍽 ♀

www.carsonridgecabins.com
1261 Wind River Road, Carson, WA USA 98610
509-427-7777 • 877-816-7908
info@carsonridgecabins.com

Member Since 2012

Washington Carson

Owners/Innkeeper
Pete and Latisha Steadman/Staci Addison

Relax and rejuvenate in the privacy of your own cabin complete with a luxurious, hand-carved log bed, hydrotherapy spa tub for two, spacious walk-in dual-head shower, open beamed ceilings, and large windows that capture spectacular views. Enjoy a glass of wine curled up in a comfy leather chair near the fireplace. Read a book or gaze at the stars, relaxing on the front porch swing. Stroll around the landscaped gardens or take a hike to visit one of the spectacular nearby waterfalls. Soothe your tired muscles with an in-cabin massage or fragrant soak in your private spa tub. Thoughtful extras enhance your stay - bathrobes, Gilchrist & Soames products, bath salts, candles, mini-kitchenette, iPod dock, Direct TV, DVDs, games and books. No wonder Carson Ridge has been named "Top 10 Most Romantic Inns in the Country," "Editors Pick of Best Inns to Celebrate Romance," "Best in the West" and "Best of the Gorge." At Carson Ridge the setting, the cabins and personalized spa services blend perfectly to create an atmosphere of utter relaxation and escape. What are you waiting for?

Rates
Summer $245 - $415; Winter $225 - $375; Call the innkeeper for specials!
Number of Rooms: 10

Cuisine
Enjoy breakfast in the dining room or in comfort of your cabin. Savor hot entreès, such as crème brulee french toast and bacon, cheese & tomato quiche, or enjoy lighter options including homemade granola and seasonal fruits.

Nearest Airport
Portland International (PDX) is a 45 minute drive through the Columbia River Gorge, right past Multnomah Falls!

SelectRegistry.com

Colette's Bed & Breakfast

www.colettes.com
339 Finn Hall Road, Port Angeles, WA USA 98362
360-457-9197 • 877-457-9777
colettes@colettes.com

Member Since 2003

Innkeepers/Owners
Dae & Clif Todd

Colette's is a breathtaking 10 acre oceanfront estate nestled between the majestic Olympic Range and the picturesque Strait of Juan de Fuca. This unique area is the gateway to Olympic National Park, a world of stunning coastline with booming surf, wave-manicured beaches, and sweeping vistas in every direction. Each perfect day at Colette's starts with a gourmet multi-course breakfast. Luxurious King Suites with magnificent oceanfront views, romantic fireplaces, and indulgent Jacuzzi spas for two rejuvenate guests at the end of the day. Stroll through Colette's 10 acre outdoor sanctuary which includes enchanting gardens, towering cedars and lush evergreen forest. Fodor's Pacific Northwest – "Top Choice" for the Olympic Peninsula. Frommer's Washington – "Deliciously Romantic...Exceedingly Luxurious." Karen Brown's Guide Pacific Northwest- "Top Pick" and "Greatest Value Award." Best Places to Kiss Pacific Northwest – "Utopian Oceanfront Hideaway." Fine Gardening Magazine – "Front Cover." AAA rated – "4 Diamond Luxury." Sunset Magazine – "Top 10 / Olympic Peninsula."

Rates
Luxury King Suites $195/$395. Number of Rooms: 5

Cuisine
Our chef has created an exciting variety of culinary delights. Enjoy your multi-course, gourmet breakfast served with a panoramic view of the Strait of Juan de Fuca and the San Juan Islands.

Nearest Airport
Seattle and Port Angeles

♿ 🍴

George Washington Inn

www.georgewashingtoninn.com
939 Finn Hall Road, Port Angeles, WA USA 98362
360-452-5207 • 360-477-5314
info@georgewashingtoninn.com

Member Since 2014

Owners/Innkeepers
Dan and Janet Abbott

Located on a working lavender farm and sitting on a high bluff overlooking the Strait of Juan de Fuca with the majestic Olympic Mountains to the south, George Washington Inn offers breathtaking panoramic views from every window! Luxury king rooms feature crisp cotton sheets, quality linens, two-person spa tubs, romantic all-season fireplaces, HDTV, free Wi-Fi, and the best views on the Peninsula. Olympic National Park (including Hurricane Ridge and the Hoh Rain Forest), Lake Crescent, the Dungeness Wildlife Refuge, west coast beaches, and so much more await your enjoyment and exploration.

Designed as an exterior replica of George & Martha Washington's Mount Vernon, the spacious interior and modern amenities pair with colonial furnishings, inviting you to step back in time and relax. The inn's upstairs veranda and main floor piazza offer spectacular oceanfront views, eagles soar overhead, deer stroll across the lawn, and ocean breezes refresh the mind and body. The sun sets in a spectacular array of color, and the lights of Victoria, Canada, twinkle in the night sky.

Rates
Deluxe ocean view suites with private entrance: $250-$350. Luxury mountain view rooms: $225-$280. Ground floor ocean view room (accommodates most handicap needs), third person possible with daybed: $250-$350. Breakfast included. Number of Rooms: 5

Cuisine
Full hot breakfast, often featuring lavender, served on the oceanfront piazza during peak season, at the dining table during quiet season. Fresh & local fruits, traditional entrees, fresh-baked sweet rolls, specialty coffee. Cookies in the evening.

Nearest Airport
Seattle-Tacoma International Airport (SeaTac)

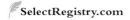
SelectRegistry.com

Shafer Baillie Mansion

www.sbmansion.com
907 14th Ave East, Seattle, WA USA 98112
206-322-4654 • 800-985-4654 • Fax: 206-329-4654
sbmansion@gmail.com   *Member Since 2012*

Owners/Innkeepers
Ana Lena Melka & Mark Mayhle

The Shafer Baillie Mansion is conveniently located in the Capitol Hill neighborhood of Seattle. In 1979, the house was opened to the public as a bed and breakfast. Mark Mayhle and Ana Lena Melka, owners since 2004, have completed an extensive top-to-bottom restoration of the property and brought it back to its original elegance, but with a completely updated 21st century infrastructure.

Amazing grandeur and craftsmanship is built into each room of this extraordinary home, giving the sense of a luxury hotel from a time gone by. Elegance is found in every detail; from original fixtures, hand-carved woodwork, and ornate fireplaces to private baths in every guest room.

Rates
$139-$239. Minimum stay September through May: 2 nights for reservations including Fri or Sat night. Minimum stay June-August: 2 nights Sun-Thurs, 3 nights for reservations including Fri or Sat night. Minimum stay Holidays:3 nights. Number of Rooms: 8

Cuisine
European style continental breakfast. Served buffet style in the oak paneled dining room, we feature smoked salmon, prosciutto, hard boiled eggs, hot and cold cereals, yogurts, fresh fruit, pastries, and assorted breads. Coffee & Tea available 24hrs.

Nearest Airport
Seattle Tacoma International- 20 min via taxi or car.

Shelburne Inn & China Beach Retreat

ふ 101 101 101 ⑨

www.shelburneinn.com or www.chinabeachretreat.com
P.O. Box 250, 4415 Pacific Hwy, Seaview, WA USA 98644
360-642-2442 • 800-INN-1896 • Fax: 360-642-8904
innkeeper@theshelburneinn.com

Member Since 1988

Washington

Seaview

Approved

Innkeepers/Owners
David Campiche and Laurie Anderson

A long, unspoiled stretch of wild Pacific seacoast is just a short walk from this inviting inn, established in 1896. Vintage stained glass windows and antiques accentuate the decor. A sumptuous breakfast is complimentary. The restaurant and pub offer musical entertainment at various times throughout the year. Innovative cuisine and a discriminating wine list have brought international recognition. Wireless Internet. Outdoor activities abound, including The Discovery Trail which parallels the majestic Pacific Ocean. Explore the western end of the Lewis & Clark trail from China Beach Retreat and its Audubon Cottage near Cape Disappointment State Park and two 100-plus-year-old lighthouses. Selected as one of the 'West's Best Small Inns' by Sunset Magazine. Featured in Martha Stewart Living magazine, The New York Times, 'a perfectly restored, impeccably run stronghold of antiques, fireplaces and stained glass for which the word "gem" is overused but unavoidable,' AAA Three Diamond-rated.

Retreat, relax and rejuvenate in this most welcoming of inns.

Rates
13 Rooms $139/$179 B&B; 2 Suites $199 B&B. Off-site waterside B&B; 2 Rooms $199 B&B; 1 Suite $229 B&B. Audubon Cottage: $289 B&B. Group Rates for Business Retreats and lodging/dining packages available Sun-Thurs, Oct-June.
Number of Rooms: 19

Cuisine
Gourmet Regional Cuisine features the best seasonal and local ingredients. Restaurant and Pub offer breakfast, lunch and dinner featuring fine NW wines, microbrewed beer and liquor. Innkeepers' Breakfast served daily and offers creative preparations.

Nearest Airport
Astoria, Oregon

Willcox House Country Inn

www.willcoxhouse.com
2390 Tekiu Pt. Rd. NW, Seabeck, WA USA 98380
800-725-9477 • 360-830-4492
willcoxhouse@silverlink.net

Member Since 1993

Washington

Seabeck

Innkeepers/Owners
Cecilia and Phillip Hughes

The Willcox House Country Inn is surrounded by the forest and overlooks the sparkling waters of Hood Canal. Located between Seattle and the Olympic mountains, this 1930s mansion offers guests peace and tranquility.

From your private table in the dining room enjoy the spectacular view of the water and the Olympic Peninsula. The inn is furnished with antiques and period pieces for relaxation and comfort. Relax by the fire in the great room, play a game of pool in the game room or watch a movie in the theater. The terrace and the library are great places to enjoy a glass of wine in the afternoon. Five guest rooms, all with private baths, overlook the water and the Olympic mountains.

Beautiful gardens host a champion Japanese maple tree and two fish ponds. Walk the oyster laden saltwater beach looking for driftwood and wildlife. Golfing, birding, and hiking are nearby.

The combination of Native American, Scandinavian, Military, and world class garden attractions make Kitsap County an easy-to-tour destination rich in history and diversity.

Rates
Guest rooms have different amenities (fireplace $279, double spa tub $259, balcony $249) $189/$279 B&B. Open year-round. Number of Rooms: 5

Cuisine
Breakfast, afternoon wine and cheese are included. The three course dinner is available by reservation only. All dining is private table. Extensive wine list. Beer is available. Complimentary hot beverages.

Nearest Airport
Seattle (SEA) Interstate 5 south to Tacoma; Hwy 16 to Bremerton; web site for specific mileage to inn 1&1/2 hours

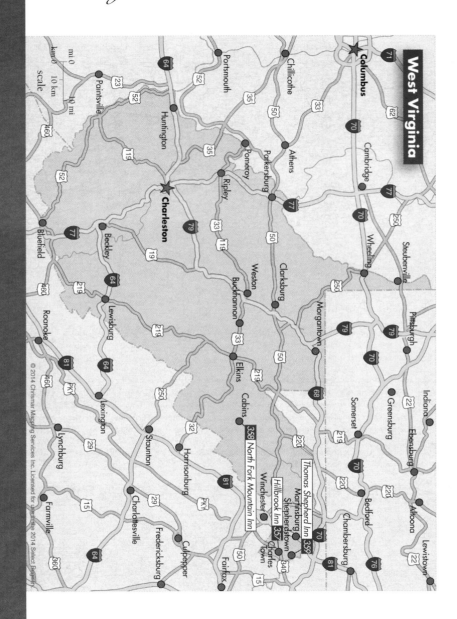

West Virginia

West Virginia

Columbus

Thomas Shepherd Inn 359
Martinsburg
Shepherdstown
Hillbrook Inn 357
Charles Town

358 North Fork Mountain Inn

© 2014 Christmas Mapping Services Inc. Licensed for use by the 2014 Select Registry.

356

SelectRegistry.com

Hillbrook Inn

www.hillbrookinn.com
4490 Summit Point Road, Charles Town, WV United States 25414
800-304-4223 • 304-725-4223
info@hillbrookinn.com

Member Since 2012

West Virginia

Charles Town

Innkeepers/Owners
Christopher and Carissa Zanella

Picture a European style country house hotel cascading down a limestone ridge on eight levels, with 2000 panes of glass flooding the interior with light. Imagine the rich patina of old wood, the gleam of polished brass, and the deep jewel tones of oriental carpets.

Imagine, too, Flemish oils, African masks, a library lined with books, a relaxing spa, and a fine dining restaurant on the premises. Add the flicker of candles and the warmth of a fire. A love seat. An intimate table for two. A quiet place to be alone together. Gardens bursting with color, a meandering stream, and ducks on the pond. The gold of autumn. The beauty of a winter storm. And a spectacular three or five course dinner featuring fragrant herbs from our garden and vegetables from a nearby farm. Sophisticated and elegant, yet unpretentious. A truly romantic getaway in West Virginia's beautiful eastern panhandle, located only an hour away from Washington D.C.

Rates
Rates: $189-$409. Each room offers an eclectic range of style and also features a private bath, iPad™, and Keurig™ coffee maker. Please see our website for room-specific information. Number of Rooms: 18

Cuisine
Indulge in a sumptuous dining experience. We use only the freshest ingredients to create daily chef's choice Prix Fixe menus that accommodate the dietary needs of our guests. Gourmet breakfast served daily. Advance reservations required for dinner.

Nearest Airport
Dulles (IAD) 1 hr; Baltimore (BWI) 1 hr 15 minutes.

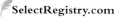

North Fork Mountain Inn

www.northforkmtninn.com
235 Canyon View Lane, Smoke Hole Road, Cabins, WV USA 26855
304–257–1108
info@northforkmtninn.com

Member Since 2007

West Virginia

Cabins

Innkeepers/Owners
Ed & Carol Fischer

We invite you to come and enjoy the natural beauty of the area in a quiet, relaxing atmosphere. Enjoy a gourmet breakfast as you start your day. Spend the day hiking in the Monongahela Forest or enjoying a spectacular view of the mountains & valleys from a rocker on the Inn's front porch. It is like taking a journey back in time to a simpler, slower paced world. Located only three hours from the Washington DC area. The Inn is located 7.6 miles up a paved mountain road with a view of Smoke Hole Canyon and six different mountains. The three story log Inn is of white pine construction with native field stone fireplaces. Each guest room is uniquely decorated with rustic elegance. Guest common areas include comfortable chairs & sofas, book & movie libraries, DirecTV, billiard table, microwave, refrigerator, and board games. Excellent fishing nearby. Enjoy fine dining with award winning chef & master sommelier. Finish your day relaxing in the hot tub under a blanket of stars. Massages available on site. Conference area available for weddings, family gatherings, or meetings.

Rates
7 Rooms, $150/$190. Two suites with king bed & loft, $245. Separate 1 Bedroom Cabin with full kitchen, $180. Gourmet breakfast included. Children under 12 welcome in the suites or cabin. Pets allowed in cabin. Number of Rooms: 10

Cuisine
Gourmet breakfast included. Fine dining w/wine tasting on Saturday evening, casual dining on other evenings, gourmet picnic baskets available for lunch or dinner. Ed is a master sommelier and an award winning chef in the Great American Seafood Cookoff.

Nearest Airport
Grant County Airport; nearest large airports are Washington Dulles(IAD), Baltimore (BWI), and Pittsburgh (PIT)

Thomas Shepherd Inn

www.thomasshepherdinn.com
300 W. German Street, P.O. Box 3634, Shepherdstown, WV USA 25443
888-889-8952 • 304-876-3715
info@thomasshepherdinn.com   *Member Since 2006*

Innkeepers/Owners
Lauren & Dave Duh

We invite you to stay in our bed & breakfast inn, with six 'inviting, well kept and beautifully decorated' guest rooms (all located on the 2nd floor) with luxe bathrobes, bedside chocolates, private baths, central air and Wi-Fi. Built in 1868, the inn has offered gracious hospitality to guests for over 30 years. Relax in front of the living room fireplace or on the back porch overlooking the garden; start your day with a generous homemade breakfast. Room amenities include comfy robes and bedside chocolates. Shepherdstown, a hidden gem for weary urbanites, is less than two hours from Washington, DC or Baltimore. The town has a vibrant cultural scene, ranging from premiere plays at the Contemporary American Theater Festival to music venues and festivals featuring diverse musicians and artists. A variety of locally-owned shops and restaurants fill the historic buildings on nearby German Street. Rich U.S. history is only minutes away at Antietam Battlefield or Harpers Ferry. Biking, hiking and water sports abound along the C&O Canal Path, the Potomac and the Shenandoah Rivers.

Rates
$170-$210 Friday-Sunday; $145-$190 Monday-Thursday, not including taxes, single or double occupancy. Two night minimum stay required on Saturdays and holidays. Not suitable for pets or children under 12. No smoking inside inn. Number of Rooms: 6

Cuisine
Full hot homemade breakfast daily w/fruit, entree, meat, baked goods; early beverage service; special diets welcomed. Hot beverages available all day; afternoon snacks. Walk to many locally-owned fine dining and casual restaurants on German Street.

Nearest Airport
BWI and Dulles airports - 70 miles. Parking beside and behind the Inn on Duke Street (corner of German Street).

Wisconsin

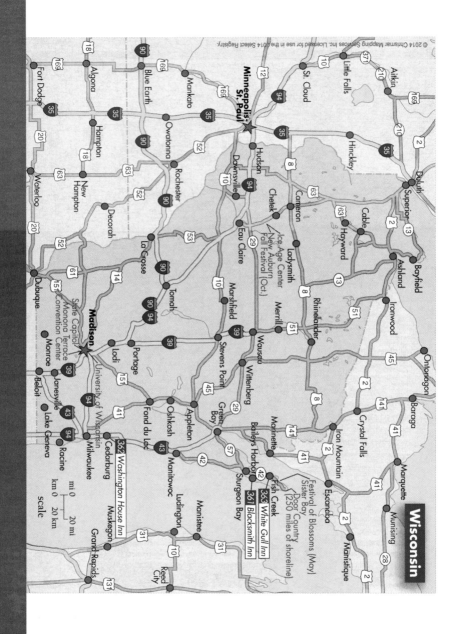

Blacksmith Inn On the Shore

www.theblacksmithinn.com
8152 Highway 57, Baileys Harbor, WI USA 54202
800-769-8619 • 920-839-9222
relax@theblacksmithinn.com

Member Since 2002

Innkeepers/Owners
Joan Holliday and Bryan Nelson

Awaken to waves lapping the shore as the morning light glistens on the water. Linger over breakfast. Kayak the harbor. Hike the adjacent Ridges Wildlife Sanctuary. Laze in your hammock. Bike a sleepy backroad to Cana Island Lighthouse. Bask in your whirlpool as you take in the warm glow of the fire. Stroll to village restaurants and shops. Serene water views, private balconies, hammocks, in-room whirlpools, fireplaces, fine linens, down pillows, satellite TV/DVD/CD, DVD library, wireless Internet, iPod dock, in-room refrigerators, complimentary use of kayaks, stand-up paddleboards, bikes and a bottomless cookie jar! Door County offers art galleries, antiquing, music, theater, lighthouses and miles and miles of shoreline. Adults Only, Smoke-Free.

Rates
High Season: Rooms $245/$305, Cottage $255/$445; 'Tween Season: Rooms $175/$255, Cottage $205/$370; Quiet Season: Rooms $145/$245, Cottage $155/$295. Number of Rooms: 16

Cuisine
Guests enjoy a homemade continental breakfast from the shared balcony overlooking the harbor or they may load up a tray at their leisure and breakfast on their own private balcony.

Nearest Airport
Green Bay (GRB) - Hwy 172 E. 8 miles to Hwy 43 N. 5 miles to Hwy 57 N. 63 miles. (90 minute drive)

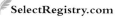

♿ 🍽   🍷
Washington House Inn

www.washingtonhouseinn.com
W62 N573 Washington Avenue, Cedarburg, WI USA 53012
888-554-0515 • 262-375-3550 • Fax: 262-375-9422
info@washingtonhouseinn.com   *Member Since 2007*

Wisconsin

Cedarburg

Innkeeper
Wendy J. Porterfield

Listed on the National Register of Historic Places, Washington House Inn successfully blends the charm and romance of days past with the amenities and conveniences expected by today's discriminating travelers. 34 rooms with luxury bedding include whirlpools (single and double), steam baths, antiques, fireplaces, flat-screen TVs and free in-room Internet. Guests are invited to enjoy a complimentary evening wine and cheese tasting featuring award-winning wines from local Cedar Creek Winery, and a sampling of Wisconsin cheeses. For a little extra pampering, the inn offers sauna facilities. Located in the heart of Cedarburg's Historic District, the inn offers elegant lodging within walking distance of shopping, dining and entertainment options, including the Ozaukee Interurban Trail (30 miles of paved trail for hiking or biking), making the Washington House Inn the place to stay in Historic Cedarburg. Within a 15 minute drive are five golf courses. The inn is also perfect for small groups such as wedding parties, family reunions, small meetings and business retreats.

Rates
Open year round. Rates $139 to $329. Number of Rooms: 34

Cuisine
Enjoy our expanded continental breakfast buffet. Thoughtfully prepared for you each morning by staff bakers and served in our Gathering Room, or if you prefer, delivered to your guest room.

Nearest Airport
General Mitchell International

White Gull Inn

www.whitegullinn.com
4225 Main Street, P.O. Box 160, Fish Creek, WI USA 54212
800-625-8813 • 920-868-3517 • Fax: 920-868-2367
innkeeper@whitegullinn.com

Member Since 1979

Innkeepers/Owners
Andy & Jan Coulson

Established in 1896, this white clapboard inn is tucked away in the scenic bayside village of Fish Creek on Wisconsin's Door Peninsula. Antiques, fireplaces and meticulously restored and exquisitely decorated rooms, suites and cottages provide a warm and romantic atmosphere. Several suites feature double whirlpool baths. Renowned for award winning breakfasts, sumptuous lunches and candlelit dinners, the inn is famous for its traditional Door County fish boils, featuring locally caught Lake Michigan whitefish cooked outside over an open fire. With its back to a bluff and its face to the bay of Green Bay, Fish Creek today is a stroll around village with historic buildings housing numerous art galleries, shops and restaurants. A natural harbor filled with majestic yachts in summer separates the village from Peninsula State Park, Wisconsin's largest and most beautiful park. Within a few minutes of the inn, guests will find spectacular sunsets, theater, music festivals, antique stores and every imaginable recreational activity, from golf and fishing to wind surfing and kayaking.

Rates
6 Rooms, $170/$245; 7 Suites, $245/$295; 4 Cottages (1, 2 and 4 bedroom), $260/$490. Open all year. Number of Rooms: 17

Cuisine
Full breakfast included. Lunch daily. Dinner from the menu Monday, Tuesday, Thursday in summer, Saturday through Thursday in winter. Traditional Door County fish boils featuring local Lake Michigan whitefish served other evenings. Open to public.

Nearest Airport
Austin Straubel International Airport, Green Bay (75 miles)

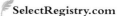

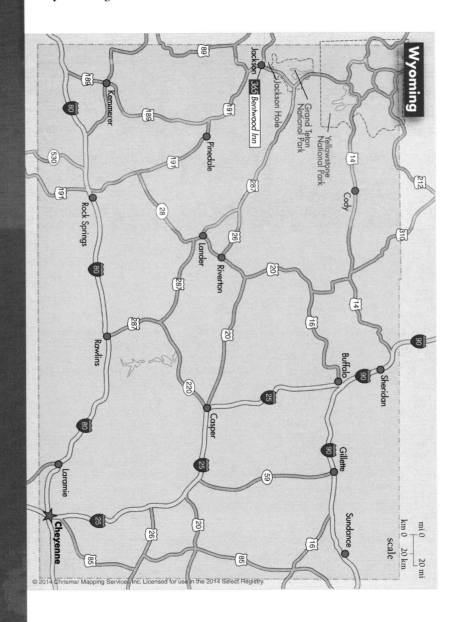

Wyoming

Wyoming

Jackson

365 Bentwood Inn

Jackson Hole

Grand Teton National Park

Yellowstone National Park

Cody

Kemmerer

Pinedale

Rock Springs

Lander

Riverton

Buffalo

Sheridan

Rawlins

Gillette

Casper

Laramie

Sundance

Cheyenne

scale

mi 0   20 mi
km 0   20 km

SelectRegistry.com

Bentwood Inn

www.bentwoodinn.com
P.O. Box 561, 4250 Raven Haven Road, Jackson, WY USA 83001
307-739-1411 • Fax: 307-739-2453
info@bentwoodinn.com

Member Since 2008

Wyoming Jackson

Innkeepers
Rachel Bechhoefer and Neil Reilley

This luxurious and iconic lodge in Jackson Hole is nestled on 3 acres of solitude in a grove of towering cottonwoods. Let the Bentwood Inn be your gateway to Yellowstone. The log home affords views of the Teton Range and is minutes from Grand Teton National Park. Built of massive 200 year-old timbers salvaged from the Yellowstone fire, the inn boasts 6,000 sq ft of Western hospitality. As you step into the Great Room, you are greeted by the three-story river-rock fireplace, a warm and inviting space where you can spend a quiet afternoon with a book or a snowy evening among friends. Our deluxe guest rooms feature a king bed, fireplace, jetted tub, quality linens, towels, and robes, cable TV, and a private deck or balcony. A hearty breakfast starts each new day of adventure in the mountains. In the afternoon, share the day's experiences with new friends over appetizers and refreshments- served on our expansive decks in summer, or in front of the fireplace in winter. A stone's throw from the Snake River, this is the ideal location to launch your Teton and Yellowstone vacation.

Rates
$195/$350 by season. Adventure travel and romantic getaway packages offered. We host business meetings and events. Ask about having your wedding or honeymoon in this scenic destination. Impromptu guests may include resident moose. Number of Rooms: 5

Cuisine
A homemade breakfast as hearty as Wyoming and artisanal appetizers with a creative twist included in your stay. Optional bistro dinners feature offerings from local ranches, farms, and markets. Special dietary needs tastefully accommodated.

Nearest Airport
Jackson Hole (JAC) 18 mi. Idaho Falls (IDA) 85 mi. Salt Lake City (SLC) 250 mi.

Canada

SELECT REGISTRY represents the finest inns, B&Bs, and unique small hotels North America has to offer. We are proud to include among our members a number of exceptional Canadian properties. To our Canadian guests, we say, "Our innkeepers stand ready to welcome you during your travels, whether it is to the States or within Canada." To our American guests, we say, "Why not see what Canada has to offer?"

In these uncertain times, when crossing oceans is worrisome, nothing beats the exhilarating feeling of visiting an exciting new country in the security and comfort of your own car. Yes, for many millions of Americans, Canada is just a short drive away—and yet it is a whole new world!

Le SELECT REGISTRY représente plusieurs auberges, cafés-couettes et petits hôtels des plus distingués en Amérique du Nord. Nous sommes fiers de pouvoir compter parmi nos membres plusieurs des plus beaux établissements canadiens. À tous les voyageurs, canadiens-français, nous vous souhaitons de merveilleux sejours dans les auberges de prestige du SELECT REGISTRY.

SelectRegistry.com

There are the breathtaking vistas, mountain wildlife, Asian food and totem poles of British Columbia, the "foodie" paradise of the Niagara Peninsula (Canada's Napa Valley) and the Eastern Townships of Quebec, replete with friendly wineries and raw milk cheeses. There are festivals galore, museums, parks and world-class shopping in Toronto and Montreal as well as the fascinating culture of the Province of Quebec where French-Canadians take food and fun very, very seriously.

Many travelers have experienced all four seasons of the Northland (the winters are sunnier and less cold than you think). Traveling east to west, it would be hard to declare a regional winner. Some Canadians modestly claim to be the most hospitable of innkeepers, and a critic can't easily challenge that assertion.

Superb food, wine and service can be expected at the Canadian inns of the SELECT REGISTRY. Understated luxury, too. But above all, they offer you an exclusive glimpse of the best of Canada: its forests, crystalline lakes, affordable golf and skiing and cosmopolitan, secure and friendly cities. The Northland beckons!

Nova Scotia

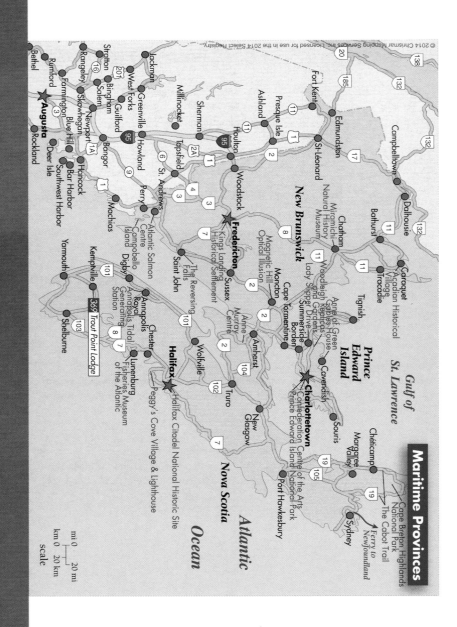

Maritime Provinces

New Brunswick

Prince Edward Island

Nova Scotia

Gulf of St. Lawrence

Atlantic Ocean

Bethel
Rumford
Augusta
Rockland
Deer Isle
Southwest Harbor
Bar Harbor
Hancock
Blue Hill
Machias
Bangor
Newport
Skowhegan
Farmington
Rangeley
Salem
Bingham
Stratton
West Forks
Greenville
Guilford
Howland
Tapsfield
St. Andrews
Perry
Campobello Island
Atlantic Salmon Centre
Deer Isle
Jackman
Millinocket
Sherman
Ashland
Presque Isle
Fort Kent
Edmundston
St-Léonard
Woodstock
Houlton
Kings Landing Historical Settlement
Fredericton
The Reversing Falls
Saint John
Sussex Centre
Magnetic Hill Optical Illusion
Chatham
Miramichi Natural History Museum
Woodleigh Replicas
Lady Slipper Drive
Anne of Green Gables House
Moncton
Cape Tormentine
Summerside Border
Tignish
Bathurst
Caraquet
Acadian Historical Village
Tracadie
Dalhousie
Campbellton
Yarmouth
Kempville
Digby
Annapolis Royal
Annapolis Tidal Generating Station
Chester
Lunenburg
Fisheries Museum of the Atlantic
Peggy's Cove Village & Lighthouse
Halifax Citadel National Historic Site
Halifax
Wolfville
Anne Murray Centre
Amherst
Truro
New Glasgow
Port Hawkesbury
Charlottetown
Confederation Centre of the Arts
Prince Edward Island National Park
Cavendish
Souris
Margaree Valley
Cheticamp
Cape Breton Highlands National Park
The Cabot Trail
Ferry to Newfoundland
Sydney
Shelburne
Trout Point Lodge

mi 0 — 20 mi
km 0 — 20 km
scale

🍴 🍴 🍴 ♀

Trout Point Lodge Of Nova Scotia

www.troutpoint.com
189 Trout Point Road, Kemptville, NS Canada B0W 1Y0
902–761–2142 • 877–812–0112 • Fax: 800-980-0713
troutpoint@foodvacation.com   *Member Since 2013*

Nova Scotia

Kemptville

AWARD
OF
EXCELLENCE
2013

Chef/Innkeepers
Vaughan Perret & Charles Leary

Understated luxury in the heart of Canada's eastern wilderness! Nestled next to 2 rivers, immediately adjacent to the inconceivably vast Tobeatic Wilderness Area of Nova Scotia, Trout Point is the most superb wilderness lodge in Atlantic Canada, offering remarkable hospitality and designed for absolute Haute Rustic comfort. Positioned so that every room boasts water views, Trout Point shelters its guests in an utterly civilized outpost amidst the Acadian Forest. The enchanting location & spacious accommodations make for a memorable luxury hideaway.

Each stay also holds myriad possibilities for vacation adventures, with or without a guide: kayaking, hiking, snow-shoeing, wilderness safaris, river swimming, star gazing, mountain bikes as well as sauna, hot tub, and in-room massage. Guests benefit from the mineral water freely flowing from the taps, pristine air quality and total absence of night-time light pollution. There's Acadian villages, whale watching, sea kayaking, beaches, historic towns, & great golf nearby. - Parks Canada Sustainable Tourism Award - 5 Green Keys.

Rates
From $139 to $459 depending on unit and season - Trout Point offers comfortable Rooms, Junior Suites & Suites as well as 2 cottages. Number of Rooms: 13

Cuisine
Rated 9/10 by the London Telegraph, Trout Point's cuisine is a standout experience, including the best local seafood. The Lodge's kitchen deftly interprets Atlantic French Acadian cuisine from traditional recipes & seasonal sources of local delicacies.

Nearest Airport
Halifax (YHZ) for commercial flights
Yarmouth International for charter or private planes

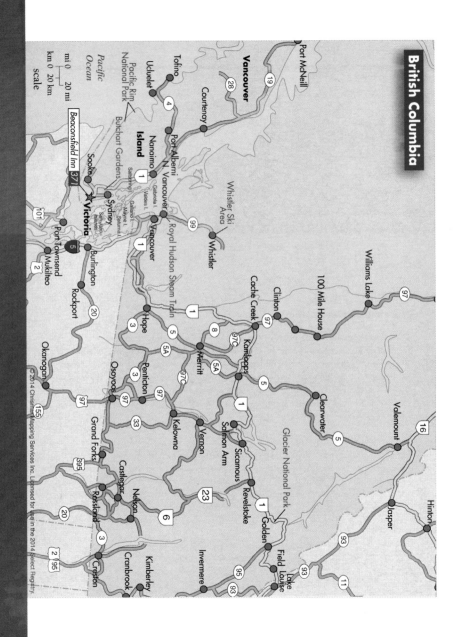

British Columbia

Vancouver

Port McNeill

Tofino
Ucluelet
Pacific Rim National Park
Butchart Gardens
Courtenay
Port Alberni
N. Vancouver
Nanaimo
Island
Gabriola I.
Saltspring I.
Galiano I.
Mayne I.
San Juan I.
Shaw I.
Sidney
Victoria
Sooke
Beaconsfield Inn 37
Pacific Ocean
mi 0   20 mi
km 0   20 km
scale

Whistler Ski Area
Whistler
Royal Hudson Steam Train
Vancouver
Burlington
Port Townsend
Muckileo
Rockport
Okanogan

Williams Lake
100 Mile House
Clinton
Cache Creek
Kamloops
Clearwater
Valemount
Jasper
Hinton

Hope
Merritt
Penticton
Osoyoos
Grand Forks
Rossland
Castlegar
Nelson
Creston
Cranbrook
Kimberley
Invermere
Golden
Field
Lake Louise
Revelstoke
Sicamous
Salmon Arm
Vernon
Kelowna
Glacier National Park

© 2014 Christman Mapping Services Inc. Licensed for use in the 2014 Select Registry.

SelectRegistry.com

Beaconsfield Inn

www.beaconsfieldinn.com
998 Humboldt St., Victoria, BC, Canada Canada
888-884-4044 • 250-384-4044 • Fax: 250-384-4052
info@beaconsfieldinn.com

Member Since 1994

Proprietors
Mark and Diana Havin

We invite you to our award-winning Edwardian Inn built in 1905. Located only four blocks from Victoria's Inner Harbor, the Beaconsfield Inn is the ultimate in charm, luxury and romance. Enjoy antique furnishings, stately guest and common rooms, spectacular stained glass windows, feather beds with down comforters and fireplaces in all rooms. Jacuzzis in most rooms. The Beaconsfield Inn is situated on a quiet, tree-lined street a short 10 minute stroll to downtown and the inner harbour with all its shopping, restaurants and tourist attractions. Afternoon tea, coffee and fresh baked treats. Evening sherry hour. Awake to our gourmet full breakfasts each morning. The Beaconsfield Inn has been awarded a 5 star rating from Canada Select.

Rates
5 Deluxe Rooms, $109/$295 CDN; 4 Suites, $199/$299 CDN. Open year-round.
Number of Rooms: 9

Cuisine
Full gourmet style breakfast. Afternoon fresh baked treats, selection of teas and freshly brewed coffee. Evening sherry hour.

Nearest Airport
Victoria International. Or downtown inner harbour - Float Planes from Vancouver.

The Stafford Smith Award

Rick Litchfield and Bev Davis

Over the years, Stafford Smith of Stafford's Bay View inn in Petoskey, Michigan, has been a mentor, leader, innovator, and supporter of the industry and of SELECT REGISTRY, in particular.

In 1972, when Association founder Norman Simpson transitioned his book, *Country Inns and Back Roads*, to a nonprofit organization of select innkeepers (then The Independent Innkeepers Association), he chose Stafford to be the first President of the group. In the years since, Stafford and his wife Janice have been fixtures in the association, lending their enthusiasm, expertise, and support to other innkeepers, and helping to keep the institutional memory of the IIA/SELECT REGISTRY intact and alive.

It was therefore extremely appropriate that, in 1999, the organization chose to make Stafford Smith the first recipient of an award bearing his name.

Recipients of the Stafford Smith Award must meet an extensive list of criteria including:
- Longstanding member of SELECT REGISTRY
- A mentor to fellow innkeepers
- SELECT REGISTRY Committee/Board involvement
- Participates at SELECT REGISTRY Division Meetings and Annual Meetings
- A leader in the industry
- A leader in their community
- Strong allegiance to SELECT REGISTRY

The award itself is shaped in the form of a bronze plate, and was originally inspired by a poem, representing the power and effect of one leaf, one act, one person. The tree bends over the sterling silver pond and one leaf drops on the water's surface. The ripples encircle the leaf in all directions and spread over the entire surface of the water.

The award, conferred on only a few qualified innkeepers, is reserved for those who've made an exceptional contribution to SELECT REGISTRY, the innkeeping industry and their communities. This honor is SELECT REGISTRY's equivalent of a lifetime achievement award. Only a handful of individuals qualify to receive it.

In addition to Stafford Smith, Norm and Kathryn Kinney (2004) and Phyllis Murray (2008) have received the prestigious award. They were joined in 2012 by longtime innkeeper veterans Rick Litchfield and Bev Davis, co-owners of the Captain Lord Mansion (see photo).

All who have experienced exceptional hospitality in inns throughout North America owe these individuals a debt of gratitude for helping to encourage and to preserve the standards of industry excellence that thousands of guests have come to expect from SELECT REGISTRY.

SelectRegistry.com

Vacation of a Lifetime:

In early January of 2014, we awarded three lucky winners the Vacation of a Lifetime, a FREE overnight stay at each of our nearly 350 SELECT REGISTRY inns and B&Bs across North America. That's a year's worth of FREE lodging and it could be yours! In 2015, we will again be drawing winners for Select Registry's Vacation of a Lifetime.

Entering the sweepstakes is easy and no purchase is necessary. Once you register for the SELECT REGISTRY Rewards program, you're automatically entered. It's that simple. Plus, for each Quill Point you earn with a night's stay at a SELECT REGISTRY inn or B&B, you'll also earn an additional entry in the drawing. The more times you stay, the better your chance of winning.

Visit **www.selectregistry.com/Vacation-of-a-Lifetime.asp** for official contest rules.

Bill & Pam O'Brian
Pen Argyl, PA

Michele Chandler & Bob Gilfoil, Toronto, CA

Michael Hubbard & Sossi Chungrian,
Montreal, CA

SelectRegistry.com

Visit our New Website
www.Comphy.com

As the industry leader in luxury microfiber linens, Comphy Company currently outfits thousands of Bed and Breakfasts around the country. Learn more about our products by visiting our all-new interactive website.

Our website allows you to design the bed of your dreams. Select fabrics, mix products and match styles to your own décor. Even change the color of your bedroom walls.

Account Executive Shantell Denson
B&B, Boutique Inns, Vacation Rentals, and Dude Ranches

Comphy Company, "changing the world, one bed at a time."

Credits

We appreciate the photo skills of everyone who contributed to this book. Some member inns have provided photographs without photographic credits, and other images are unidentified. If you're not listed here, we extend our thanks. We will be pleased to publish a credit if it is furnished to Select Registry. Many of the images/inns featured in the book were provided by Jumping Rocks Photography, George W. Gardner Associates, Tim Shellmer, Brad Wittman, Doug Plummer, Laurie Anderson. Other photo credits available upon request.

Select Registry, Distinguished Inns of North America, 501 E. Michigan Avenue, Marshall, MI 49068. Phone: 800.344.5244, Fax: 269.789.0970. Copyright Select Registry, 2012. All rights reserved. Printed in the U.S.A. Select Registry assumes no liability for the accuracy of the information contained herein. At the time of this printing we assumed all information was correct. Information for individual Inn pages has been provided by the member properties. Select Registry is a membership marketing organization and has no ownership role or policy-making authority with respect to its members.

From time to time, the composition of our membership changes. For an up-to-date list of our current membership please go online at *www.selectregistry.com*. Please note that only current members are entitled to redeem Select Registry gift certificates and loyalty rewards. To assure a safe and happy trip, please call ahead to verify times, prices, Inn policies, etc.

Contributing writers: Keith Kehlbeck, Stafford & Janet Smith, Stafford's Bayview Inn. Canadian copy: Steve Stafford. Design: Haas-Wittmann Design. Maps: Chrismar Mapping Services Inc. Production: Cadmus Media Works. /Cenveo Publisher Services. Guidebook Project Coordinator/Editor: Keith Kehlbeck. Publisher: Select Registry, Distinguished Inns of North America.

Join our loyalty program and get updates on new properties, valuable information from Select Registry and track your Quills online: *www.selectregistry.com/rewards*

Follow us on Facebook *www.facebook.com/SelectRegistry*

Index by Inn

Index by Inn

Index by Inn

Index by Inn

"There's an App for that!"

For those who have smartphones, Apps have become so cheap, fun and useful that they are actually becoming more popular than the Internet, say statisticians. Apps have actually overtaken the Web in terms of the number of minutes users spend per day. It's a huge change for the connected world.

After all, these days, there really is an app for everything, from smartphone downloads to keep you entertained to useful tools to find lodging.

The SELECT REGISTRY Mobile App *is* a great combination of our guidebook and our website.

Some of its features are:

Show Inns Nearby:

- Automatically locates the inns closest to you for those last minute reservations.
- Has options to show inns within 25, 50, 75, 100, 150, 250, and 500 miles.

Find an Inn:

- Provides a search similar to the powerful inn search functionality on the SELECT REGISTRY website.
- Filter by inn name, city, state, location type, price and amenities.

Discover SELECT REGISTRY:

- Learn about the "SELECT REGISTRY Inn Experience"
- See the events calendar
- View Packages and Specials
- Plan an Event
- Visit the online gift shop
- Use travel tools
- Access the latest digital guidebook

What makes this App even better…it's free! Visit our website today to learn more about our Mobile App, or download it from the App Store or on Google play.

Get the App.
Find the inn.
Experience the
difference.

SelectRegistry.com